COUNTDOWN TO
ADVENTURE

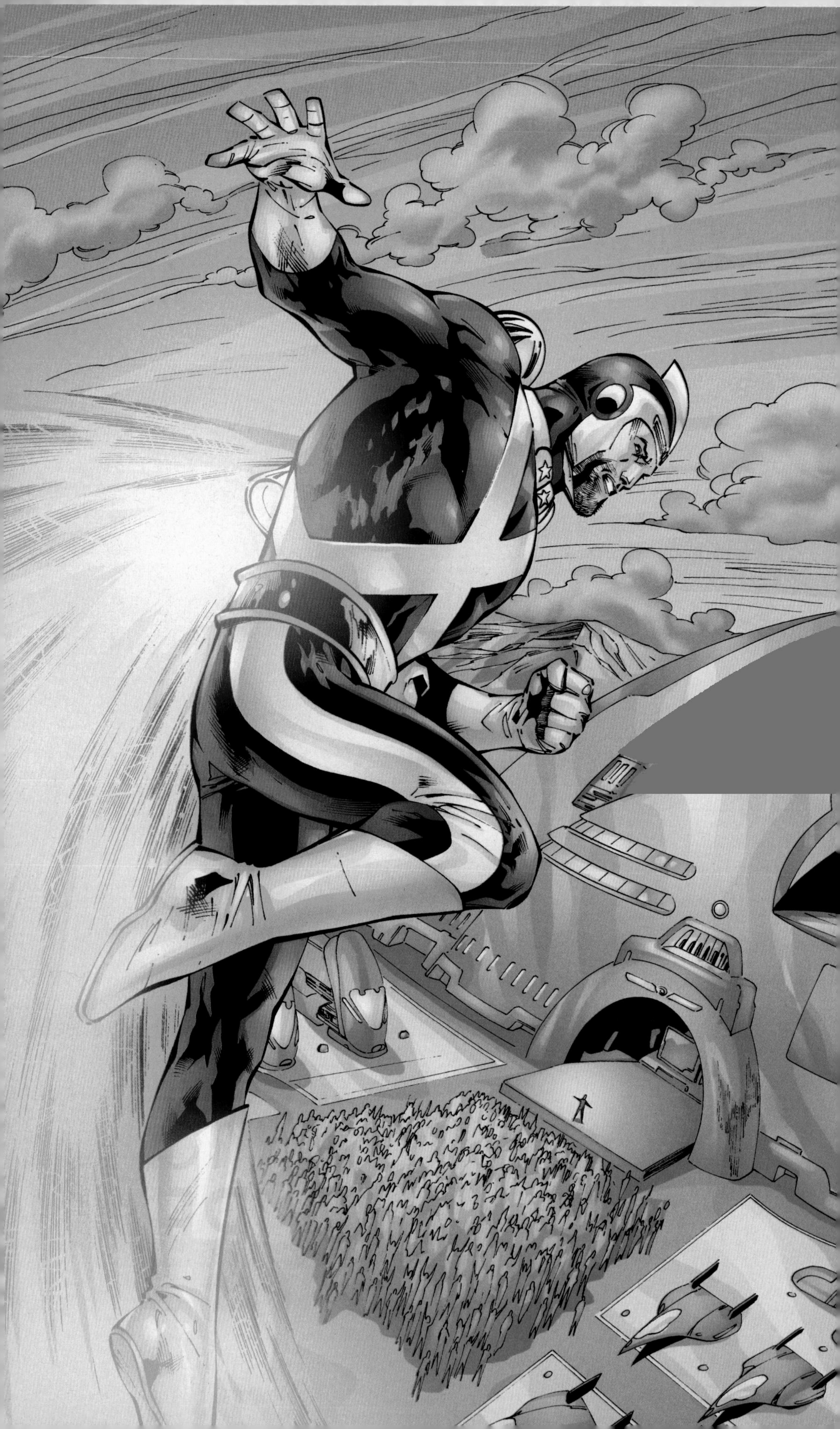

COUNTDOWN TO
ADVENTURE

ADAM BEECHEN

Writer

EDDY BARROWS *(Chapters 1-3)*
ALLAN GOLDMAN *(Chapters 4-8)*

Pencillers

JULIO FERREIRA

with JAY LEISTEN, OCLAIR ALBERT & WILSON MAGALHAES

Inkers

TANYA & RICHARD HORIE

Colorists

PHIL BALSMAN • SWANDS • ROB LEIGH
SAL CIPRIANO

Letterers

Cover by Ivan Reis & Oclair Albert, with Rod Reis.
Publication design by Brainchild Studios/NYC.

COUNTDOWN TO ADVENTURE
Published by DC Comics. Cover and compilation Copyright ©
2008 DC Comics. All Rights Reserved.

Originally published in single magazine form in COUNTDOWN
TO ADVENTURE 1-8. Copyright © 2007, 2008 DC Comics.
All Rights Reserved. All characters, their distinctive likenesses
and related elements featured in this publication are trademarks
of DC Comics. The stories, characters and incidents featured in
this publication are entirely fictional. DC Comics does not read
or accept unsolicited submissions of ideas, stories or artwork.

DC Comics, 1700 Broadway, New York, NY 10019
A Warner Bros. Entertainment Company
Printed in Canada. First Printing.
ISBN: 978-1-4012-1823-2

Cast of Characters

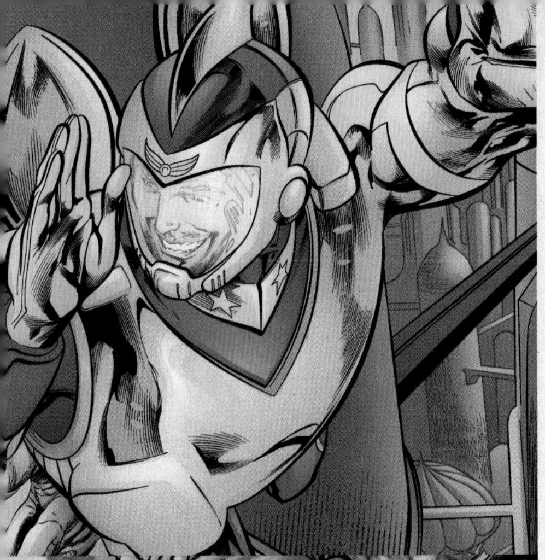

ADAM STRANGE

In his former life as an archaeologist, Adam was transported by the teleportation device known as the Zeta Beam from Earth to the planet Rann. There he became the planet's guardian and champion, and fell in love with the Rannian woman Alanna. Despite technological limitations that frequently kept him far from her, they formed a family and had a daughter, Aleea — the first child born on Rann in decades.

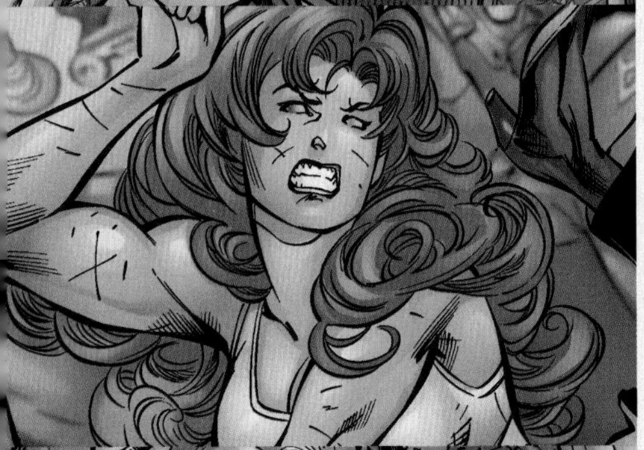

STARFIRE

Princess Koriand'r, heir to the throne of the paradise planet Tamaran, was betrayed and enslaved through the schemes of her jealous older sister Komand'r. After years of toil and abuse she escaped to Earth, where Kory (as she's known to her friends) used her solar-powered abilities of flight and energy blasts to fight alongside the Teen Titans. Trained as a warrior, she is as proud and dangerous as she is beautiful.

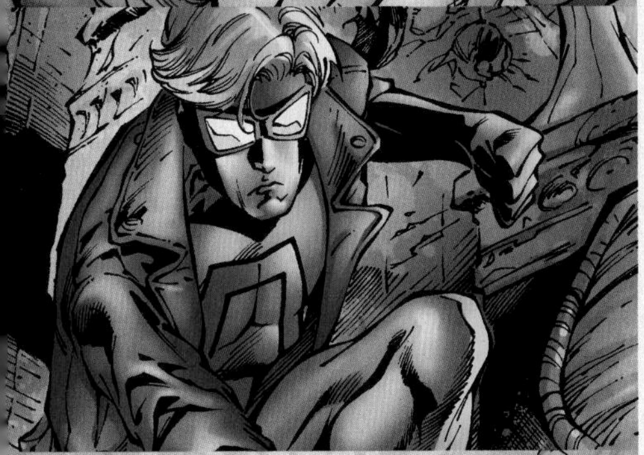

ANIMAL MAN

Contact with a crashed alien spacecraft granted friendly family man Buddy Baker the ability to tap into the morphogenetic field, which links all forms of animal life. By doing so he can access the innate abilities of any animal on Earth. Despite adventures that have led to startling revelations about not just man's relationship to animals but the nature of the universe itself, Buddy's priority remains his beloved wife Ellen, son Cliff and daughter Maxine, whom he supports by working as a stuntman.

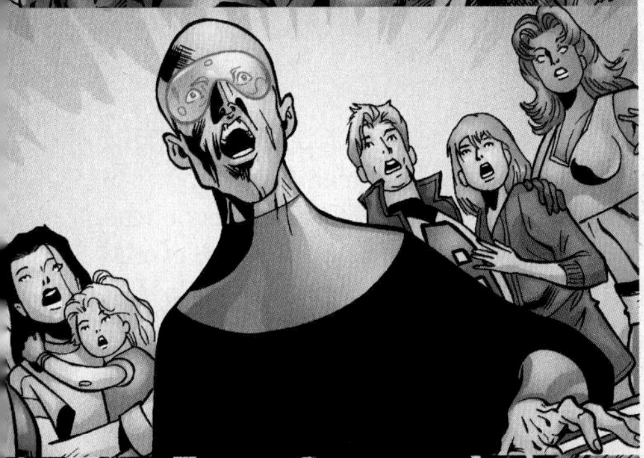

SARDATH

Chief scientist of Rann and father of Adam Strange's wife Alanna, Sardath invented Zeta Beam teleportation technology and its large-scale counterpart, the Omega Beam. It was this latter innovation that enabled Rann's move to the same solar system as the planet Thanagar, an event which the Thanagarians erroneously believed to be the cause of their planet's destruction. Sardath made Rann a refuge for the now-homeless Thanagarians and has sought peace between the two warring races ever since.

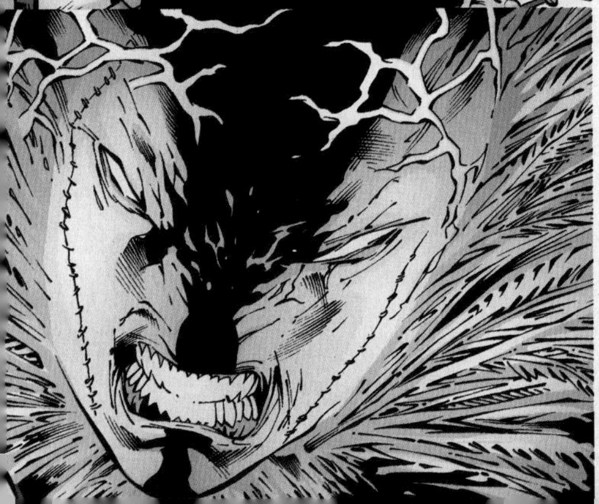

LADY STYX

A brutal tyrant of unknown origin, Lady Styx waged a campaign of terror against scores of worlds, converting their inhabitants into worshipful slaves and slaughtering all who refused to "believe in her." Thought dead following a battle with Animal Man, Adam Strange and Starfire — whom she'd sought to destroy for a full year — she has since resurfaced to menace heroes throughout the cosmos, frequently manifesting in the most unexpected of ways.

Previously...

WHEN A CRISIS OF INFINITE PROPORTIONS THREATENS ALL OF EXISTENCE, ADAM STRANGE, STARFIRE AND ANIMAL MAN ARE AMONG THE HEROES WHO SET OFF TO INVESTIGATE A HOLE IN THE FABRIC OF REALITY.

There they encounter and defeat Alexander Luthor, a former hero from an alternate dimension who sought to remake the universe to his liking.

But an accident involving Zeta Beam teleportation technology after the battle leaves Strange with no eyes, and he blasts the three heroes far from their homes. They spend the next year lost in space, soon becoming targets of a brutal tyrant called Lady Styx and her legions of zombie-like followers.

With the help of their unlikely allies Lobo — the last Czarnian, a lethal bounty hunter turned religious guru — and the Emerald Head of Ekron — original owner of the powerful Emerald Eye of Ekron and designated Green Lantern of a space sector destroyed by Lady Styx — the trio manage to defeat the murderous Styx, erroneously believing her killed.

But their victory is bittersweet: Infected by a neurotoxin, Animal Man is killed, while Strange and Starfire are forced to flee from Styx's relentless followers. With Strange blind, Starfire

badly wounded and their damaged ship on a collision course with a sun, they are saved at the last minute by the sentient planet Green Lantern Mogo.

Adam Strange returns to his adopted planet Rann for a reunion with his daughter Aleea and wife Alanna — who equips him with a new, enhanced set of eyes. Meanwhile, the still not fully recovered Starfire travels to Earth to bring the trademark jacket of her fallen friend Animal Man to his wife as a memento. Little does she know that Animal Man has been resurrected by the powerful alien race who gave him his powers and returned home himself, using the power of the alien creatures called sun-eaters to fly back to Earth.

Animal Man's family, who believed him dead, throws him a welcome home party — but it's interrupted by the furious followers of Lady Styx, who traced Animal Man to his home seeking vengeance. Fortunately, Starfire arrives at that very moment and defeats the attackers, only to finally succumb to exhaustion and collapse when she sees Animal Man alive and well...

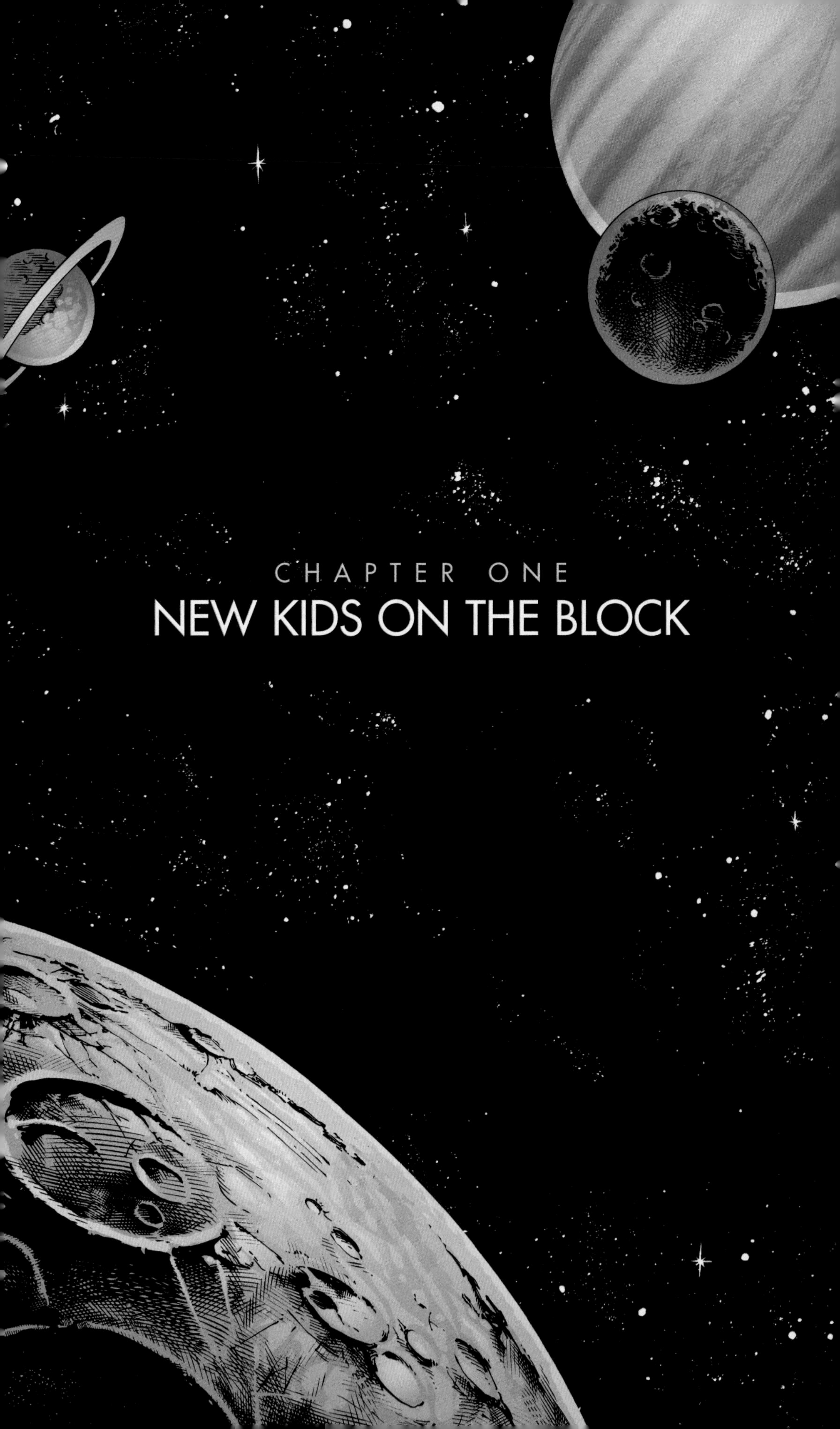

CHAPTER ONE

NEW KIDS ON THE BLOCK

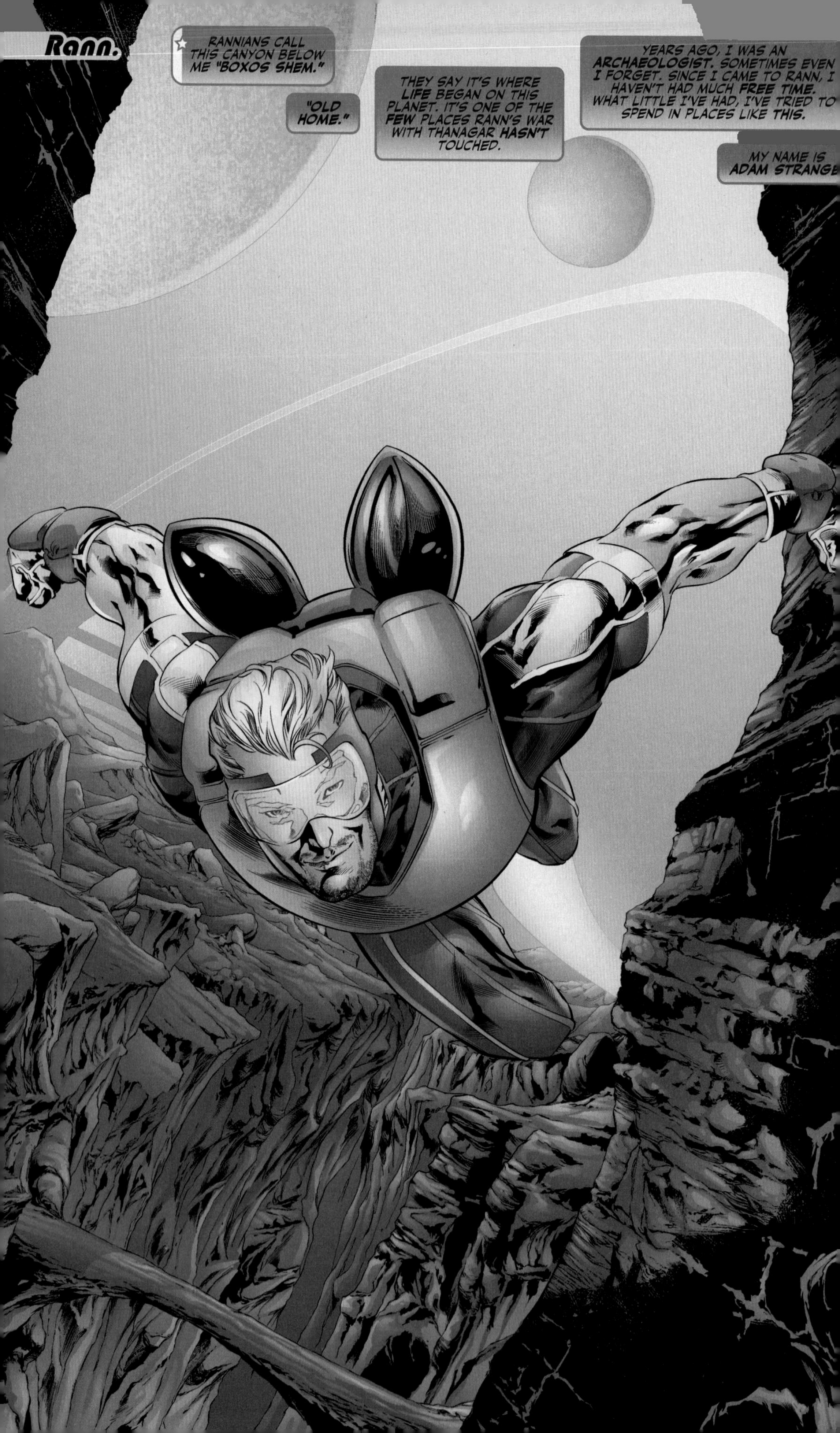
Rann.
RANNIANS CALL THIS CANYON BELOW ME "BOXOS SHEM."
"OLD HOME."
THEY SAY IT'S WHERE LIFE BEGAN ON THIS PLANET. IT'S ONE OF THE FEW PLACES RANN'S WAR WITH THANAGAR HASN'T TOUCHED.
YEARS AGO, I WAS AN ARCHAEOLOGIST. SOMETIMES EVEN I FORGET. SINCE I CAME TO RANN, I HAVEN'T HAD MUCH FREE TIME. WHAT LITTLE I'VE HAD, I'VE TRIED TO SPEND IN PLACES LIKE THIS.
MY NAME IS ADAM STRANGE

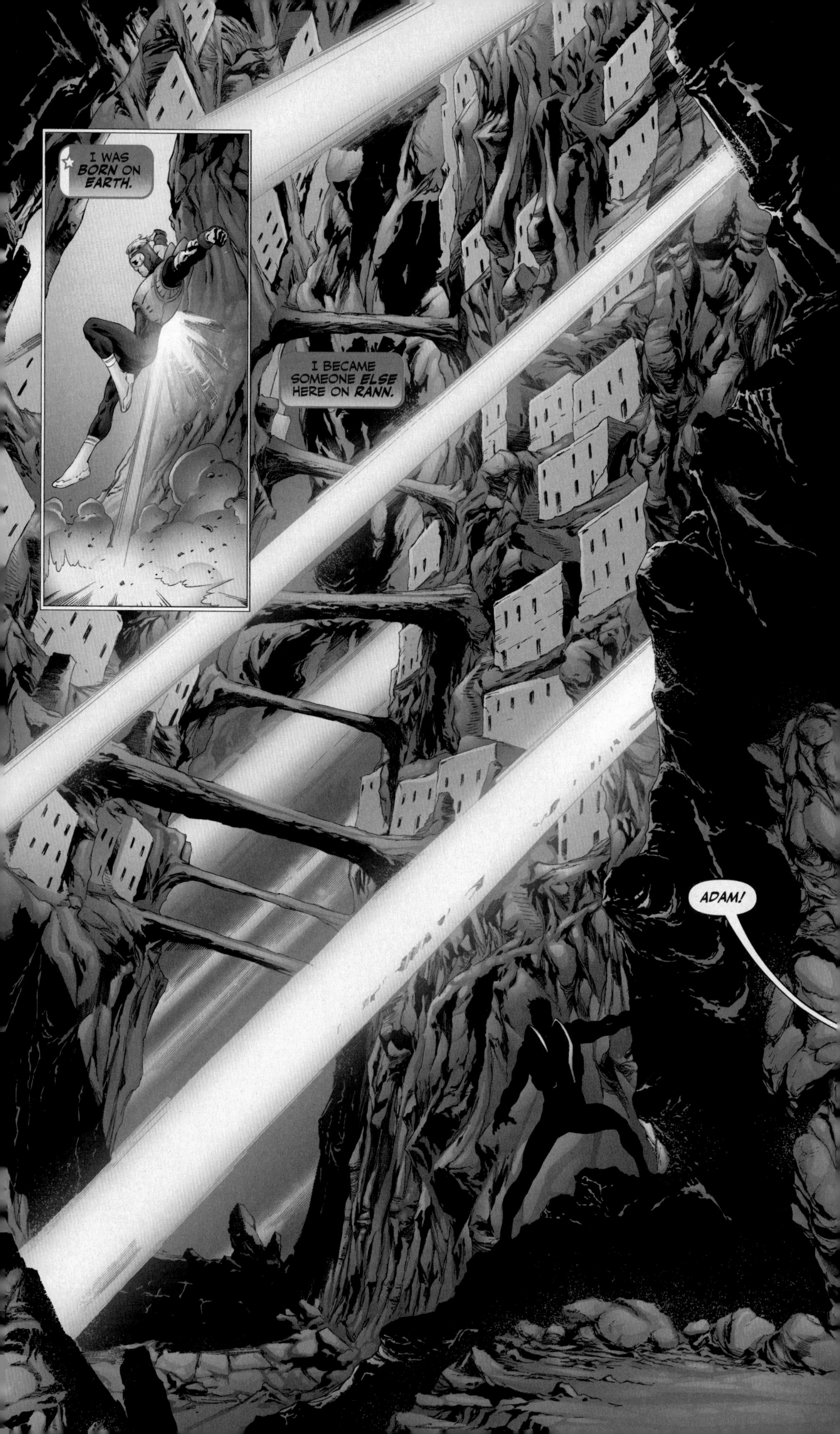
I WAS BORN ON EARTH.
I BECAME SOMEONE ELSE HERE ON RANN.
ADAM!

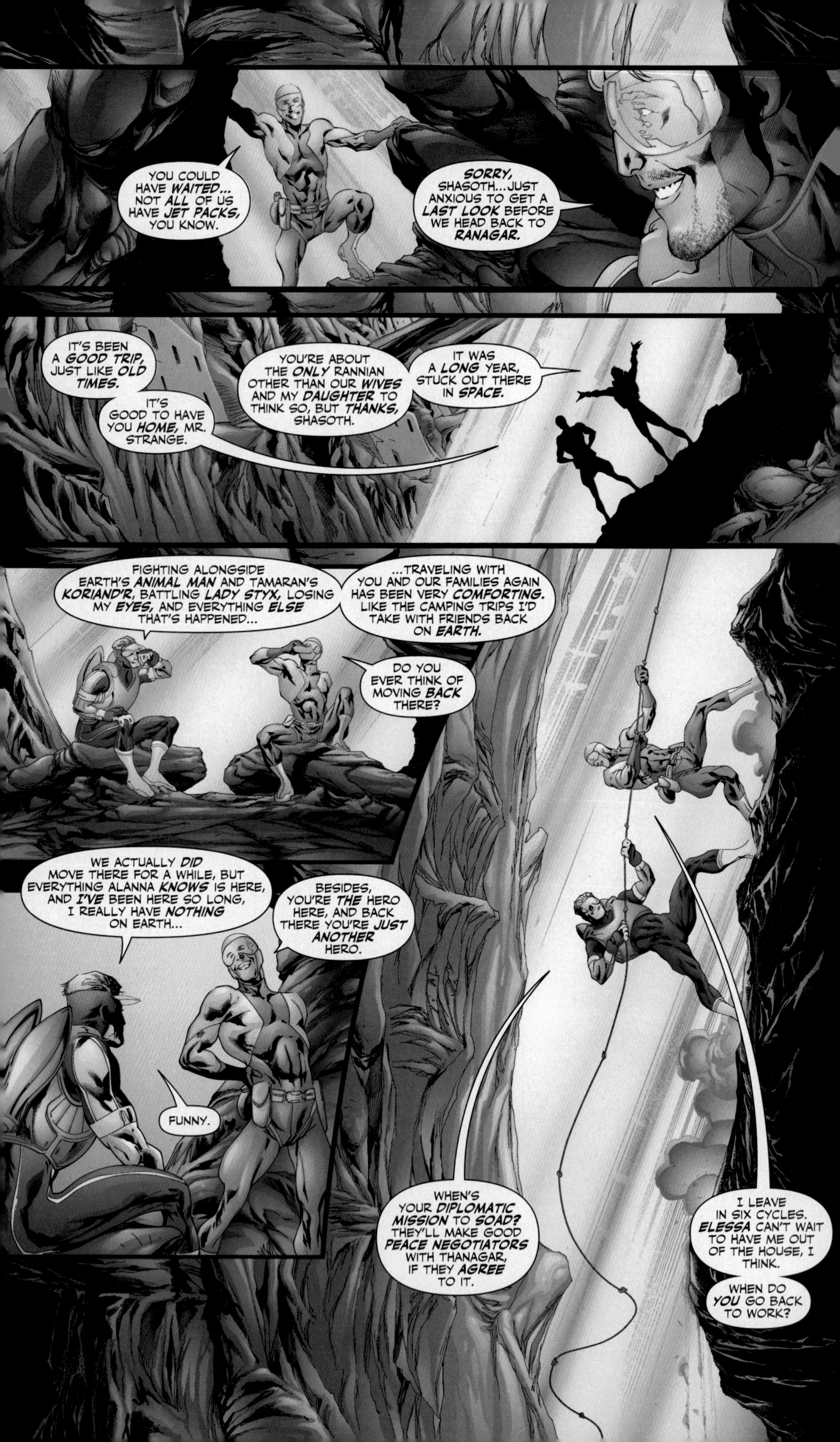
YOU COULD HAVE WAITED... NOT ALL OF US HAVE JET PACKS, YOU KNOW.
SORRY, SHASOTH...JUST ANXIOUS TO GET A LAST LOOK BEFORE WE HEAD BACK TO RANAGAR.
IT'S BEEN A GOOD TRIP, JUST LIKE OLD TIMES.
IT'S GOOD TO HAVE YOU HOME, MR. STRANGE.
YOU'RE ABOUT THE ONLY RANNIAN OTHER THAN OUR WIVES AND MY DAUGHTER TO THINK SO, BUT THANKS, SHASOTH.
IT WAS A LONG YEAR, STUCK OUT THERE IN SPACE.
FIGHTING ALONGSIDE EARTH'S ANIMAL MAN AND TAMARAN'S KORIAND'R, BATTLING LADY STYX, LOSING MY EYES, AND EVERYTHING ELSE THAT'S HAPPENED...
...TRAVELING WITH YOU AND OUR FAMILIES AGAIN HAS BEEN VERY COMFORTING. LIKE THE CAMPING TRIPS I'D TAKE WITH FRIENDS BACK ON EARTH.
DO YOU EVER THINK OF MOVING BACK THERE?
WE ACTUALLY DID MOVE THERE FOR A WHILE, BUT EVERYTHING ALANNA KNOWS IS HERE, AND I'VE BEEN HERE SO LONG, I REALLY HAVE NOTHING ON EARTH...
BESIDES, YOU'RE THE HERO HERE, AND BACK THERE YOU'RE JUST ANOTHER HERO.
FUNNY.
WHEN'S YOUR DIPLOMATIC MISSION TO SOAD? THEY'LL MAKE GOOD PEACE NEGOTIATORS WITH THANAGAR, IF THEY AGREE TO IT.
I LEAVE IN SIX CYCLES. ELESSA CAN'T WAIT TO HAVE ME OUT OF THE HOUSE, I THINK.
WHEN DO YOU GO BACK TO WORK?

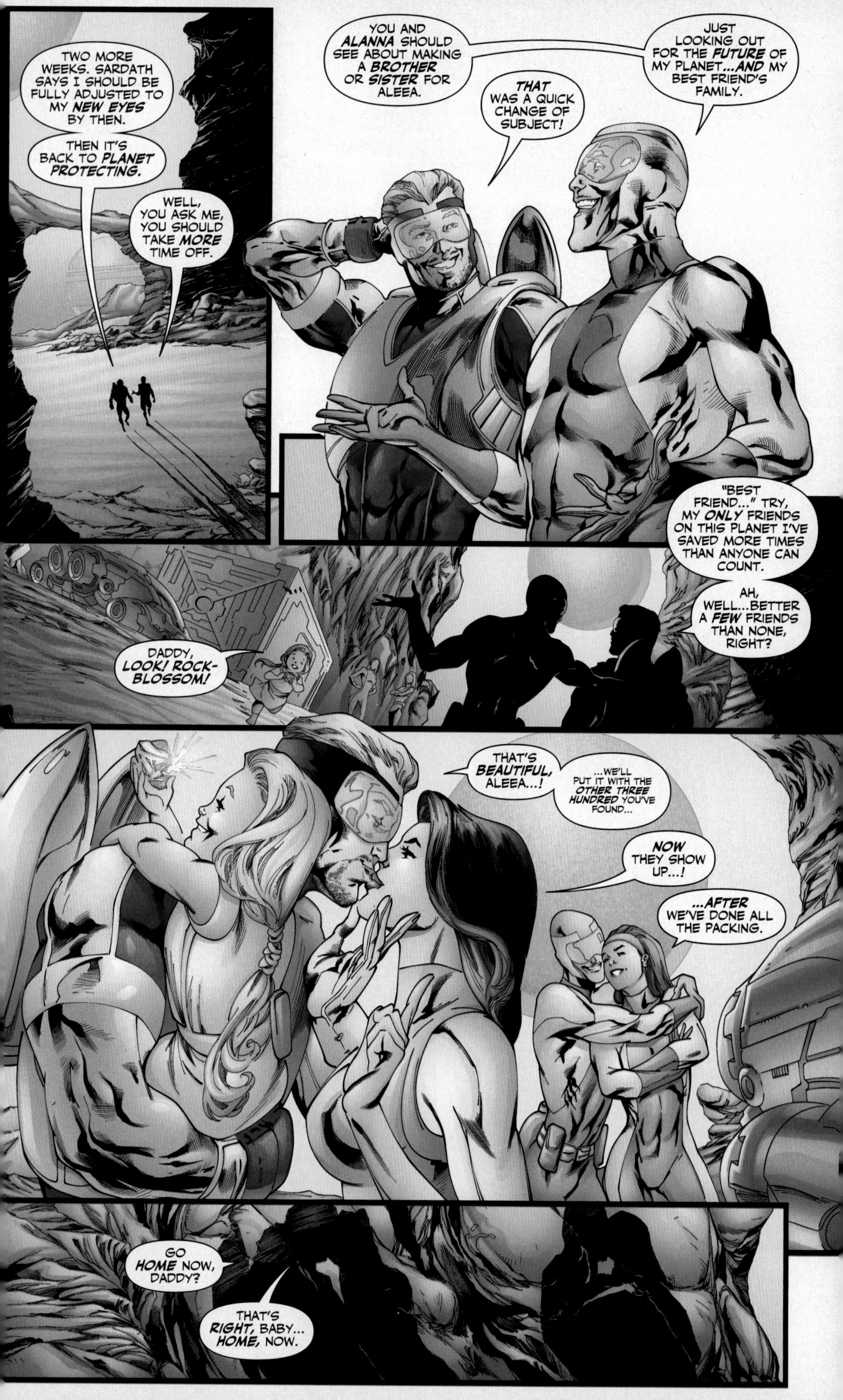
TWO MORE WEEKS. SARDATH SAYS I SHOULD BE FULLY ADJUSTED TO MY NEW EYES BY THEN.
THEN IT'S BACK TO PLANET PROTECTING.
WELL, YOU ASK ME, YOU SHOULD TAKE MORE TIME OFF.
YOU AND ALANNA SHOULD SEE ABOUT MAKING A BROTHER OR SISTER FOR ALEEA.
THAT WAS A QUICK CHANGE OF SUBJECT!
JUST LOOKING OUT FOR THE FUTURE OF MY PLANET...AND MY BEST FRIEND'S FAMILY.
"BEST FRIEND..." TRY, MY ONLY FRIENDS ON THIS PLANET I'VE SAVED MORE TIMES THAN ANYONE CAN COUNT.
AH, WELL...BETTER A FEW FRIENDS THAN NONE, RIGHT?
DADDY, LOOK! ROCK-BLOSSOM!
THAT'S BEAUTIFUL, ALEEA...!
...WE'LL PUT IT WITH THE OTHER THREE HUNDRED YOU'VE FOUND...
NOW THEY SHOW UP...!
...AFTER WE'VE DONE ALL THE PACKING.
GO HOME NOW, DADDY?
THAT'S RIGHT, BABY... HOME, NOW.

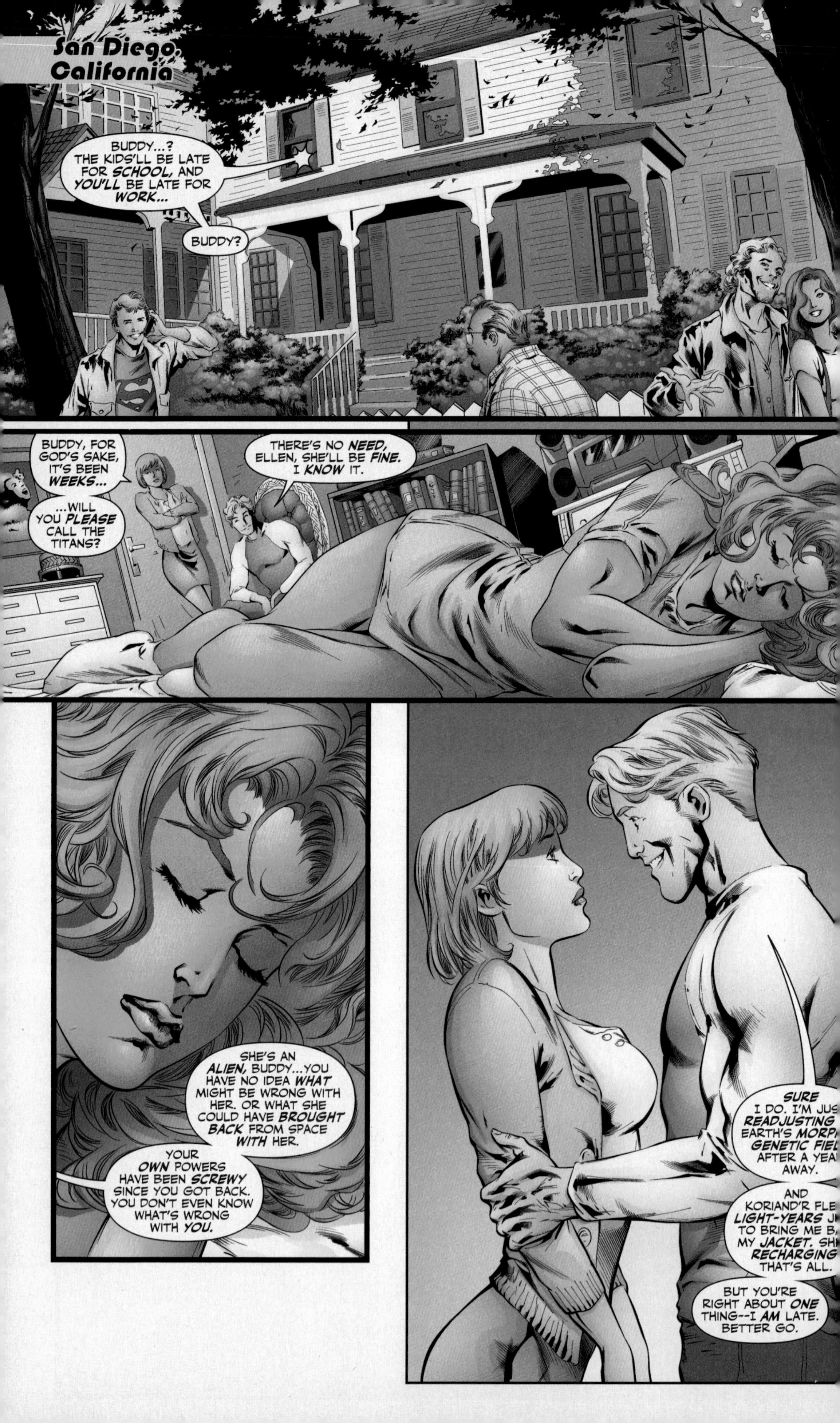
San Diego, California
BUDDY...? THE KIDS'LL BE LATE FOR SCHOOL, AND YOU'LL BE LATE FOR WORK...
BUDDY?
BUDDY, FOR GOD'S SAKE, IT'S BEEN WEEKS...
...WILL YOU PLEASE CALL THE TITANS?
THERE'S NO NEED, ELLEN, SHE'LL BE FINE. I KNOW IT.
SHE'S AN ALIEN, BUDDY...YOU HAVE NO IDEA WHAT MIGHT BE WRONG WITH HER. OR WHAT SHE COULD HAVE BROUGHT BACK FROM SPACE WITH HER.
YOUR OWN POWERS HAVE BEEN SCREWY SINCE YOU GOT BACK. YOU DON'T EVEN KNOW WHAT'S WRONG WITH YOU.
SURE I DO. I'M JUS READJUSTING EARTH'S MORP GENETIC FIEL AFTER A YEA AWAY.
AND KORIAND'R FLE LIGHT-YEARS J TO BRING ME B MY JACKET. SH RECHARGING THAT'S ALL.
BUT YOU'RE RIGHT ABOUT ONE THING--I AM LATE. BETTER GO.

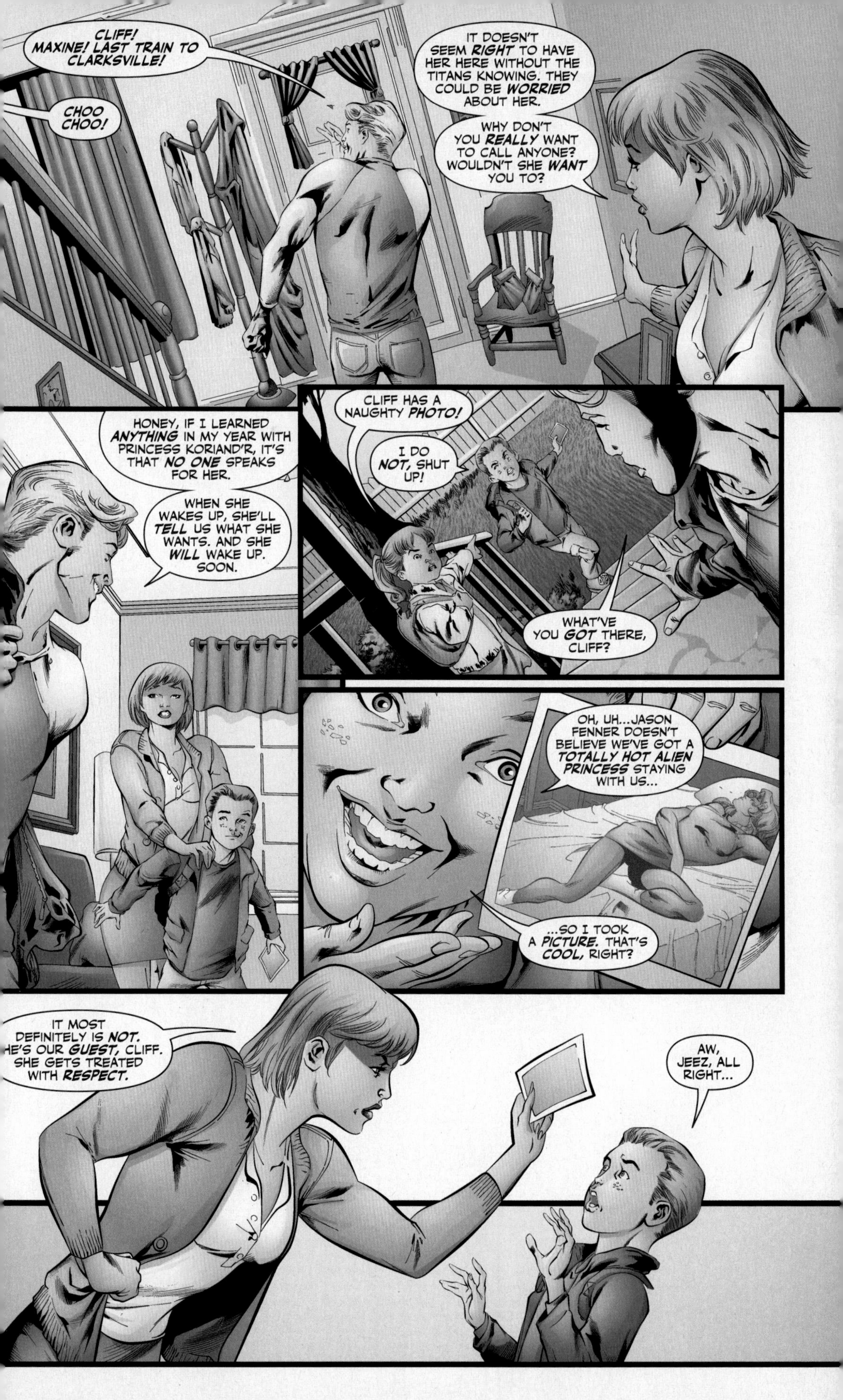
CLIFF! MAXINE! LAST TRAIN TO CLARKSVILLE!
CHOO CHOO!
IT DOESN'T SEEM RIGHT TO HAVE HER HERE WITHOUT THE TITANS KNOWING. THEY COULD BE WORRIED ABOUT HER.
WHY DON'T YOU REALLY WANT TO CALL ANYONE? WOULDN'T SHE WANT YOU TO?
HONEY, IF I LEARNED ANYTHING IN MY YEAR WITH PRINCESS KORIAND'R, IT'S THAT NO ONE SPEAKS FOR HER.
WHEN SHE WAKES UP, SHE'LL TELL US WHAT SHE WANTS. AND SHE WILL WAKE UP. SOON.
CLIFF HAS A NAUGHTY PHOTO!
I DO NOT, SHUT UP!
WHAT'VE YOU GOT THERE, CLIFF?
OH, UH...JASON FENNER DOESN'T BELIEVE WE'VE GOT A TOTALLY HOT ALIEN PRINCESS STAYING WITH US...
...SO I TOOK A PICTURE. THAT'S COOL, RIGHT?
IT MOST DEFINITELY IS NOT. HE'S OUR GUEST, CLIFF. SHE GETS TREATED WITH RESPECT.
AW, JEEZ, ALL RIGHT...

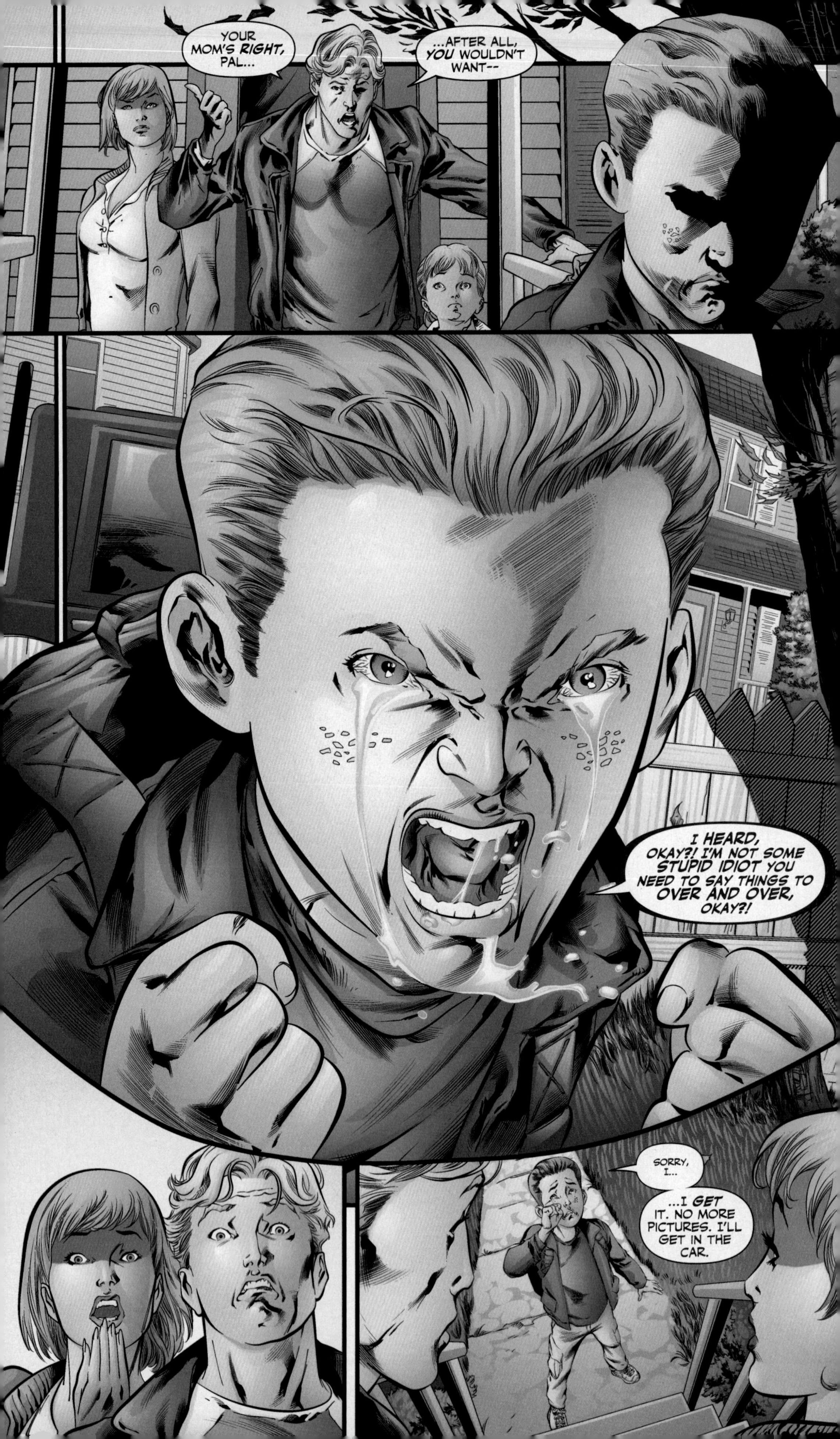
YOUR MOM'S **RIGHT**, PAL...
...AFTER ALL, **YOU** WOULDN'T WANT--
I **HEARD**, OKAY?! I'M NOT SOME **STUPID IDIOT** YOU NEED TO SAY THINGS TO **OVER AND OVER**, OKAY?!
SORRY, I...
...I **GET** IT. NO MORE PICTURES. I'LL GET IN THE CAR.

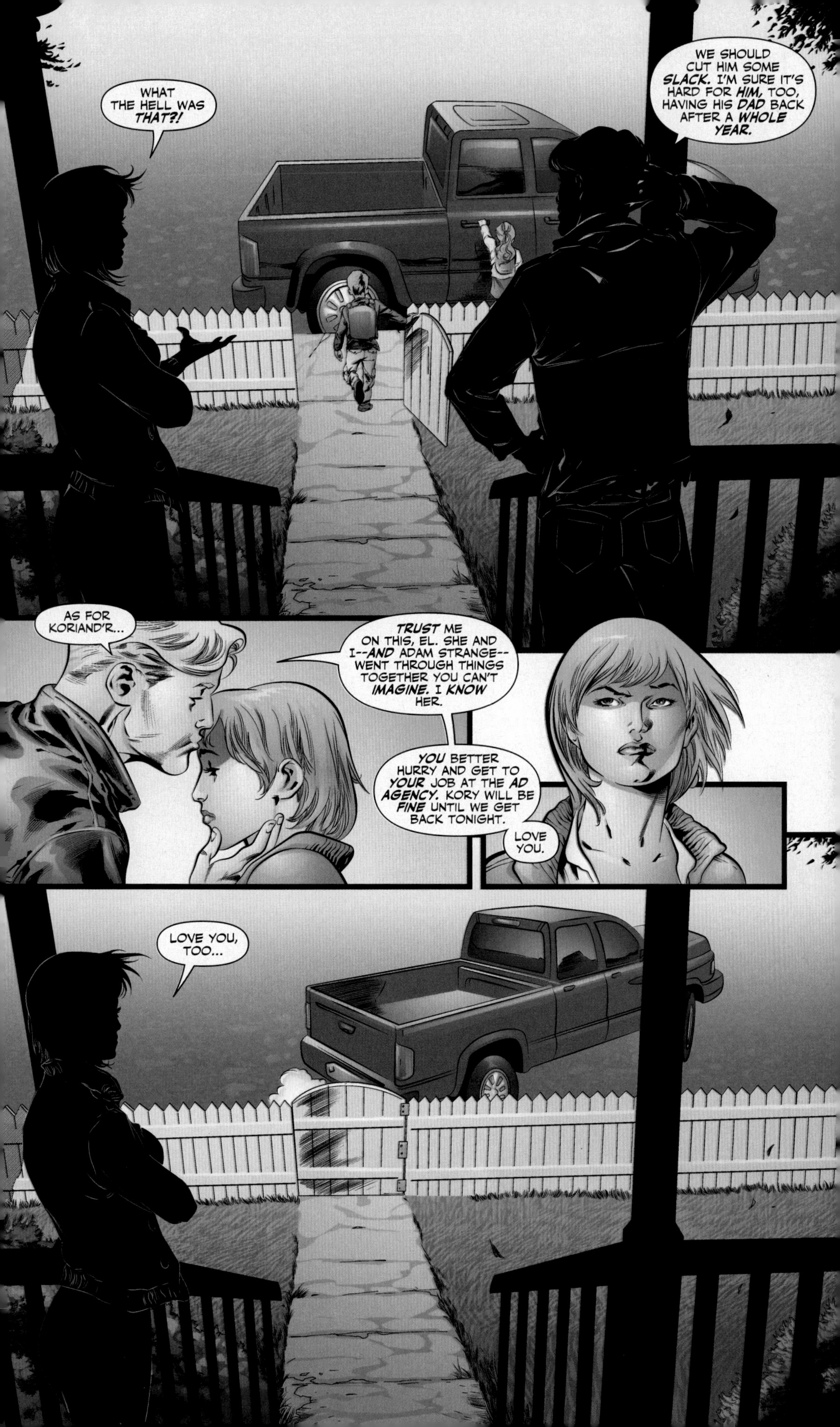
WHAT THE HELL WAS THAT?!
WE SHOULD CUT HIM SOME SLACK. I'M SURE IT'S HARD FOR HIM, TOO, HAVING HIS DAD BACK AFTER A WHOLE YEAR.
AS FOR KORIAND'R...
TRUST ME ON THIS, EL. SHE AND I--AND ADAM STRANGE--WENT THROUGH THINGS TOGETHER YOU CAN'T IMAGINE. I KNOW HER.
YOU BETTER HURRY AND GET TO YOUR JOB AT THE AD AGENCY. KORY WILL BE FINE UNTIL WE GET BACK TONIGHT.
LOVE YOU.
LOVE YOU, TOO...

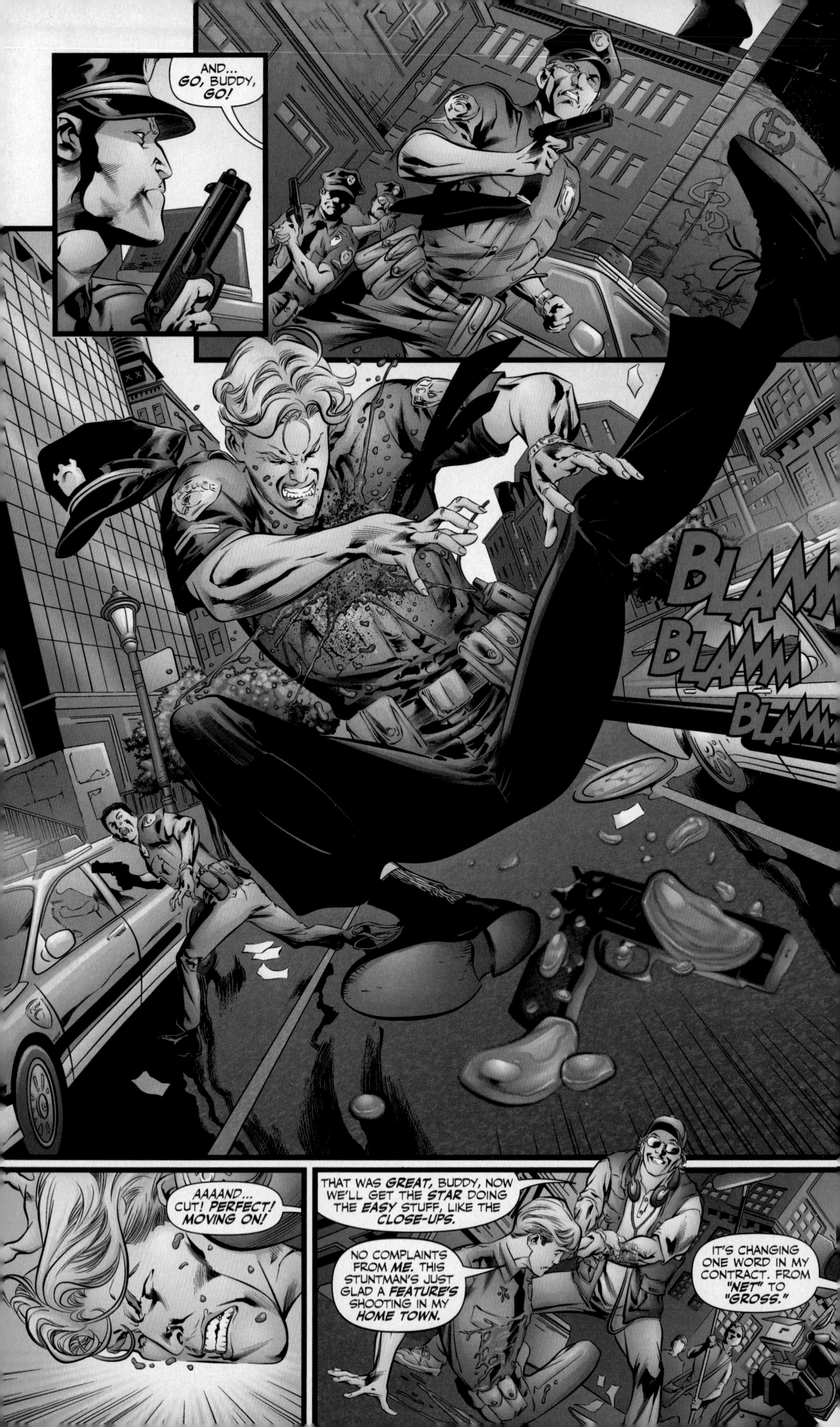
AND... GO, BUDDY, GO!
BLAMM
BLAMM
BLAMM
AAAAND... CUT! PERFECT! MOVING ON!
THAT WAS GREAT, BUDDY, NOW WE'LL GET THE STAR DOING THE EASY STUFF, LIKE THE CLOSE-UPS.
NO COMPLAINTS FROM ME. THIS STUNTMAN'S JUST GLAD A FEATURE'S SHOOTING IN MY HOME TOWN.
IT'S CHANGING ONE WORD IN MY CONTRACT. FROM "NET" TO "GROSS."

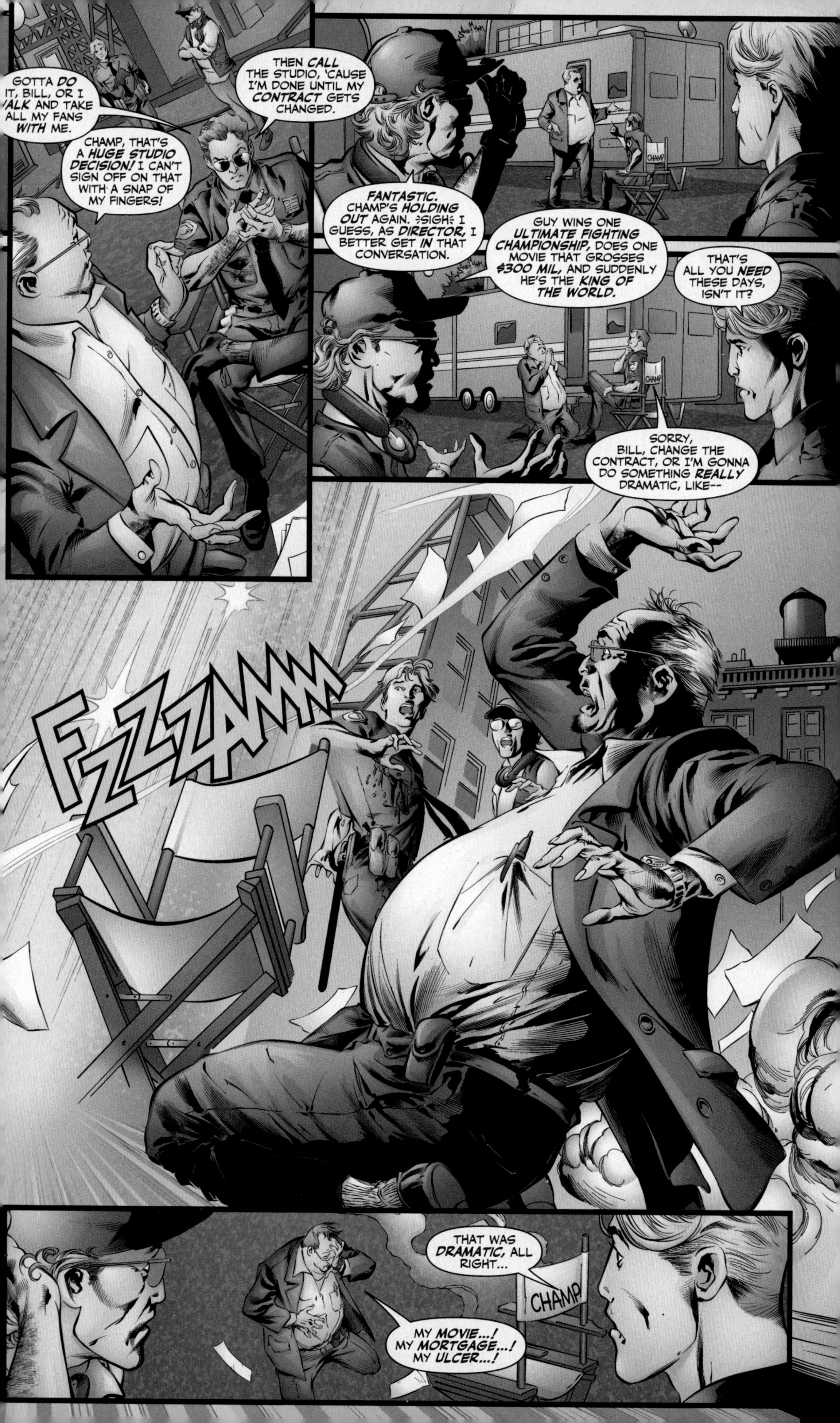

GOTTA DO IT, BILL, OR I WALK AND TAKE ALL MY FANS WITH ME.
THEN CALL THE STUDIO, 'CAUSE I'M DONE UNTIL MY CONTRACT GETS CHANGED.
CHAMP, THAT'S A HUGE STUDIO DECISION! I CAN'T SIGN OFF ON THAT WITH A SNAP OF MY FINGERS!
FANTASTIC. CHAMP'S HOLDING OUT AGAIN. *SIGH* I GUESS, AS DIRECTOR, I BETTER GET IN THAT CONVERSATION.
CHAMP
GUY WINS ONE ULTIMATE FIGHTING CHAMPIONSHIP, DOES ONE MOVIE THAT GROSSES $300 MIL, AND SUDDENLY HE'S THE KING OF THE WORLD.
THAT'S ALL YOU NEED THESE DAYS, ISN'T IT?
CHAMP
SORRY, BILL, CHANGE THE CONTRACT, OR I'M GONNA DO SOMETHING REALLY DRAMATIC, LIKE--
FZZZAMMM
THAT WAS DRAMATIC, ALL RIGHT...
CHAMP
MY MOVIE...! MY MORTGAGE...! MY ULCER...!

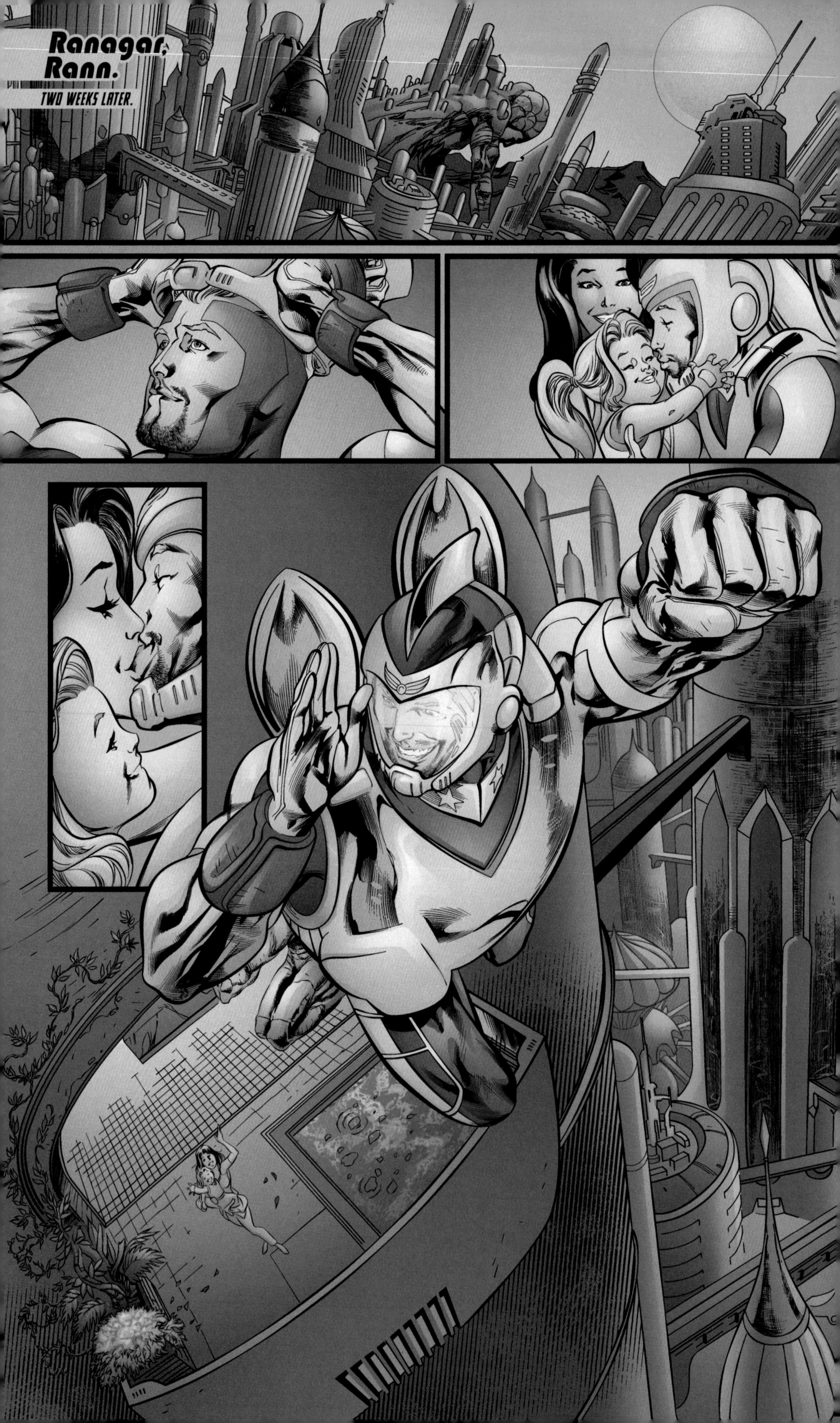
Ranagar, Rann.
TWO WEEKS LATER.

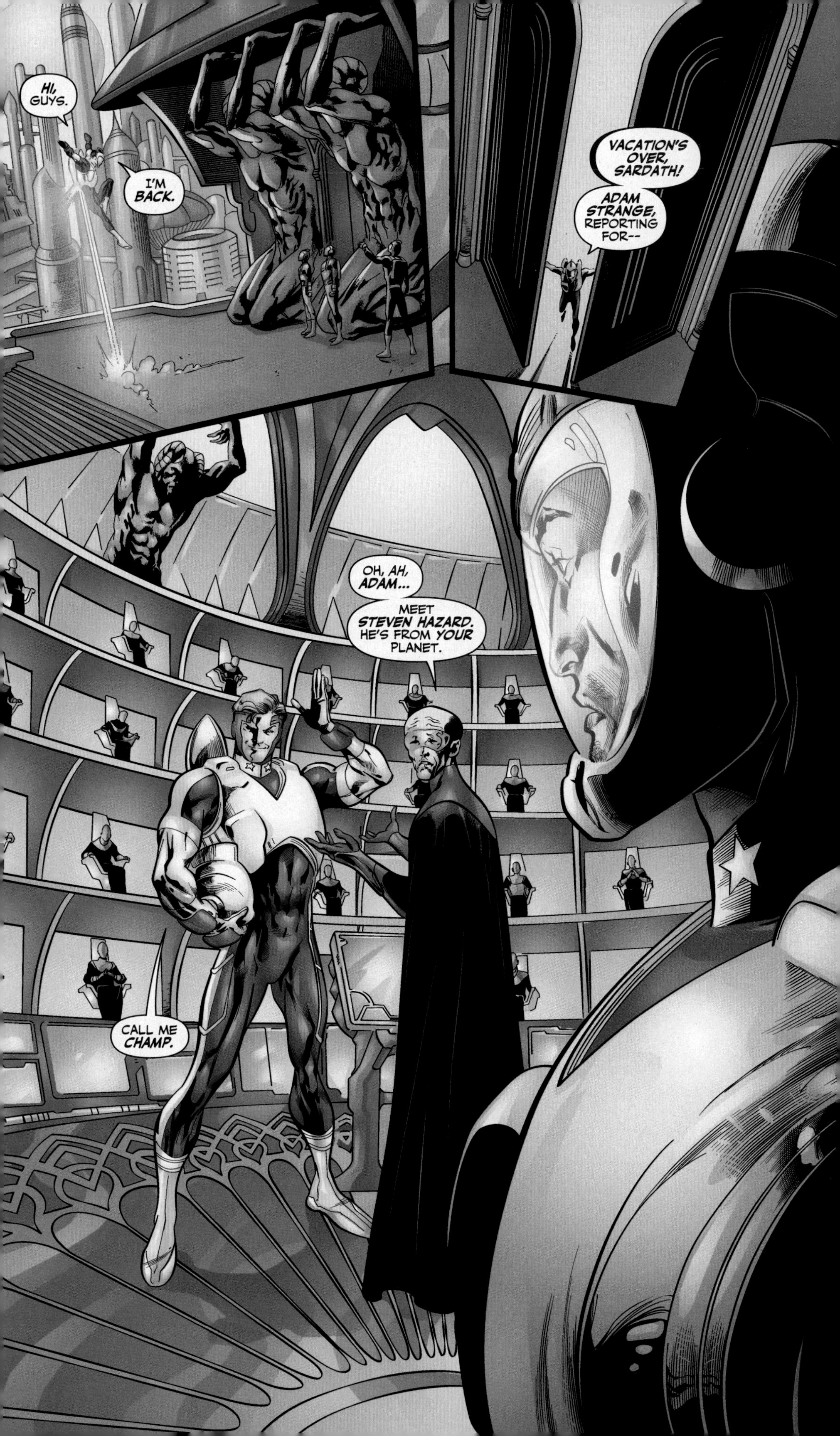
HI, GUYS.
I'M BACK.
VACATION'S OVER, SARDATH!
ADAM STRANGE, REPORTING FOR--
OH, AH, ADAM...
MEET STEVEN HAZARD. HE'S FROM YOUR PLANET.
CALL ME CHAMP.

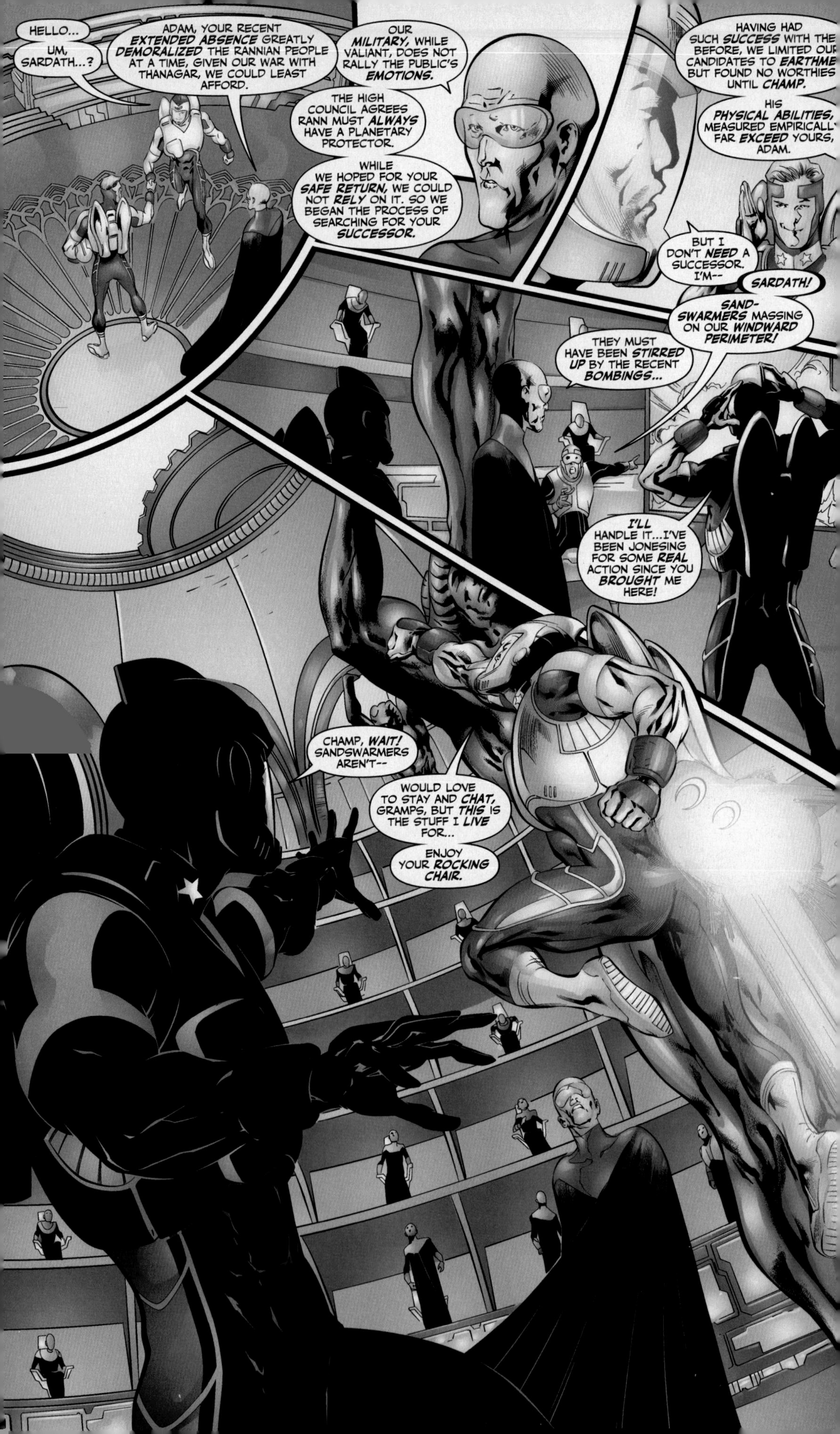
HELLO... UM, SARDATH...?
ADAM, YOUR RECENT EXTENDED ABSENCE GREATLY DEMORALIZED THE RANNIAN PEOPLE AT A TIME, GIVEN OUR WAR WITH THANAGAR, WE COULD LEAST AFFORD.
OUR MILITARY, WHILE VALIANT, DOES NOT RALLY THE PUBLIC'S EMOTIONS.
THE HIGH COUNCIL AGREES RANN MUST ALWAYS HAVE A PLANETARY PROTECTOR.
WHILE WE HOPED FOR YOUR SAFE RETURN, WE COULD NOT RELY ON IT. SO WE BEGAN THE PROCESS OF SEARCHING FOR YOUR SUCCESSOR.
HAVING HAD SUCH SUCCESS WITH THE BEFORE, WE LIMITED OUR CANDIDATES TO EARTHME BUT FOUND NO WORTHIES UNTIL CHAMP.
HIS PHYSICAL ABILITIES, MEASURED EMPIRICALL FAR EXCEED YOURS, ADAM.
BUT I DON'T NEED A SUCCESSOR. I'M--
SARDATH!
SAND-SWARMERS MASSING ON OUR WINDWARD PERIMETER!
THEY MUST HAVE BEEN STIRRED UP BY THE RECENT BOMBINGS...
I'LL HANDLE IT...I'VE BEEN JONESING FOR SOME REAL ACTION SINCE YOU BROUGHT ME HERE!
CHAMP, WAIT! SANDSWARMERS AREN'T--
WOULD LOVE TO STAY AND CHAT, GRAMPS, BUT THIS IS THE STUFF I LIVE FOR...
ENJOY YOUR ROCKING CHAIR.

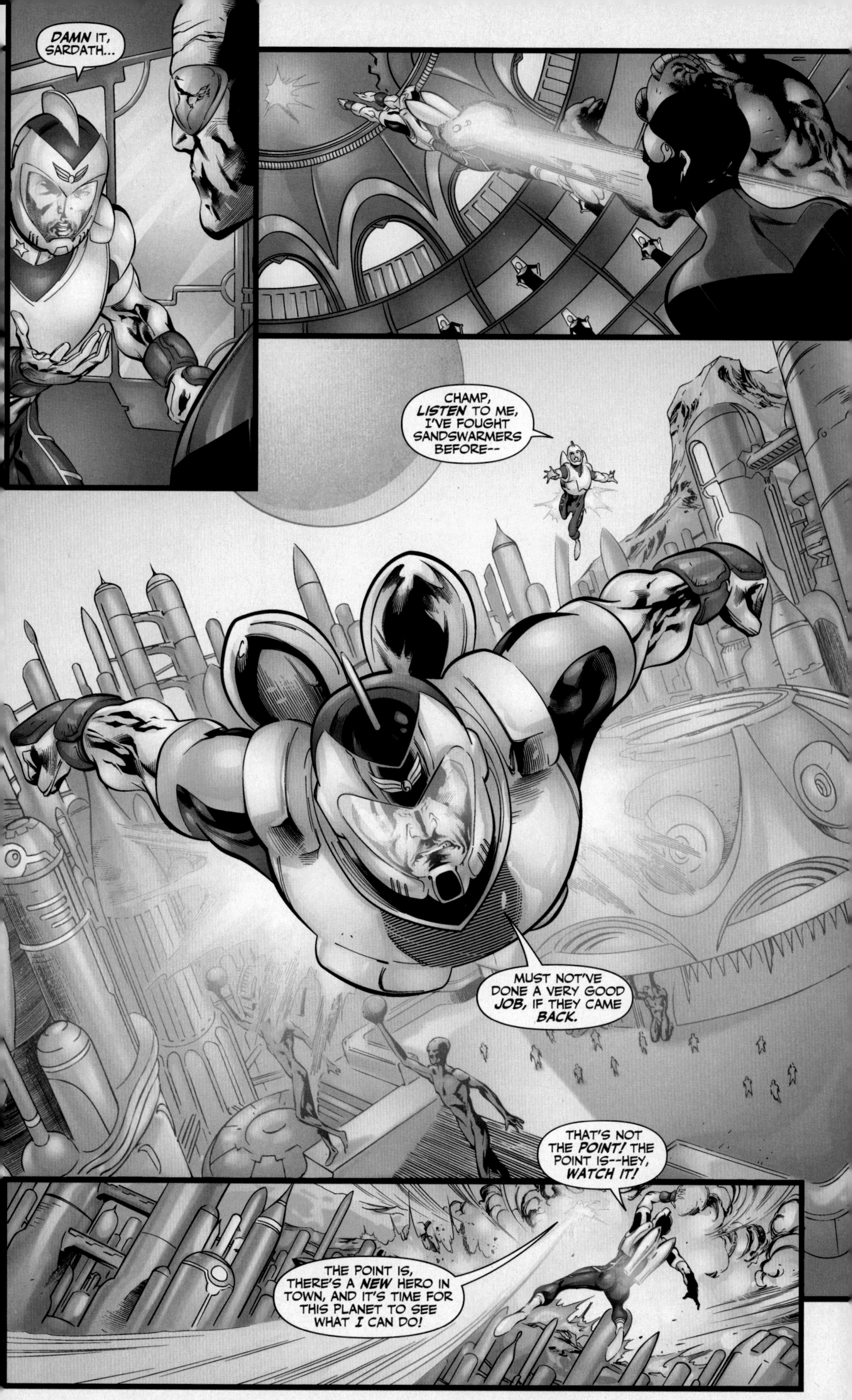
DAMN IT, SARDATH...
CHAMP, LISTEN TO ME, I'VE FOUGHT SANDSWARMERS BEFORE--
MUST NOT'VE DONE A VERY GOOD JOB, IF THEY CAME BACK.
THAT'S NOT THE POINT! THE POINT IS--HEY, WATCH IT!
THE POINT IS, THERE'S A NEW HERO IN TOWN, AND IT'S TIME FOR THIS PLANET TO SEE WHAT I CAN DO!

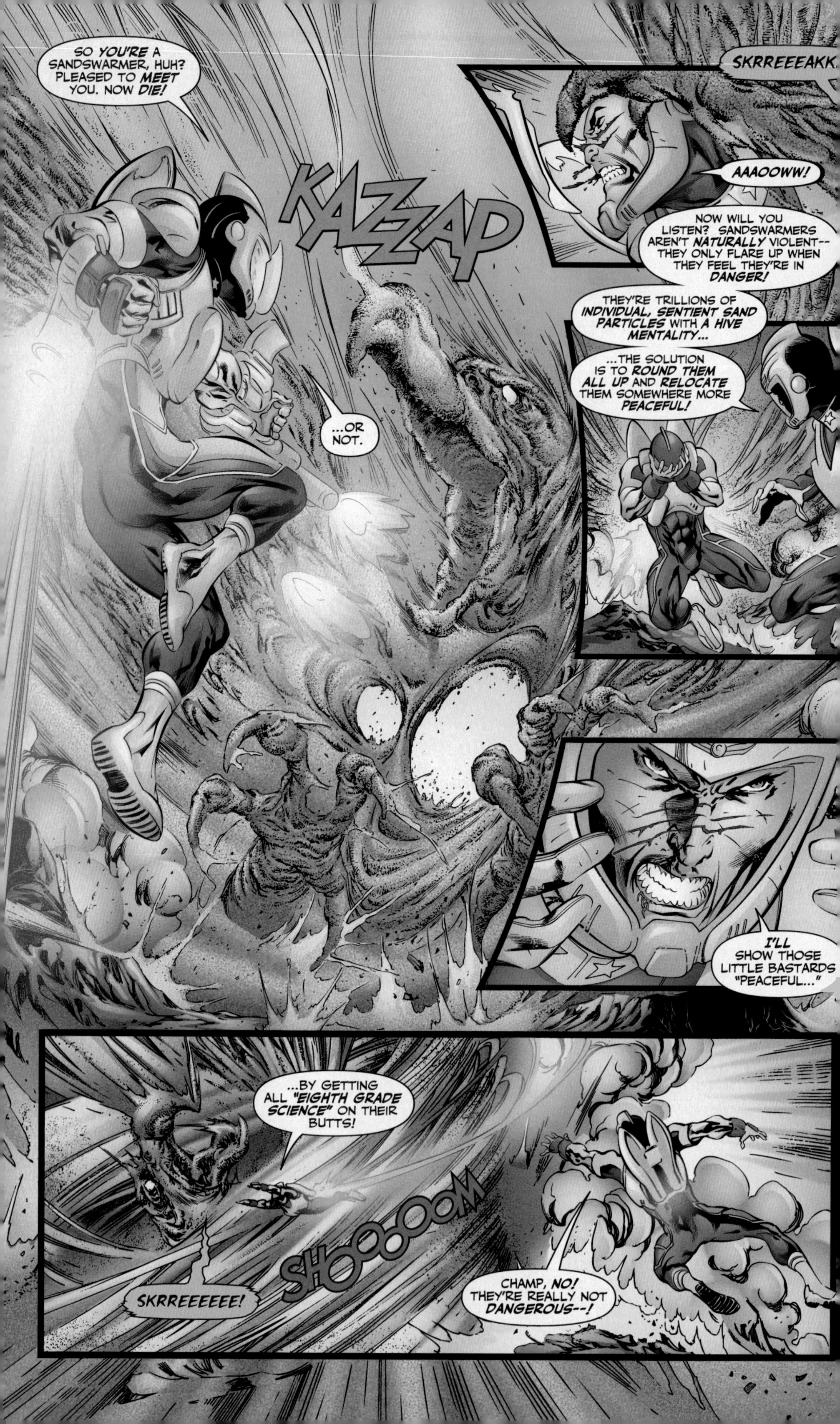
SO YOU'RE A SANDSWARMER, HUH? PLEASED TO MEET YOU. NOW DIE!
KAZZAP
...OR NOT.
SKRREEEAKK
AAAOOWW!
NOW WILL YOU LISTEN? SANDSWARMERS AREN'T NATURALLY VIOLENT-- THEY ONLY FLARE UP WHEN THEY FEEL THEY'RE IN DANGER!
THEY'RE TRILLIONS OF INDIVIDUAL, SENTIENT SAND PARTICLES WITH A HIVE MENTALITY...
...THE SOLUTION IS TO ROUND THEM ALL UP AND RELOCATE THEM SOMEWHERE MORE PEACEFUL!
I'LL SHOW THOSE LITTLE BASTARDS "PEACEFUL..."
...BY GETTING ALL "EIGHTH GRADE SCIENCE" ON THEIR BUTTS!
SHOOOOOOM
SKRREEEEEEE!
CHAMP, NO! THEY'RE REALLY NOT DANGEROUS--!

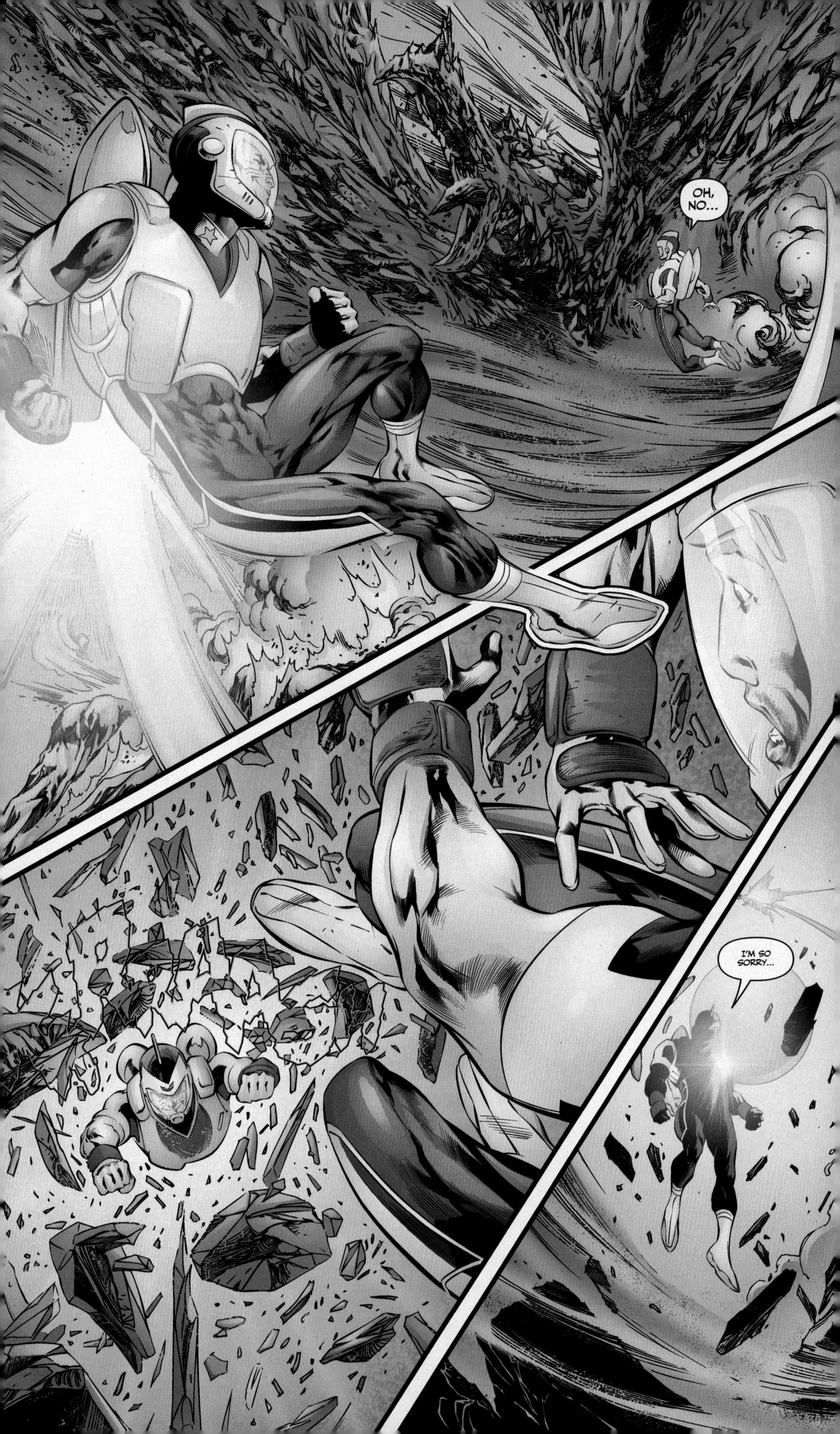
OH, NO...
I'M SO SORRY...

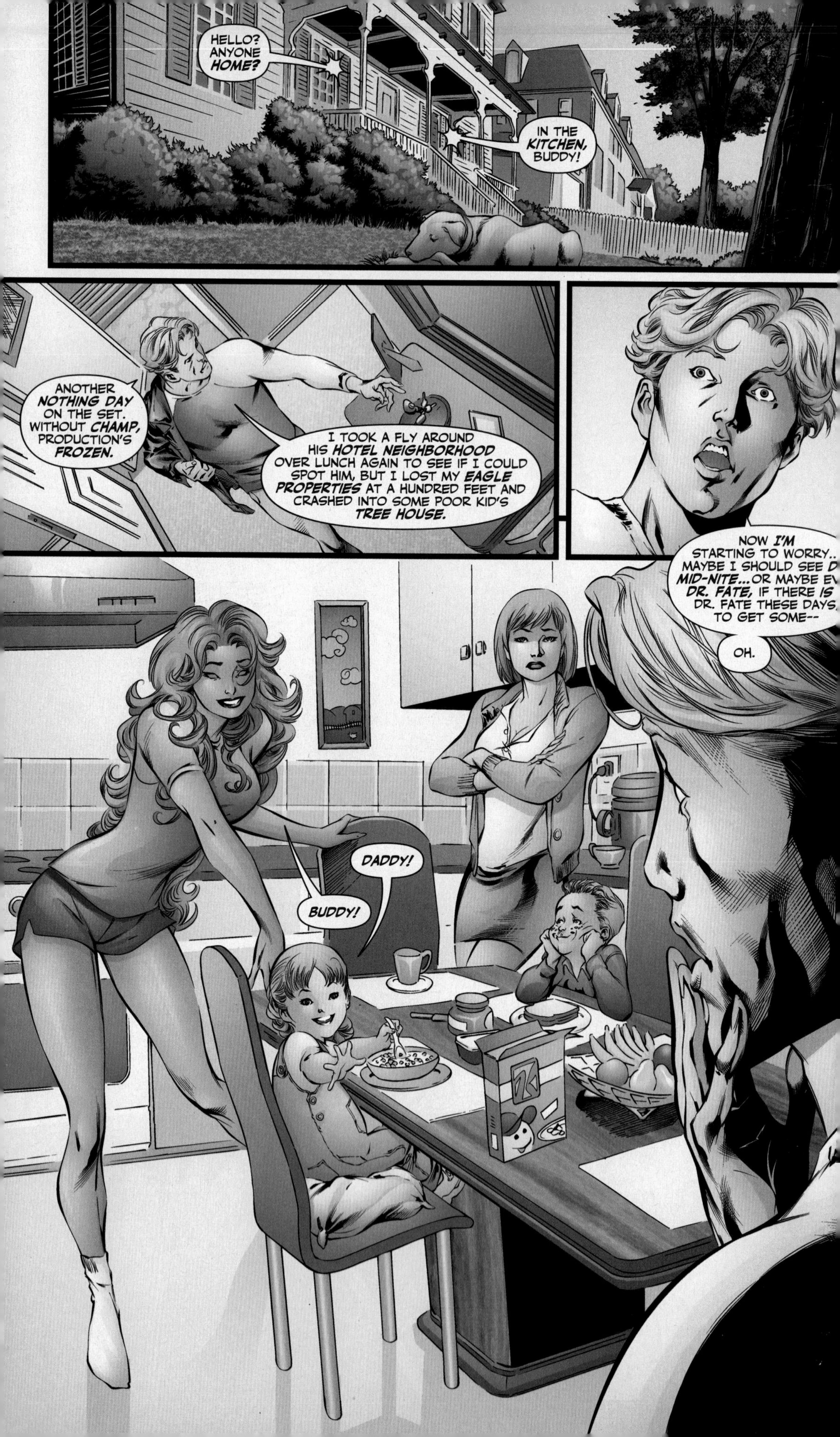
HELLO? ANYONE HOME?
IN THE KITCHEN, BUDDY!
ANOTHER NOTHING DAY ON THE SET. WITHOUT CHAMP, PRODUCTION'S FROZEN.
I TOOK A FLY AROUND HIS HOTEL NEIGHBORHOOD OVER LUNCH AGAIN TO SEE IF I COULD SPOT HIM, BUT I LOST MY EAGLE PROPERTIES AT A HUNDRED FEET AND CRASHED INTO SOME POOR KID'S TREE HOUSE.
NOW I'M STARTING TO WORRY.. MAYBE I SHOULD SEE D MID-NITE...OR MAYBE EV DR. FATE, IF THERE IS DR. FATE THESE DAYS, TO GET SOME--
OH.
DADDY!
BUDDY!

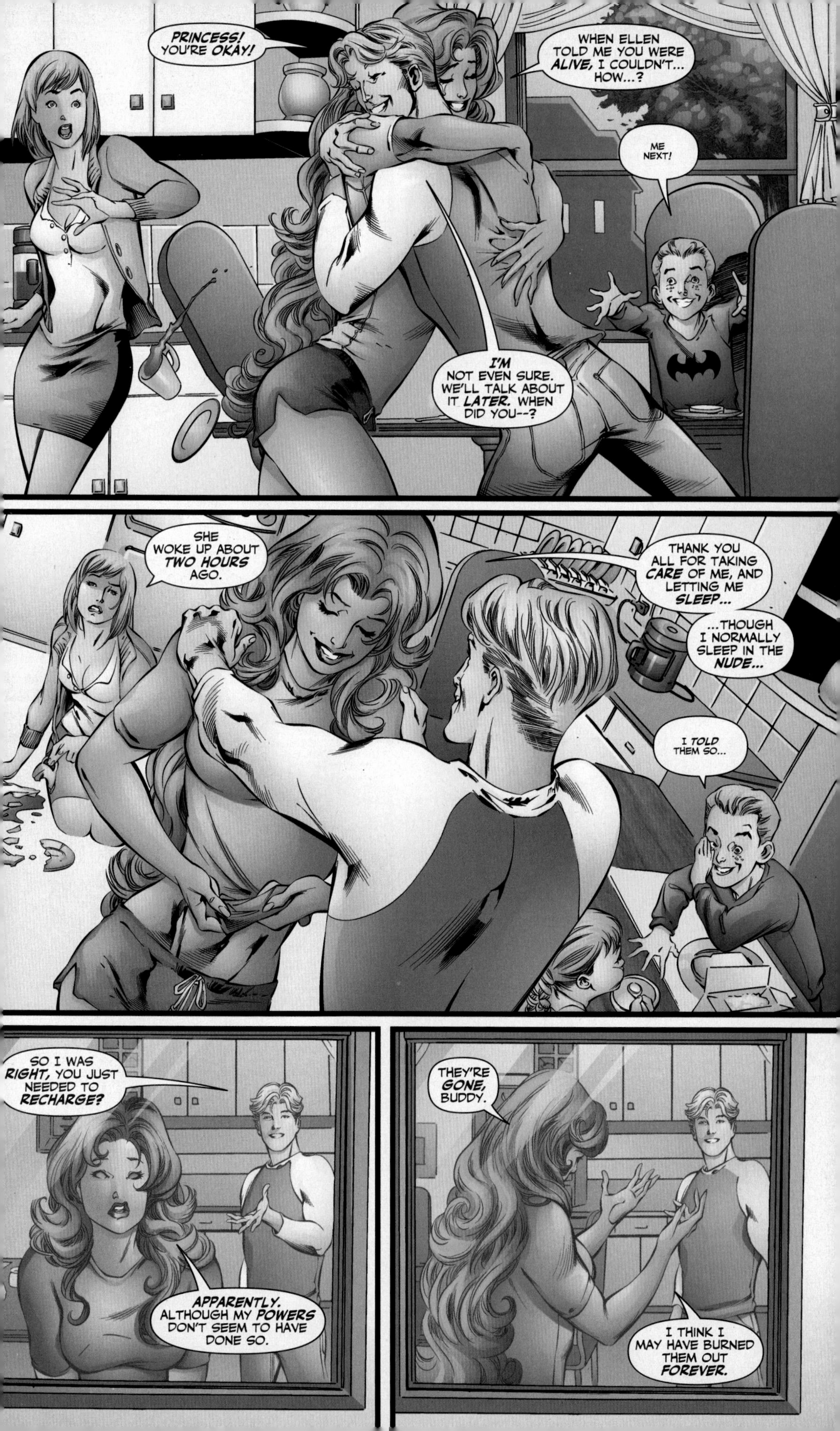
PRINCESS! YOU'RE OKAY!
WHEN ELLEN TOLD ME YOU WERE ALIVE, I COULDN'T... HOW...?
ME NEXT!
I'M NOT EVEN SURE. WE'LL TALK ABOUT IT LATER. WHEN DID YOU--?
SHE WOKE UP ABOUT TWO HOURS AGO.
THANK YOU ALL FOR TAKING CARE OF ME, AND LETTING ME SLEEP...
...THOUGH I NORMALLY SLEEP IN THE NUDE...
I TOLD THEM SO...
SO I WAS RIGHT, YOU JUST NEEDED TO RECHARGE?
APPARENTLY. ALTHOUGH MY POWERS DON'T SEEM TO HAVE DONE SO.
THEY'RE GONE, BUDDY.
I THINK I MAY HAVE BURNED THEM OUT FOREVER.

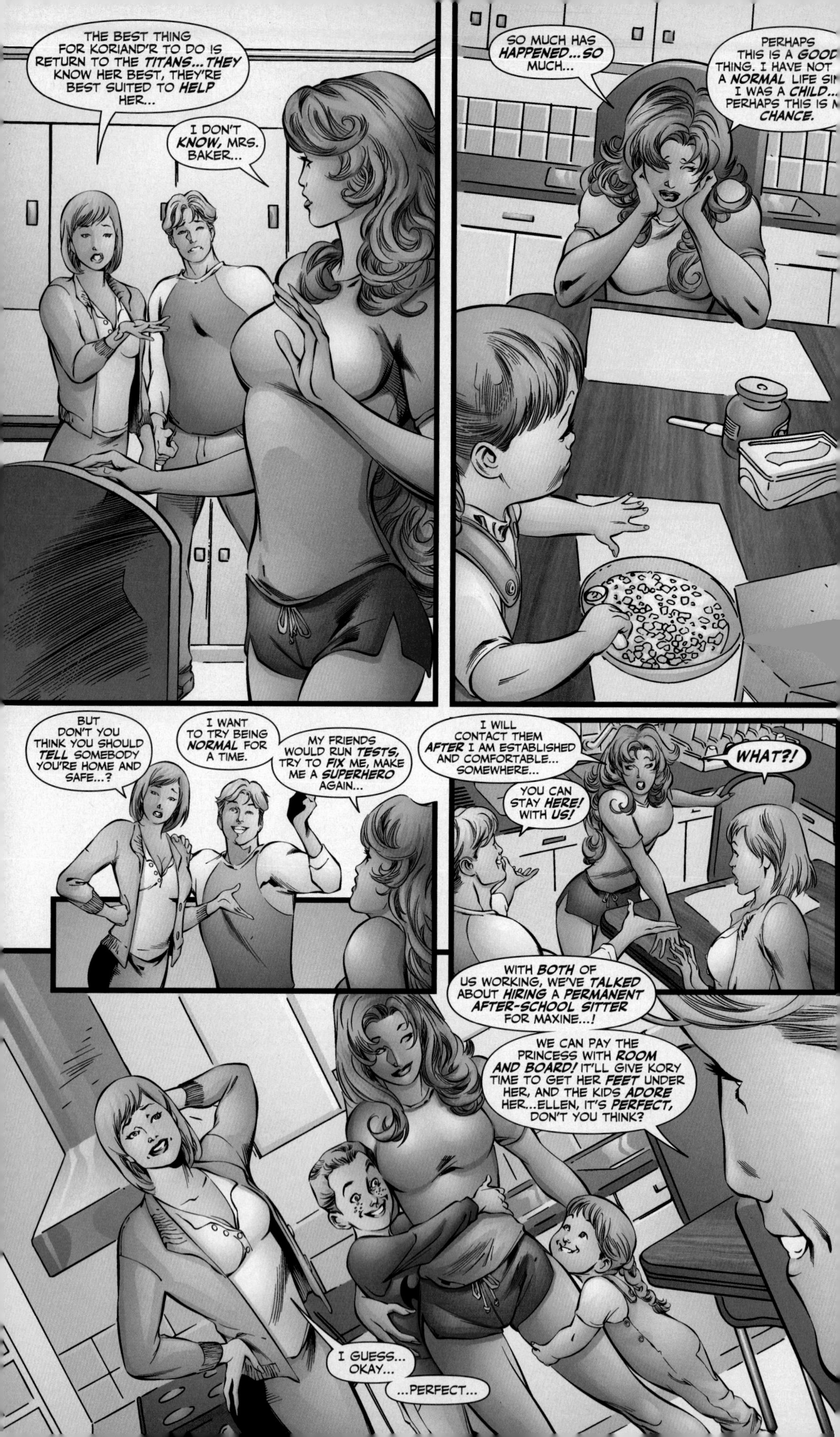
THE BEST THING FOR KORIAND'R TO DO IS RETURN TO THE TITANS... THEY KNOW HER BEST, THEY'RE BEST SUITED TO HELP HER...
I DON'T KNOW, MRS. BAKER...
SO MUCH HAS HAPPENED... SO MUCH...
PERHAPS THIS IS A GOOD THING. I HAVE NOT A NORMAL LIFE SIN I WAS A CHILD... PERHAPS THIS IS M CHANCE.
BUT DON'T YOU THINK YOU SHOULD TELL SOMEBODY YOU'RE HOME AND SAFE...?
I WANT TO TRY BEING NORMAL FOR A TIME.
MY FRIENDS WOULD RUN TESTS, TRY TO FIX ME, MAKE ME A SUPERHERO AGAIN...
I WILL CONTACT THEM AFTER I AM ESTABLISHED AND COMFORTABLE... SOMEWHERE...
WHAT?!
YOU CAN STAY HERE! WITH US!
WITH BOTH OF US WORKING, WE'VE TALKED ABOUT HIRING A PERMANENT AFTER-SCHOOL SITTER FOR MAXINE...!
WE CAN PAY THE PRINCESS WITH ROOM AND BOARD! IT'LL GIVE KORY TIME TO GET HER FEET UNDER HER, AND THE KIDS ADORE HER...ELLEN, IT'S PERFECT, DON'T YOU THINK?
I GUESS... OKAY...
...PERFECT...

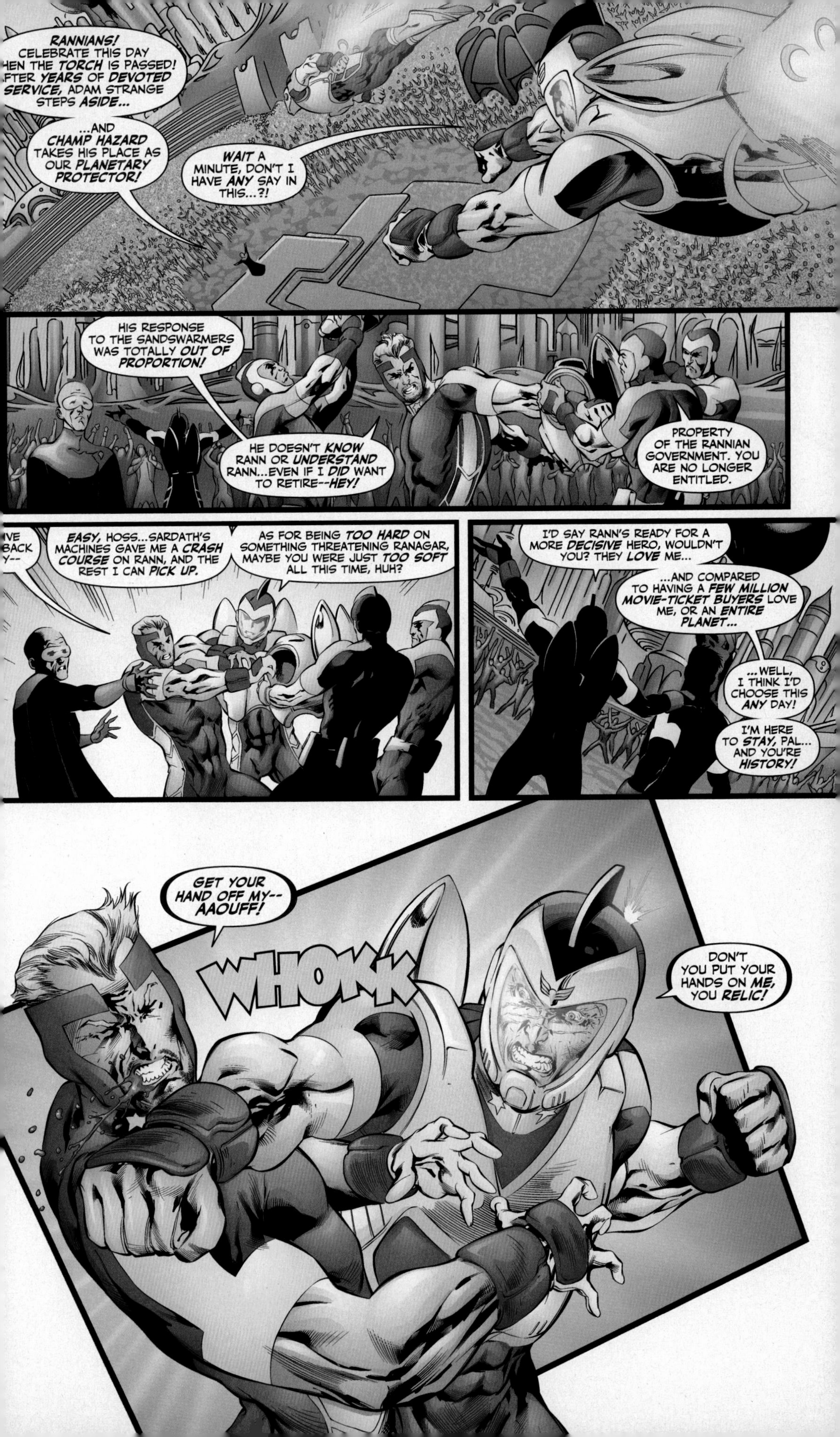

RANNIANS! CELEBRATE THIS DAY HEN THE TORCH IS PASSED! FTER YEARS OF DEVOTED SERVICE, ADAM STRANGE STEPS ASIDE...
...AND CHAMP HAZARD TAKES HIS PLACE AS OUR PLANETARY PROTECTOR!
WAIT A MINUTE, DON'T I HAVE ANY SAY IN THIS...?!
HIS RESPONSE TO THE SANDSWARMERS WAS TOTALLY OUT OF PROPORTION!
HE DOESN'T KNOW RANN OR UNDERSTAND RANN...EVEN IF I DID WANT TO RETIRE--HEY!
PROPERTY OF THE RANNIAN GOVERNMENT. YOU ARE NO LONGER ENTITLED.
VE BACK Y--
EASY, HOSS...SARDATH'S MACHINES GAVE ME A CRASH COURSE ON RANN, AND THE REST I CAN PICK UP.
AS FOR BEING TOO HARD ON SOMETHING THREATENING RANAGAR, MAYBE YOU WERE JUST TOO SOFT ALL THIS TIME, HUH?
I'D SAY RANN'S READY FOR A MORE DECISIVE HERO, WOULDN'T YOU? THEY LOVE ME...
...AND COMPARED TO HAVING A FEW MILLION MOVIE-TICKET BUYERS LOVE ME, OR AN ENTIRE PLANET...
...WELL, I THINK I'D CHOOSE THIS ANY DAY!
I'M HERE TO STAY, PAL... AND YOU'RE HISTORY!
GET YOUR HAND OFF MY-- AAOUFF!
WHOKK
DON'T YOU PUT YOUR HANDS ON ME, YOU RELIC!

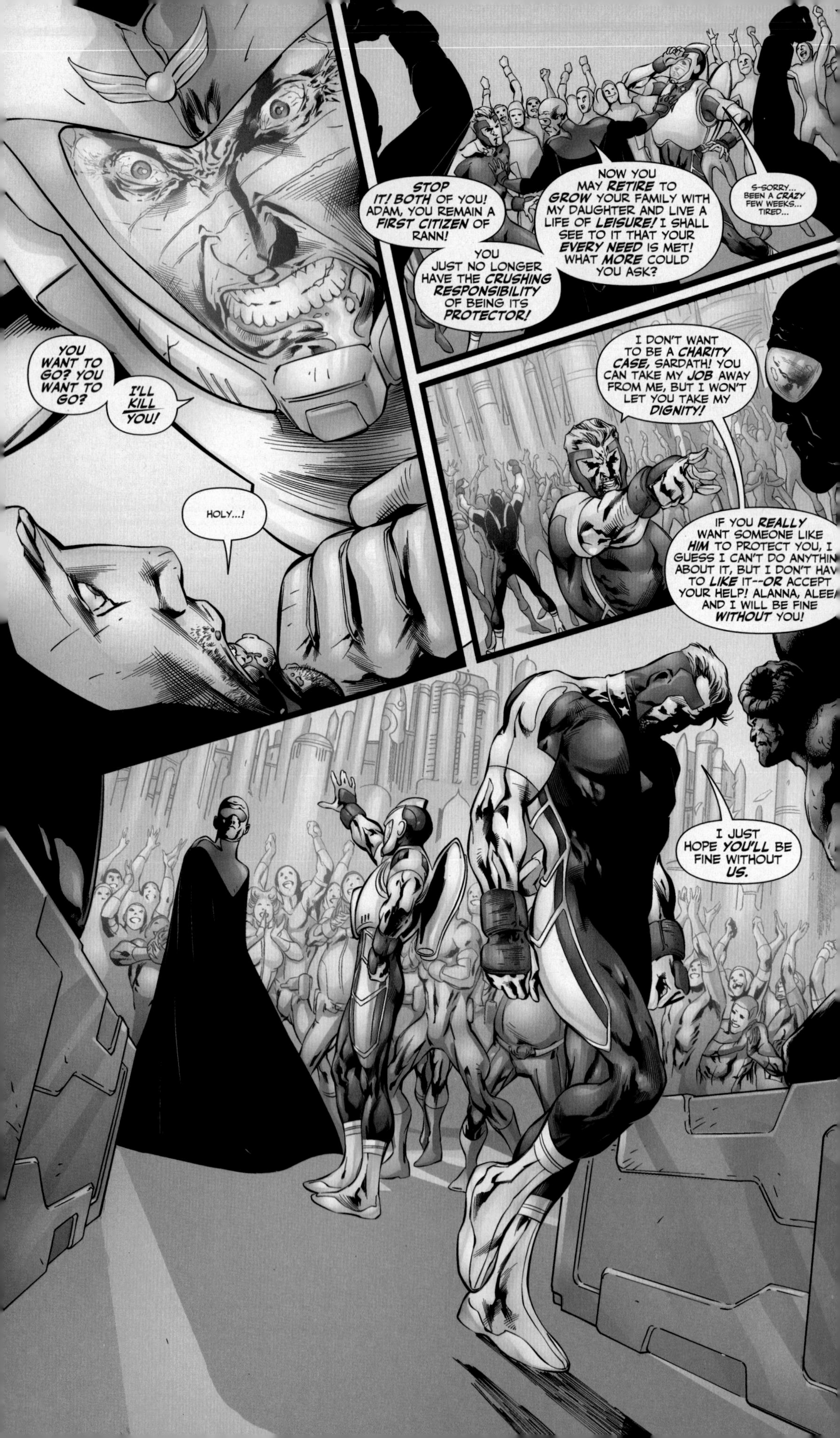

YOU WANT TO GO? YOU WANT TO GO?
I'LL KILL YOU!
HOLY...!
STOP IT! BOTH OF YOU! ADAM, YOU REMAIN A FIRST CITIZEN OF RANN!
YOU JUST NO LONGER HAVE THE CRUSHING RESPONSIBILITY OF BEING ITS PROTECTOR!
NOW YOU MAY RETIRE TO GROW YOUR FAMILY WITH MY DAUGHTER AND LIVE A LIFE OF LEISURE! I SHALL SEE TO IT THAT YOUR EVERY NEED IS MET! WHAT MORE COULD YOU ASK?
S-SORRY... BEEN A CRAZY FEW WEEKS... TIRED...
I DON'T WANT TO BE A CHARITY CASE, SARDATH! YOU CAN TAKE MY JOB AWAY FROM ME, BUT I WON'T LET YOU TAKE MY DIGNITY!
IF YOU REALLY WANT SOMEONE LIKE HIM TO PROTECT YOU, I GUESS I CAN'T DO ANYTHIN ABOUT IT, BUT I DON'T HAV TO LIKE IT--OR ACCEPT YOUR HELP! ALANNA, ALEE AND I WILL BE FINE WITHOUT YOU!
I JUST HOPE YOU'LL BE FINE WITHOUT US.

COUNTDOWN TO ADVENTURE

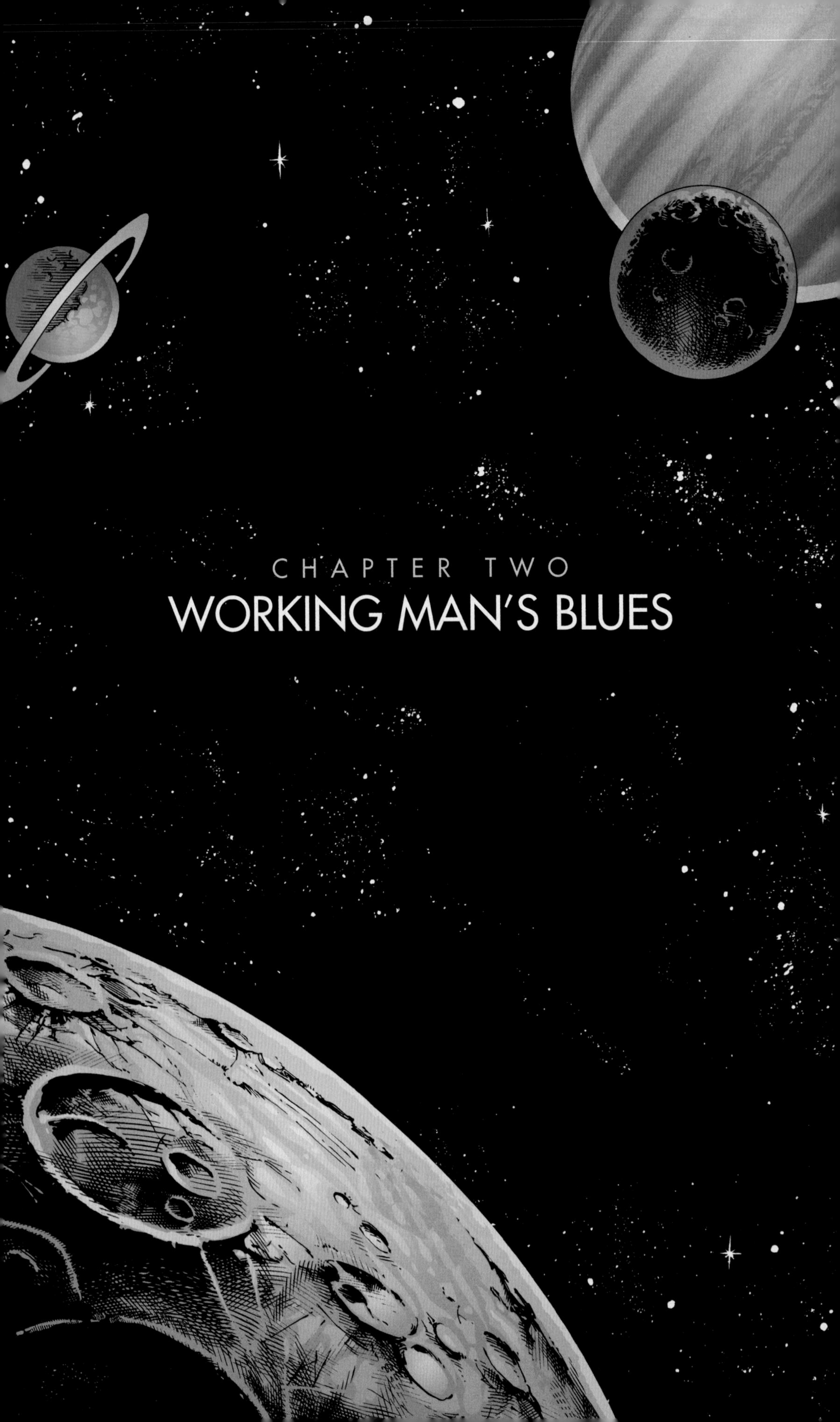

CHAPTER TWO

WORKING MAN'S BLUES

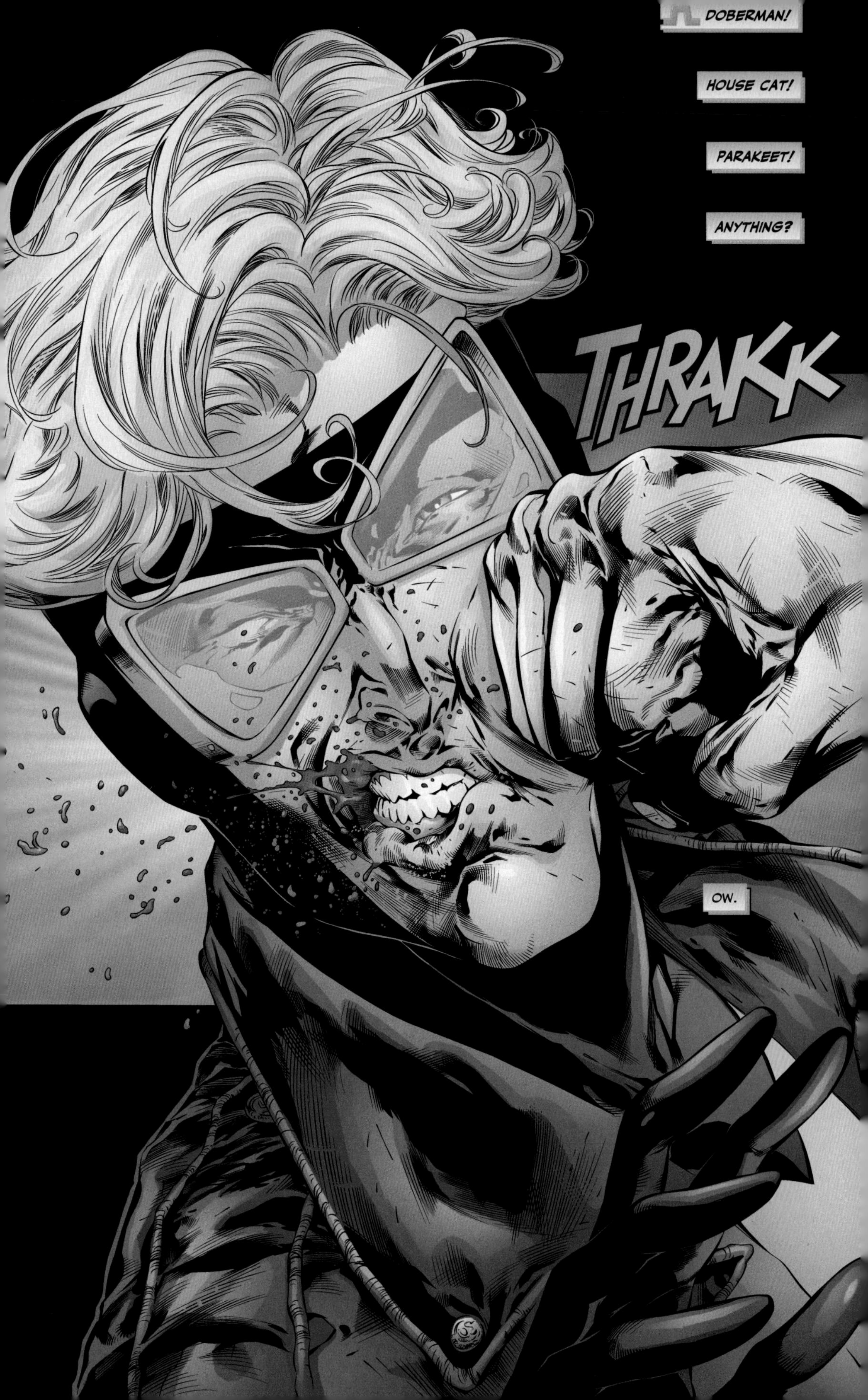
DOBERMAN!
HOUSE CAT!
PARAKEET!
ANYTHING?
THRAKK
OW.

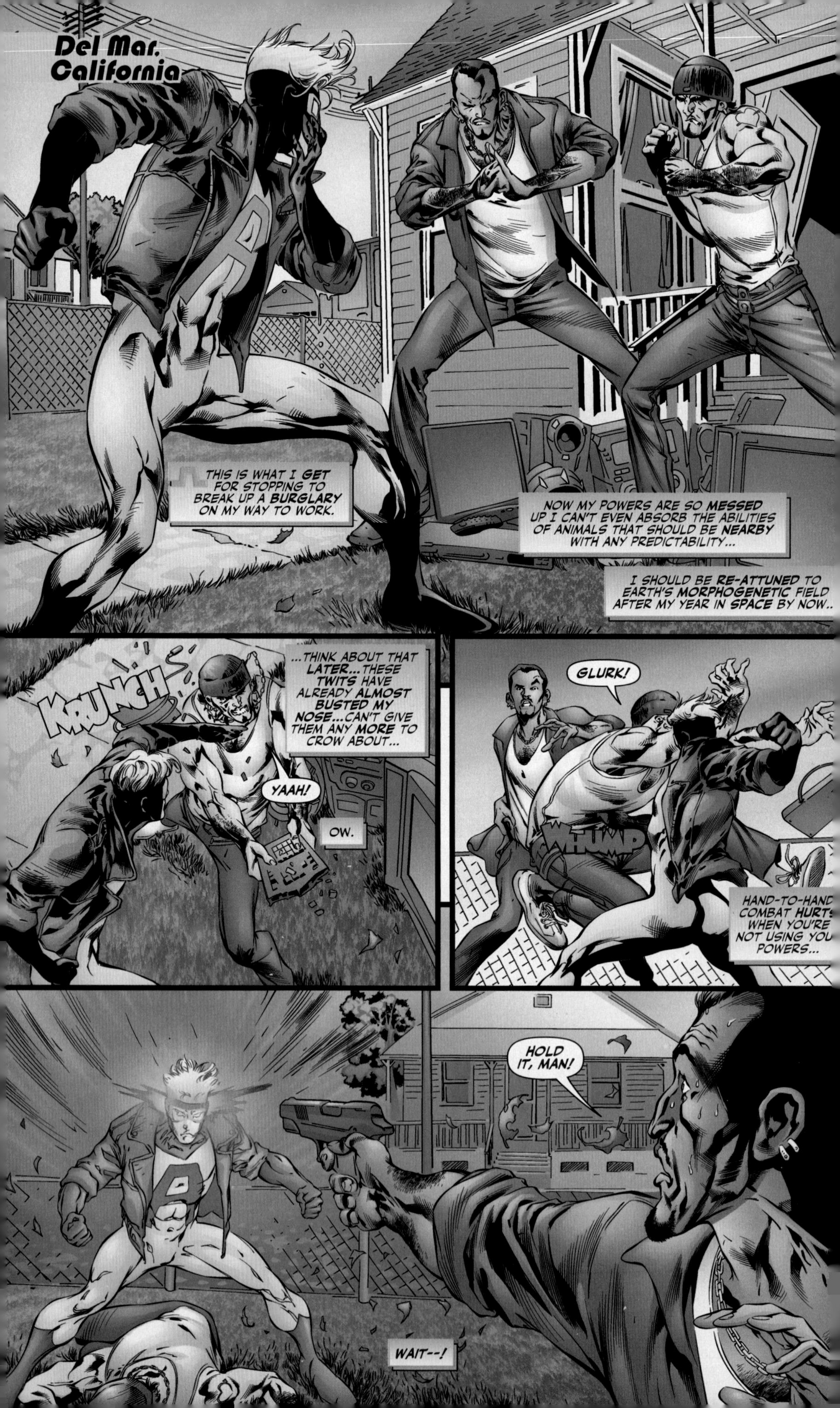
Del Mar, California
THIS IS WHAT I GET FOR STOPPING TO BREAK UP A BURGLARY ON MY WAY TO WORK.
NOW MY POWERS ARE SO MESSED UP I CAN'T EVEN ABSORB THE ABILITIES OF ANIMALS THAT SHOULD BE NEARBY WITH ANY PREDICTABILITY...
I SHOULD BE RE-ATTUNED TO EARTH'S MORPHOGENETIC FIELD AFTER MY YEAR IN SPACE BY NOW...
KRUNCH
...THINK ABOUT THAT LATER...THESE TWITS HAVE ALREADY ALMOST BUSTED MY NOSE...CAN'T GIVE THEM ANY MORE TO CROW ABOUT...
YAAH!
OW.
GLURK!
WHUMP
HAND-TO-HAND COMBAT HURTS WHEN YOU'RE NOT USING YOUR POWERS...
HOLD IT, MAN!
WAIT--!

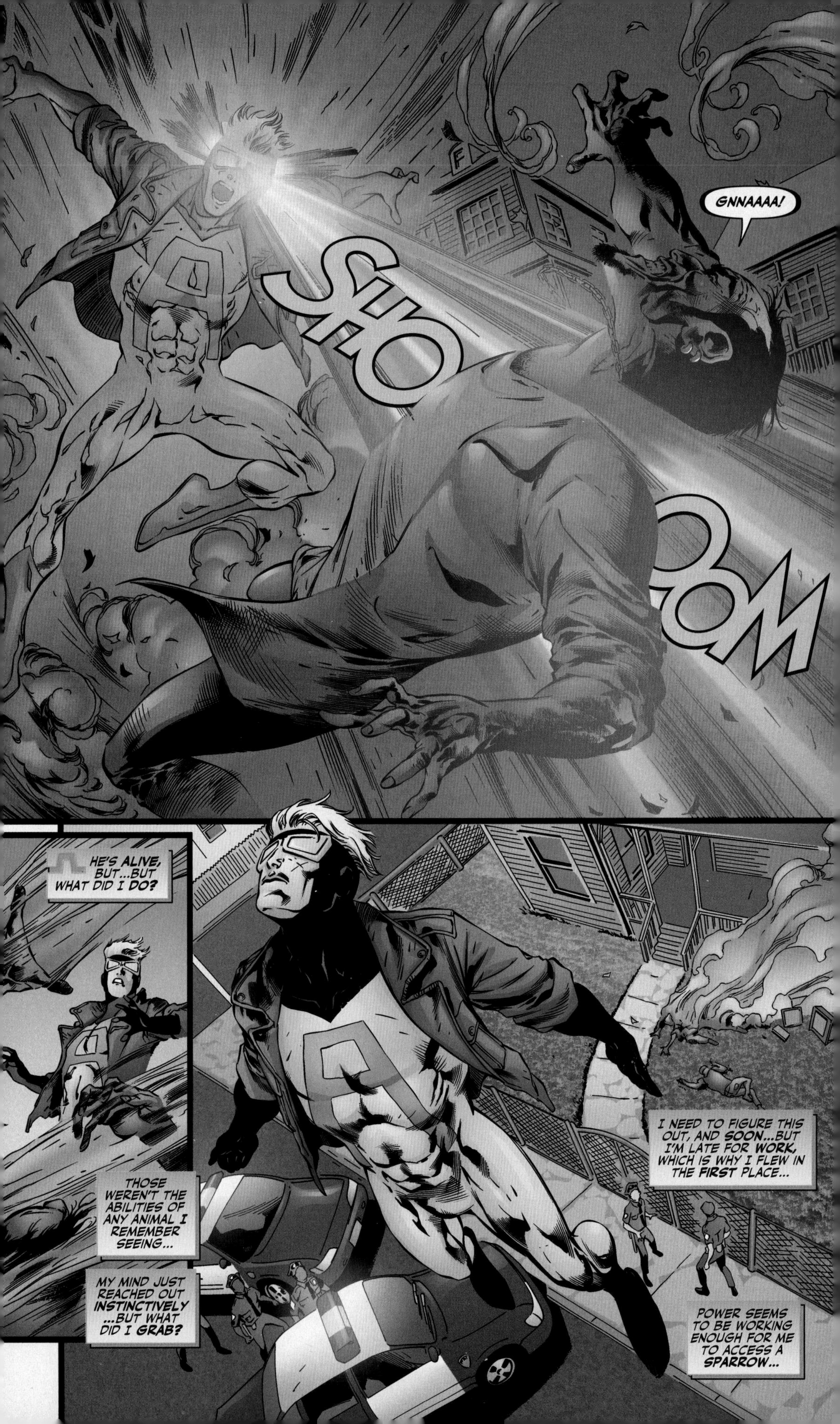
GNNAAAA!
SHOOOM
HE'S ALIVE, BUT...BUT WHAT DID I DO?
THOSE WEREN'T THE ABILITIES OF ANY ANIMAL I REMEMBER SEEING...
MY MIND JUST REACHED OUT INSTINCTIVELY ...BUT WHAT DID I GRAB?
I NEED TO FIGURE THIS OUT, AND SOON...BUT I'M LATE FOR WORK, WHICH IS WHY I FLEW IN THE FIRST PLACE...
POWER SEEMS TO BE WORKING ENOUGH FOR ME TO ACCESS A SPARROW...

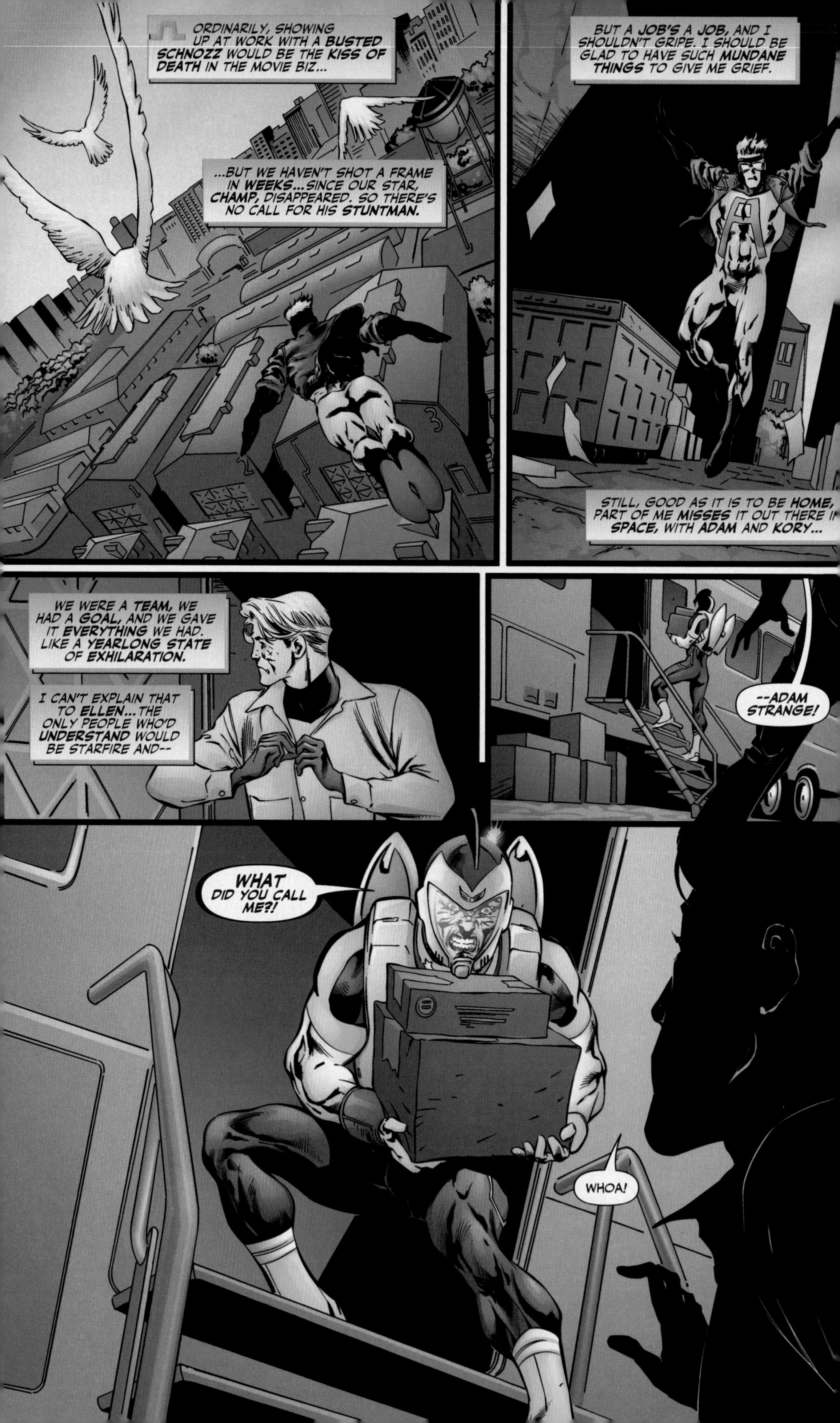
ORDINARILY, SHOWING UP AT WORK WITH A BUSTED SCHNOZZ WOULD BE THE KISS OF DEATH IN THE MOVIE BIZ...
...BUT WE HAVEN'T SHOT A FRAME IN WEEKS...SINCE OUR STAR, CHAMP, DISAPPEARED. SO THERE'S NO CALL FOR HIS STUNTMAN.
BUT A JOB'S A JOB, AND I SHOULDN'T GRIPE. I SHOULD BE GLAD TO HAVE SUCH MUNDANE THINGS TO GIVE ME GRIEF.
STILL, GOOD AS IT IS TO BE HOME, PART OF ME MISSES IT OUT THERE I SPACE, WITH ADAM AND KORY...
WE WERE A TEAM, WE HAD A GOAL, AND WE GAVE IT EVERYTHING WE HAD. LIKE A YEARLONG STATE OF EXHILARATION.
I CAN'T EXPLAIN THAT TO ELLEN...THE ONLY PEOPLE WHO'D UNDERSTAND WOULD BE STARFIRE AND--
--ADAM STRANGE!
WHAT DID YOU CALL ME?!
WHOA!

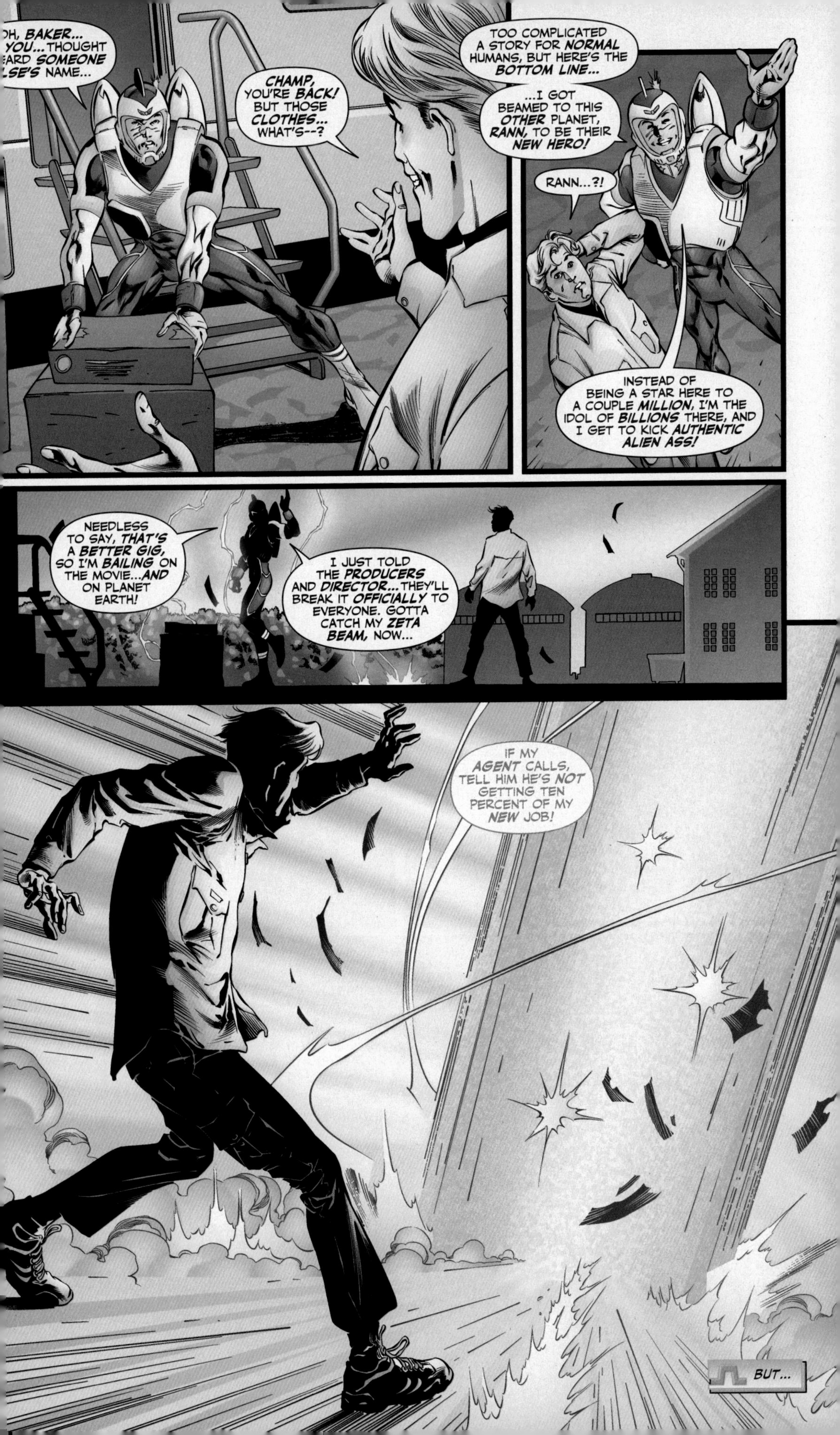

OH, BAKER... YOU... THOUGHT I HEARD SOMEONE ELSE'S NAME...
CHAMP, YOU'RE BACK! BUT THOSE CLOTHES... WHAT'S--?
TOO COMPLICATED A STORY FOR NORMAL HUMANS, BUT HERE'S THE BOTTOM LINE...
...I GOT BEAMED TO THIS OTHER PLANET, RANN, TO BE THEIR NEW HERO!
RANN...?!
INSTEAD OF BEING A STAR HERE TO A COUPLE MILLION, I'M THE IDOL OF BILLIONS THERE, AND I GET TO KICK AUTHENTIC ALIEN ASS!
NEEDLESS TO SAY, THAT'S A BETTER GIG, SO I'M BAILING ON THE MOVIE...AND ON PLANET EARTH!
I JUST TOLD THE PRODUCERS AND DIRECTOR... THEY'LL BREAK IT OFFICIALLY TO EVERYONE. GOTTA CATCH MY ZETA BEAM, NOW...
IF MY AGENT CALLS, TELL HIM HE'S NOT GETTING TEN PERCENT OF MY NEW JOB!
BUT...

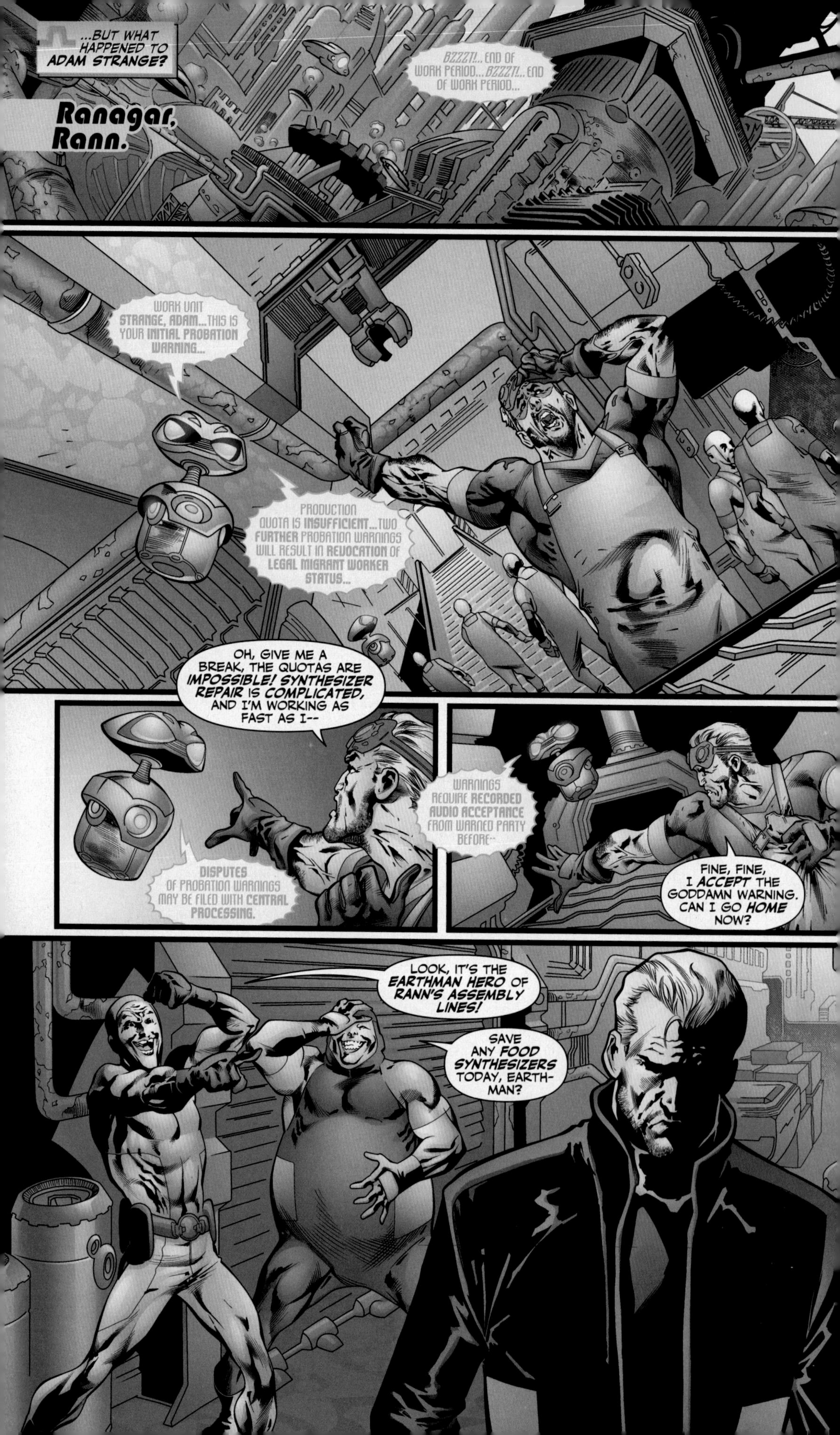

...BUT WHAT HAPPENED TO ADAM STRANGE?
Ranagar, Rann.
BZZZT!... END OF WORK PERIOD... BZZZT!... END OF WORK PERIOD...
WORK UNIT STRANGE, ADAM... THIS IS YOUR INITIAL PROBATION WARNING...
PRODUCTION QUOTA IS INSUFFICIENT... TWO FURTHER PROBATION WARNINGS WILL RESULT IN REVOCATION OF LEGAL MIGRANT WORKER STATUS...
OH, GIVE ME A BREAK, THE QUOTAS ARE IMPOSSIBLE! SYNTHESIZER REPAIR IS COMPLICATED, AND I'M WORKING AS FAST AS I--
DISPUTES OF PROBATION WARNINGS MAY BE FILED WITH CENTRAL PROCESSING.
WARNINGS REQUIRE RECORDED AUDIO ACCEPTANCE FROM WARNED PARTY BEFORE--
FINE, FINE, I ACCEPT THE GODDAMN WARNING. CAN I GO HOME NOW?
LOOK, IT'S THE EARTHMAN HERO OF RANN'S ASSEMBLY LINES!
SAVE ANY FOOD SYNTHESIZERS TODAY, EARTH-MAN?

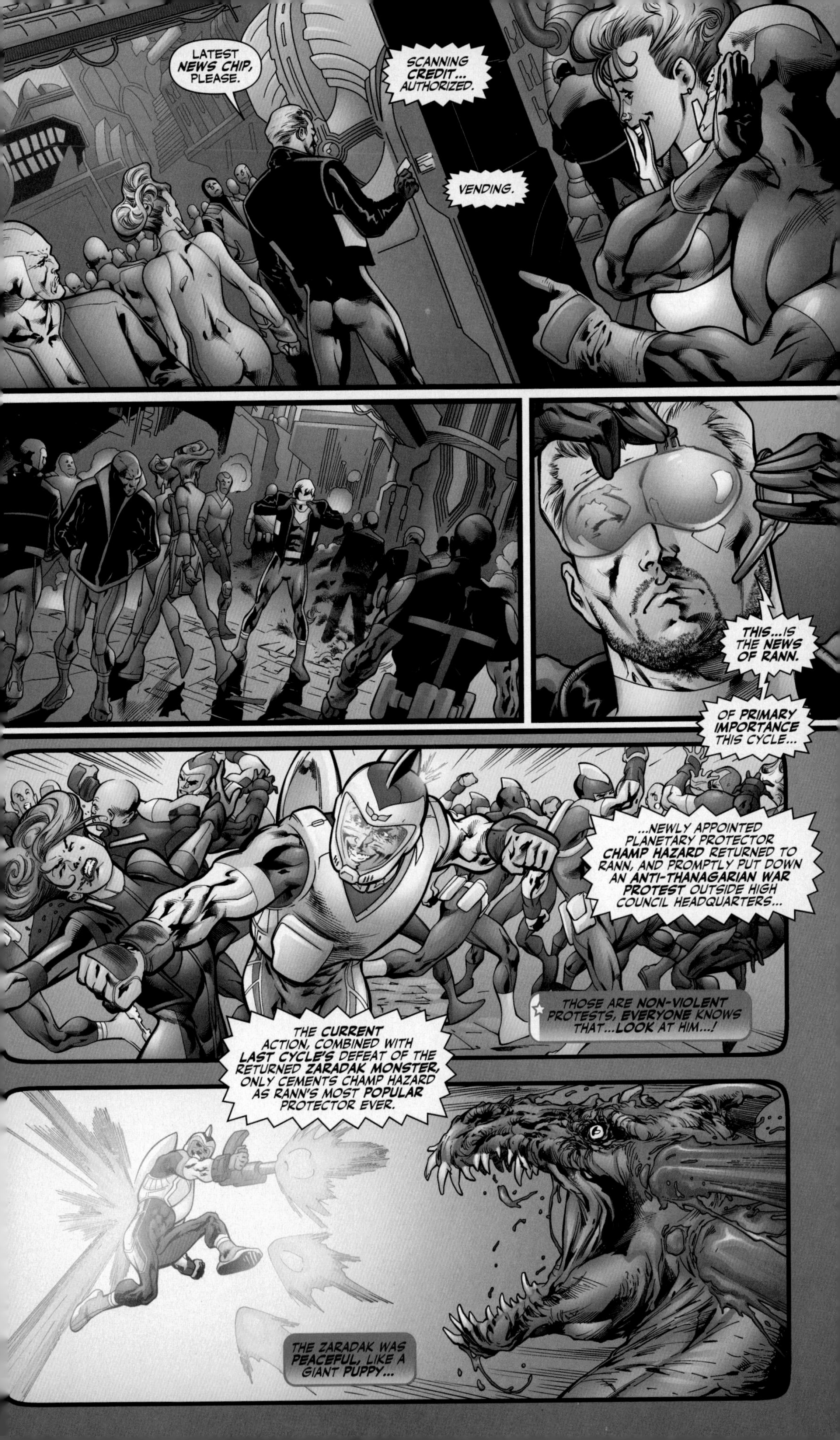
LATEST NEWS CHIP, PLEASE.
SCANNING CREDIT... AUTHORIZED.
VENDING.
THIS...IS THE NEWS OF RANN.
OF PRIMARY IMPORTANCE THIS CYCLE...
...NEWLY APPOINTED PLANETARY PROTECTOR CHAMP HAZARD RETURNED TO RANN, AND PROMPTLY PUT DOWN AN ANTI-THANAGARIAN WAR PROTEST OUTSIDE HIGH COUNCIL HEADQUARTERS...
THOSE ARE NON-VIOLENT PROTESTS, EVERYONE KNOWS THAT...LOOK AT HIM...!
THE CURRENT ACTION, COMBINED WITH LAST CYCLE'S DEFEAT OF THE RETURNED ZARADAK MONSTER, ONLY CEMENTS CHAMP HAZARD AS RANN'S MOST POPULAR PROTECTOR EVER.
THE ZARADAK WAS PEACEFUL, LIKE A GIANT PUPPY...

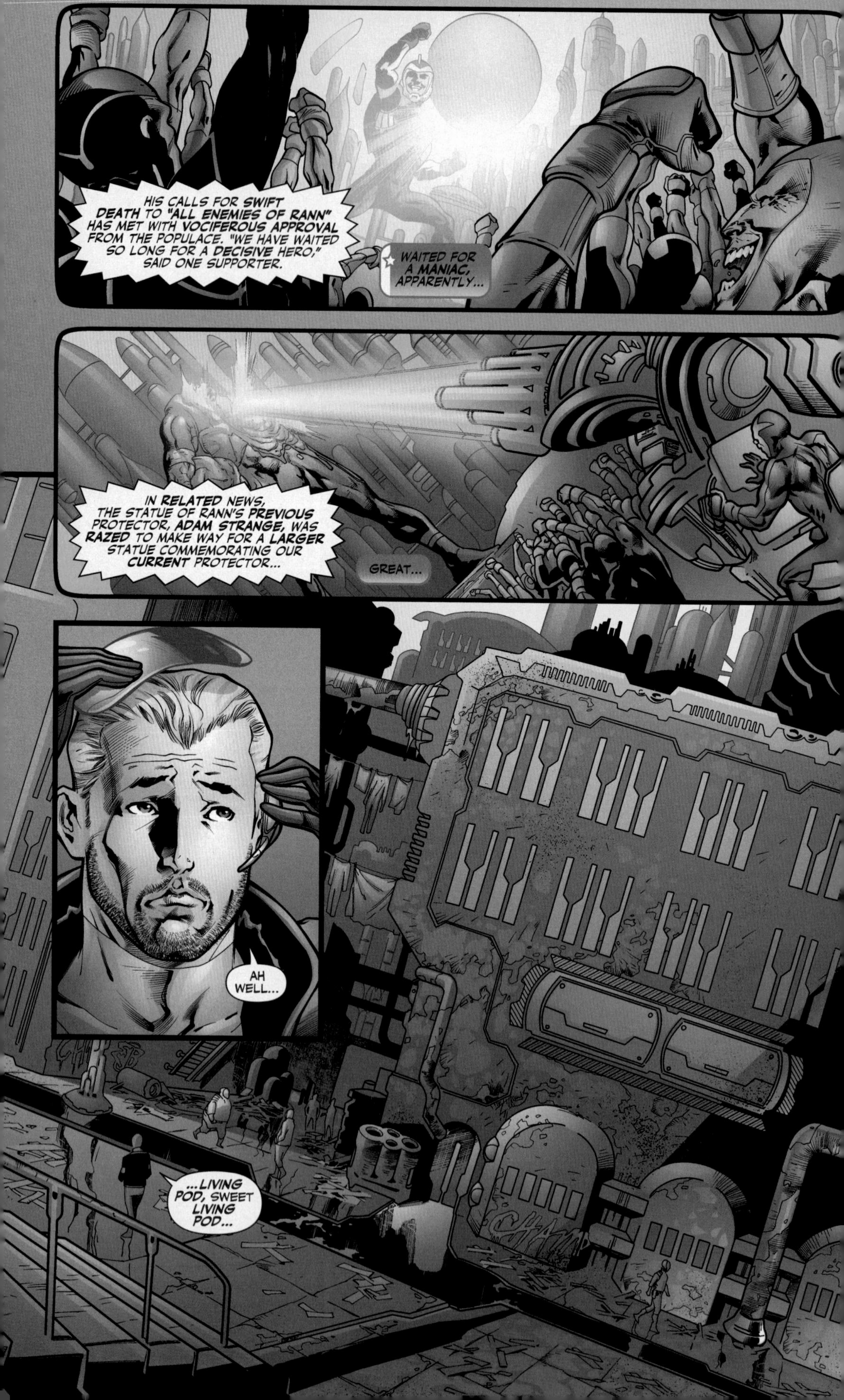
HIS CALLS FOR SWIFT DEATH TO "ALL ENEMIES OF RANN" HAS MET WITH VOCIFEROUS APPROVAL FROM THE POPULACE. "WE HAVE WAITED SO LONG FOR A DECISIVE HERO," SAID ONE SUPPORTER.
WAITED FOR A MANIAC, APPARENTLY...
IN RELATED NEWS, THE STATUE OF RANN'S PREVIOUS PROTECTOR, ADAM STRANGE, WAS RAZED TO MAKE WAY FOR A LARGER STATUE COMMEMORATING OUR CURRENT PROTECTOR...
GREAT...
AH WELL...
...LIVING POD, SWEET LIVING POD...

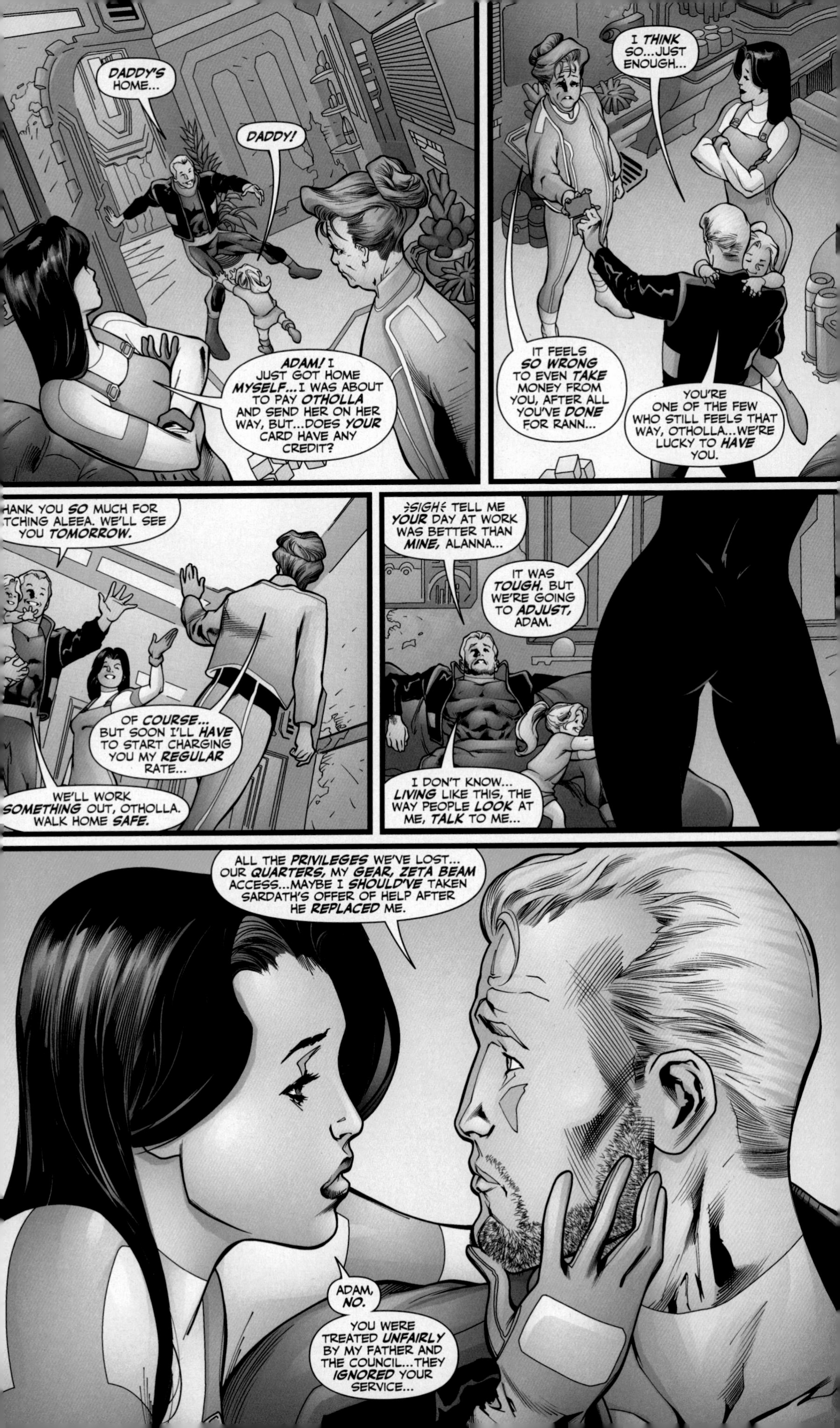
DADDY'S HOME...
DADDY!
ADAM! I JUST GOT HOME MYSELF...I WAS ABOUT TO PAY OTHOLLA AND SEND HER ON HER WAY, BUT...DOES YOUR CARD HAVE ANY CREDIT?
I THINK SO...JUST ENOUGH...
IT FEELS SO WRONG TO EVEN TAKE MONEY FROM YOU, AFTER ALL YOU'VE DONE FOR RANN...
YOU'RE ONE OF THE FEW WHO STILL FEELS THAT WAY, OTHOLLA...WE'RE LUCKY TO HAVE YOU.
HANK YOU SO MUCH FOR TCHING ALEEA. WE'LL SEE YOU TOMORROW.
OF COURSE... BUT SOON I'LL HAVE TO START CHARGING YOU MY REGULAR RATE...
WE'LL WORK SOMETHING OUT, OTHOLLA. WALK HOME SAFE.
SIGH TELL ME YOUR DAY AT WORK WAS BETTER THAN MINE, ALANNA...
IT WAS TOUGH. BUT WE'RE GOING TO ADJUST, ADAM.
I DON'T KNOW... LIVING LIKE THIS, THE WAY PEOPLE LOOK AT ME, TALK TO ME...
ALL THE PRIVILEGES WE'VE LOST... OUR QUARTERS, MY GEAR, ZETA BEAM ACCESS...MAYBE I SHOULD'VE TAKEN SARDATH'S OFFER OF HELP AFTER HE REPLACED ME.
ADAM, NO.
YOU WERE TREATED UNFAIRLY BY MY FATHER AND THE COUNCIL...THEY IGNORED YOUR SERVICE...

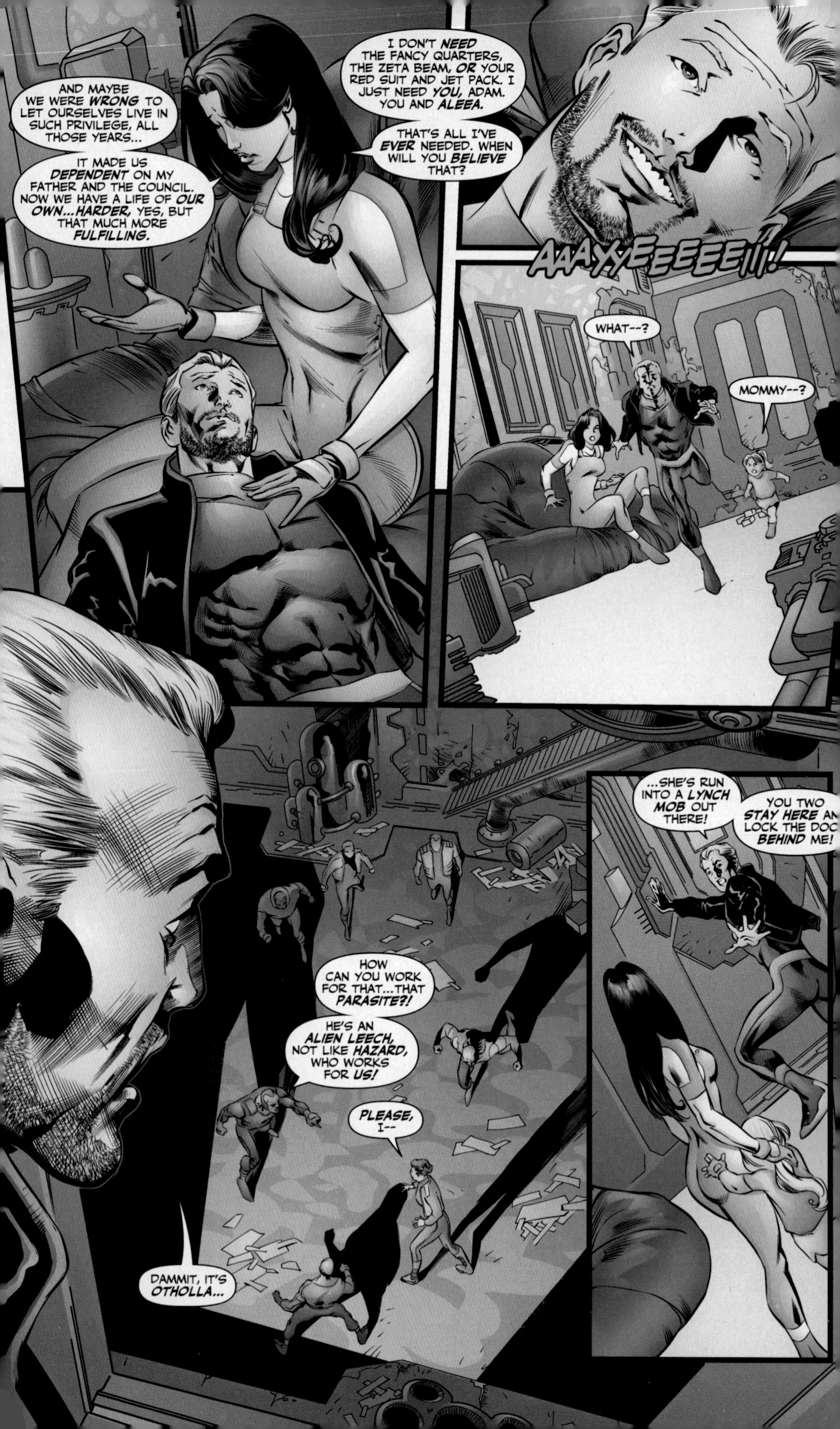
AND MAYBE WE WERE WRONG TO LET OURSELVES LIVE IN SUCH PRIVILEGE, ALL THOSE YEARS...
IT MADE US DEPENDENT ON MY FATHER AND THE COUNCIL. NOW WE HAVE A LIFE OF OUR OWN...HARDER, YES, BUT THAT MUCH MORE FULFILLING.
I DON'T NEED THE FANCY QUARTERS, THE ZETA BEAM, OR YOUR RED SUIT AND JET PACK. I JUST NEED YOU, ADAM. YOU AND ALEEA.
THAT'S ALL I'VE EVER NEEDED. WHEN WILL YOU BELIEVE THAT?
AAAYYEEEEE!!!!
WHAT--?
MOMMY--?
HOW CAN YOU WORK FOR THAT...THAT PARASITE?!
HE'S AN ALIEN LEECH, NOT LIKE HAZARD, WHO WORKS FOR US!
PLEASE, I--
DAMMIT, IT'S OTHOLLA...
...SHE'S RUN INTO A LYNCH MOB OUT THERE!
YOU TWO STAY HERE AN LOCK THE DOO BEHIND ME!

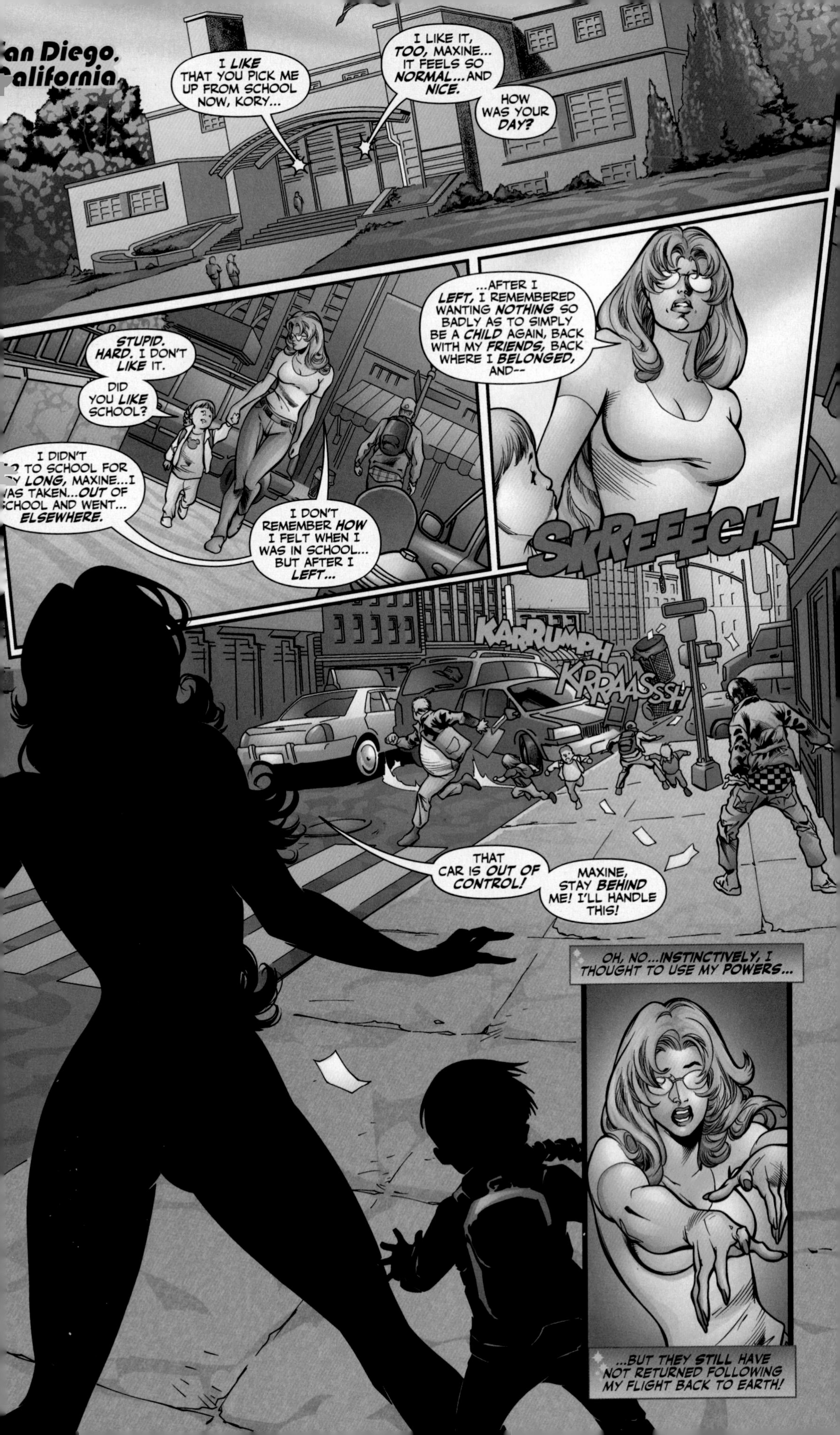
an Diego, California
I LIKE THAT YOU PICK ME UP FROM SCHOOL NOW, KORY...
I LIKE IT, TOO, MAXINE... IT FEELS SO NORMAL...AND NICE.
HOW WAS YOUR DAY?
STUPID. HARD. I DON'T LIKE IT.
DID YOU LIKE SCHOOL?
I DIDN'T TO SCHOOL FOR LONG, MAXINE...I WAS TAKEN...OUT OF SCHOOL AND WENT... ELSEWHERE.
I DON'T REMEMBER HOW I FELT WHEN I WAS IN SCHOOL... BUT AFTER I LEFT...
...AFTER I LEFT, I REMEMBERED WANTING NOTHING SO BADLY AS TO SIMPLY BE A CHILD AGAIN, BACK WITH MY FRIENDS, BACK WHERE I BELONGED, AND--
SKREEECH
KARRUMPH
KRRAASSSH
THAT CAR IS OUT OF CONTROL!
MAXINE, STAY BEHIND ME! I'LL HANDLE THIS!
OH, NO...INSTINCTIVELY, I THOUGHT TO USE MY POWERS...
...BUT THEY STILL HAVE NOT RETURNED FOLLOWING MY FLIGHT BACK TO EARTH!

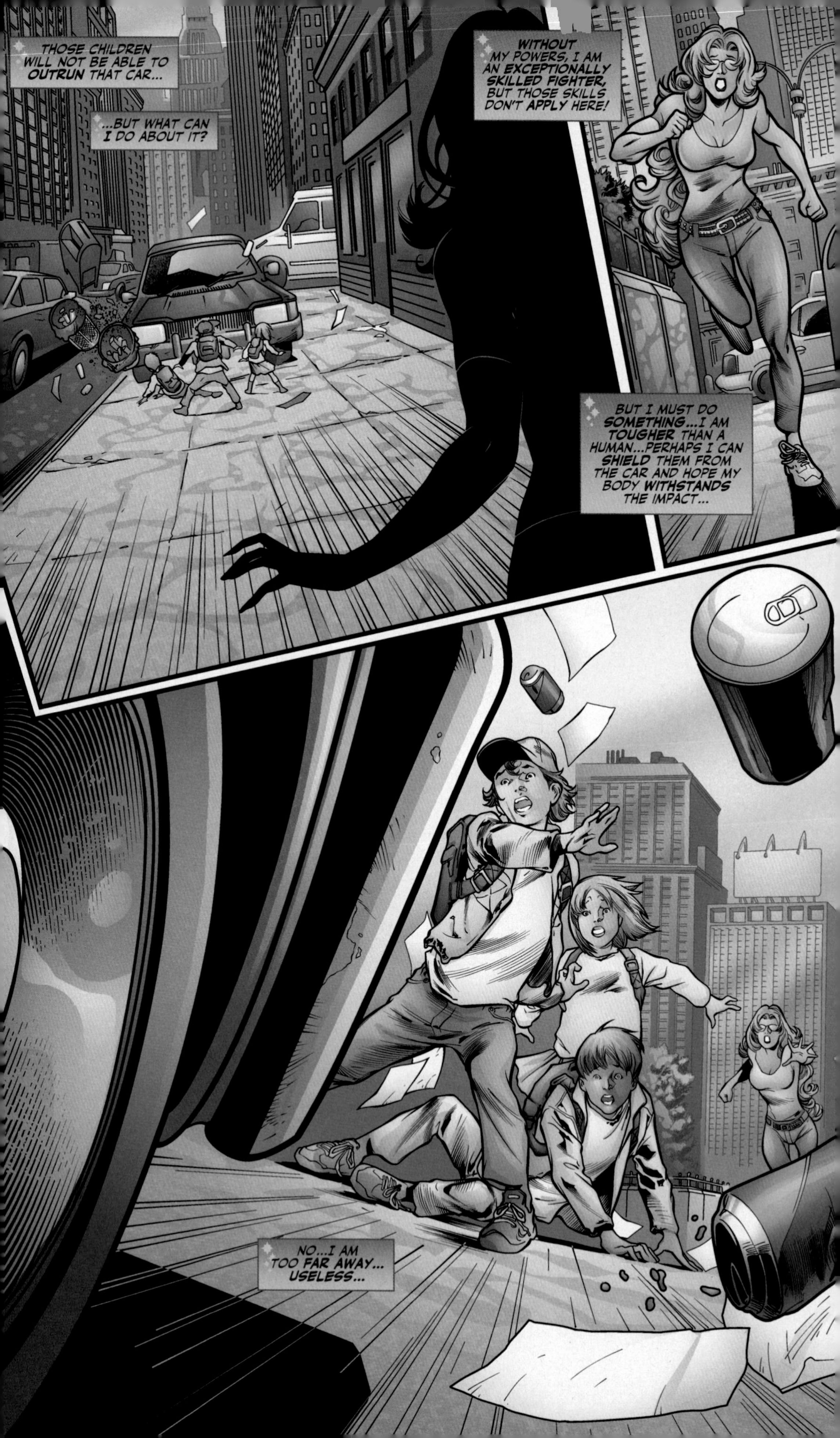
THOSE CHILDREN WILL NOT BE ABLE TO OUTRUN THAT CAR...
...BUT WHAT CAN I DO ABOUT IT?
WITHOUT MY POWERS, I AM AN EXCEPTIONALLY SKILLED FIGHTER, BUT THOSE SKILLS DON'T APPLY HERE!
BUT I MUST DO SOMETHING...I AM TOUGHER THAN A HUMAN...PERHAPS I CAN SHIELD THEM FROM THE CAR AND HOPE MY BODY WITHSTANDS THE IMPACT...
NO...I AM TOO FAR AWAY... USELESS...

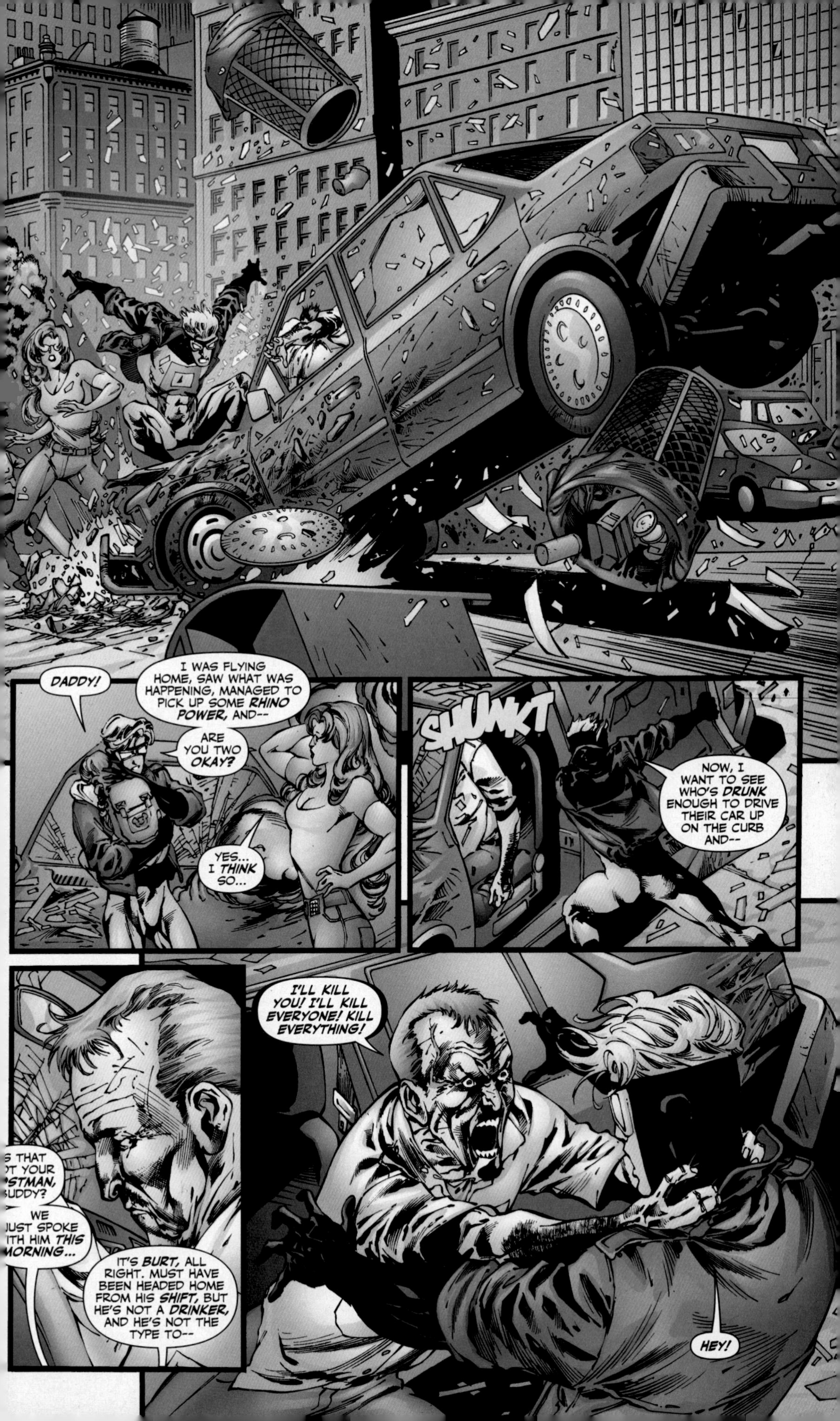
DADDY!
I WAS FLYING HOME, SAW WHAT WAS HAPPENING, MANAGED TO PICK UP SOME RHINO POWER, AND--
ARE YOU TWO OKAY?
YES... I THINK SO...
SHUNKT
NOW, I WANT TO SEE WHO'S DRUNK ENOUGH TO DRIVE THEIR CAR UP ON THE CURB AND--
I'LL KILL YOU! I'LL KILL EVERYONE! KILL EVERYTHING!
HEY!
S THAT
OT YOUR
STMAN,
UDDY?
WE
UST SPOKE
ITH HIM THIS
MORNING...
IT'S BURT, ALL RIGHT. MUST HAVE BEEN HEADED HOME FROM HIS SHIFT, BUT HE'S NOT A DRINKER, AND HE'S NOT THE TYPE TO--

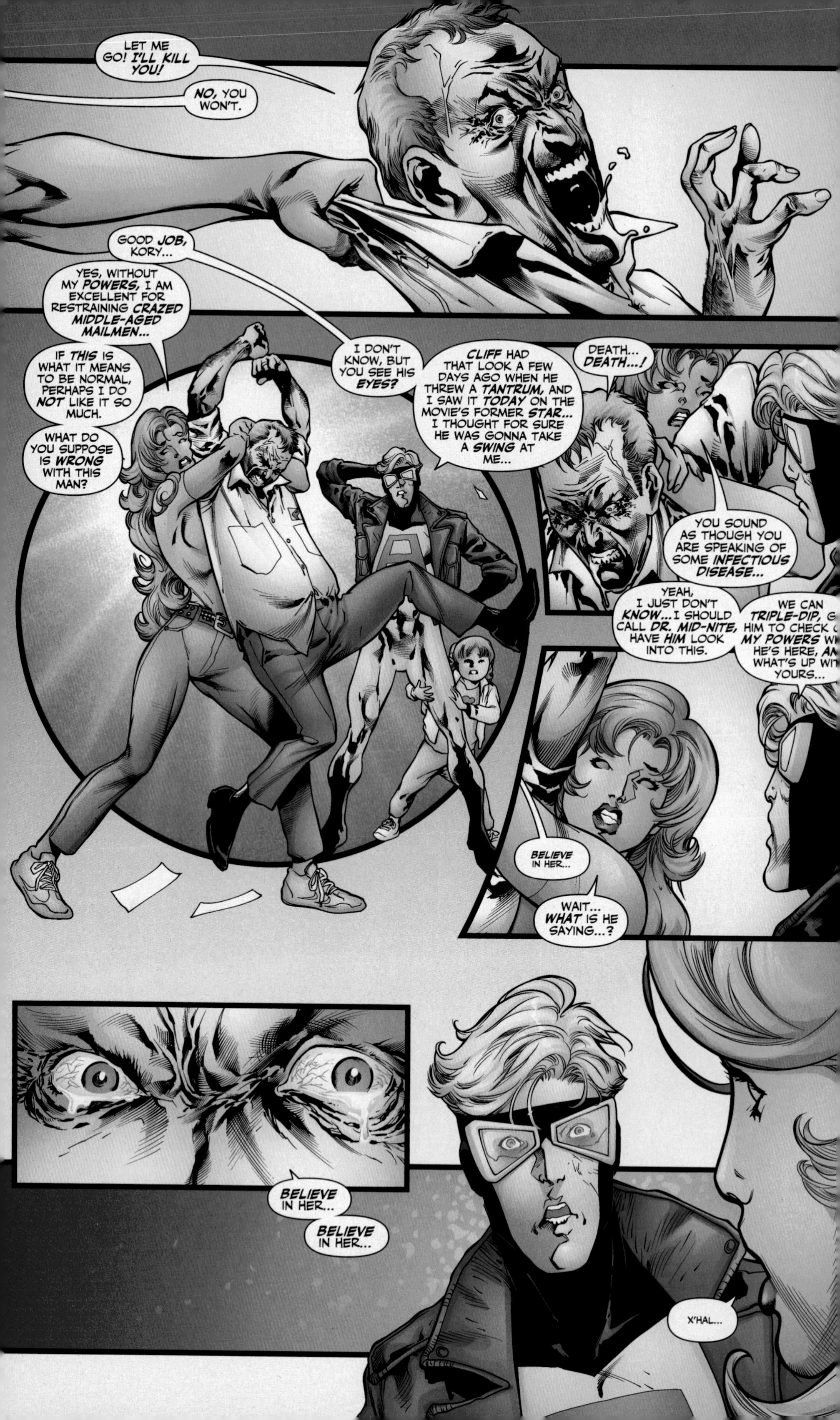

LET ME GO! I'LL KILL YOU!
NO, YOU WON'T.
GOOD JOB, KORY...
YES, WITHOUT MY POWERS, I AM EXCELLENT FOR RESTRAINING CRAZED MIDDLE-AGED MAILMEN...
IF THIS IS WHAT IT MEANS TO BE NORMAL, PERHAPS I DO NOT LIKE IT SO MUCH.
WHAT DO YOU SUPPOSE IS WRONG WITH THIS MAN?
I DON'T KNOW, BUT YOU SEE HIS EYES?
CLIFF HAD THAT LOOK A FEW DAYS AGO WHEN HE THREW A TANTRUM, AND I SAW IT TODAY ON THE MOVIE'S FORMER STAR... I THOUGHT FOR SURE HE WAS GONNA TAKE A SWING AT ME...
DEATH... DEATH...!
YOU SOUND AS THOUGH YOU ARE SPEAKING OF SOME INFECTIOUS DISEASE...
YEAH, I JUST DON'T KNOW... I SHOULD CALL DR. MID-NITE, HAVE HIM LOOK INTO THIS.
WE CAN TRIPLE-DIP, G HIM TO CHECK MY POWERS HE'S HERE, AN WHAT'S UP WI YOURS...
BELIEVE IN HER...
WAIT... WHAT IS HE SAYING...?
BELIEVE IN HER...
BELIEVE IN HER...
X'HAL...

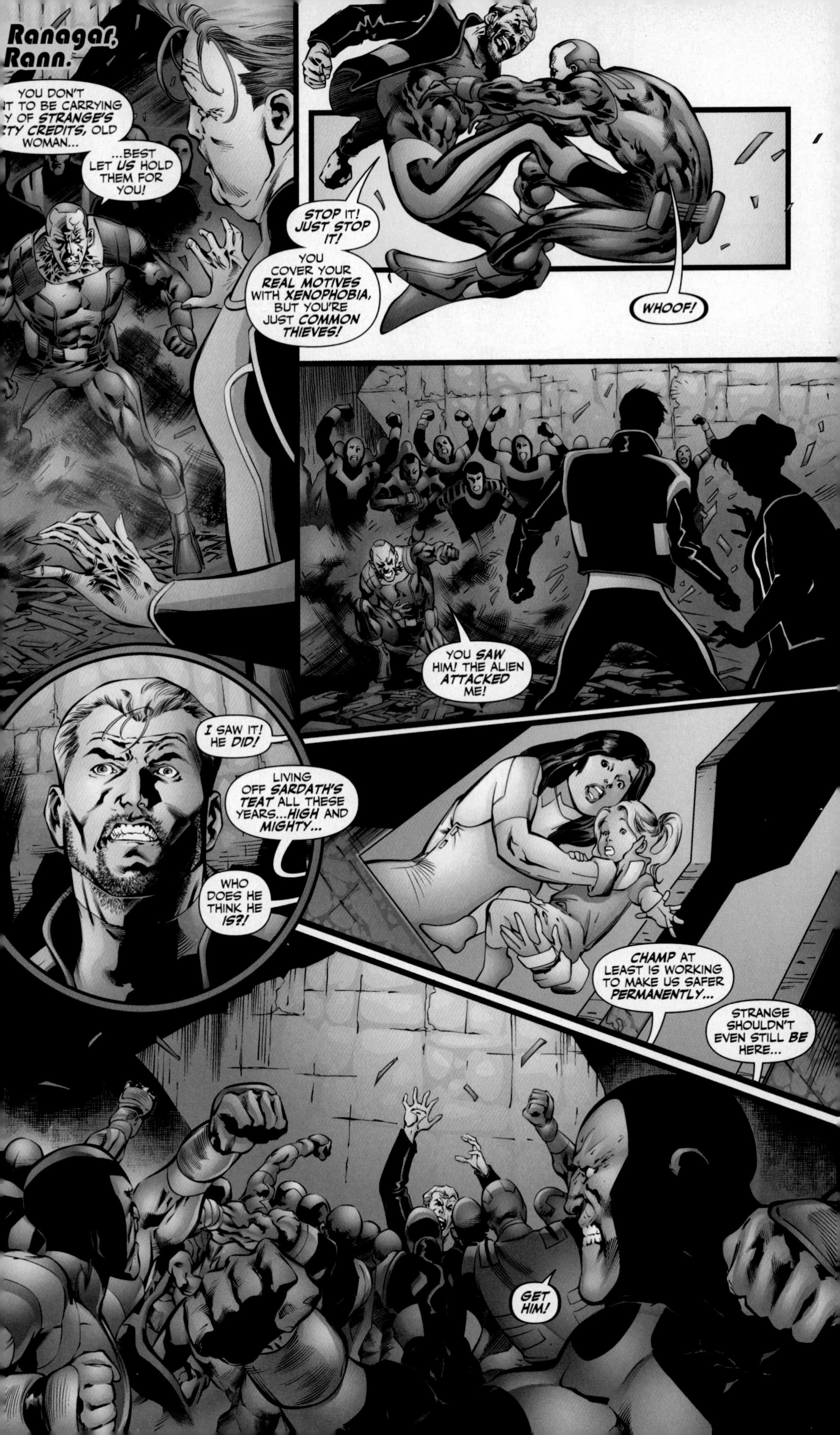

Ranagar, Rann.
YOU DON'T ...NT TO BE CARRYING ...Y OF STRANGE'S ...RTY CREDITS, OLD WOMAN...
...BEST LET US HOLD THEM FOR YOU!
STOP IT! JUST STOP IT!
YOU COVER YOUR REAL MOTIVES WITH XENOPHOBIA, BUT YOU'RE JUST COMMON THIEVES!
WHOOF!
YOU SAW HIM! THE ALIEN ATTACKED ME!
I SAW IT! HE DID!
LIVING OFF SARDATH'S TEAT ALL THESE YEARS...HIGH AND MIGHTY...
WHO DOES HE THINK HE IS?!
CHAMP AT LEAST IS WORKING TO MAKE US SAFER PERMANENTLY...
STRANGE SHOULDN'T EVEN STILL BE HERE...
GET HIM!

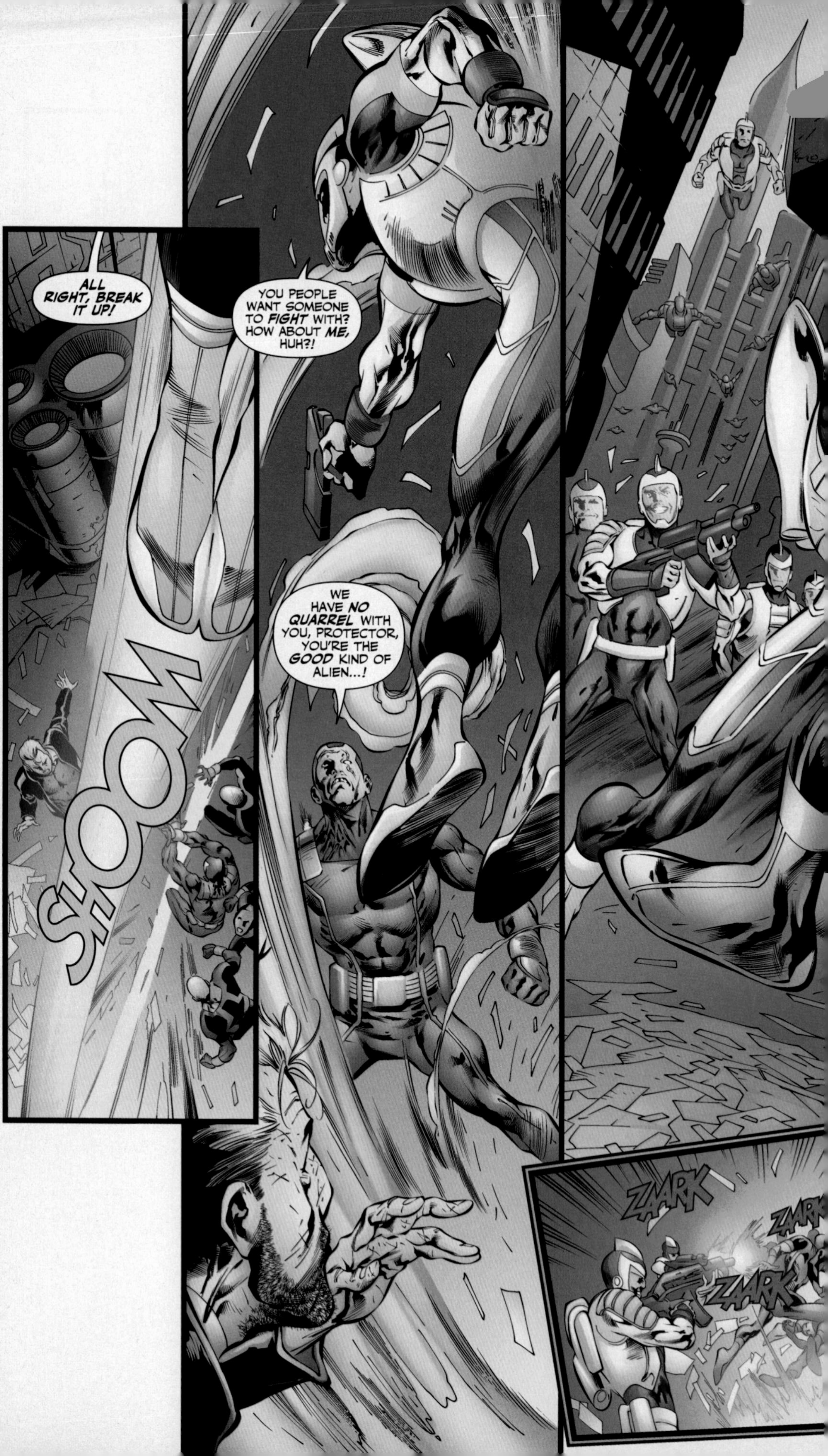
ALL RIGHT, BREAK IT UP!
SHOOM
YOU PEOPLE WANT SOMEONE TO FIGHT WITH? HOW ABOUT ME, HUH?!
WE HAVE NO QUARREL WITH YOU, PROTECTOR, YOU'RE THE GOOD KIND OF ALIEN...!
ZAARK
ZAARK
ZAARK

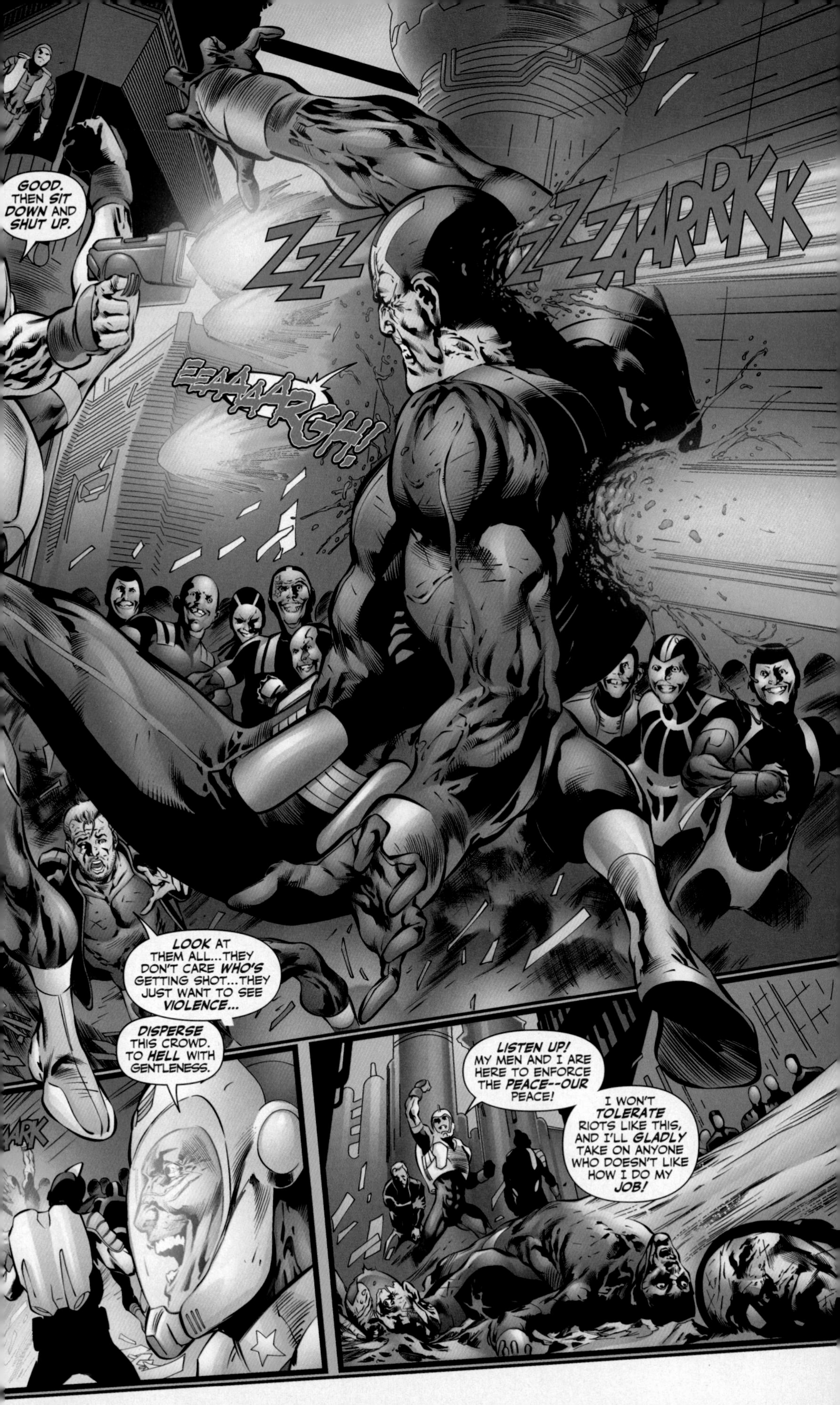
GOOD. THEN SIT DOWN AND SHUT UP.
ZZZZZZAARRRKK
EEAAAARGH!
LOOK AT THEM ALL...THEY DON'T CARE WHO'S GETTING SHOT...THEY JUST WANT TO SEE VIOLENCE...
DISPERSE THIS CROWD. TO HELL WITH GENTLENESS.
LISTEN UP! MY MEN AND I ARE HERE TO ENFORCE THE PEACE--OUR PEACE!
I WON'T TOLERATE RIOTS LIKE THIS, AND I'LL GLADLY TAKE ON ANYONE WHO DOESN'T LIKE HOW I DO MY JOB!

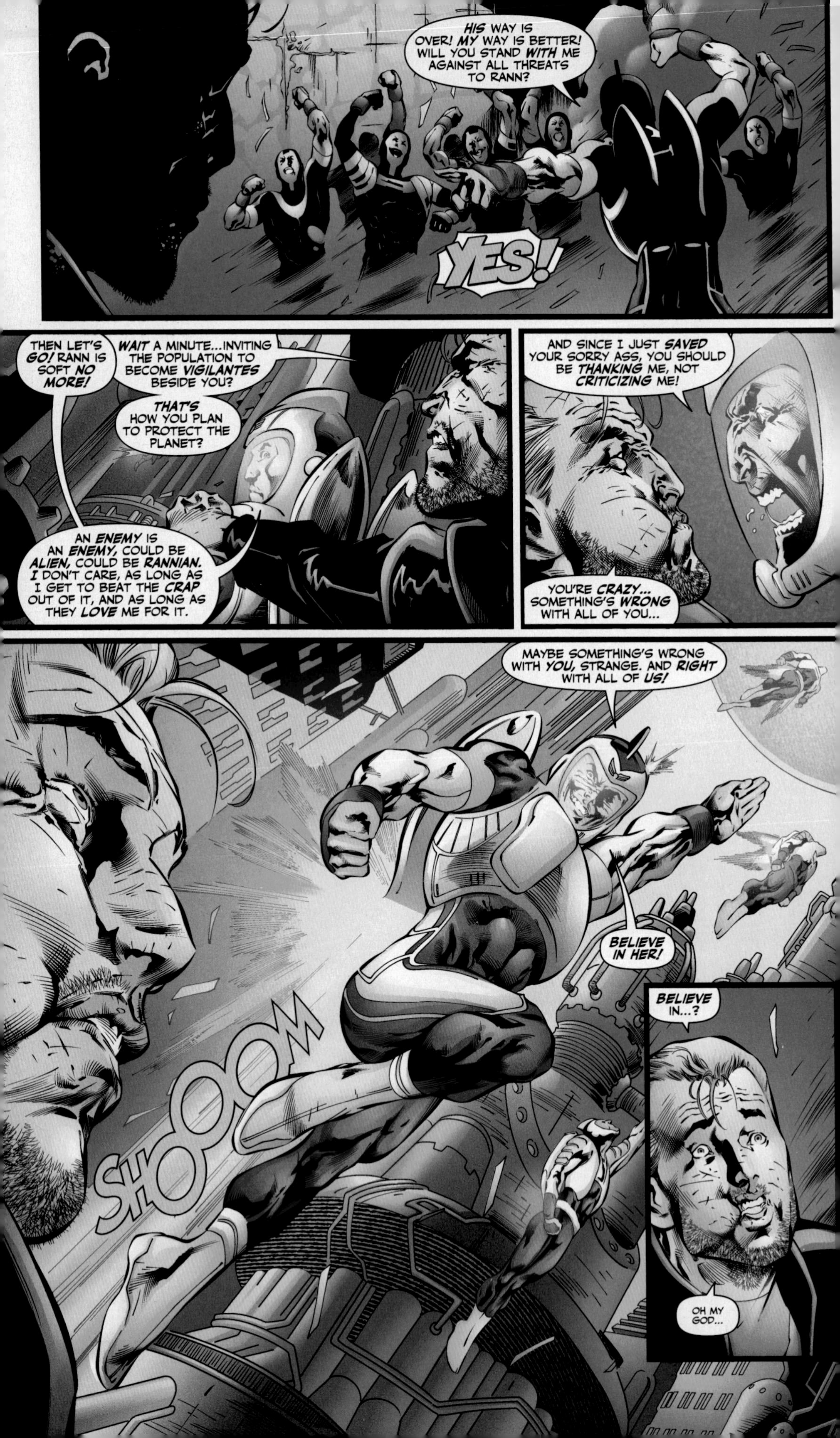
HIS WAY IS OVER! MY WAY IS BETTER! WILL YOU STAND WITH ME AGAINST ALL THREATS TO RANN?
YES!
THEN LET'S GO! RANN IS SOFT NO MORE!
WAIT A MINUTE...INVITING THE POPULATION TO BECOME VIGILANTES BESIDE YOU?
THAT'S HOW YOU PLAN TO PROTECT THE PLANET?
AN ENEMY IS AN ENEMY, COULD BE ALIEN, COULD BE RANNIAN. I DON'T CARE, AS LONG AS I GET TO BEAT THE CRAP OUT OF IT, AND AS LONG AS THEY LOVE ME FOR IT.
AND SINCE I JUST SAVED YOUR SORRY ASS, YOU SHOULD BE THANKING ME, NOT CRITICIZING ME!
YOU'RE CRAZY... SOMETHING'S WRONG WITH ALL OF YOU...
MAYBE SOMETHING'S WRONG WITH YOU, STRANGE. AND RIGHT WITH ALL OF US!
BELIEVE IN HER!
SHOOOOM
BELIEVE IN...?
OH MY GOD...

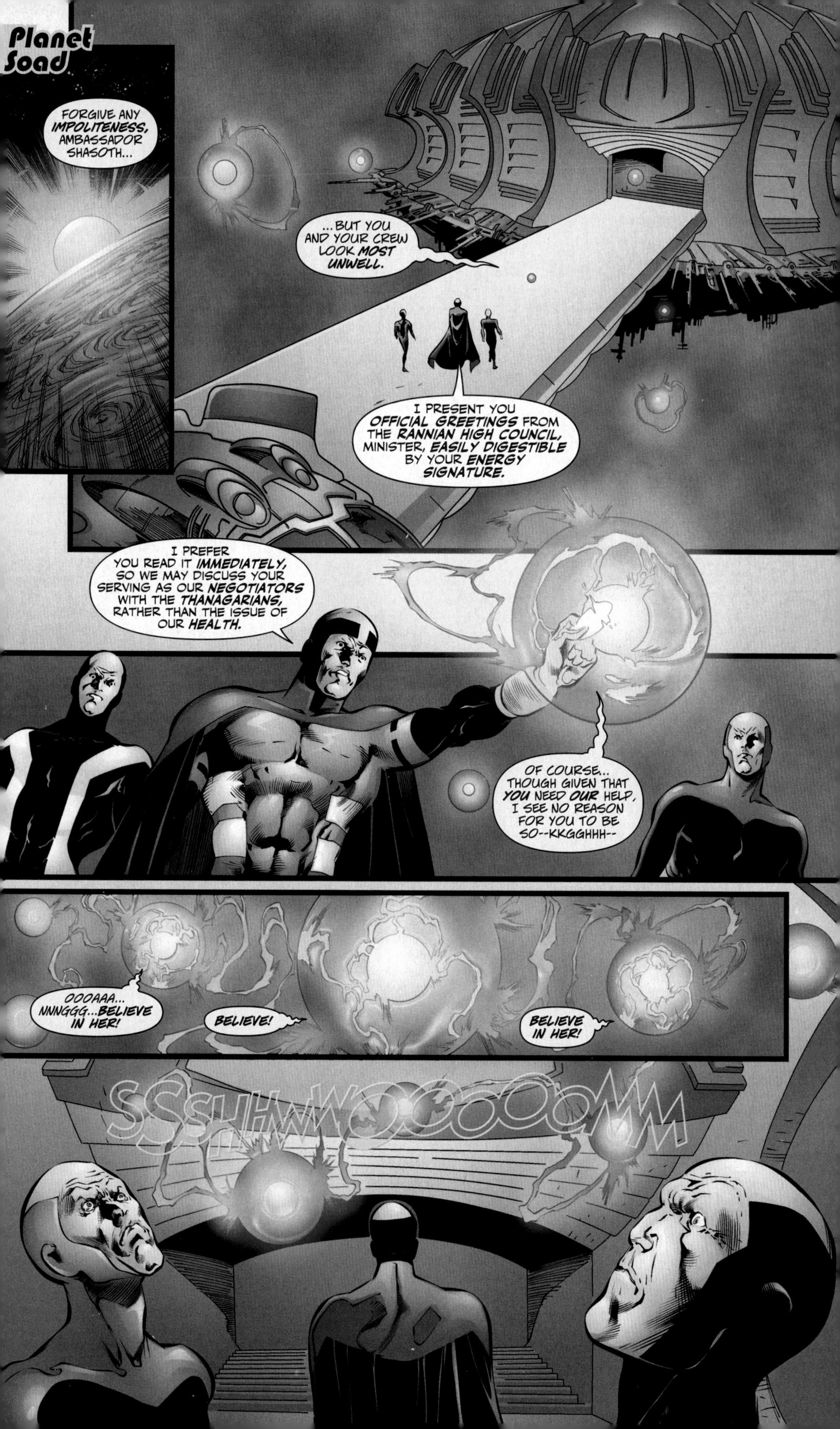
Planet Soad
FORGIVE ANY IMPOLITENESS, AMBASSADOR SHASOTH...
...BUT YOU AND YOUR CREW LOOK MOST UNWELL.
I PRESENT YOU OFFICIAL GREETINGS FROM THE RANNIAN HIGH COUNCIL, MINISTER, EASILY DIGESTIBLE BY YOUR ENERGY SIGNATURE.
I PREFER YOU READ IT IMMEDIATELY, SO WE MAY DISCUSS YOUR SERVING AS OUR NEGOTIATORS WITH THE THANAGARIANS, RATHER THAN THE ISSUE OF OUR HEALTH.
OF COURSE... THOUGH GIVEN THAT YOU NEED OUR HELP, I SEE NO REASON FOR YOU TO BE SO--KKGGHHH--
OOOAAA... NNNGGG...BELIEVE IN HER!
BELIEVE!
BELIEVE IN HER!
SSSHHWWOOOOOOMM

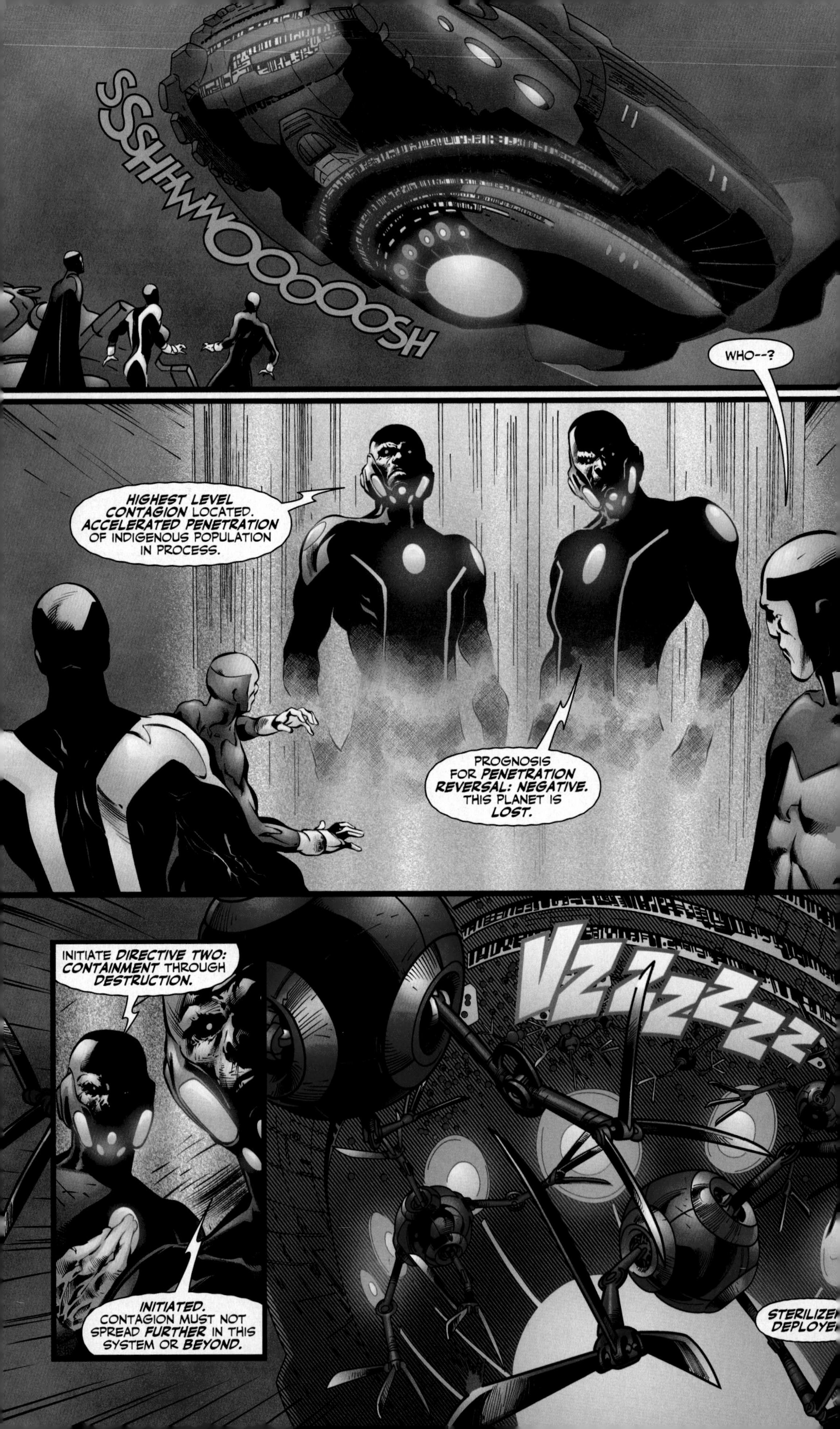
SSSHHWWOOOOOOOSH
WHO--?
HIGHEST LEVEL CONTAGION LOCATED. ACCELERATED PENETRATION OF INDIGENOUS POPULATION IN PROCESS.
PROGNOSIS FOR PENETRATION REVERSAL: NEGATIVE. THIS PLANET IS LOST.
INITIATE DIRECTIVE TWO: CONTAINMENT THROUGH DESTRUCTION.
VZZZZZZ
INITIATED. CONTAGION MUST NOT SPREAD FURTHER IN THIS SYSTEM OR BEYOND.

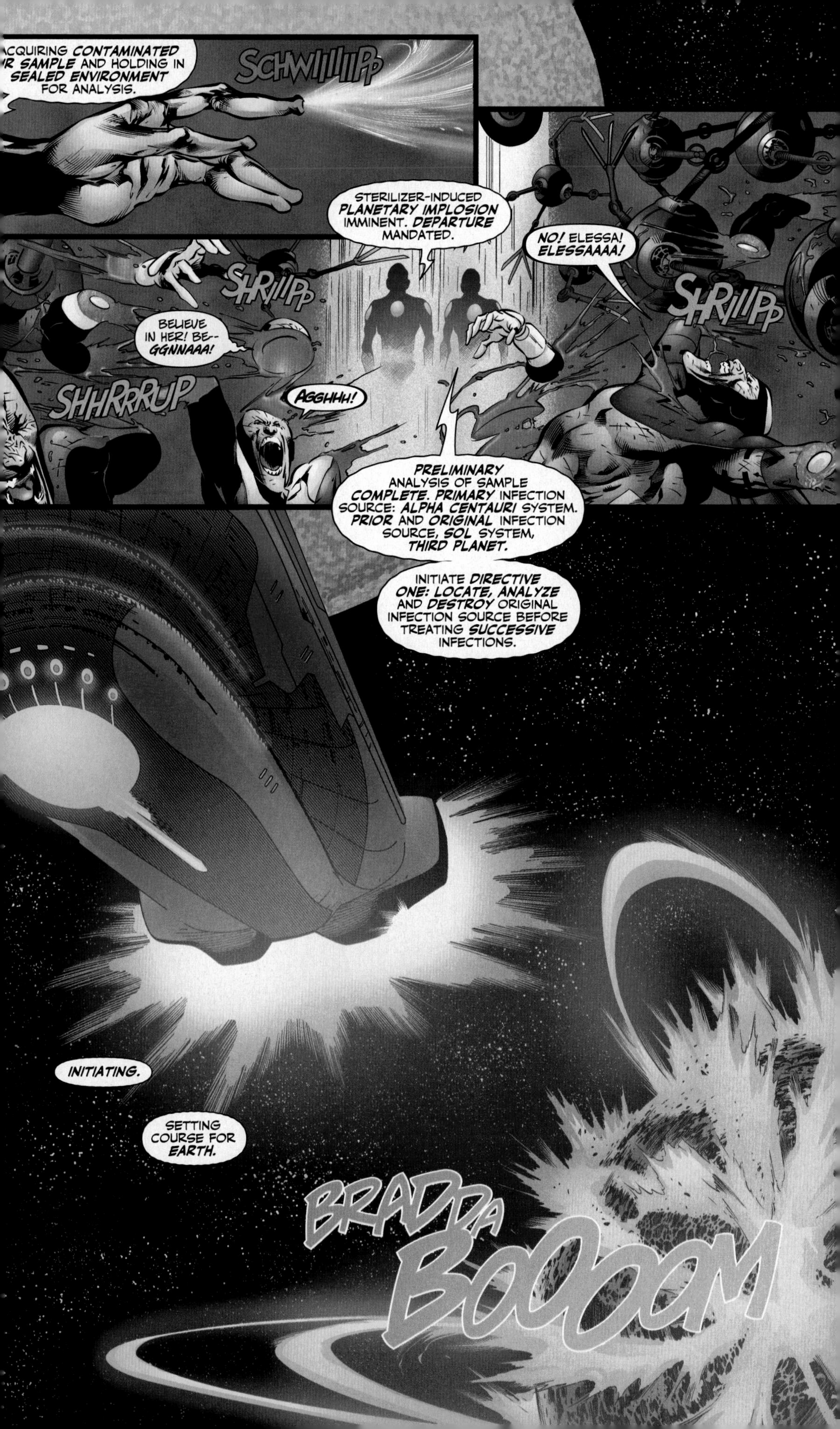
ACQUIRING CONTAMINATED [?]R SAMPLE AND HOLDING IN SEALED ENVIRONMENT FOR ANALYSIS.
SCHWIIIIIPP
STERILIZER-INDUCED PLANETARY IMPLOSION IMMINENT. DEPARTURE MANDATED.
NO! ELESSA! ELESSAAAA!
SHRIIPP
SHRIIPP
BELIEVE IN HER! BE-- GGNNAAA!
SHHRRRUP
AGGHHH!
PRELIMINARY ANALYSIS OF SAMPLE COMPLETE. PRIMARY INFECTION SOURCE: ALPHA CENTAURI SYSTEM. PRIOR AND ORIGINAL INFECTION SOURCE, SOL SYSTEM, THIRD PLANET.
INITIATE DIRECTIVE ONE: LOCATE, ANALYZE AND DESTROY ORIGINAL INFECTION SOURCE BEFORE TREATING SUCCESSIVE INFECTIONS.
INITIATING.
SETTING COURSE FOR EARTH.
BRADDA BOOOOM

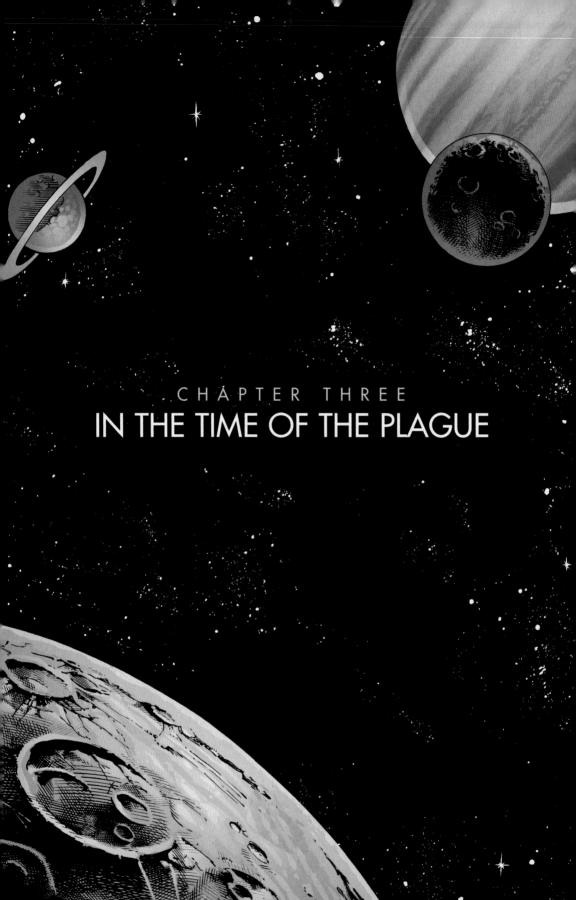

CHAPTER THREE

IN THE TIME OF THE PLAGUE

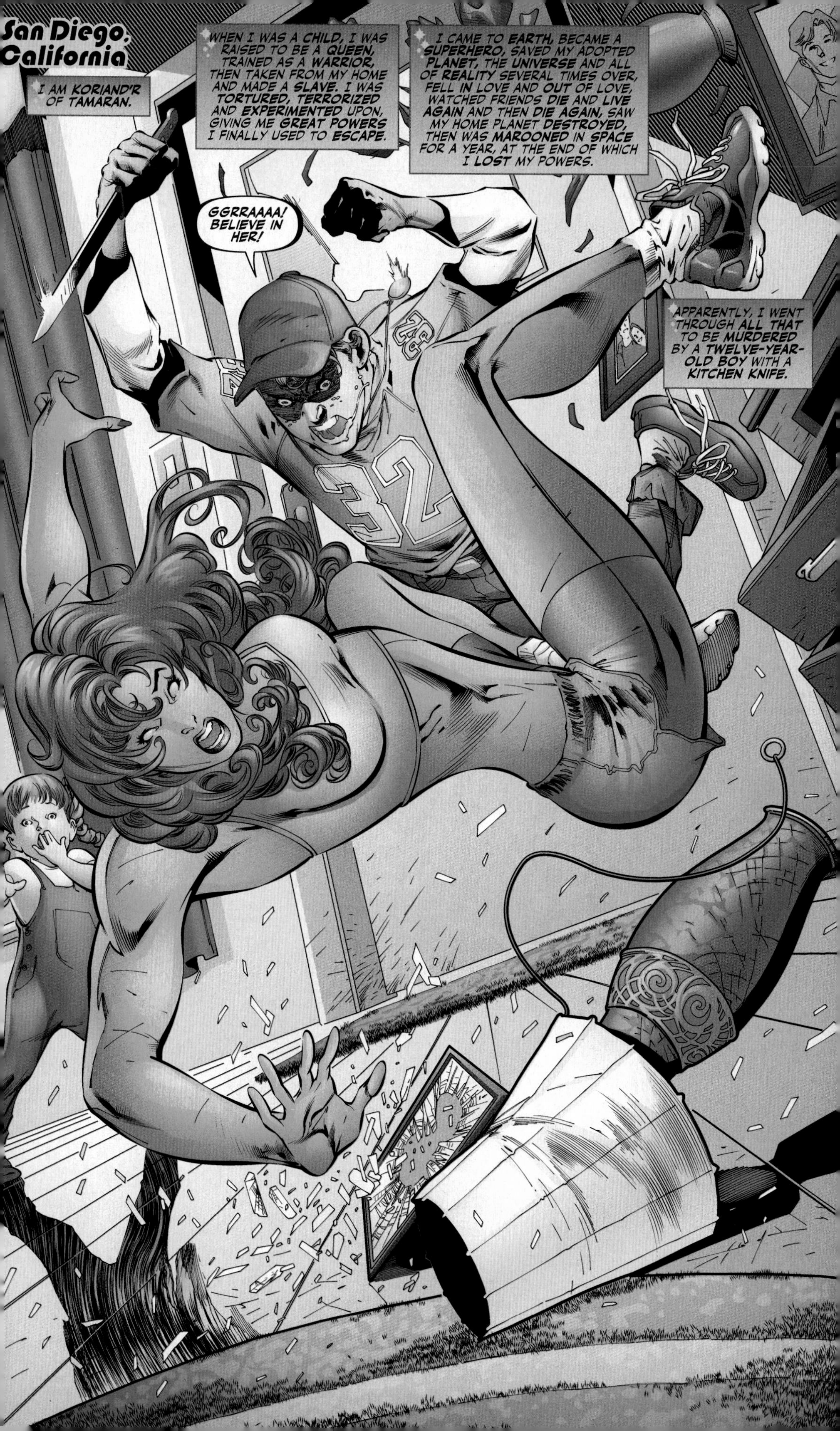
San Diego, California
I AM KORIAND'R OF TAMARAN.
WHEN I WAS A CHILD, I WAS RAISED TO BE A QUEEN, TRAINED AS A WARRIOR, THEN TAKEN FROM MY HOME AND MADE A SLAVE. I WAS TORTURED, TERRORIZED AND EXPERIMENTED UPON, GIVING ME GREAT POWERS I FINALLY USED TO ESCAPE.
I CAME TO EARTH, BECAME A SUPERHERO, SAVED MY ADOPTED PLANET, THE UNIVERSE AND ALL OF REALITY SEVERAL TIMES OVER, FELL IN LOVE AND OUT OF LOVE, WATCHED FRIENDS DIE AND LIVE AGAIN AND THEN DIE AGAIN, SAW MY HOME PLANET DESTROYED, THEN WAS MAROONED IN SPACE FOR A YEAR, AT THE END OF WHICH I LOST MY POWERS.
GGRRAAAA! BELIEVE IN HER!
APPARENTLY, I WENT THROUGH ALL THAT TO BE MURDERED BY A TWELVE-YEAR-OLD BOY WITH A KITCHEN KNIFE.

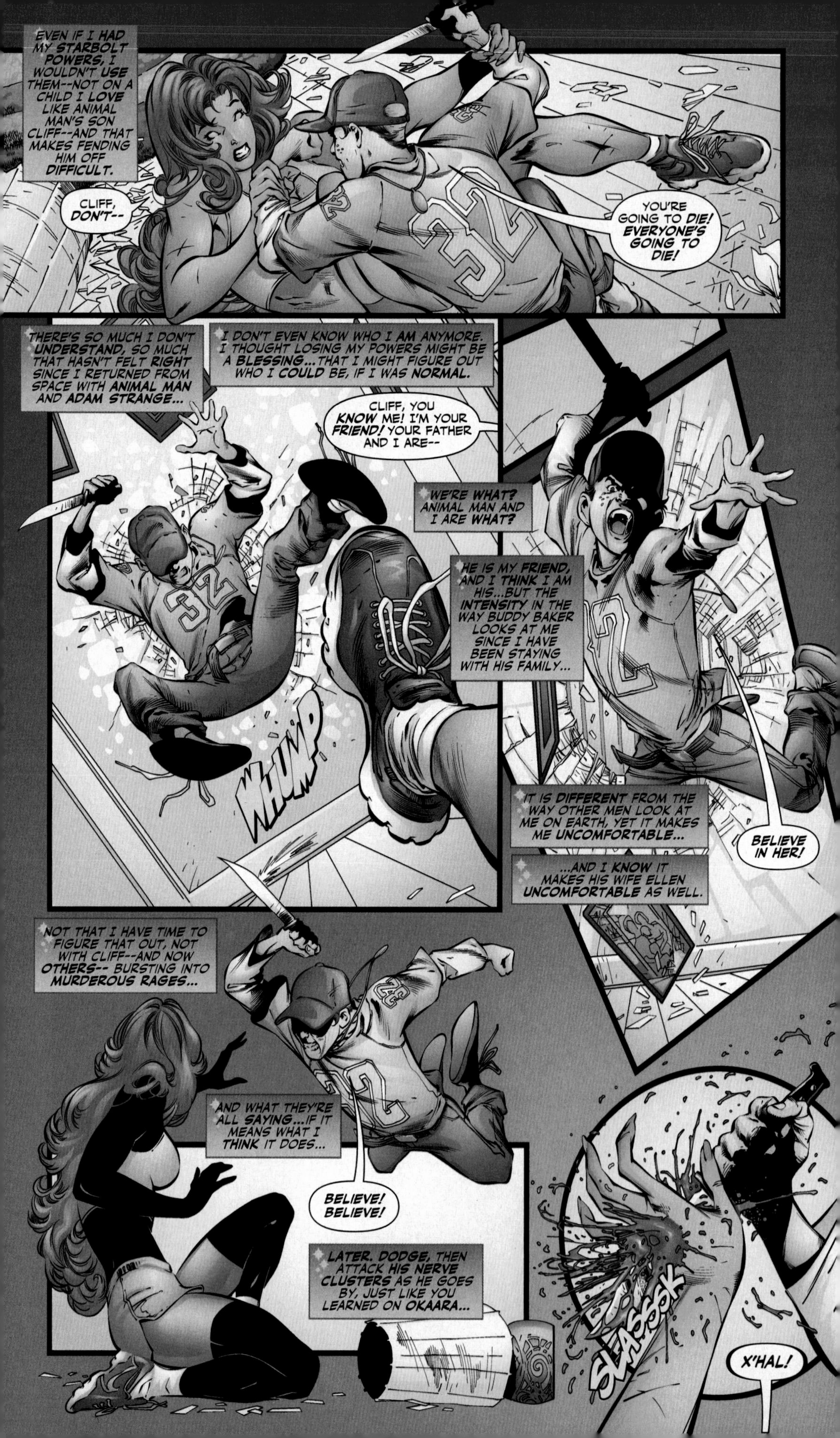
EVEN IF I HAD MY STARBOLT POWERS, I WOULDN'T USE THEM--NOT ON A CHILD I LOVE LIKE ANIMAL MAN'S SON CLIFF--AND THAT MAKES FENDING HIM OFF DIFFICULT.
CLIFF, DON'T--
YOU'RE GOING TO DIE! EVERYONE'S GOING TO DIE!
THERE'S SO MUCH I DON'T UNDERSTAND, SO MUCH THAT HASN'T FELT RIGHT SINCE I RETURNED FROM SPACE WITH ANIMAL MAN AND ADAM STRANGE...
I DON'T EVEN KNOW WHO I AM ANYMORE. I THOUGHT LOSING MY POWERS MIGHT BE A BLESSING...THAT I MIGHT FIGURE OUT WHO I COULD BE, IF I WAS NORMAL.
CLIFF, YOU KNOW ME! I'M YOUR FRIEND! YOUR FATHER AND I ARE--
WE'RE WHAT? ANIMAL MAN AND I ARE WHAT?
HE IS MY FRIEND, AND I THINK I AM HIS...BUT THE INTENSITY IN THE WAY BUDDY BAKER LOOKS AT ME SINCE I HAVE BEEN STAYING WITH HIS FAMILY...
WHUMP
IT IS DIFFERENT FROM THE WAY OTHER MEN LOOK AT ME ON EARTH, YET IT MAKES ME UNCOMFORTABLE...
...AND I KNOW IT MAKES HIS WIFE ELLEN UNCOMFORTABLE AS WELL.
BELIEVE IN HER!
NOT THAT I HAVE TIME TO FIGURE THAT OUT, NOT WITH CLIFF--AND NOW OTHERS-- BURSTING INTO MURDEROUS RAGES...
AND WHAT THEY'RE ALL SAYING...IF IT MEANS WHAT I THINK IT DOES...
BELIEVE! BELIEVE!
LATER. DODGE, THEN ATTACK HIS NERVE CLUSTERS AS HE GOES BY, JUST LIKE YOU LEARNED ON OKAARA...
SLASSSK
X'HAL!

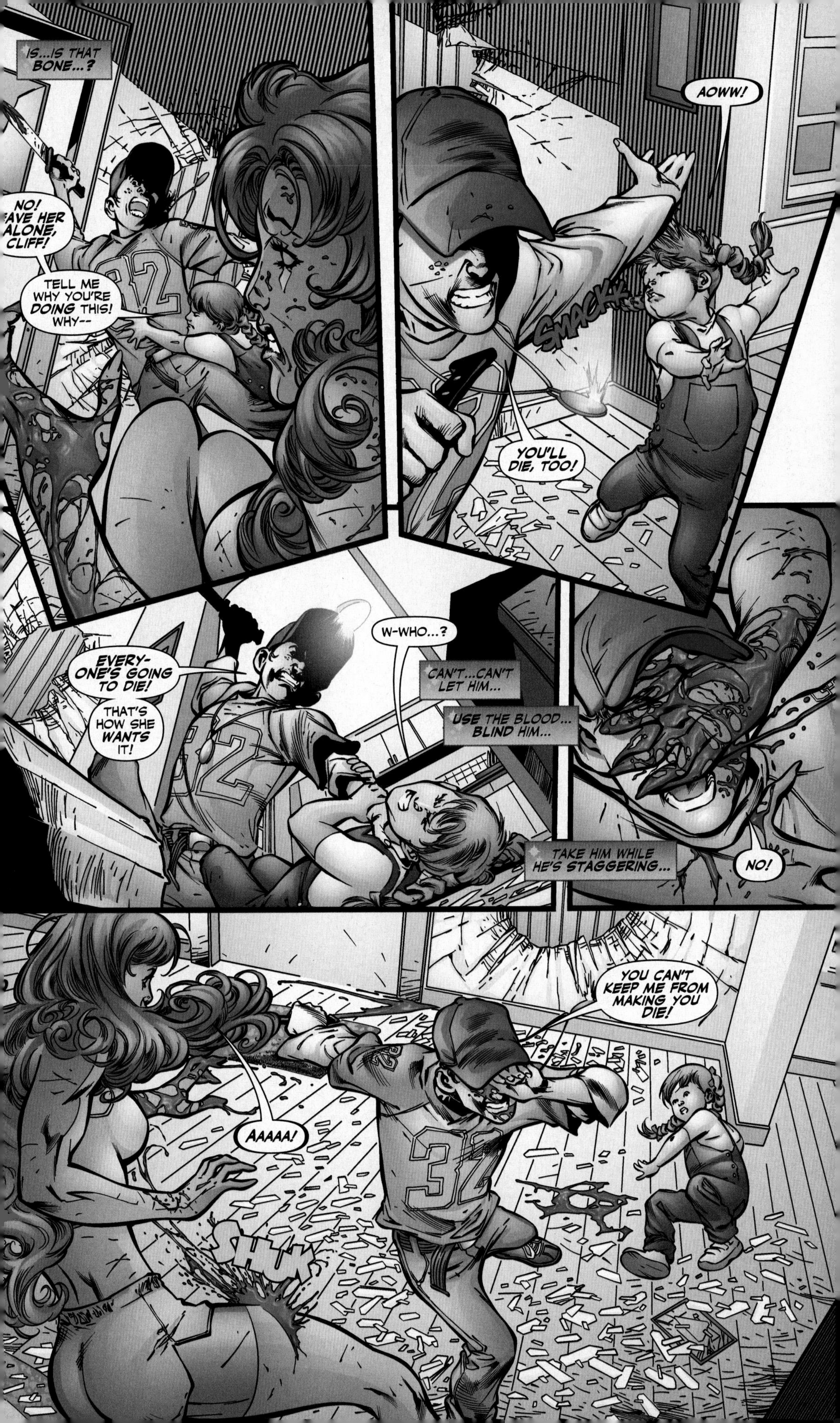
IS...IS THAT BONE...?
NO! LEAVE HER ALONE, CLIFF!
TELL ME WHY YOU'RE DOING THIS! WHY--
AOWW!
SMACKK
YOU'LL DIE, TOO!
EVERY-ONE'S GOING TO DIE!
THAT'S HOW SHE WANTS IT!
W-WHO...?
CAN'T...CAN'T LET HIM...
USE THE BLOOD... BLIND HIM...
TAKE HIM WHILE HE'S STAGGERING...
NO!
YOU CAN'T KEEP ME FROM MAKING YOU DIE!
AAAAA!
SHUK

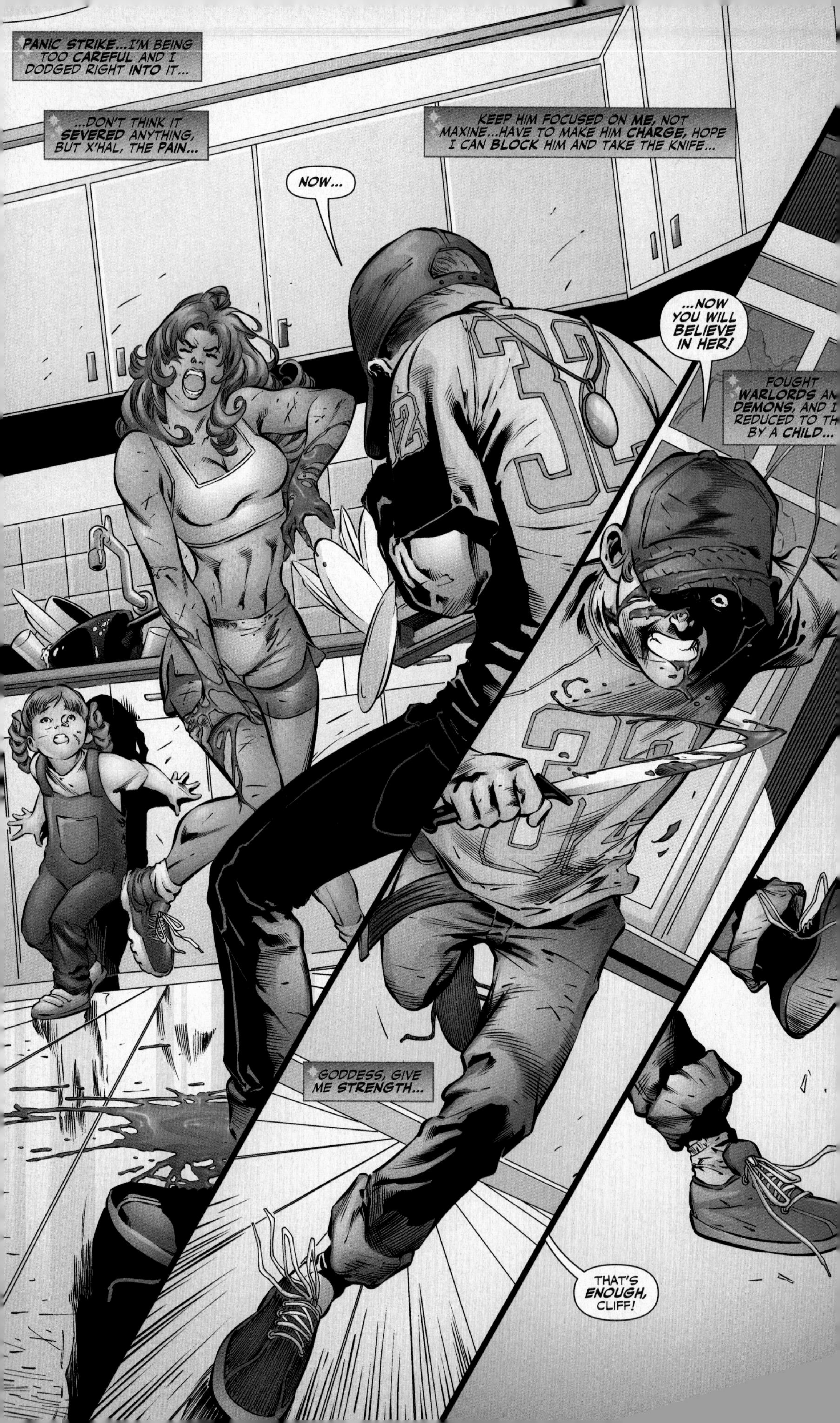
PANIC STRIKE...I'M BEING TOO CAREFUL AND I DODGED RIGHT INTO IT...
...DON'T THINK IT SEVERED ANYTHING, BUT X'HAL, THE PAIN...
KEEP HIM FOCUSED ON ME, NOT MAXINE...HAVE TO MAKE HIM CHARGE, HOPE I CAN BLOCK HIM AND TAKE THE KNIFE...
NOW...
...NOW YOU WILL BELIEVE IN HER!
FOUGHT WARLORDS AN DEMONS, AND I REDUCED TO TH BY A CHILD...
GODDESS, GIVE ME STRENGTH...
THAT'S ENOUGH, CLIFF!

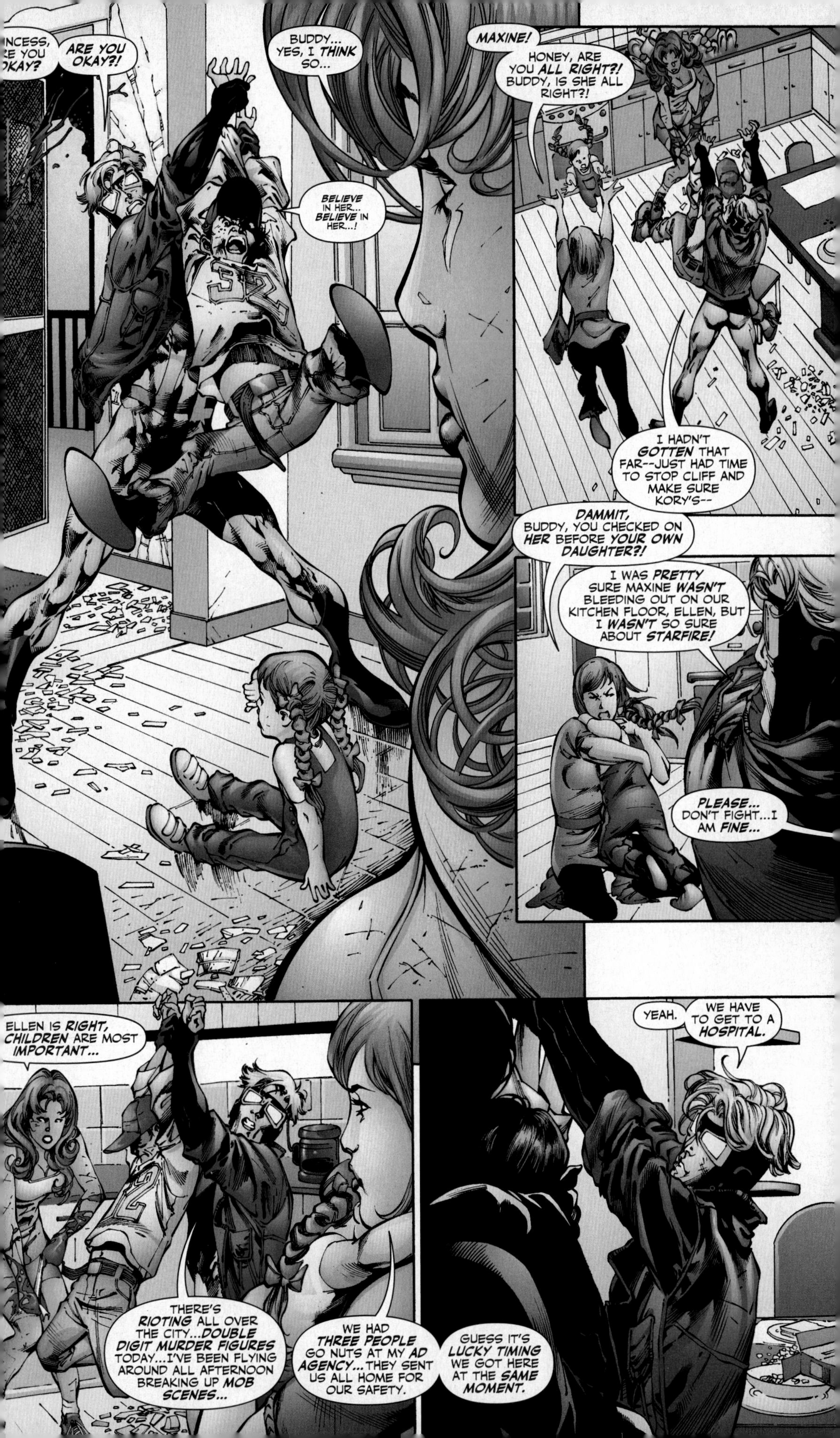

...NCESS, ...E YOU ...OKAY?
ARE YOU OKAY?!
BUDDY... YES, I THINK SO...
BELIEVE IN HER... BELIEVE IN HER...!
MAXINE!
HONEY, ARE YOU ALL RIGHT?! BUDDY, IS SHE ALL RIGHT?!
I HADN'T GOTTEN THAT FAR--JUST HAD TIME TO STOP CLIFF AND MAKE SURE KORY'S--
DAMMIT, BUDDY, YOU CHECKED ON HER BEFORE YOUR OWN DAUGHTER?!
I WAS PRETTY SURE MAXINE WASN'T BLEEDING OUT ON OUR KITCHEN FLOOR, ELLEN, BUT I WASN'T SO SURE ABOUT STARFIRE!
PLEASE... DON'T FIGHT...I AM FINE...
ELLEN IS RIGHT, CHILDREN ARE MOST IMPORTANT...
THERE'S RIOTING ALL OVER THE CITY...DOUBLE DIGIT MURDER FIGURES TODAY...I'VE BEEN FLYING AROUND ALL AFTERNOON BREAKING UP MOB SCENES...
WE HAD THREE PEOPLE GO NUTS AT MY AD AGENCY...THEY SENT US ALL HOME FOR OUR SAFETY.
GUESS IT'S LUCKY TIMING WE GOT HERE AT THE SAME MOMENT.
YEAH.
WE HAVE TO GET TO A HOSPITAL.

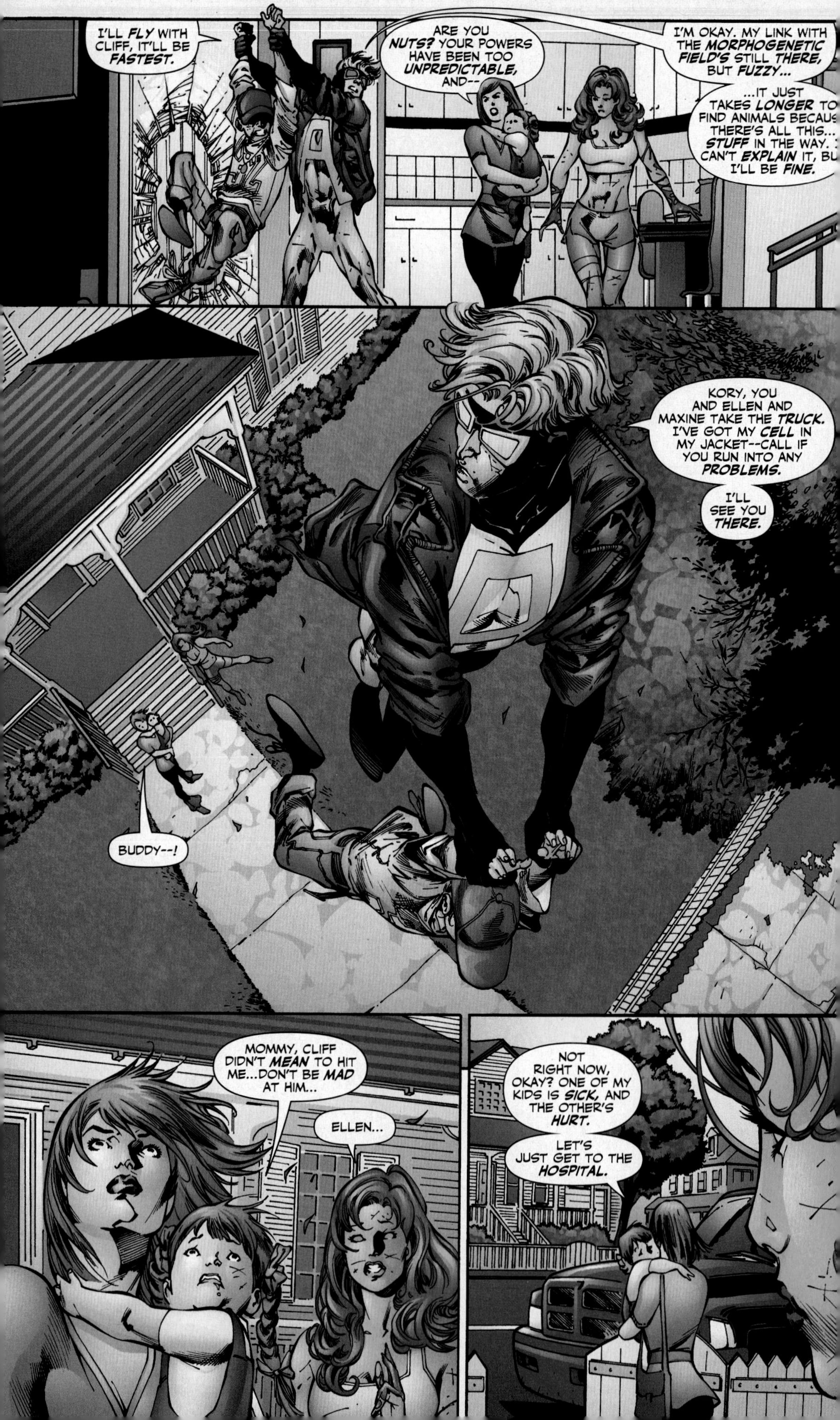
I'LL FLY WITH CLIFF, IT'LL BE FASTEST.
ARE YOU NUTS? YOUR POWERS HAVE BEEN TOO UNPREDICTABLE, AND--
I'M OKAY. MY LINK WITH THE MORPHOGENETIC FIELD'S STILL THERE, BUT FUZZY...
...IT JUST TAKES LONGER TO FIND ANIMALS BECAUSE THERE'S ALL THIS... STUFF IN THE WAY. I CAN'T EXPLAIN IT, BUT I'LL BE FINE.
KORY, YOU AND ELLEN AND MAXINE TAKE THE TRUCK. I'VE GOT MY CELL IN MY JACKET--CALL IF YOU RUN INTO ANY PROBLEMS.
I'LL SEE YOU THERE.
BUDDY--!
MOMMY, CLIFF DIDN'T MEAN TO HIT ME...DON'T BE MAD AT HIM...
ELLEN...
NOT RIGHT NOW, OKAY? ONE OF MY KIDS IS SICK, AND THE OTHER'S HURT.
LET'S JUST GET TO THE HOSPITAL.

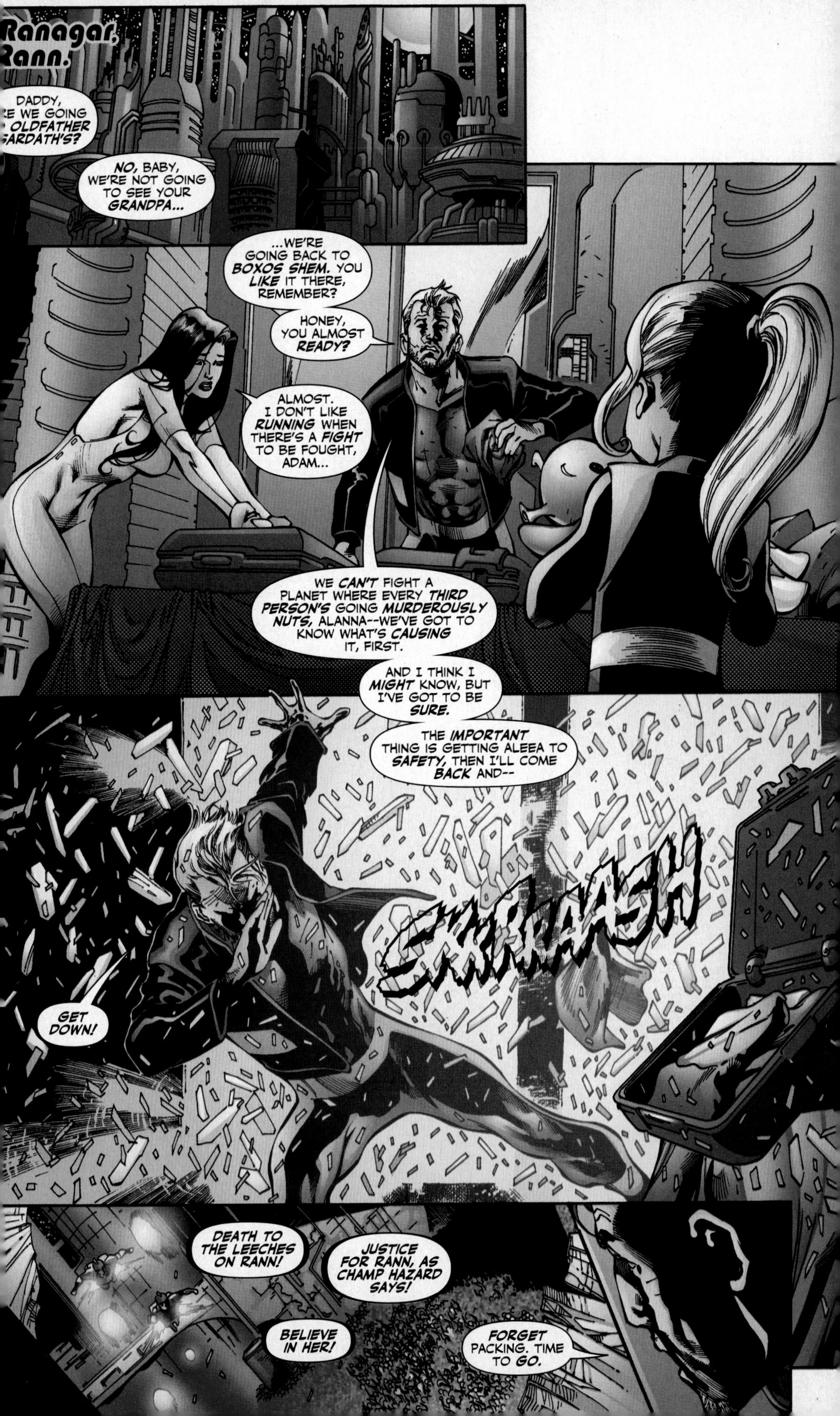

Ranagar,
Rann.
DADDY, RE WE GOING OLDFATHER ARDATH'S?
NO, BABY, WE'RE NOT GOING TO SEE YOUR GRANDPA...
...WE'RE GOING BACK TO BOXOS SHEM. YOU LIKE IT THERE, REMEMBER?
HONEY, YOU ALMOST READY?
ALMOST. I DON'T LIKE RUNNING WHEN THERE'S A FIGHT TO BE FOUGHT, ADAM...
WE CAN'T FIGHT A PLANET WHERE EVERY THIRD PERSON'S GOING MURDEROUSLY NUTS, ALANNA--WE'VE GOT TO KNOW WHAT'S CAUSING IT, FIRST.
AND I THINK I MIGHT KNOW, BUT I'VE GOT TO BE SURE.
THE IMPORTANT THING IS GETTING ALEEA TO SAFETY, THEN I'LL COME BACK AND--
GET DOWN!
DEATH TO THE LEECHES ON RANN!
JUSTICE FOR RANN, AS CHAMP HAZARD SAYS!
BELIEVE IN HER!
FORGET PACKING. TIME TO GO.

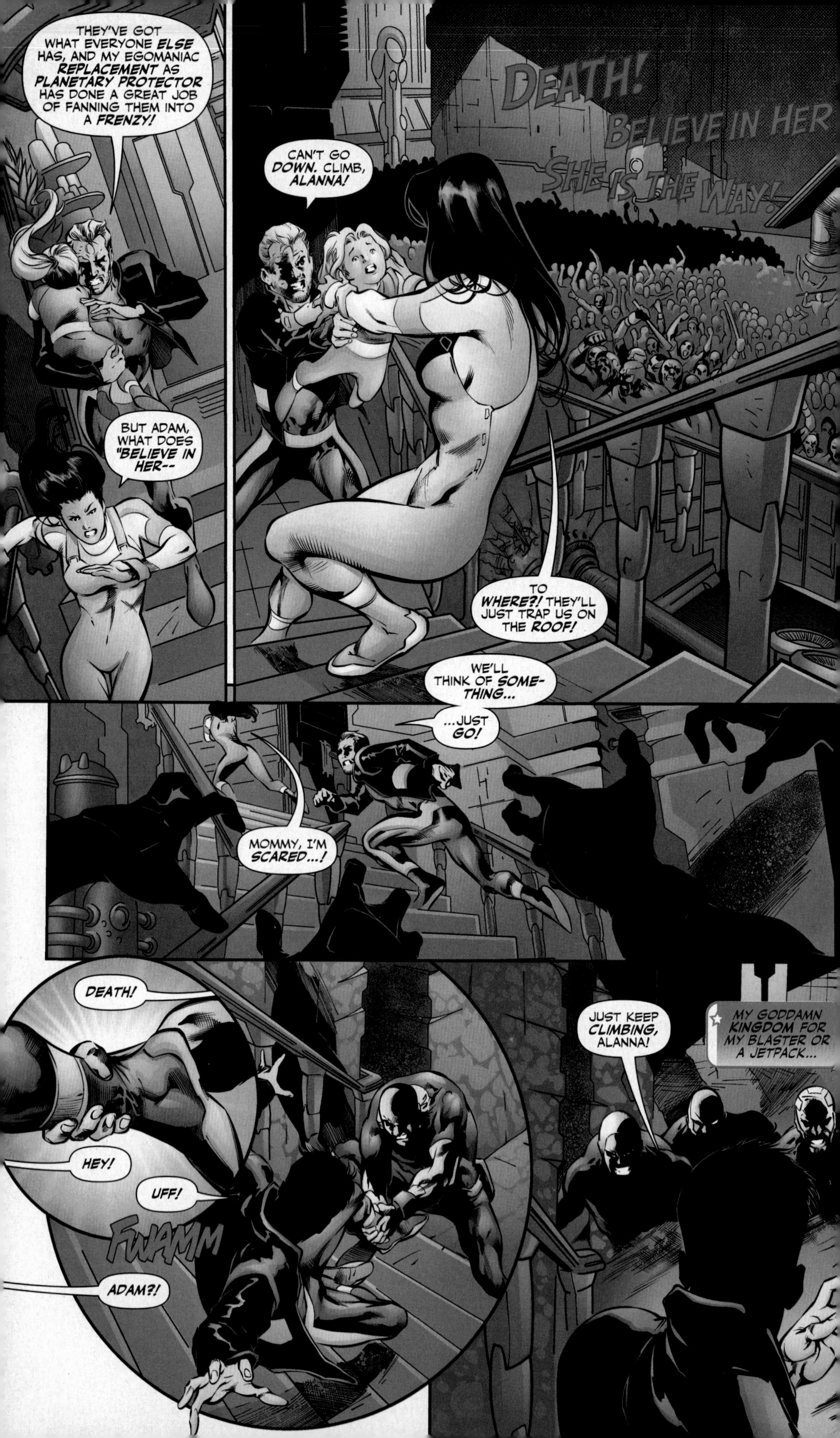
THEY'VE GOT WHAT EVERYONE ELSE HAS, AND MY EGOMANIAC REPLACEMENT AS PLANETARY PROTECTOR HAS DONE A GREAT JOB OF FANNING THEM INTO A FRENZY!
BUT ADAM, WHAT DOES "BELIEVE IN HER--
DEATH!
BELIEVE IN HER
SHE IS THE WAY!
CAN'T GO DOWN. CLIMB, ALANNA!
TO WHERE?! THEY'LL JUST TRAP US ON THE ROOF!
WE'LL THINK OF SOME-THING...
...JUST GO!
MOMMY, I'M SCARED...!
DEATH!
HEY!
UFF!
FWAMM
ADAM?!
JUST KEEP CLIMBING, ALANNA!
MY GODDAMN KINGDOM FOR MY BLASTER OR A JETPACK...

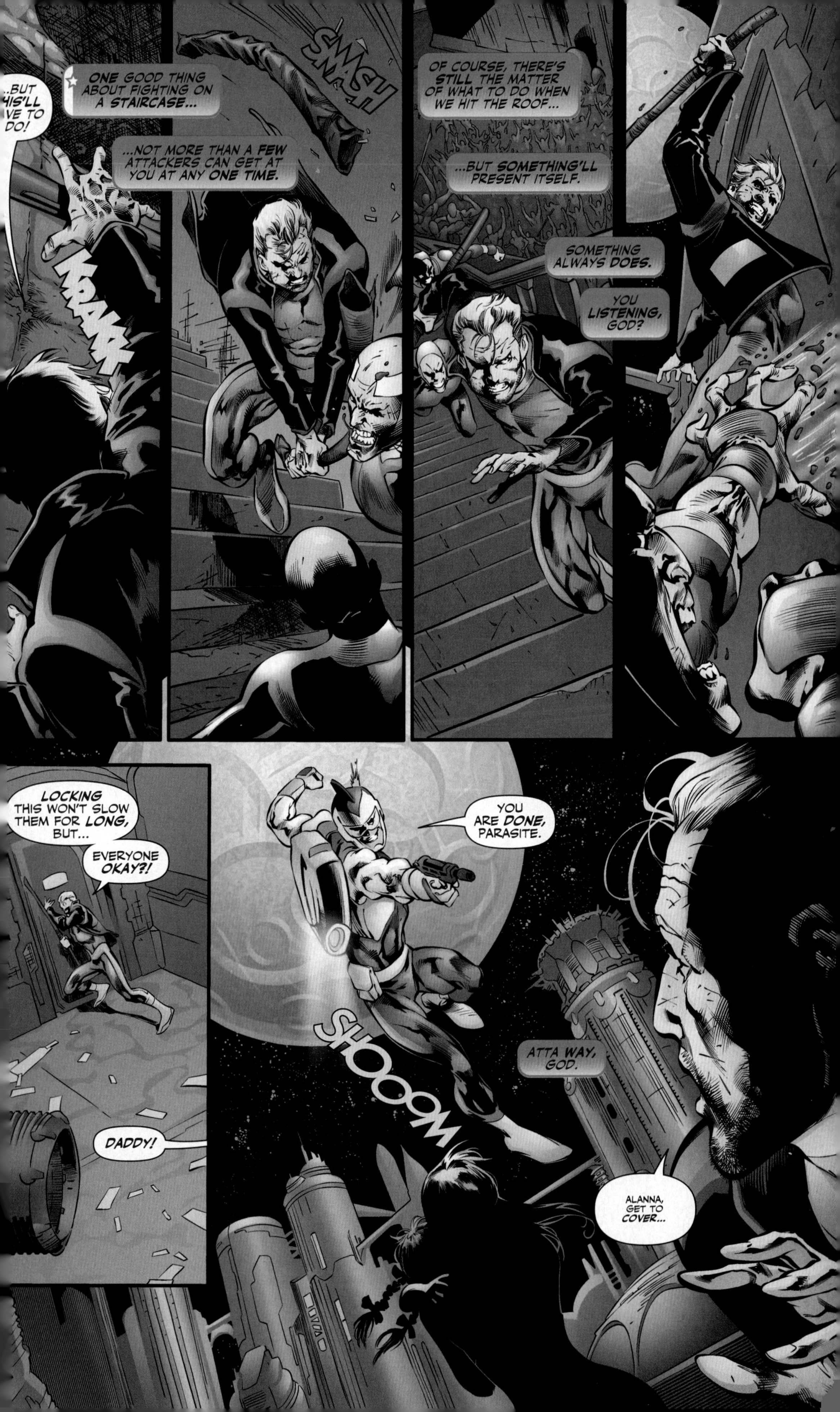
..BUT HIS'LL VE TO DO!
ONE GOOD THING ABOUT FIGHTING ON A STAIRCASE...
...NOT MORE THAN A FEW ATTACKERS CAN GET AT YOU AT ANY ONE TIME.
KRAAK
SMASH
OF COURSE, THERE'S STILL THE MATTER OF WHAT TO DO WHEN WE HIT THE ROOF...
...BUT SOMETHING'LL PRESENT ITSELF.
SOMETHING ALWAYS DOES.
YOU LISTENING, GOD?
LOCKING THIS WON'T SLOW THEM FOR LONG, BUT...
EVERYONE OKAY?!
DADDY!
YOU ARE DONE, PARASITE.
SHOOOM
ATTA WAY, GOD.
ALANNA, GET TO COVER...

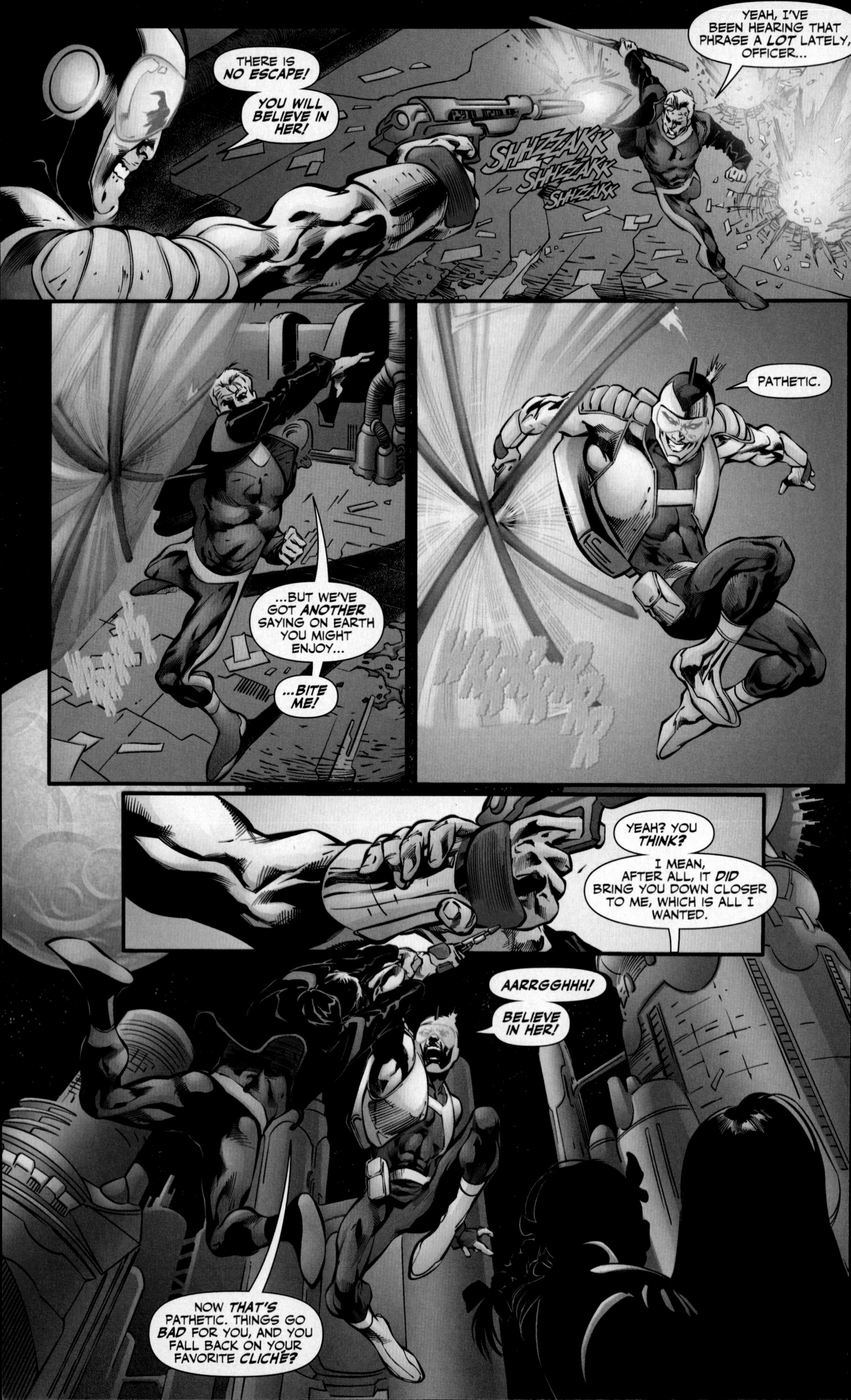
YEAH, I'VE BEEN HEARING THAT PHRASE A *LOT* LATELY, OFFICER...
THERE IS *NO ESCAPE!*
YOU WILL BELIEVE IN HER!
SHHZZAKK SHHZZAKK SHHZZAKK
...BUT WE'VE GOT *ANOTHER* SAYING ON EARTH YOU MIGHT ENJOY...
...BITE ME!
PATHETIC.
YEAH? YOU *THINK?*
I MEAN, AFTER ALL, IT *DID* BRING YOU DOWN CLOSER TO ME, WHICH IS ALL I WANTED.
AARRGGHHH!
BELIEVE IN HER!
NOW *THAT'S* PATHETIC. THINGS GO *BAD* FOR YOU, AND YOU FALL BACK ON YOUR FAVORITE *CLICHÉ?*

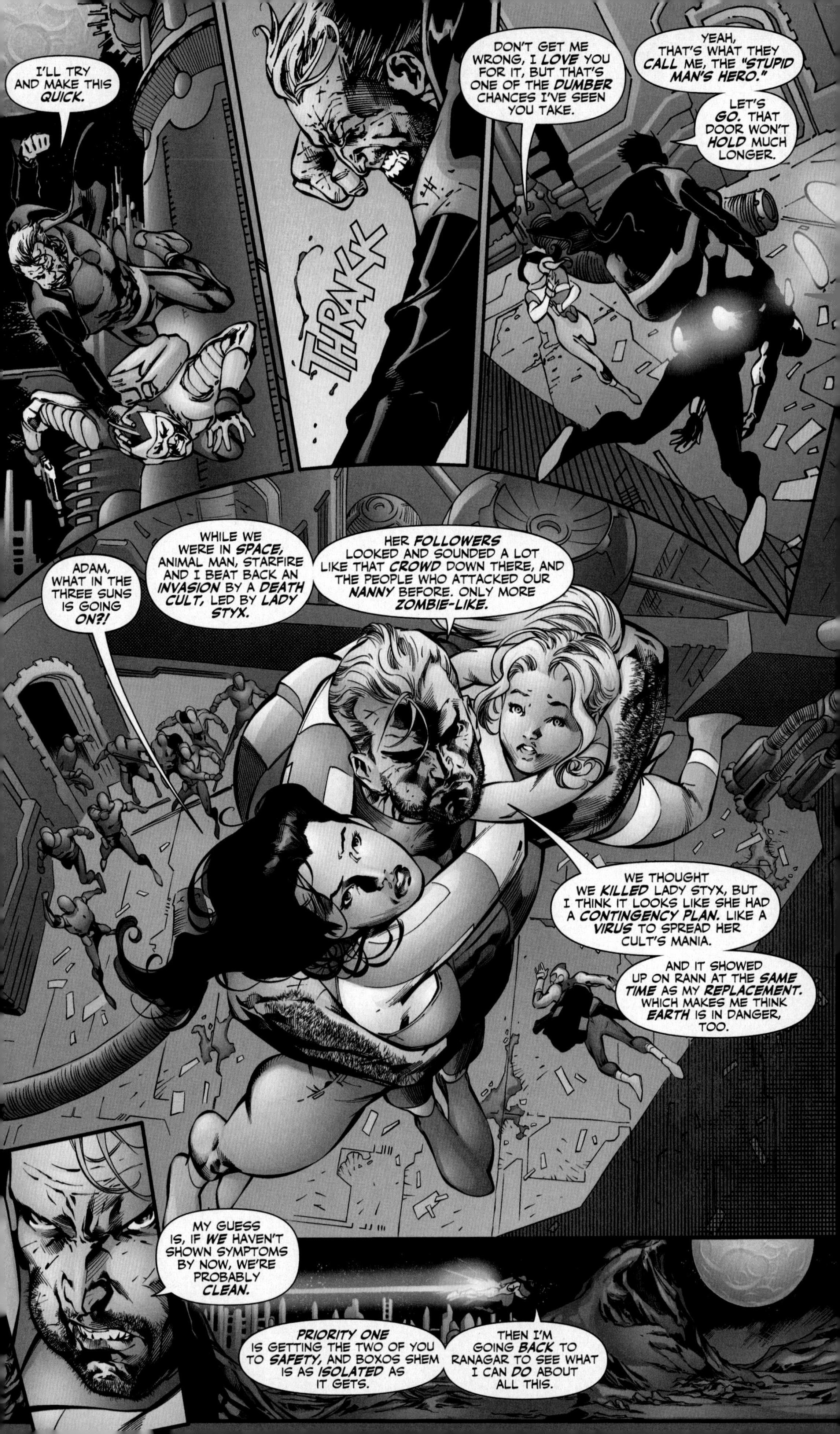
I'LL TRY AND MAKE THIS QUICK.
THRAKK
DON'T GET ME WRONG, I LOVE YOU FOR IT, BUT THAT'S ONE OF THE DUMBER CHANCES I'VE SEEN YOU TAKE.
YEAH, THAT'S WHAT THEY CALL ME, THE "STUPID MAN'S HERO."
LET'S GO. THAT DOOR WON'T HOLD MUCH LONGER.
ADAM, WHAT IN THE THREE SUNS IS GOING ON?!
WHILE WE WERE IN SPACE, ANIMAL MAN, STARFIRE AND I BEAT BACK AN INVASION BY A DEATH CULT, LED BY LADY STYX.
HER FOLLOWERS LOOKED AND SOUNDED A LOT LIKE THAT CROWD DOWN THERE, AND THE PEOPLE WHO ATTACKED OUR NANNY BEFORE. ONLY MORE ZOMBIE-LIKE.
WE THOUGHT WE KILLED LADY STYX, BUT I THINK IT LOOKS LIKE SHE HAD A CONTINGENCY PLAN. LIKE A VIRUS TO SPREAD HER CULT'S MANIA.
AND IT SHOWED UP ON RANN AT THE SAME TIME AS MY REPLACEMENT. WHICH MAKES ME THINK EARTH IS IN DANGER, TOO.
MY GUESS IS, IF WE HAVEN'T SHOWN SYMPTOMS BY NOW, WE'RE PROBABLY CLEAN.
PRIORITY ONE IS GETTING THE TWO OF YOU TO SAFETY, AND BOXOS SHEM IS AS ISOLATED AS IT GETS.
THEN I'M GOING BACK TO RANAGAR TO SEE WHAT I CAN DO ABOUT ALL THIS.

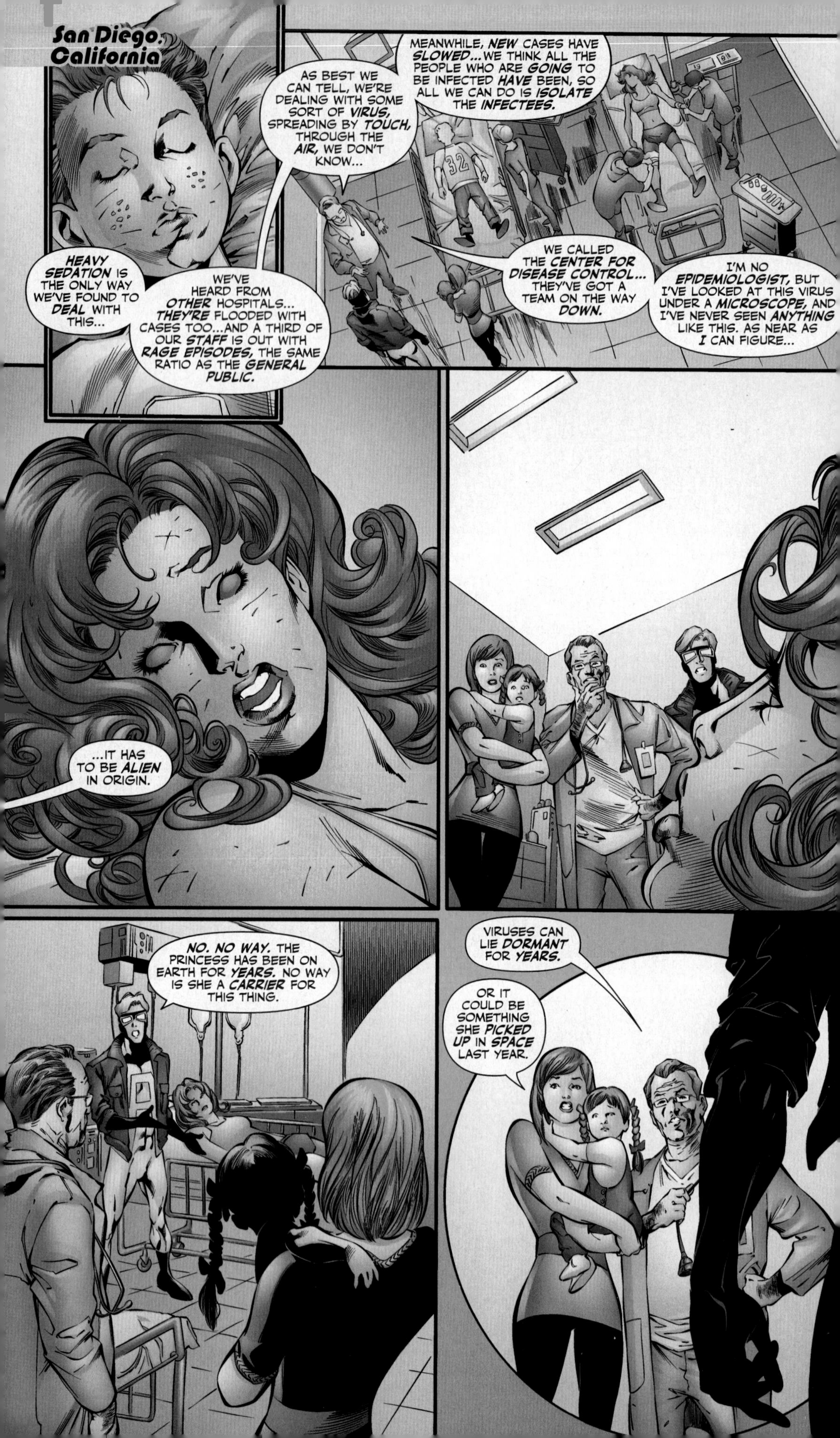
San Diego, California
HEAVY SEDATION IS THE ONLY WAY WE'VE FOUND TO DEAL WITH THIS...
WE'VE HEARD FROM OTHER HOSPITALS... THEY'RE FLOODED WITH CASES TOO...AND A THIRD OF OUR STAFF IS OUT WITH RAGE EPISODES, THE SAME RATIO AS THE GENERAL PUBLIC.
AS BEST WE CAN TELL, WE'RE DEALING WITH SOME SORT OF VIRUS, SPREADING BY TOUCH, THROUGH THE AIR, WE DON'T KNOW...
MEANWHILE, NEW CASES HAVE SLOWED... WE THINK ALL THE PEOPLE WHO ARE GOING TO BE INFECTED HAVE BEEN, SO ALL WE CAN DO IS ISOLATE THE INFECTEES.
WE CALLED THE CENTER FOR DISEASE CONTROL... THEY'VE GOT A TEAM ON THE WAY DOWN.
I'M NO EPIDEMIOLOGIST, BUT I'VE LOOKED AT THIS VIRUS UNDER A MICROSCOPE, AND I'VE NEVER SEEN ANYTHING LIKE THIS. AS NEAR AS I CAN FIGURE...
...IT HAS TO BE ALIEN IN ORIGIN.
NO. NO WAY. THE PRINCESS HAS BEEN ON EARTH FOR YEARS. NO WAY IS SHE A CARRIER FOR THIS THING.
VIRUSES CAN LIE DORMANT FOR YEARS.
OR IT COULD BE SOMETHING SHE PICKED UP IN SPACE LAST YEAR.

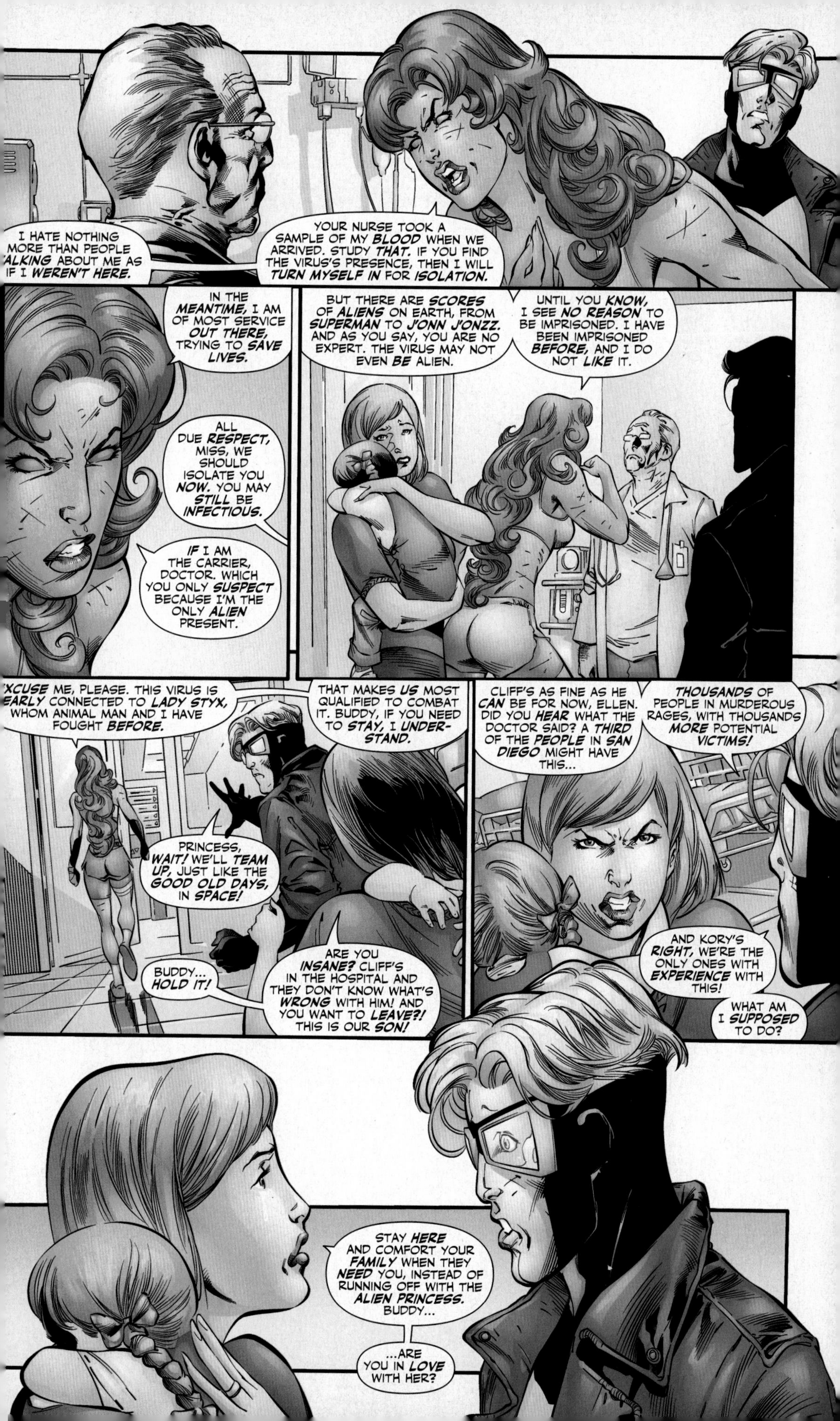

I HATE NOTHING MORE THAN PEOPLE TALKING ABOUT ME AS IF I WEREN'T HERE.
YOUR NURSE TOOK A SAMPLE OF MY BLOOD WHEN WE ARRIVED. STUDY THAT. IF YOU FIND THE VIRUS'S PRESENCE, THEN I WILL TURN MYSELF IN FOR ISOLATION.
IN THE MEANTIME, I AM OF MOST SERVICE OUT THERE, TRYING TO SAVE LIVES.
ALL DUE RESPECT, MISS, WE SHOULD ISOLATE YOU NOW. YOU MAY STILL BE INFECTIOUS.
IF I AM THE CARRIER, DOCTOR. WHICH YOU ONLY SUSPECT BECAUSE I'M THE ONLY ALIEN PRESENT.
BUT THERE ARE SCORES OF ALIENS ON EARTH, FROM SUPERMAN TO J'ONN J'ONZZ. AND AS YOU SAY, YOU ARE NO EXPERT. THE VIRUS MAY NOT EVEN BE ALIEN.
UNTIL YOU KNOW, I SEE NO REASON TO BE IMPRISONED. I HAVE BEEN IMPRISONED BEFORE, AND I DO NOT LIKE IT.
XCUSE ME, PLEASE. THIS VIRUS IS EARLY CONNECTED TO LADY STYX, WHOM ANIMAL MAN AND I HAVE FOUGHT BEFORE.
THAT MAKES US MOST QUALIFIED TO COMBAT IT. BUDDY, IF YOU NEED TO STAY, I UNDER-STAND.
PRINCESS, WAIT! WE'LL TEAM UP, JUST LIKE THE GOOD OLD DAYS, IN SPACE!
BUDDY... HOLD IT!
ARE YOU INSANE? CLIFF'S IN THE HOSPITAL AND THEY DON'T KNOW WHAT'S WRONG WITH HIM! AND YOU WANT TO LEAVE?! THIS IS OUR SON!
CLIFF'S AS FINE AS HE CAN BE FOR NOW, ELLEN. DID YOU HEAR WHAT THE DOCTOR SAID? A THIRD OF THE PEOPLE IN SAN DIEGO MIGHT HAVE THIS...
THOUSANDS OF PEOPLE IN MURDEROUS RAGES, WITH THOUSANDS MORE POTENTIAL VICTIMS!
AND KORY'S RIGHT, WE'RE THE ONLY ONES WITH EXPERIENCE WITH THIS!
WHAT AM I SUPPOSED TO DO?
STAY HERE AND COMFORT YOUR FAMILY WHEN THEY NEED YOU, INSTEAD OF RUNNING OFF WITH THE ALIEN PRINCESS. BUDDY...
...ARE YOU IN LOVE WITH HER?

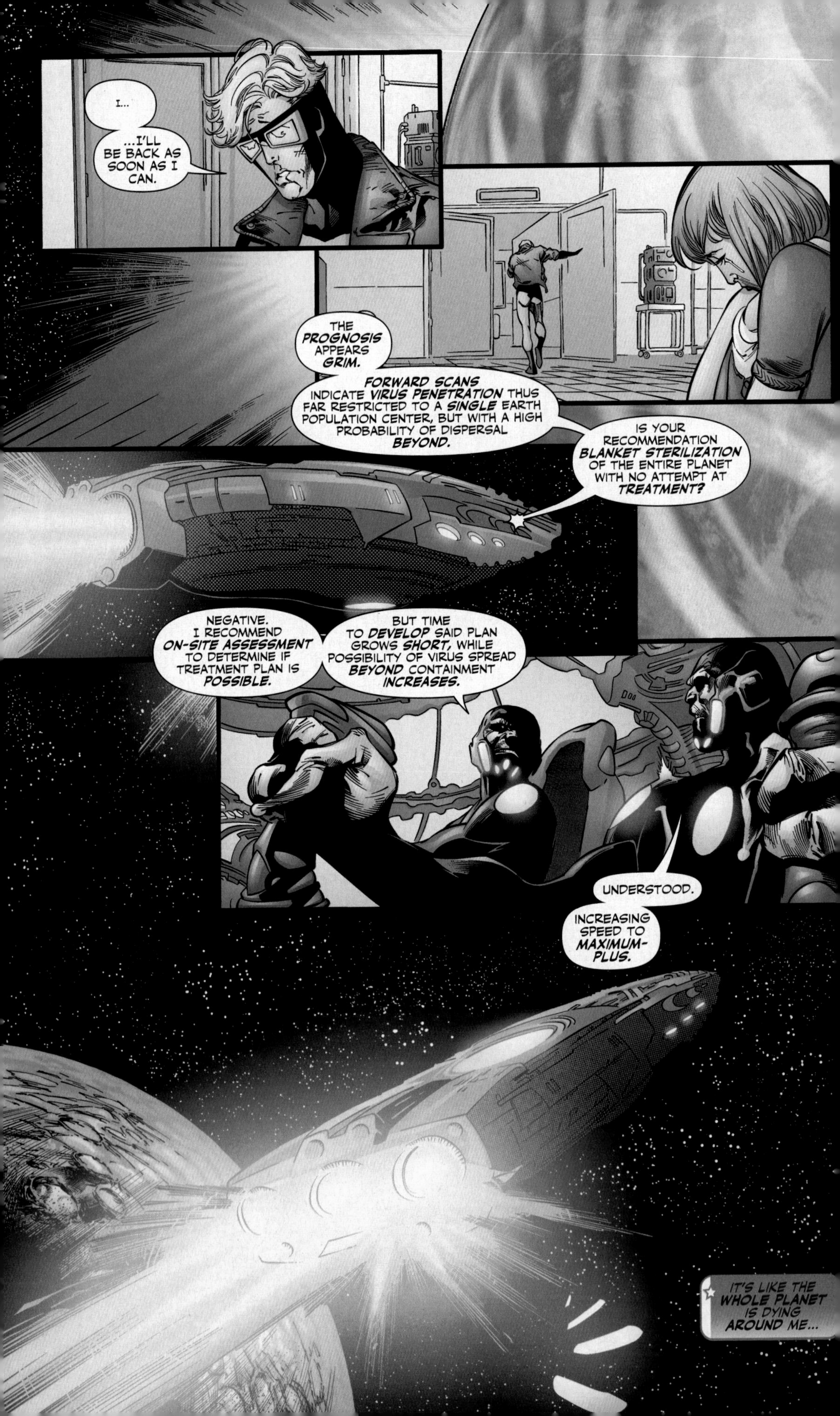
I...
...I'LL BE BACK AS SOON AS I CAN.
THE PROGNOSIS APPEARS GRIM.
FORWARD SCANS INDICATE VIRUS PENETRATION THUS FAR RESTRICTED TO A SINGLE EARTH POPULATION CENTER, BUT WITH A HIGH PROBABILITY OF DISPERSAL BEYOND.
IS YOUR RECOMMENDATION BLANKET STERILIZATION OF THE ENTIRE PLANET WITH NO ATTEMPT AT TREATMENT?
NEGATIVE. I RECOMMEND ON-SITE ASSESSMENT TO DETERMINE IF TREATMENT PLAN IS POSSIBLE.
BUT TIME TO DEVELOP SAID PLAN GROWS SHORT, WHILE POSSIBILITY OF VIRUS SPREAD BEYOND CONTAINMENT INCREASES.
UNDERSTOOD.
INCREASING SPEED TO MAXIMUM-PLUS.
IT'S LIKE THE WHOLE PLANET IS DYING AROUND ME...

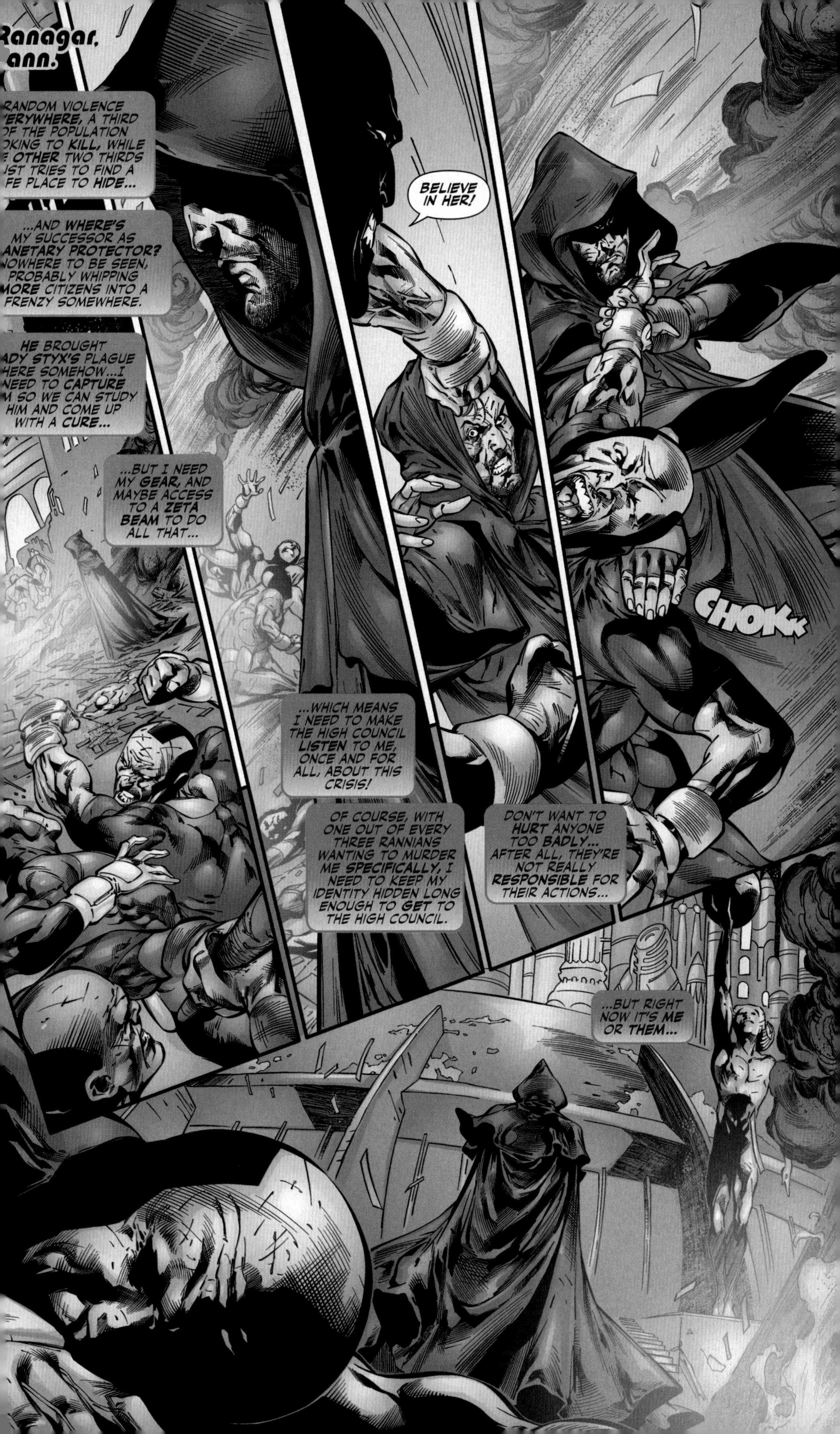

Ranagar, ann.
RANDOM VIOLENCE ERYWHERE, A THIRD OF THE POPULATION OKING TO KILL, WHILE E OTHER TWO THIRDS UST TRIES TO FIND A FE PLACE TO HIDE...
...AND WHERE'S MY SUCCESSOR AS ANETARY PROTECTOR? NOWHERE TO BE SEEN, PROBABLY WHIPPING MORE CITIZENS INTO A FRENZY SOMEWHERE.
HE BROUGHT ADY STYX'S PLAGUE HERE SOMEHOW...I NEED TO CAPTURE M SO WE CAN STUDY HIM AND COME UP WITH A CURE...
...BUT I NEED MY GEAR, AND MAYBE ACCESS TO A ZETA BEAM TO DO ALL THAT...
BELIEVE IN HER!
...WHICH MEANS I NEED TO MAKE THE HIGH COUNCIL LISTEN TO ME, ONCE AND FOR ALL, ABOUT THIS CRISIS!
OF COURSE, WITH ONE OUT OF EVERY THREE RANNIANS WANTING TO MURDER ME SPECIFICALLY, I NEED TO KEEP MY IDENTITY HIDDEN LONG ENOUGH TO GET TO THE HIGH COUNCIL.
CHOKK
DON'T WANT TO HURT ANYONE TOO BADLY... AFTER ALL, THEY'RE NOT REALLY RESPONSIBLE FOR THEIR ACTIONS...
...BUT RIGHT NOW IT'S ME OR THEM...

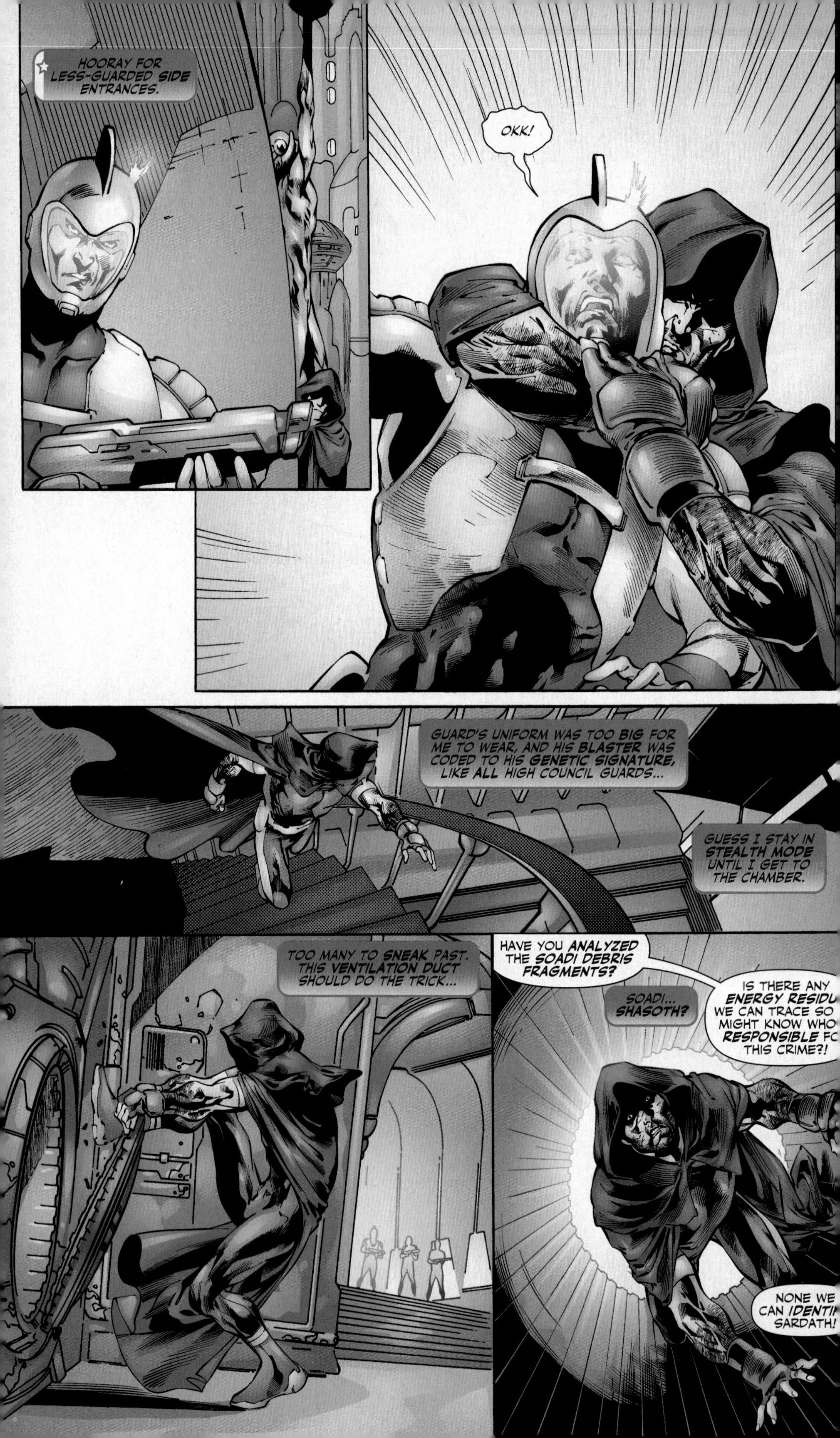
HOORAY FOR LESS-GUARDED SIDE ENTRANCES.
OKK!
GUARD'S UNIFORM WAS TOO BIG FOR ME TO WEAR, AND HIS BLASTER WAS CODED TO HIS GENETIC SIGNATURE, LIKE ALL HIGH COUNCIL GUARDS...
GUESS I STAY IN STEALTH MODE UNTIL I GET TO THE CHAMBER.
TOO MANY TO SNEAK PAST. THIS VENTILATION DUCT SHOULD DO THE TRICK...
HAVE YOU ANALYZED THE SOADI DEBRIS FRAGMENTS?
SOADI... SHASOTH?
IS THERE ANY ENERGY RESIDU WE CAN TRACE SO MIGHT KNOW WHO RESPONSIBLE FO THIS CRIME?!
NONE WE CAN IDENTI SARDATH!

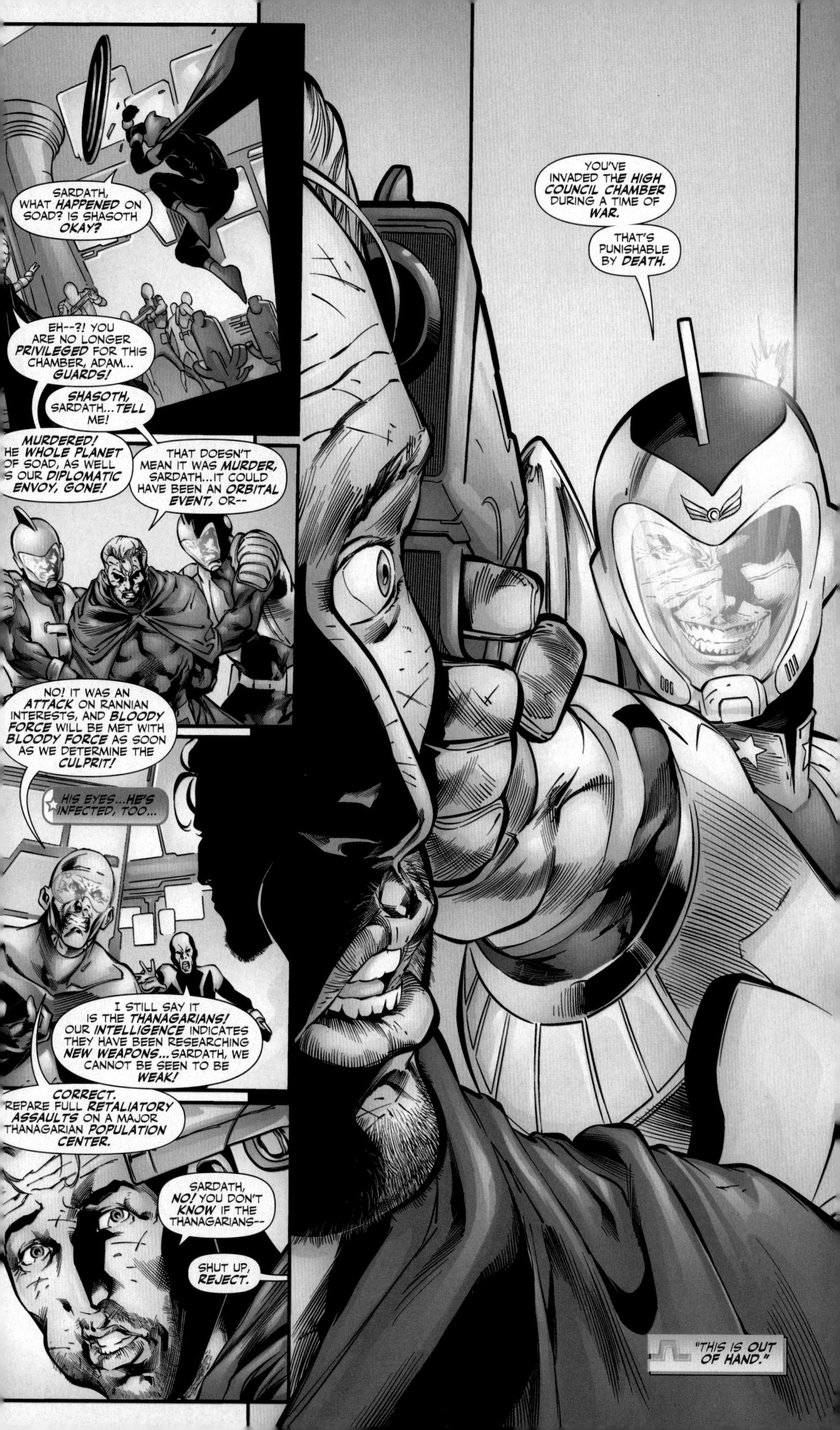

SARDATH, WHAT HAPPENED ON SOAD? IS SHASOTH OKAY?
EH--?! YOU ARE NO LONGER PRIVILEGED FOR THIS CHAMBER, ADAM... GUARDS!
SHASOTH, SARDATH...TELL ME!
MURDERED! THE WHOLE PLANET OF SOAD, AS WELL AS OUR DIPLOMATIC ENVOY, GONE!
THAT DOESN'T MEAN IT WAS MURDER, SARDATH...IT COULD HAVE BEEN AN ORBITAL EVENT, OR--
NO! IT WAS AN ATTACK ON RANNIAN INTERESTS, AND BLOODY FORCE WILL BE MET WITH BLOODY FORCE AS SOON AS WE DETERMINE THE CULPRIT!
HIS EYES...HE'S INFECTED, TOO...
I STILL SAY IT IS THE THANAGARIANS! OUR INTELLIGENCE INDICATES THEY HAVE BEEN RESEARCHING NEW WEAPONS...SARDATH, WE CANNOT BE SEEN TO BE WEAK!
CORRECT. PREPARE FULL RETALIATORY ASSAULTS ON A MAJOR THANAGARIAN POPULATION CENTER.
SARDATH, NO! YOU DON'T KNOW IF THE THANAGARIANS--
SHUT UP, REJECT.
YOU'VE INVADED THE HIGH COUNCIL CHAMBER DURING A TIME OF WAR.
THAT'S PUNISHABLE BY DEATH.
"THIS IS OUT OF HAND."

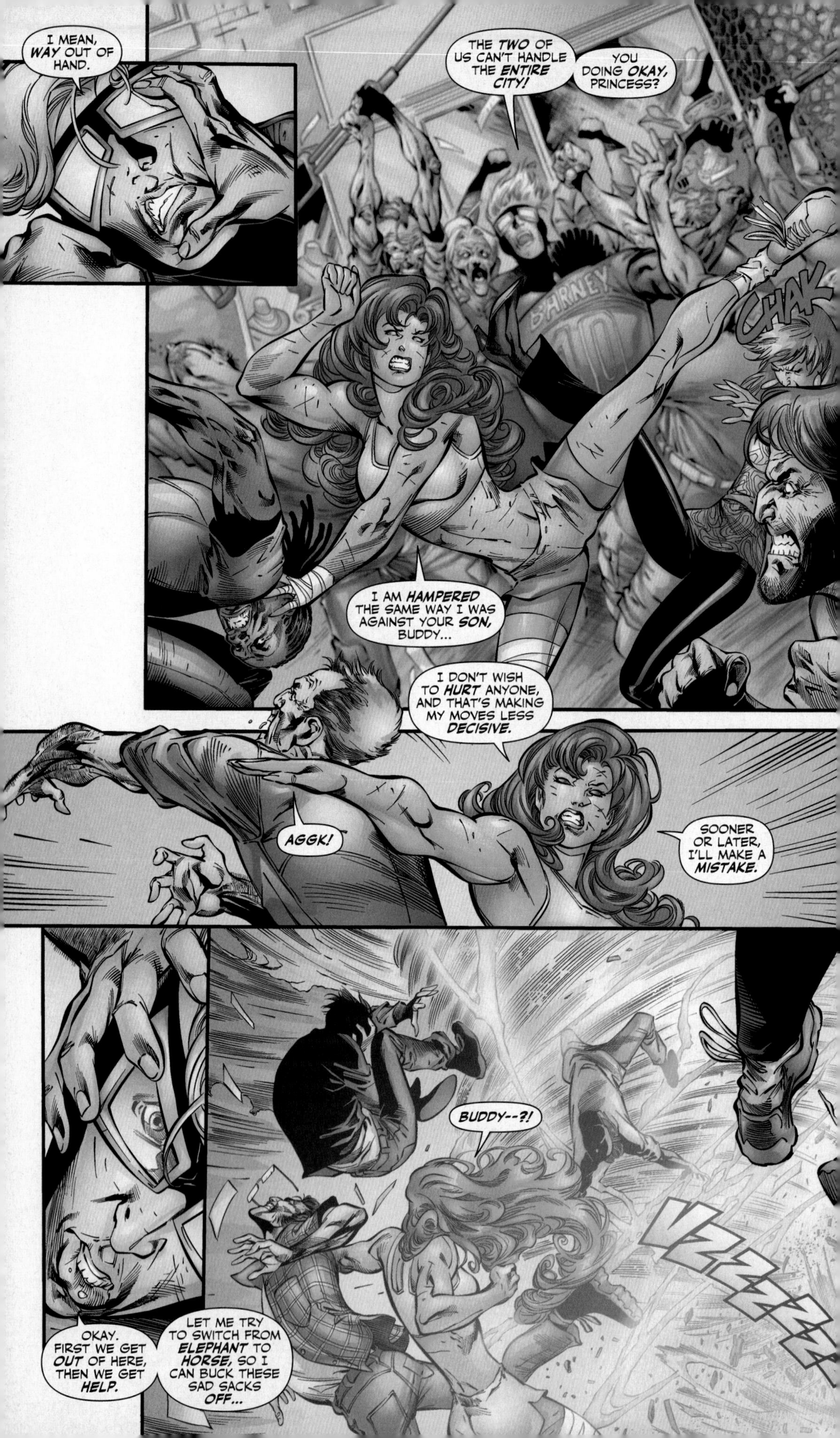
I MEAN, WAY OUT OF HAND.
THE TWO OF US CAN'T HANDLE THE ENTIRE CITY!
YOU DOING OKAY, PRINCESS?
CHAK
I AM HAMPERED THE SAME WAY I WAS AGAINST YOUR SON, BUDDY...
I DON'T WISH TO HURT ANYONE, AND THAT'S MAKING MY MOVES LESS DECISIVE.
AGGK!
SOONER OR LATER, I'LL MAKE A MISTAKE.
BUDDY--?!
OKAY. FIRST WE GET OUT OF HERE, THEN WE GET HELP.
LET ME TRY TO SWITCH FROM ELEPHANT TO HORSE, SO I CAN BUCK THESE SAD SACKS OFF...

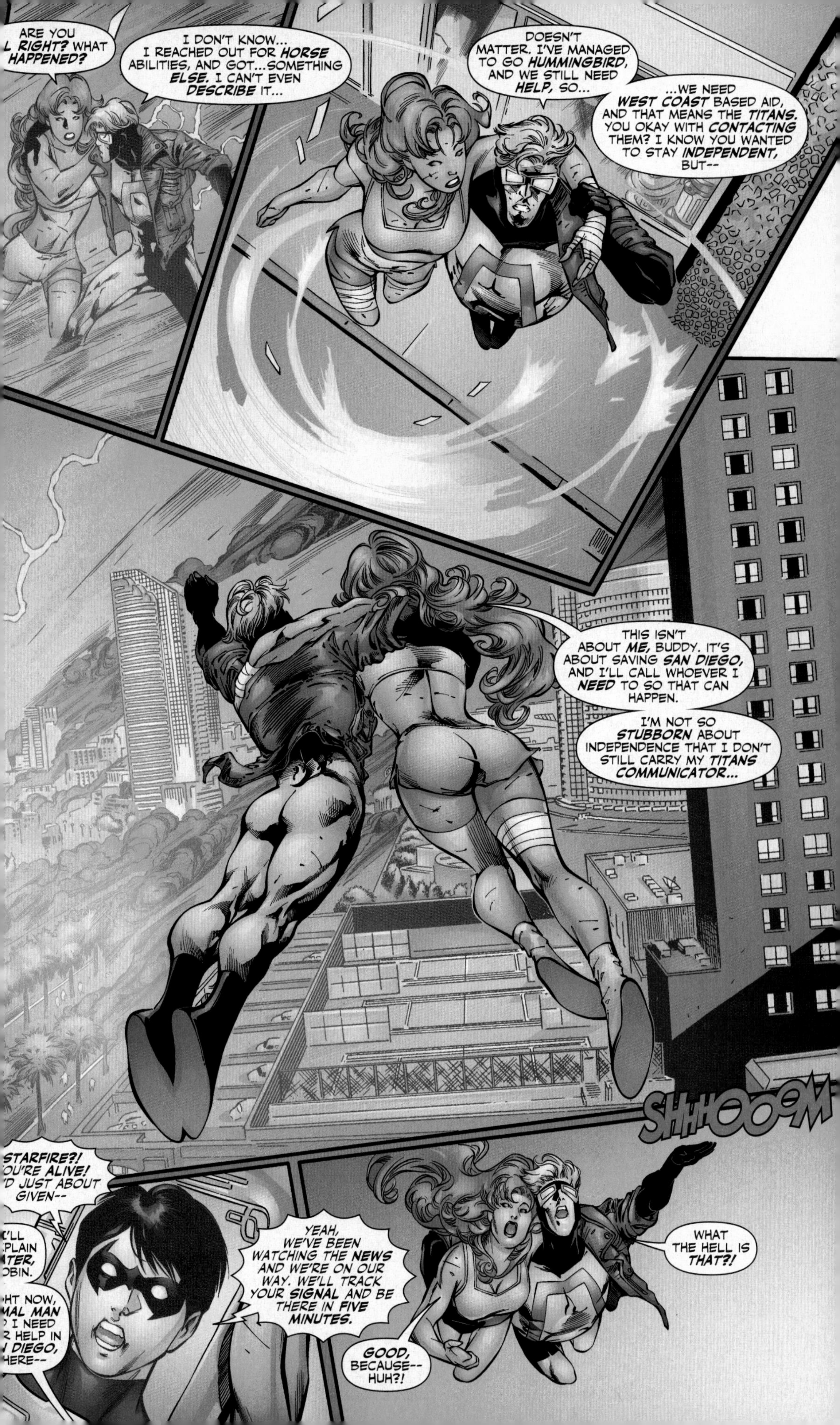
ARE YOU L RIGHT? WHAT HAPPENED?
I DON'T KNOW... I REACHED OUT FOR HORSE ABILITIES, AND GOT...SOMETHING ELSE. I CAN'T EVEN DESCRIBE IT...
DOESN'T MATTER. I'VE MANAGED TO GO HUMMINGBIRD, AND WE STILL NEED HELP, SO...
...WE NEED WEST COAST BASED AID, AND THAT MEANS THE TITANS. YOU OKAY WITH CONTACTING THEM? I KNOW YOU WANTED TO STAY INDEPENDENT, BUT--
THIS ISN'T ABOUT ME, BUDDY. IT'S ABOUT SAVING SAN DIEGO, AND I'LL CALL WHOEVER I NEED TO SO THAT CAN HAPPEN.
I'M NOT SO STUBBORN ABOUT INDEPENDENCE THAT I DON'T STILL CARRY MY TITANS COMMUNICATOR...
SHHHOOOM
STARFIRE?! OU'RE ALIVE! 'D JUST ABOUT GIVEN--
'LL PLAIN TER, OBIN.
HT NOW, MAL MAN I NEED R HELP IN DIEGO, HERE--
YEAH, WE'VE BEEN WATCHING THE NEWS AND WE'RE ON OUR WAY. WE'LL TRACK YOUR SIGNAL AND BE THERE IN FIVE MINUTES.
GOOD, BECAUSE-- HUH?!
WHAT THE HELL IS THAT?!

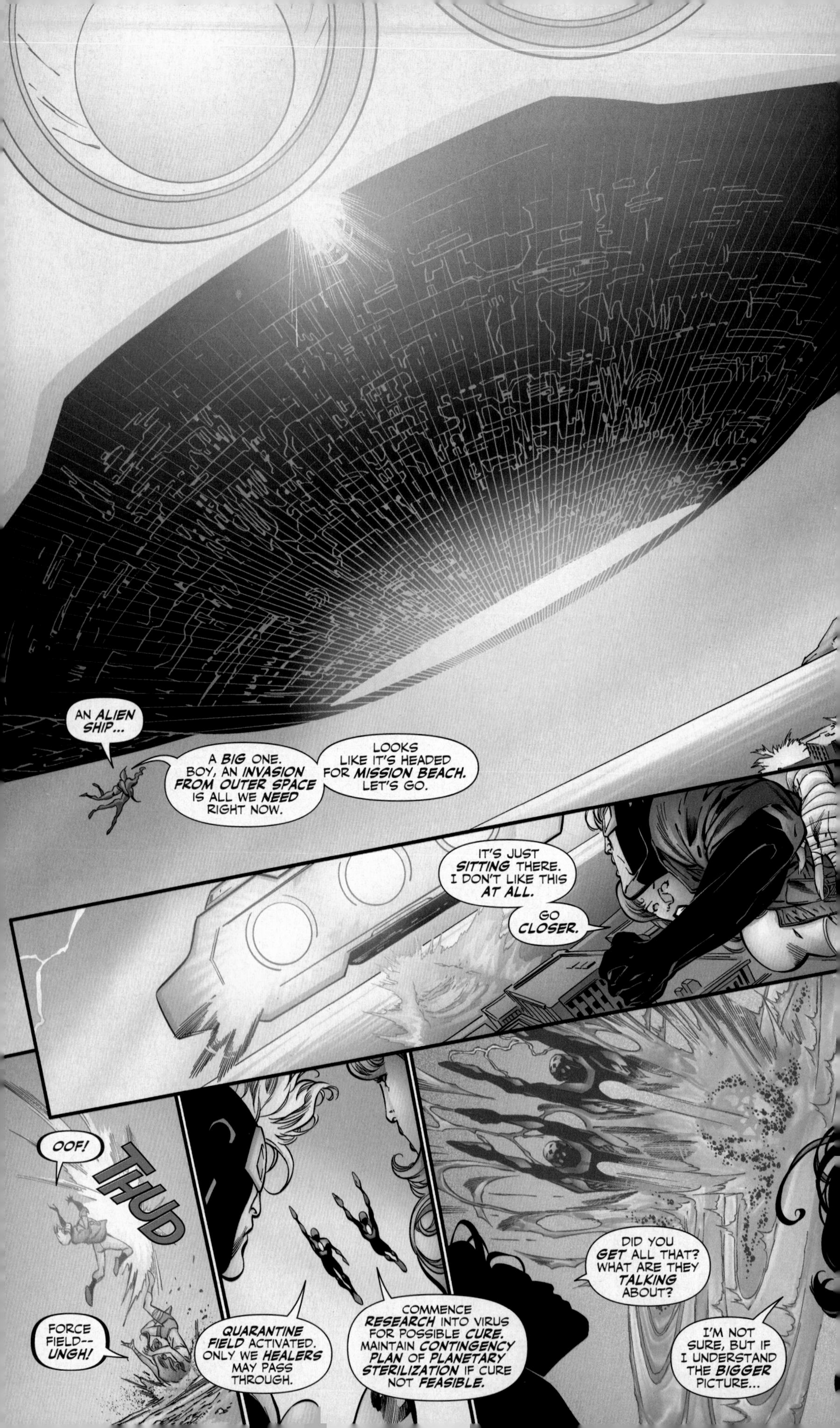
AN ALIEN SHIP...
A BIG ONE. BOY, AN INVASION FROM OUTER SPACE IS ALL WE NEED RIGHT NOW.
LOOKS LIKE IT'S HEADED FOR MISSION BEACH. LET'S GO.
IT'S JUST SITTING THERE. I DON'T LIKE THIS AT ALL.
GO CLOSER.
OOF!
THUD
FORCE FIELD-- UNGH!
QUARANTINE FIELD ACTIVATED. ONLY WE HEALERS MAY PASS THROUGH.
COMMENCE RESEARCH INTO VIRUS FOR POSSIBLE CURE. MAINTAIN CONTINGENCY PLAN OF PLANETARY STERILIZATION IF CURE NOT FEASIBLE.
DID YOU GET ALL THAT? WHAT ARE THEY TALKING ABOUT?
I'M NOT SURE, BUT IF I UNDERSTAND THE BIGGER PICTURE...

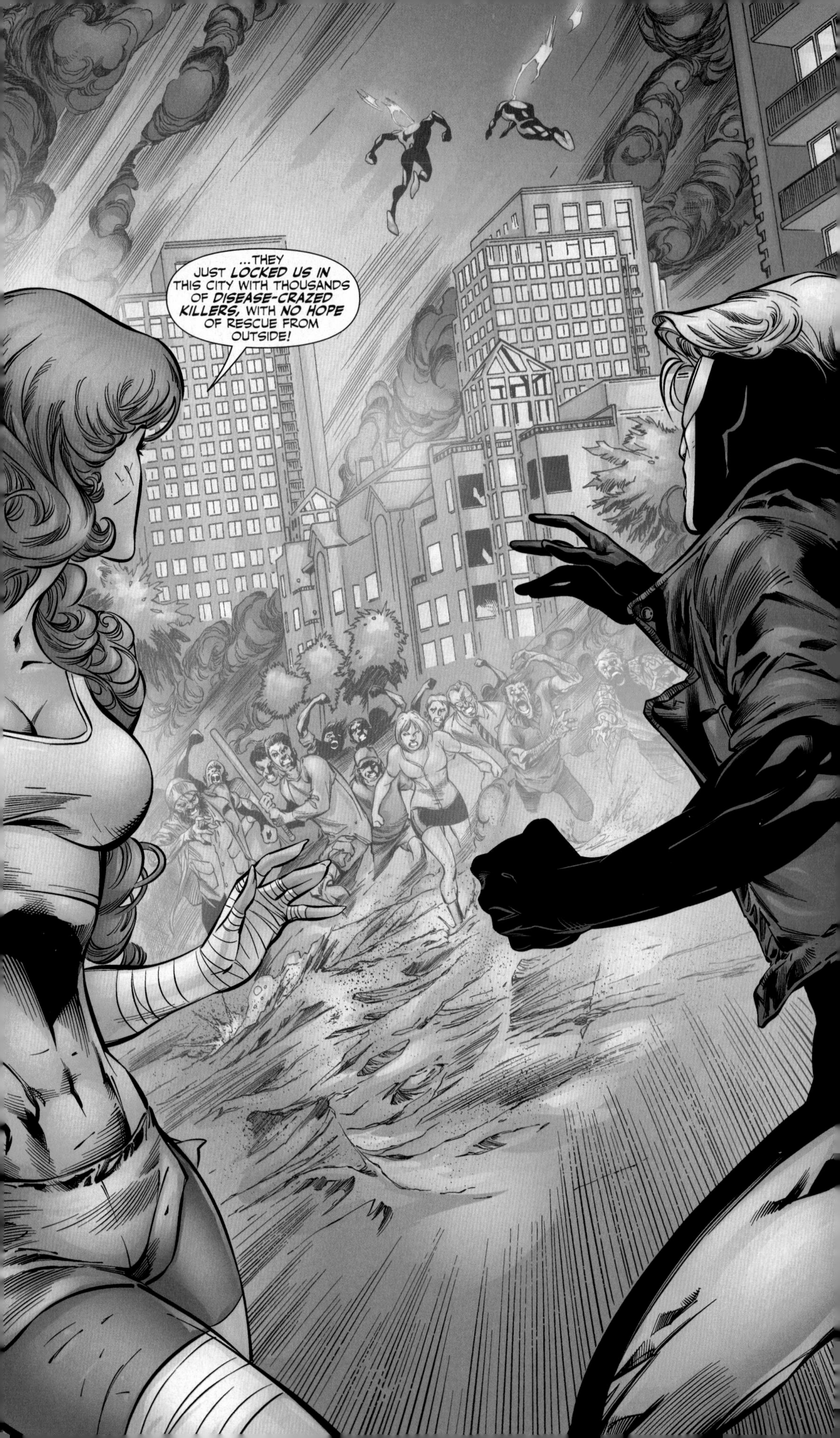
...THEY JUST LOCKED US IN THIS CITY WITH THOUSANDS OF DISEASE-CRAZED KILLERS, WITH NO HOPE OF RESCUE FROM OUTSIDE!

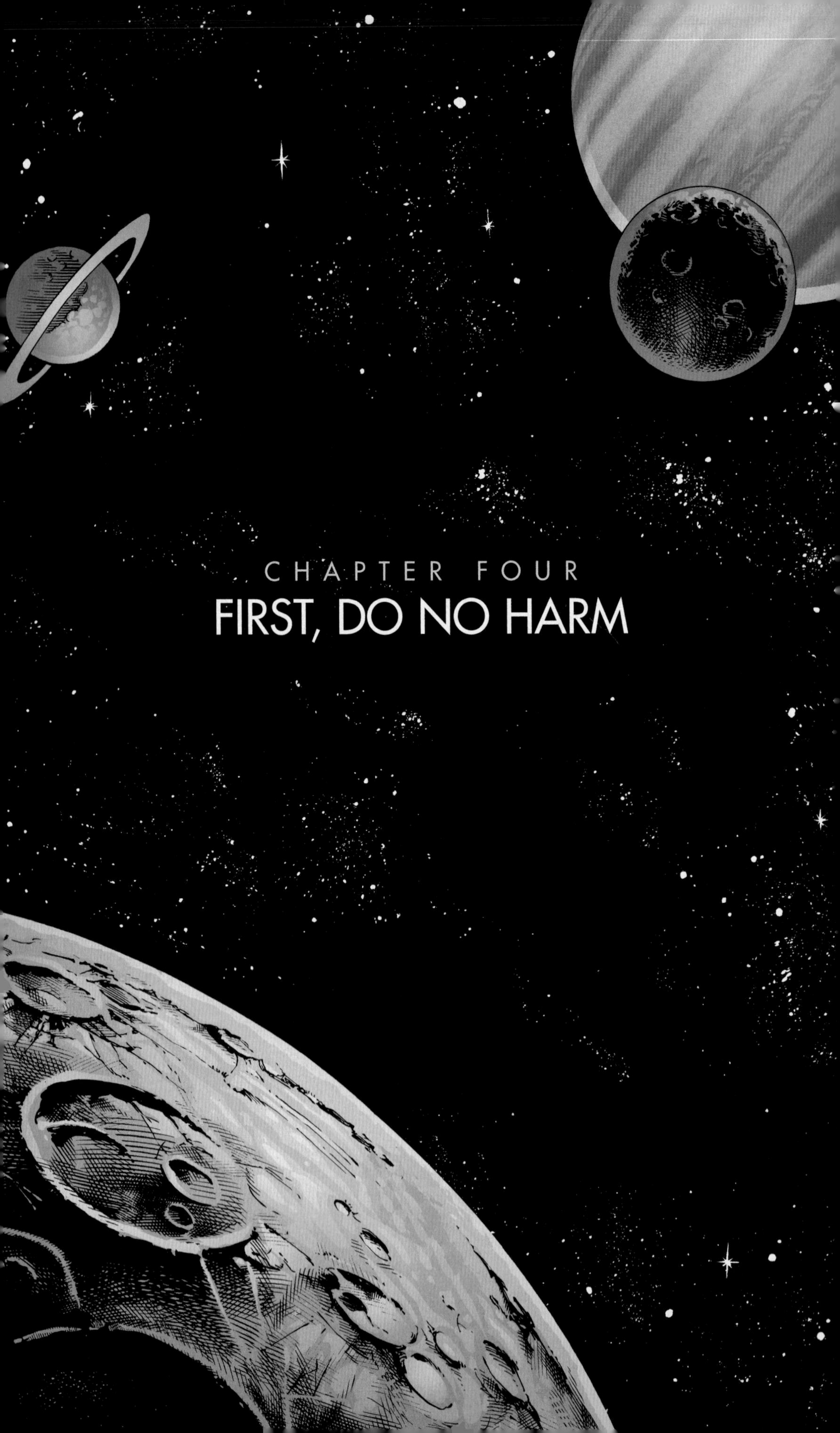

CHAPTER FOUR
FIRST, DO NO HARM

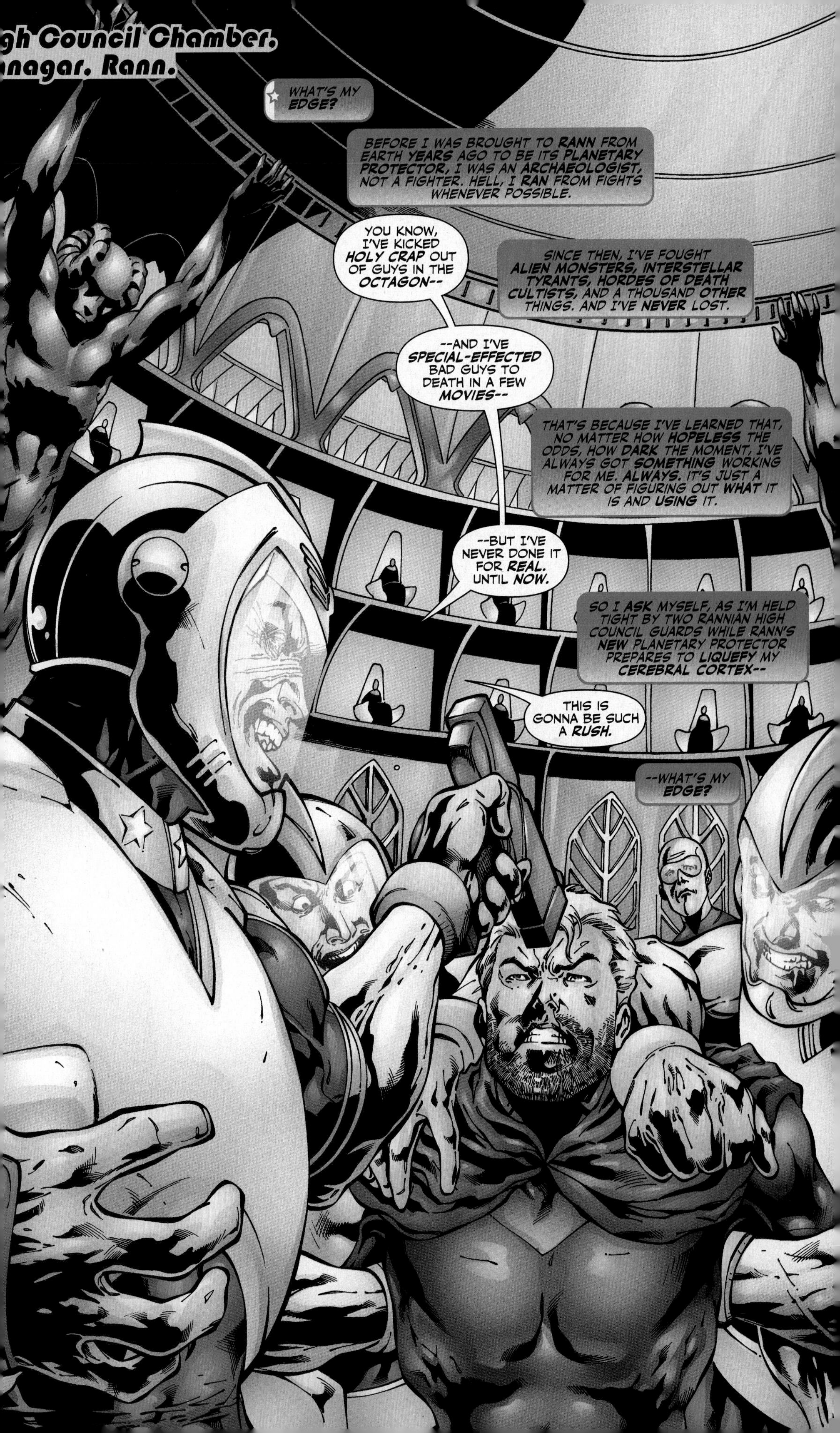

gh Council Chamber, nagar, Rann.
WHAT'S MY EDGE?
BEFORE I WAS BROUGHT TO RANN FROM EARTH YEARS AGO TO BE ITS PLANETARY PROTECTOR, I WAS AN ARCHAEOLOGIST, NOT A FIGHTER. HELL, I RAN FROM FIGHTS WHENEVER POSSIBLE.
YOU KNOW, I'VE KICKED HOLY CRAP OUT OF GUYS IN THE OCTAGON--
SINCE THEN, I'VE FOUGHT ALIEN MONSTERS, INTERSTELLAR TYRANTS, HORDES OF DEATH CULTISTS, AND A THOUSAND OTHER THINGS. AND I'VE NEVER LOST.
--AND I'VE SPECIAL-EFFECTED BAD GUYS TO DEATH IN A FEW MOVIES--
THAT'S BECAUSE I'VE LEARNED THAT, NO MATTER HOW HOPELESS THE ODDS, HOW DARK THE MOMENT, I'VE ALWAYS GOT SOMETHING WORKING FOR ME. ALWAYS. IT'S JUST A MATTER OF FIGURING OUT WHAT IT IS AND USING IT.
--BUT I'VE NEVER DONE IT FOR REAL. UNTIL NOW.
SO I ASK MYSELF, AS I'M HELD TIGHT BY TWO RANNIAN HIGH COUNCIL GUARDS WHILE RANN'S NEW PLANETARY PROTECTOR PREPARES TO LIQUEFY MY CEREBRAL CORTEX--
THIS IS GONNA BE SUCH A RUSH.
--WHAT'S MY EDGE?

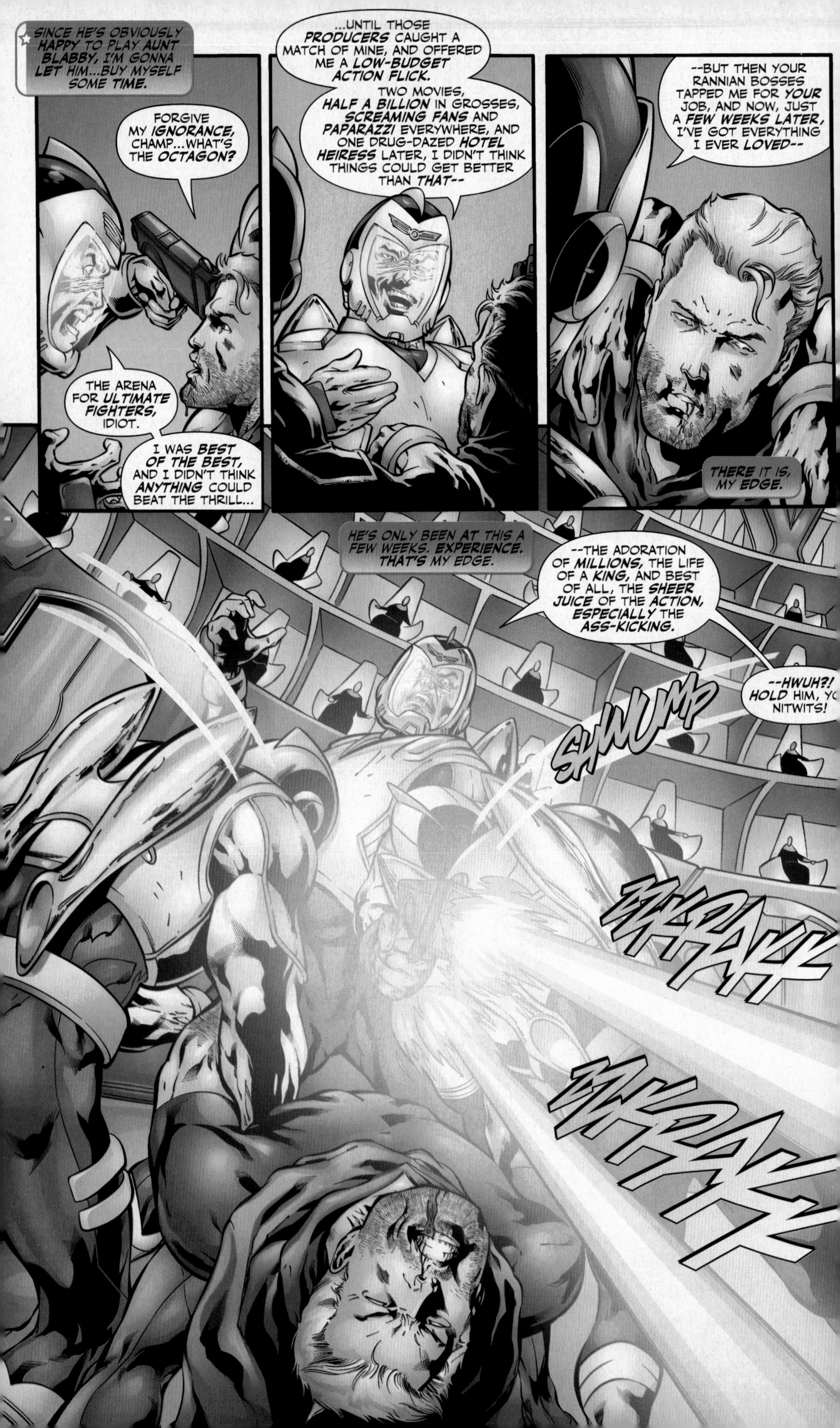
SINCE HE'S OBVIOUSLY HAPPY TO PLAY AUNT BLABBY, I'M GONNA LET HIM...BUY MYSELF SOME TIME.
FORGIVE MY IGNORANCE, CHAMP...WHAT'S THE OCTAGON?
THE ARENA FOR ULTIMATE FIGHTERS, IDIOT.
I WAS BEST OF THE BEST, AND I DIDN'T THINK ANYTHING COULD BEAT THE THRILL...
...UNTIL THOSE PRODUCERS CAUGHT A MATCH OF MINE, AND OFFERED ME A LOW-BUDGET ACTION FLICK.
TWO MOVIES, HALF A BILLION IN GROSSES, SCREAMING FANS AND PAPARAZZI EVERYWHERE, AND ONE DRUG-DAZED HOTEL HEIRESS LATER, I DIDN'T THINK THINGS COULD GET BETTER THAN THAT--
--BUT THEN YOUR RANNIAN BOSSES TAPPED ME FOR YOUR JOB, AND NOW, JUST A FEW WEEKS LATER, I'VE GOT EVERYTHING I EVER LOVED--
THERE IT IS, MY EDGE.
HE'S ONLY BEEN AT THIS A FEW WEEKS. EXPERIENCE. THAT'S MY EDGE.
--THE ADORATION OF MILLIONS, THE LIFE OF A KING, AND BEST OF ALL, THE SHEER JUICE OF THE ACTION, ESPECIALLY THE ASS-KICKING.
SHWUMP
--HWUH?! HOLD HIM, YO NITWITS!
KKRAKK
KKRAKK

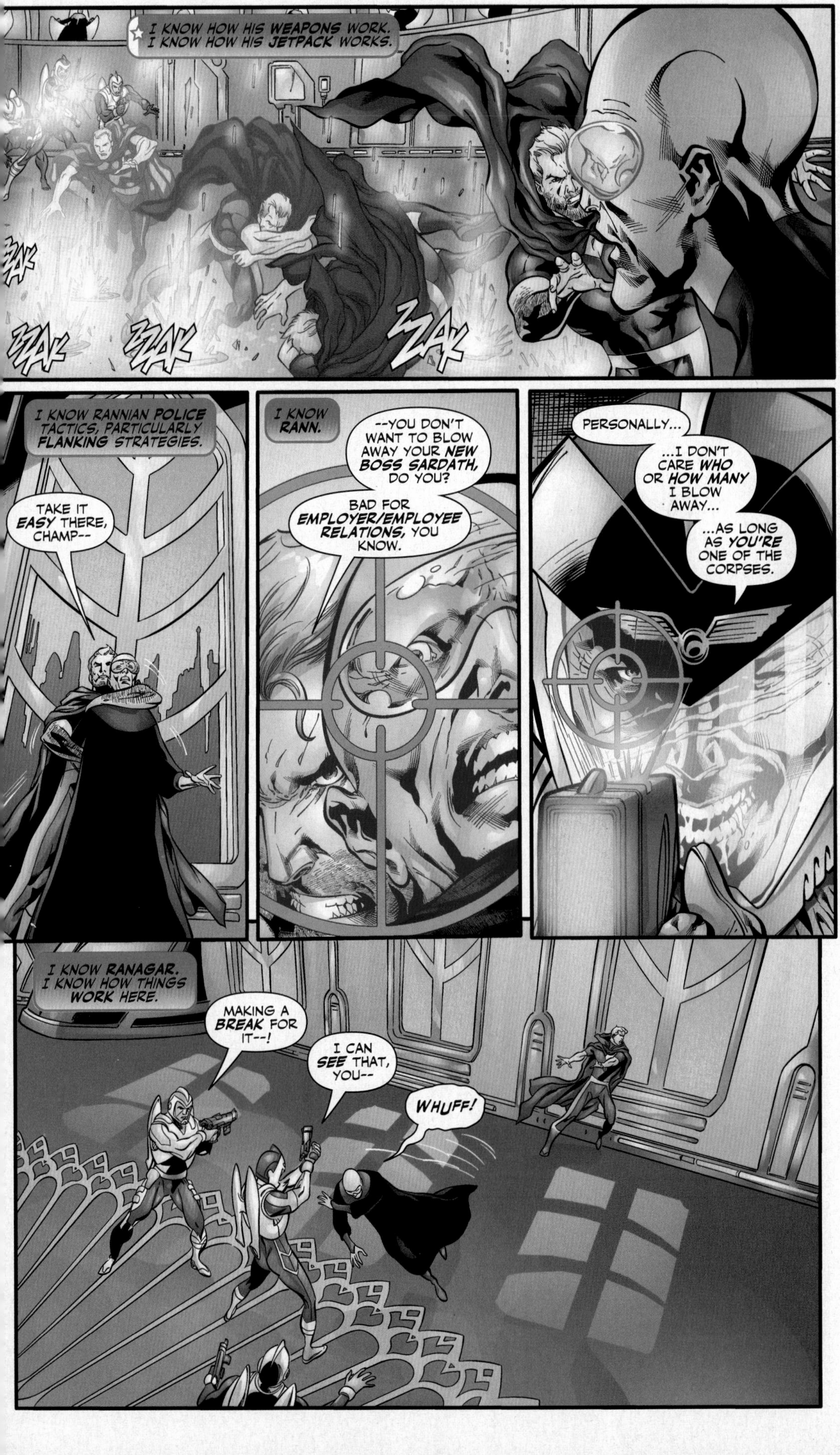
I KNOW HOW HIS WEAPONS WORK. I KNOW HOW HIS JETPACK WORKS.
ZZAK
ZZAK
ZZAK
ZZAK
I KNOW RANNIAN POLICE TACTICS, PARTICULARLY FLANKING STRATEGIES.
TAKE IT EASY THERE, CHAMP--
I KNOW RANN.
--YOU DON'T WANT TO BLOW AWAY YOUR NEW BOSS SARDATH, DO YOU?
BAD FOR EMPLOYER/EMPLOYEE RELATIONS, YOU KNOW.
PERSONALLY...
...I DON'T CARE WHO OR HOW MANY I BLOW AWAY...
...AS LONG AS YOU'RE ONE OF THE CORPSES.
I KNOW RANAGAR. I KNOW HOW THINGS WORK HERE.
MAKING A BREAK FOR IT--!
I CAN SEE THAT, YOU--
WHUFF!

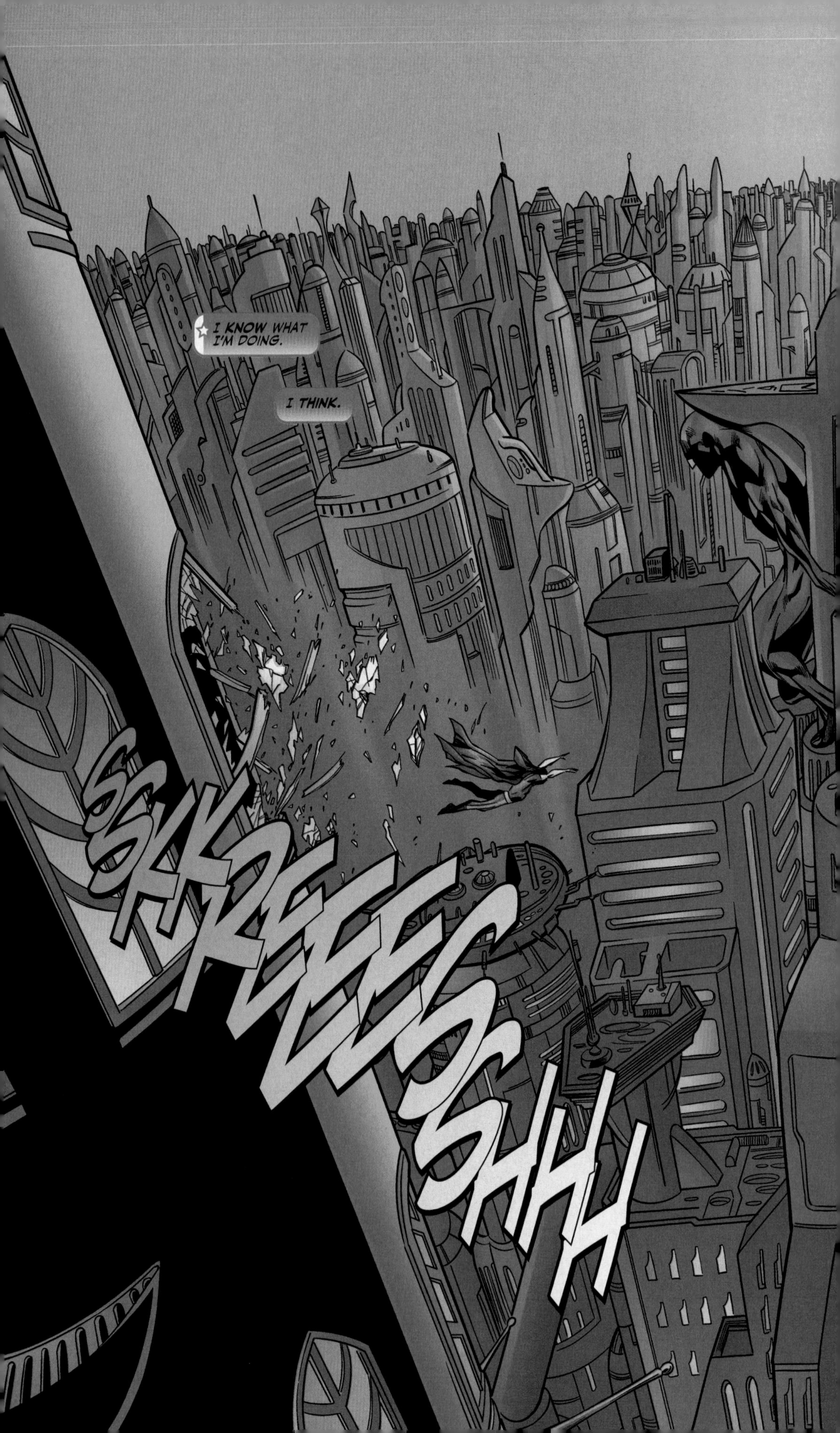
I KNOW WHAT I'M DOING.
I THINK.
SKKREEESHHH

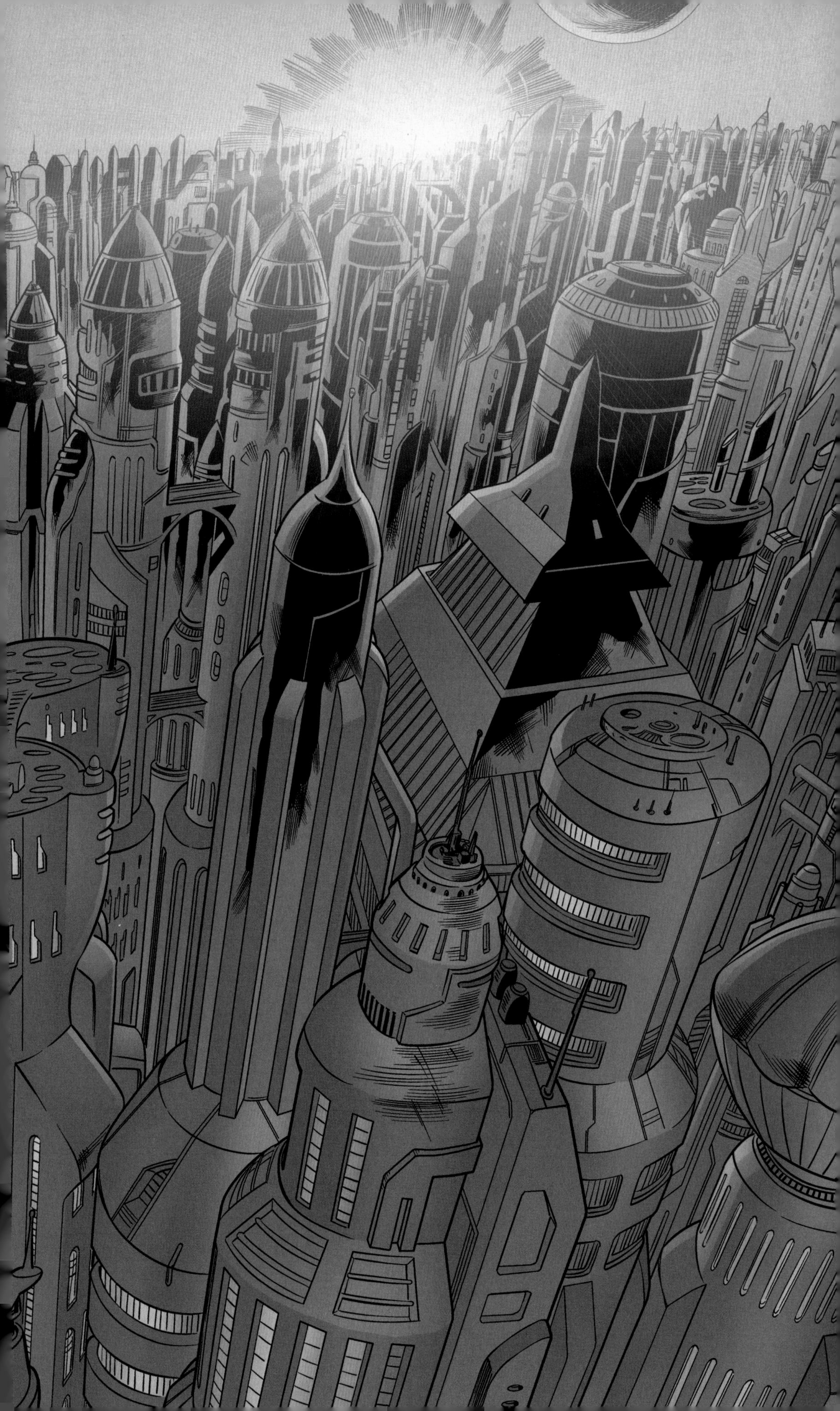

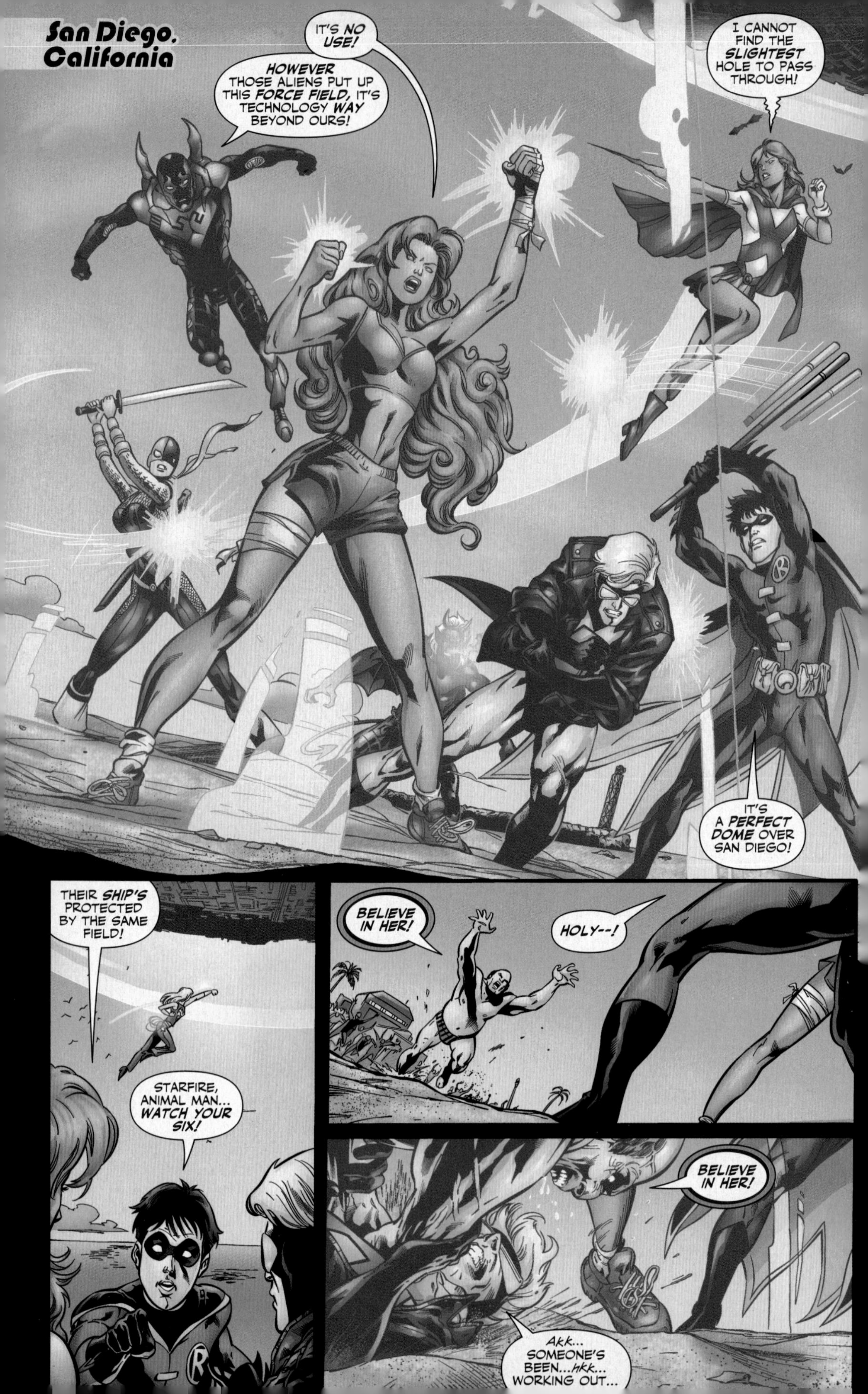
San Diego, California
HOWEVER THOSE ALIENS PUT UP THIS FORCE FIELD, IT'S TECHNOLOGY WAY BEYOND OURS!
IT'S NO USE!
I CANNOT FIND THE SLIGHTEST HOLE TO PASS THROUGH!
IT'S A PERFECT DOME OVER SAN DIEGO!
THEIR SHIP'S PROTECTED BY THE SAME FIELD!
STARFIRE, ANIMAL MAN... WATCH YOUR SIX!
BELIEVE IN HER!
HOLY--!
BELIEVE IN HER!
Akk... SOMEONE'S BEEN...hkk... WORKING OUT...

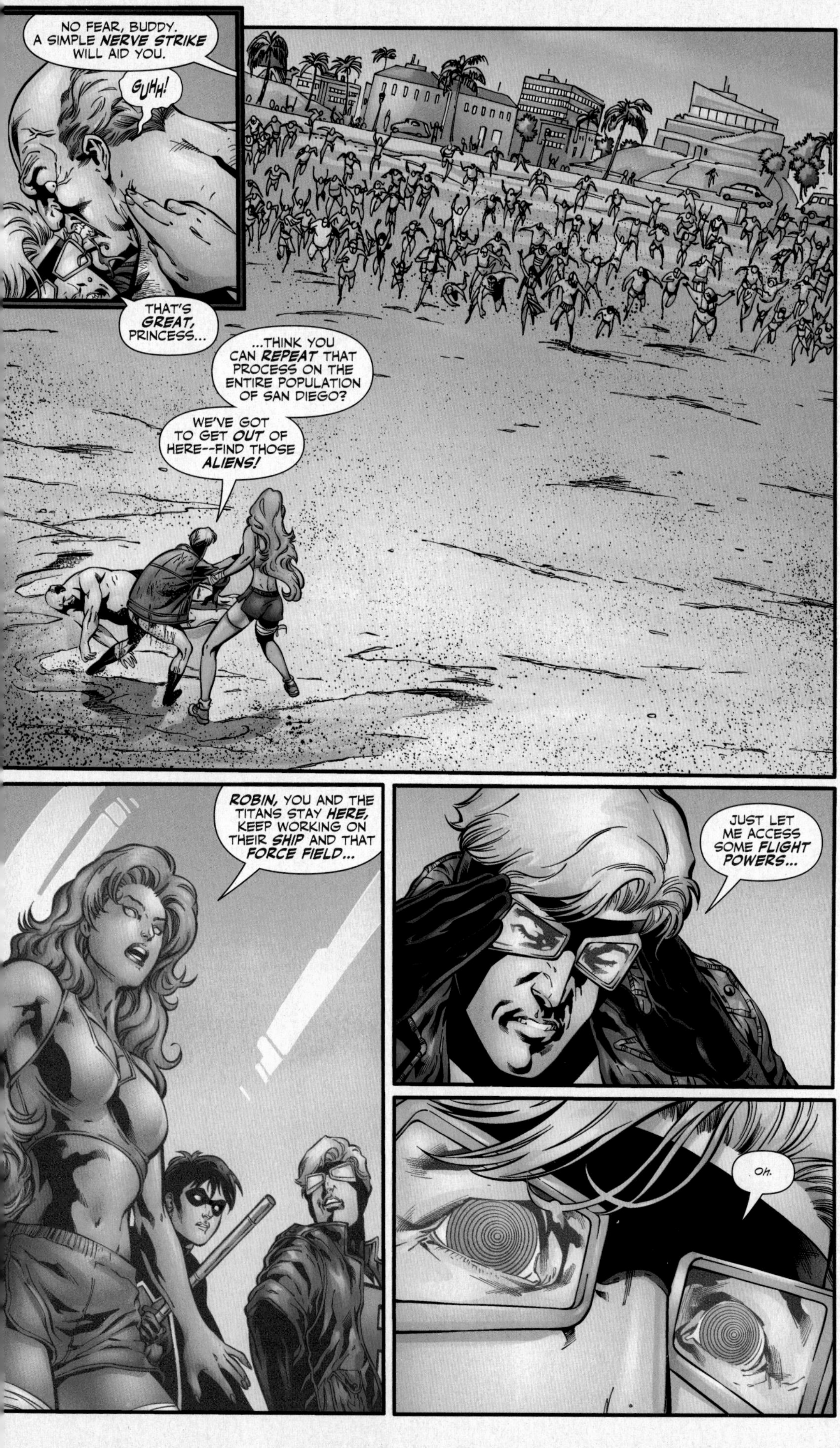
NO FEAR, BUDDY. A SIMPLE NERVE STRIKE WILL AID YOU.
GUHH!
THAT'S GREAT, PRINCESS...
...THINK YOU CAN REPEAT THAT PROCESS ON THE ENTIRE POPULATION OF SAN DIEGO?
WE'VE GOT TO GET OUT OF HERE--FIND THOSE ALIENS!
ROBIN, YOU AND THE TITANS STAY HERE, KEEP WORKING ON THEIR SHIP AND THAT FORCE FIELD...
JUST LET ME ACCESS SOME FLIGHT POWERS...
Oh.

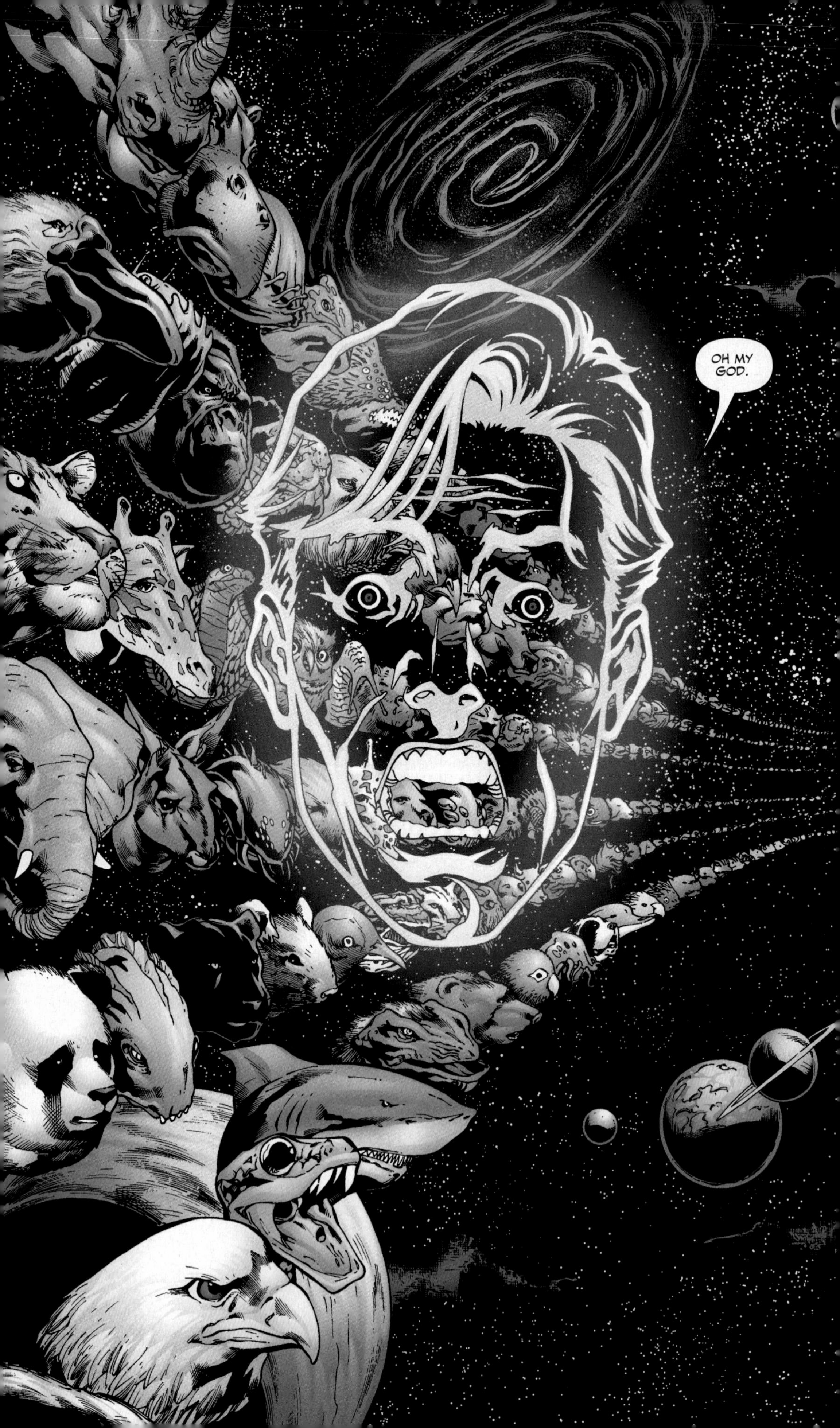
OH MY GOD.

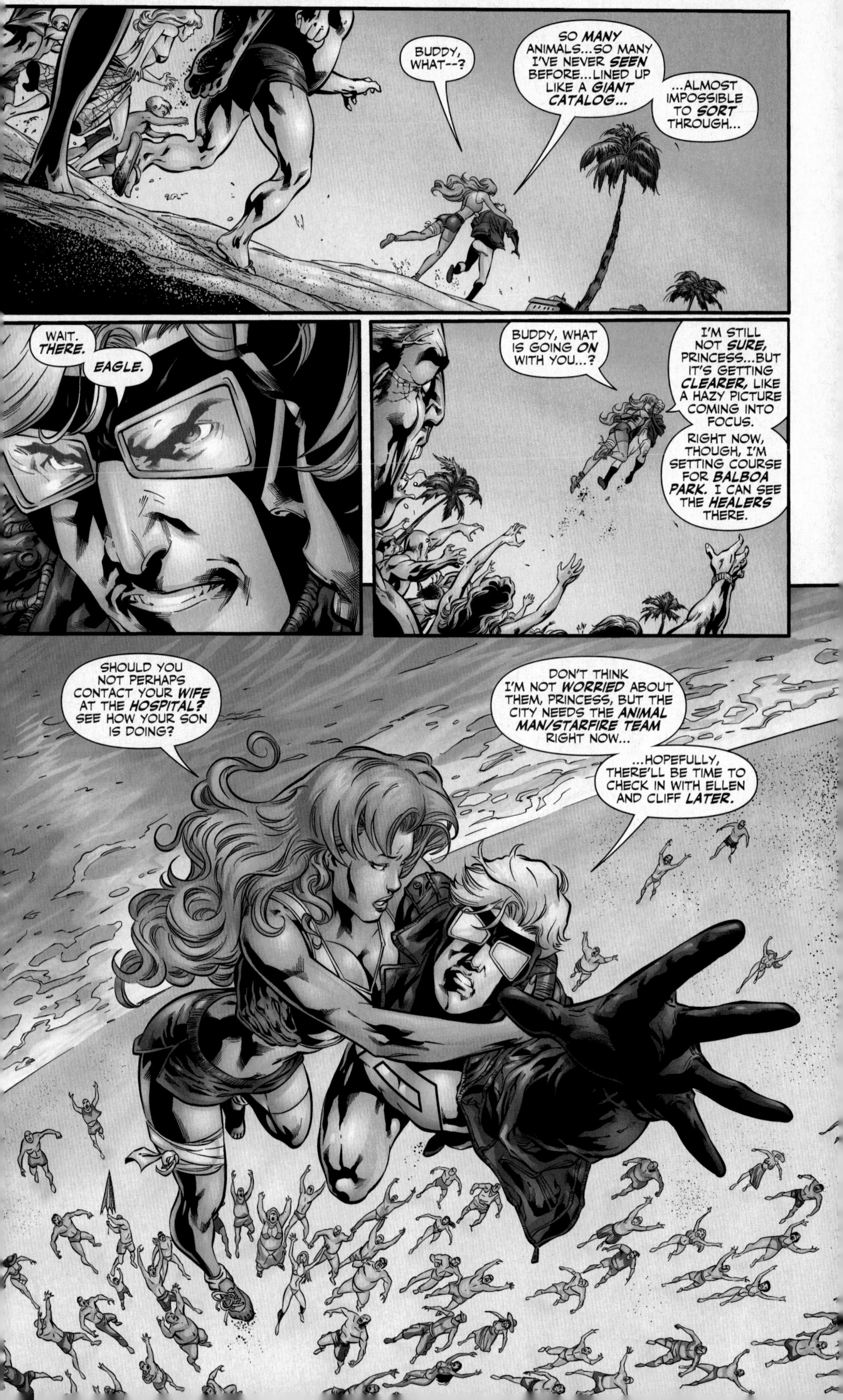
BUDDY, WHAT--?
SO MANY ANIMALS...SO MANY I'VE NEVER SEEN BEFORE...LINED UP LIKE A GIANT CATALOG...
...ALMOST IMPOSSIBLE TO SORT THROUGH...
WAIT. THERE.
EAGLE.
BUDDY, WHAT IS GOING ON WITH YOU...?
I'M STILL NOT SURE, PRINCESS...BUT IT'S GETTING CLEARER, LIKE A HAZY PICTURE COMING INTO FOCUS.
RIGHT NOW, THOUGH, I'M SETTING COURSE FOR BALBOA PARK. I CAN SEE THE HEALERS THERE.
SHOULD YOU NOT PERHAPS CONTACT YOUR WIFE AT THE HOSPITAL? SEE HOW YOUR SON IS DOING?
DON'T THINK I'M NOT WORRIED ABOUT THEM, PRINCESS, BUT THE CITY NEEDS THE ANIMAL MAN/STARFIRE TEAM RIGHT NOW...
...HOPEFULLY, THERE'LL BE TIME TO CHECK IN WITH ELLEN AND CLIFF LATER.

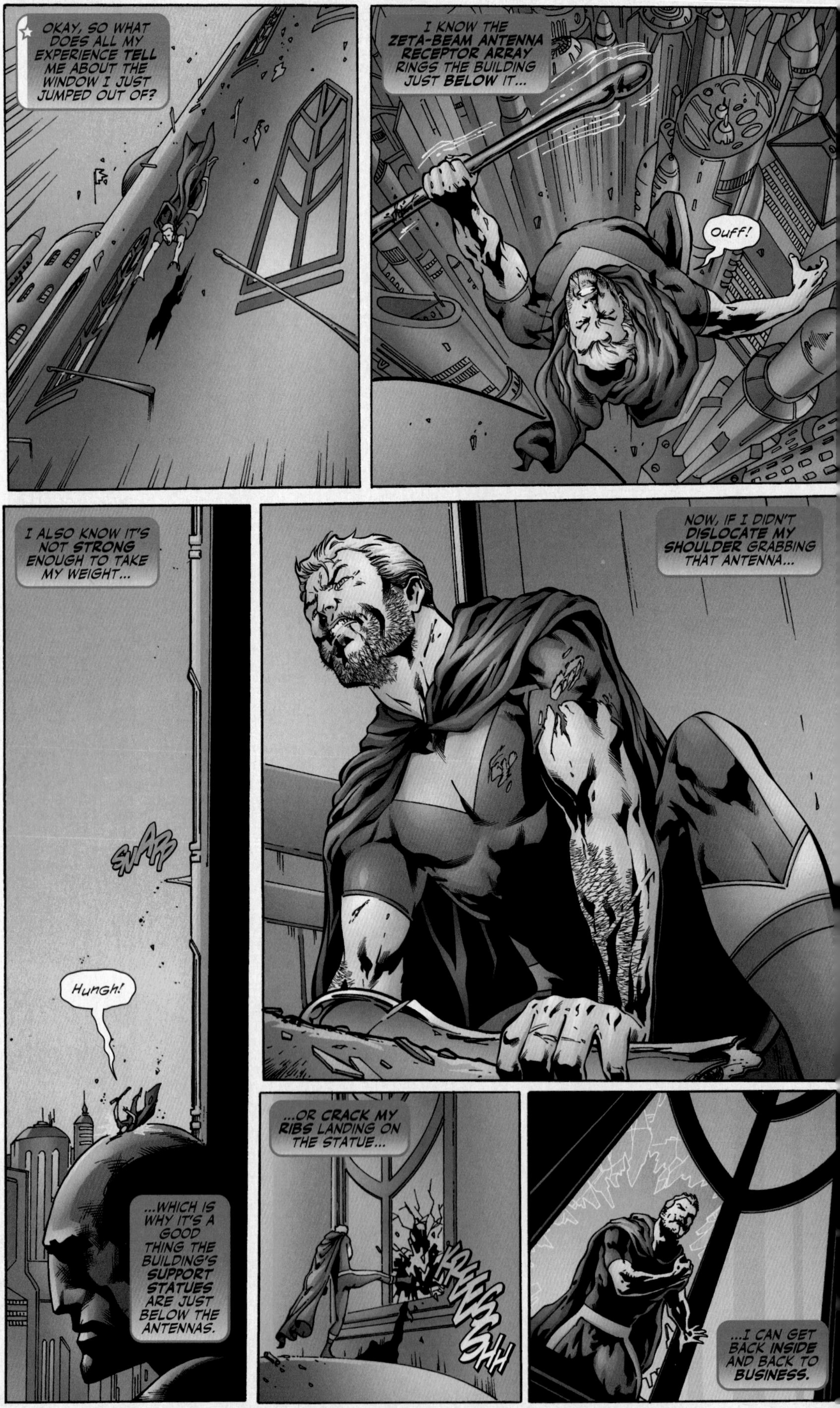
OKAY, SO WHAT DOES ALL MY EXPERIENCE TELL ME ABOUT THE WINDOW I JUST JUMPED OUT OF?
I KNOW THE ZETA-BEAM ANTENNA RECEPTOR ARRAY RINGS THE BUILDING JUST BELOW IT...
Ouff!
I ALSO KNOW IT'S NOT STRONG ENOUGH TO TAKE MY WEIGHT...
SNAP
Hungh!
...WHICH IS WHY IT'S A GOOD THING THE BUILDING'S SUPPORT STATUES ARE JUST BELOW THE ANTENNAS.
NOW, IF I DIDN'T DISLOCATE MY SHOULDER GRABBING THAT ANTENNA...
...OR CRACK MY RIBS LANDING ON THE STATUE...
KRASSSHH
...I CAN GET BACK INSIDE AND BACK TO BUSINESS.

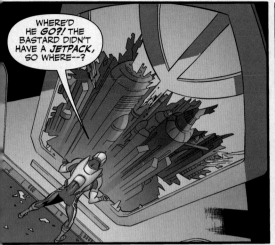

WHERE'D HE GO?! THE BASTARD DIDN'T HAVE A JETPACK, SO WHERE--?

THAT BROKEN ANTENNA...

SEARCH THIS BUILDING! EVERY FLOOR!

TELL EVERYONE-- SHOOT ON SIGHT! ANYTHING THAT EVEN LOOKS LIKE STRANGE, BURN IT TO ASH!

BUT WE...BUT WE KILL FOR HER...

BELIEVE IN HER...

OF COURSE, KILL FOR HER! I BELIEVE IN HER, TOO!

BUT KILL FOR ME AS WELL! I'M YOUR PLANETARY PROTECTOR!

I'M THE ONLY ONE WORTHY OF HER LOVE!

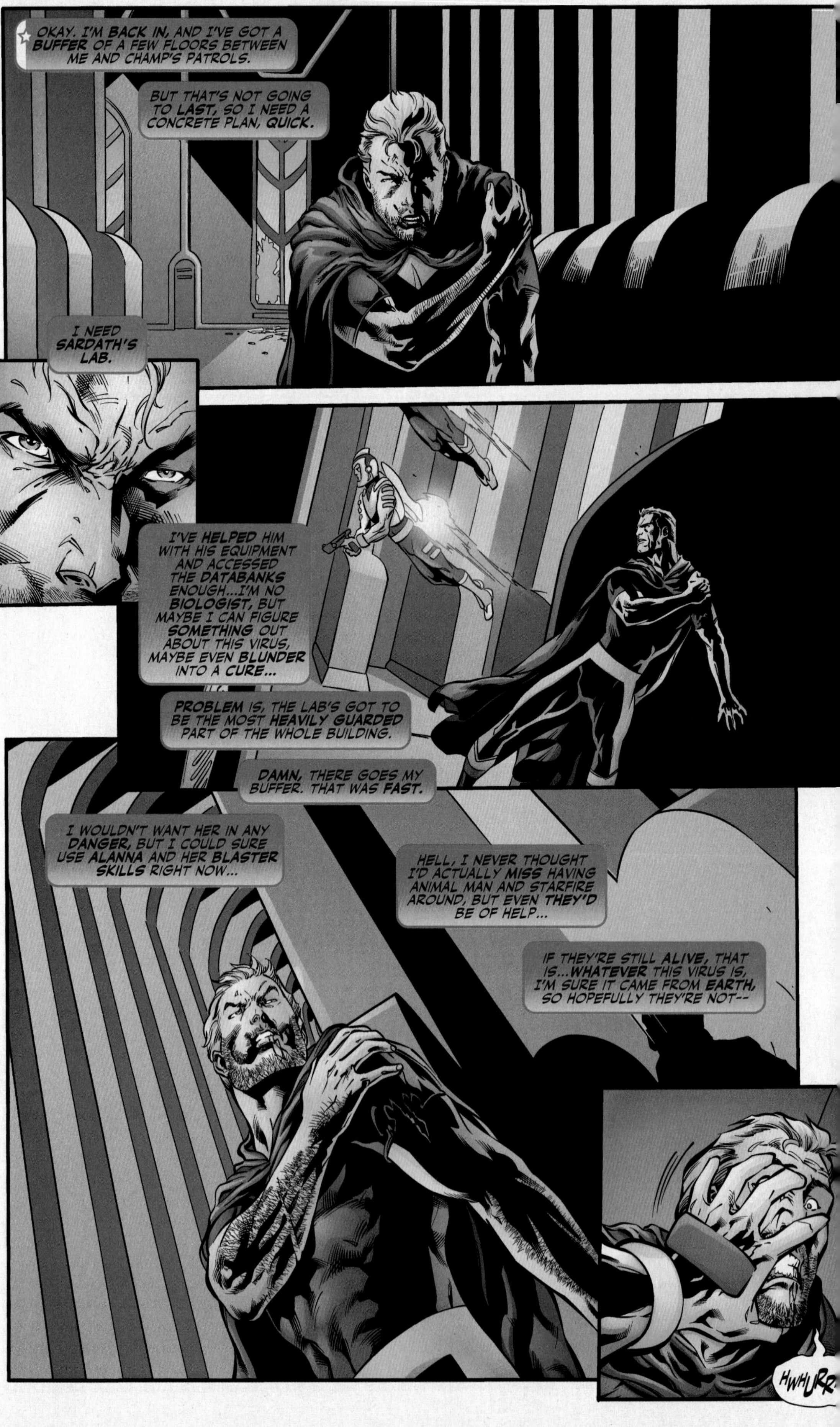
OKAY. I'M BACK IN, AND I'VE GOT A BUFFER OF A FEW FLOORS BETWEEN ME AND CHAMP'S PATROLS.
BUT THAT'S NOT GOING TO LAST, SO I NEED A CONCRETE PLAN, QUICK.
I NEED SARDATH'S LAB.
I'VE HELPED HIM WITH HIS EQUIPMENT AND ACCESSED THE DATABANKS ENOUGH...I'M NO BIOLOGIST, BUT MAYBE I CAN FIGURE SOMETHING OUT ABOUT THIS VIRUS, MAYBE EVEN BLUNDER INTO A CURE...
PROBLEM IS, THE LAB'S GOT TO BE THE MOST HEAVILY GUARDED PART OF THE WHOLE BUILDING.
DAMN, THERE GOES MY BUFFER. THAT WAS FAST.
I WOULDN'T WANT HER IN ANY DANGER, BUT I COULD SURE USE ALANNA AND HER BLASTER SKILLS RIGHT NOW...
HELL, I NEVER THOUGHT I'D ACTUALLY MISS HAVING ANIMAL MAN AND STARFIRE AROUND, BUT EVEN THEY'D BE OF HELP...
IF THEY'RE STILL ALIVE, THAT IS...WHATEVER THIS VIRUS IS, I'M SURE IT CAME FROM EARTH, SO HOPEFULLY THEY'RE NOT--
HWHURR

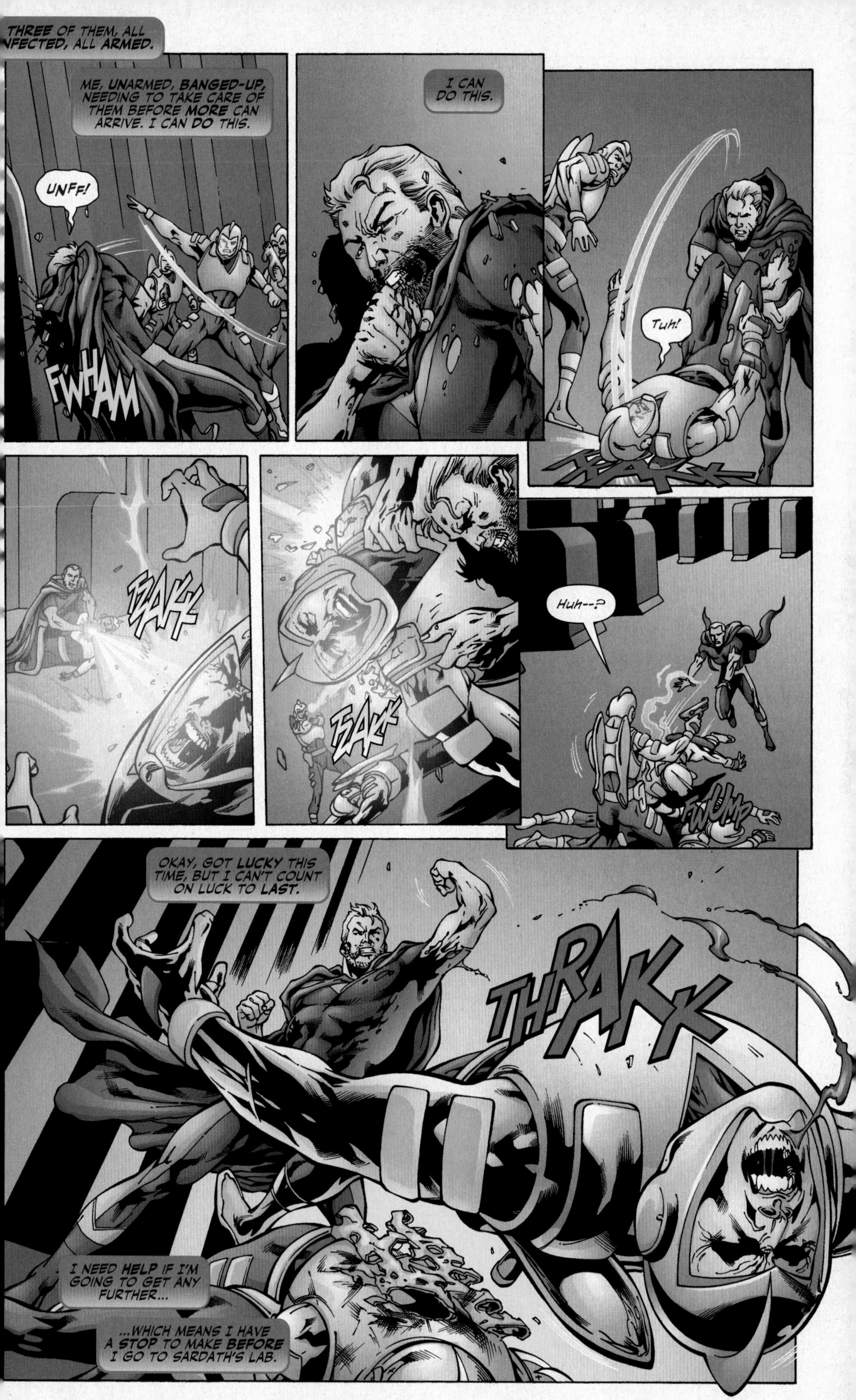
THREE OF THEM, ALL INFECTED, ALL ARMED.
ME, UNARMED, BANGED-UP, NEEDING TO TAKE CARE OF THEM BEFORE MORE CAN ARRIVE. I CAN DO THIS.
UNFF!
FWHAM
I CAN DO THIS.
Tuh!
TZAKK
TZAKK
TZAKK
Huh--?
FWUMP
OKAY, GOT LUCKY THIS TIME, BUT I CAN'T COUNT ON LUCK TO LAST.
THRAKK
I NEED HELP IF I'M GOING TO GET ANY FURTHER...
...WHICH MEANS I HAVE A STOP TO MAKE BEFORE I GO TO SARDATH'S LAB.

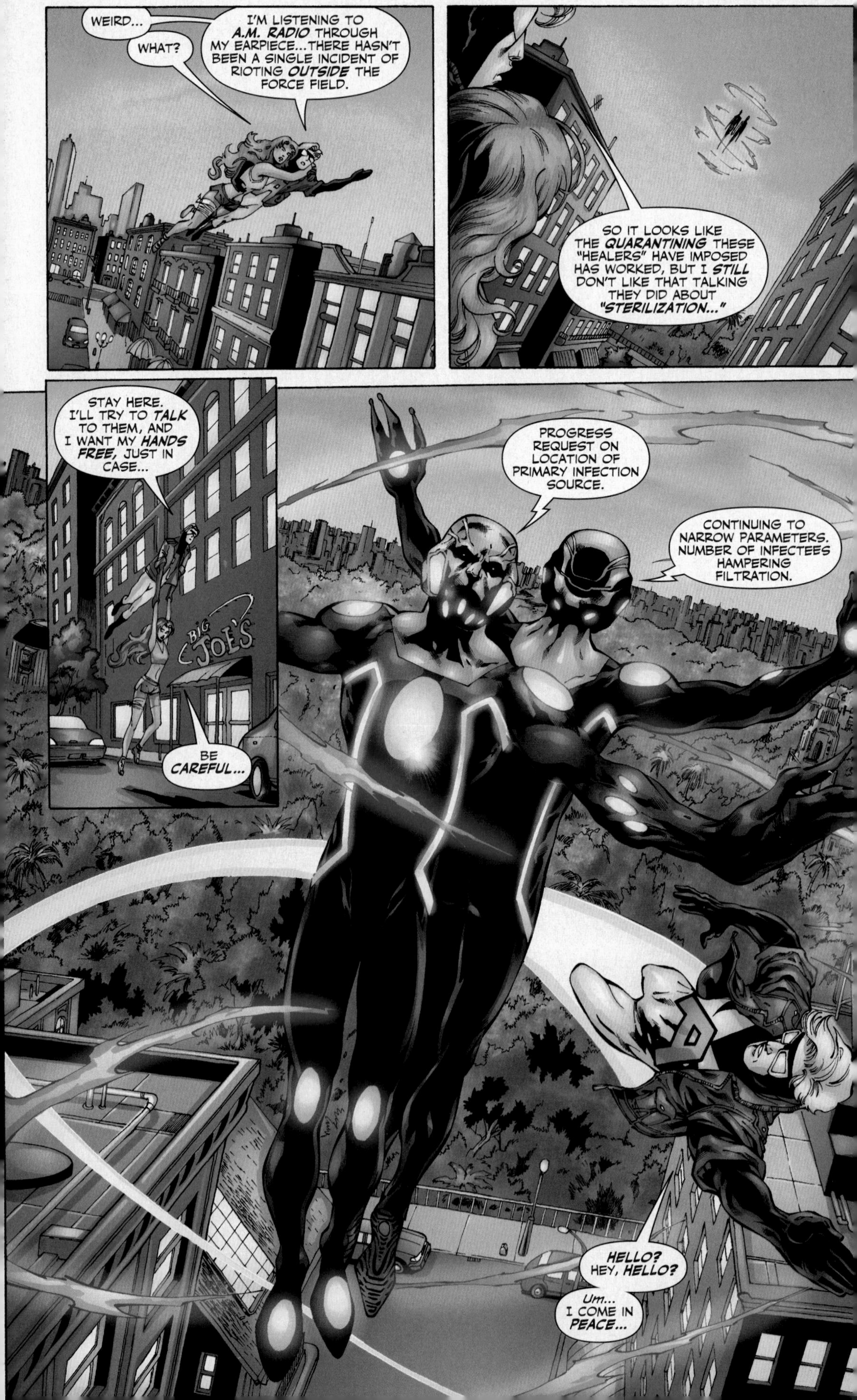
WEIRD...
WHAT?
I'M LISTENING TO A.M. RADIO THROUGH MY EARPIECE...THERE HASN'T BEEN A SINGLE INCIDENT OF RIOTING OUTSIDE THE FORCE FIELD.
SO IT LOOKS LIKE THE QUARANTINING THESE "HEALERS" HAVE IMPOSED HAS WORKED, BUT I STILL DON'T LIKE THAT TALKING THEY DID ABOUT "STERILIZATION..."
STAY HERE. I'LL TRY TO TALK TO THEM, AND I WANT MY HANDS FREE, JUST IN CASE...
BIG JOE'S
BE CAREFUL...
PROGRESS REQUEST ON LOCATION OF PRIMARY INFECTION SOURCE.
CONTINUING TO NARROW PARAMETERS. NUMBER OF INFECTEES HAMPERING FILTRATION.
HELLO? HEY, HELLO?
Um... I COME IN PEACE...

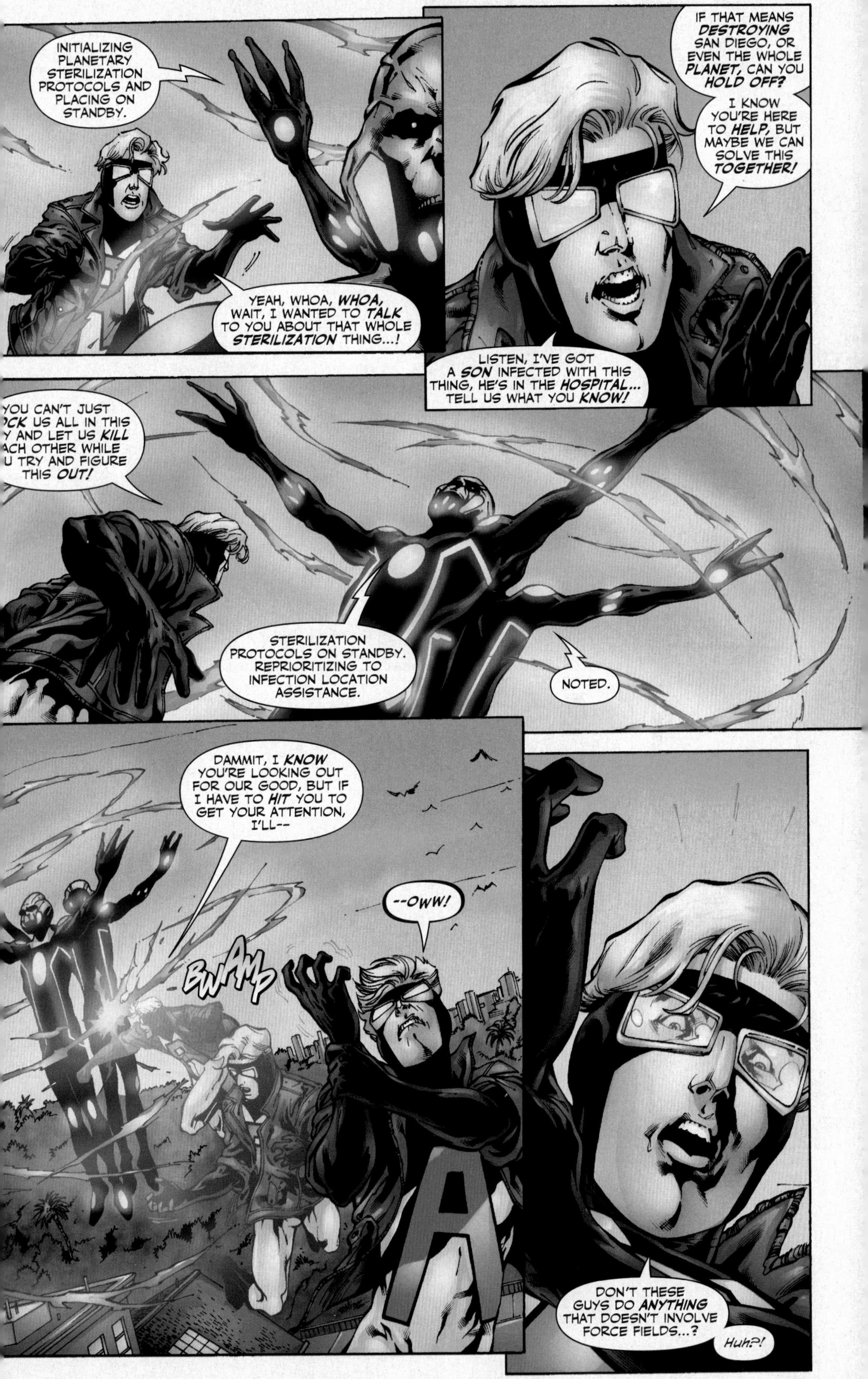
INITIALIZING PLANETARY STERILIZATION PROTOCOLS AND PLACING ON STANDBY.
YEAH, WHOA, WHOA, WAIT, I WANTED TO TALK TO YOU ABOUT THAT WHOLE STERILIZATION THING...!
IF THAT MEANS DESTROYING SAN DIEGO, OR EVEN THE WHOLE PLANET, CAN YOU HOLD OFF?
I KNOW YOU'RE HERE TO HELP, BUT MAYBE WE CAN SOLVE THIS TOGETHER!
LISTEN, I'VE GOT A SON INFECTED WITH THIS THING, HE'S IN THE HOSPITAL... TELL US WHAT YOU KNOW!
YOU CAN'T JUST OCK US ALL IN THIS Y AND LET US KILL ACH OTHER WHILE U TRY AND FIGURE THIS OUT!
STERILIZATION PROTOCOLS ON STANDBY. REPRIORITIZING TO INFECTION LOCATION ASSISTANCE.
NOTED.
DAMMIT, I KNOW YOU'RE LOOKING OUT FOR OUR GOOD, BUT IF I HAVE TO HIT YOU TO GET YOUR ATTENTION, I'LL--
--OWW!
BWAMP
DON'T THESE GUYS DO ANYTHING THAT DOESN'T INVOLVE FORCE FIELDS...?
Huh?!

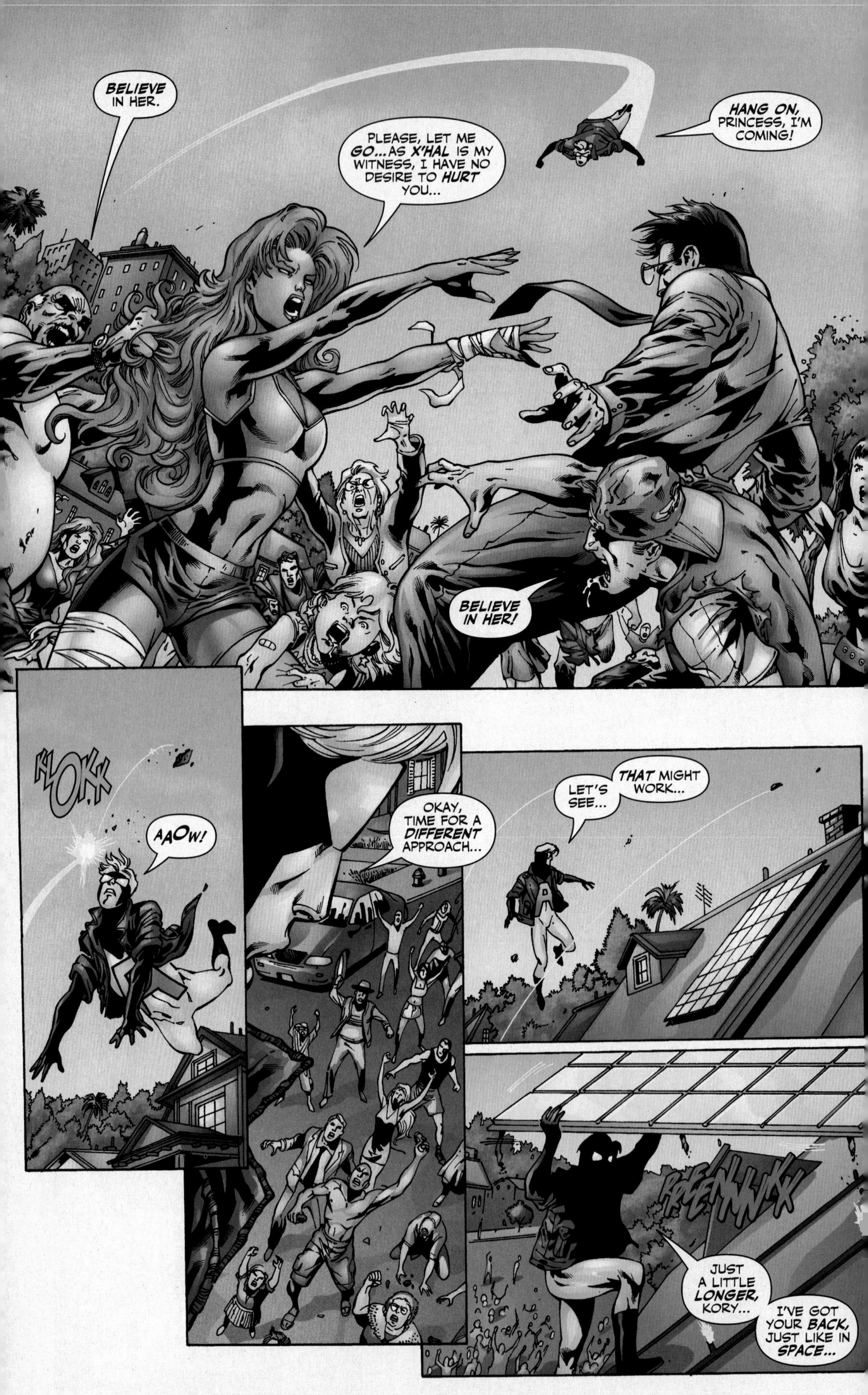

BELIEVE IN HER.
PLEASE, LET ME GO...AS X'HAL IS MY WITNESS, I HAVE NO DESIRE TO HURT YOU...
HANG ON, PRINCESS, I'M COMING!
BELIEVE IN HER!
KLOKK
AAOW!
OKAY, TIME FOR A DIFFERENT APPROACH...
LET'S SEE...
THAT MIGHT WORK...
KRRRENNNKK
JUST A LITTLE LONGER, KORY...
I'VE GOT YOUR BACK, JUST LIKE IN SPACE...

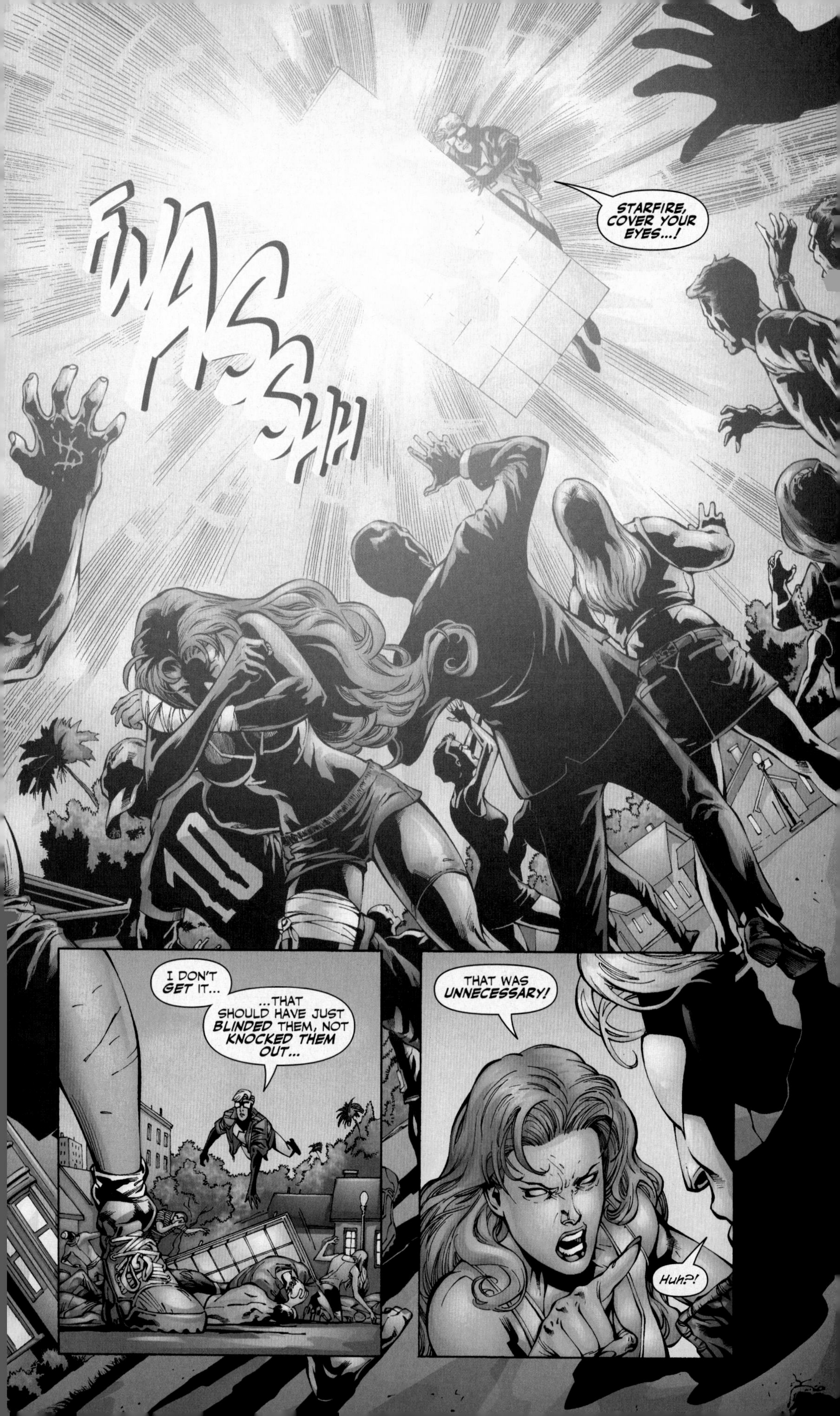

STARFIRE, COVER YOUR EYES...!
I DON'T GET IT...
...THAT SHOULD HAVE JUST BLINDED THEM, NOT KNOCKED THEM OUT...
THAT WAS UNNECESSARY!
Huh?!

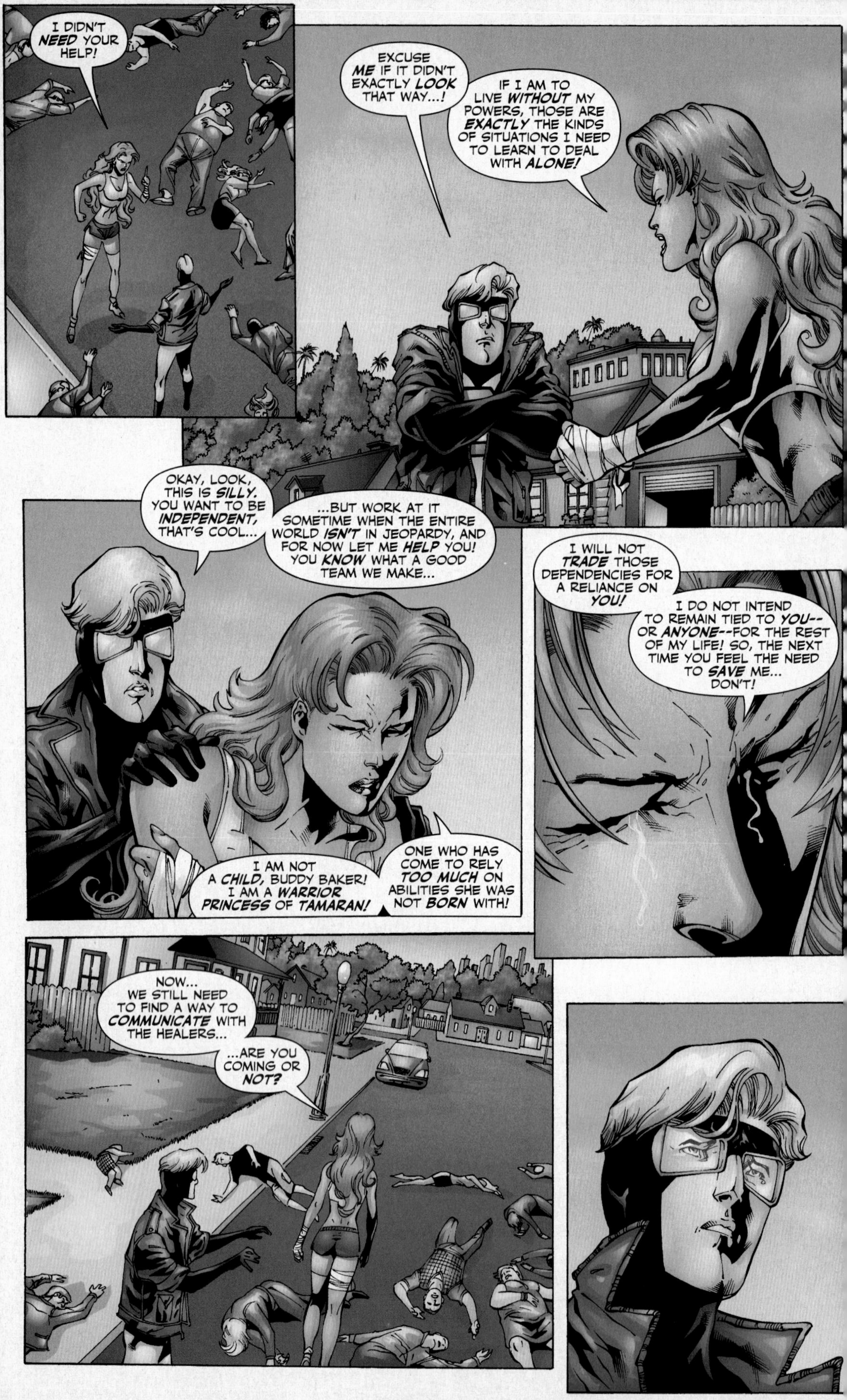
I DIDN'T NEED YOUR HELP!
EXCUSE ME IF IT DIDN'T EXACTLY LOOK THAT WAY...!
IF I AM TO LIVE WITHOUT MY POWERS, THOSE ARE EXACTLY THE KINDS OF SITUATIONS I NEED TO LEARN TO DEAL WITH ALONE!
OKAY, LOOK, THIS IS SILLY. YOU WANT TO BE INDEPENDENT, THAT'S COOL...
...BUT WORK AT IT SOMETIME WHEN THE ENTIRE WORLD ISN'T IN JEOPARDY, AND FOR NOW LET ME HELP YOU! YOU KNOW WHAT A GOOD TEAM WE MAKE...
I AM NOT A CHILD, BUDDY BAKER! I AM A WARRIOR PRINCESS OF TAMARAN!
ONE WHO HAS COME TO RELY TOO MUCH ON ABILITIES SHE WAS NOT BORN WITH!
I WILL NOT TRADE THOSE DEPENDENCIES FOR A RELIANCE ON YOU!
I DO NOT INTEND TO REMAIN TIED TO YOU--OR ANYONE--FOR THE REST OF MY LIFE! SO, THE NEXT TIME YOU FEEL THE NEED TO SAVE ME... DON'T!
NOW... WE STILL NEED TO FIND A WAY TO COMMUNICATE WITH THE HEALERS...
...ARE YOU COMING OR NOT?

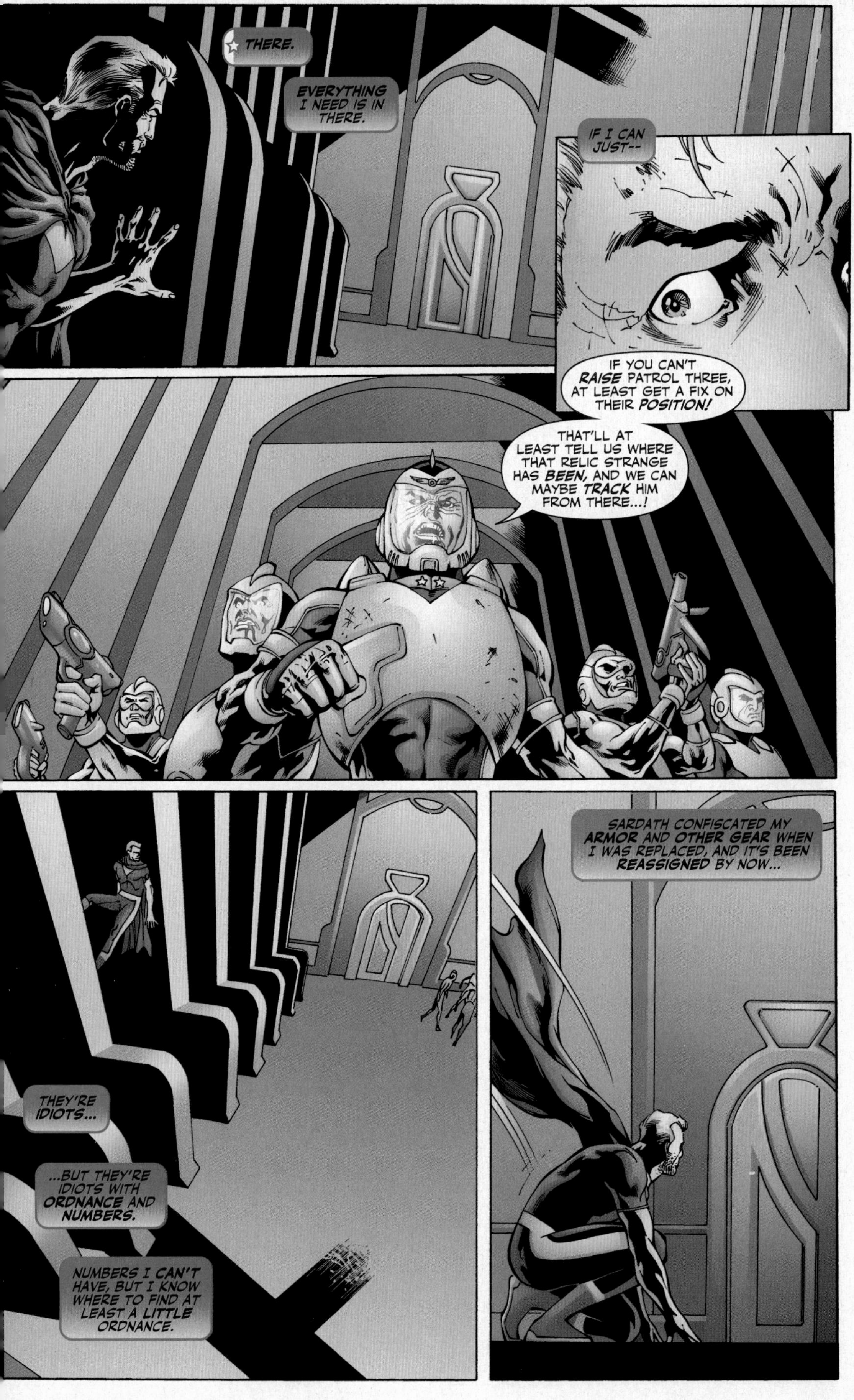
THERE.
EVERYTHING I NEED IS IN THERE.
IF I CAN JUST--
IF YOU CAN'T RAISE PATROL THREE, AT LEAST GET A FIX ON THEIR POSITION!
THAT'LL AT LEAST TELL US WHERE THAT RELIC STRANGE HAS BEEN, AND WE CAN MAYBE TRACK HIM FROM THERE...!
THEY'RE IDIOTS...
...BUT THEY'RE IDIOTS WITH ORDNANCE AND NUMBERS.
NUMBERS I CAN'T HAVE, BUT I KNOW WHERE TO FIND AT LEAST A LITTLE ORDNANCE.
SARDATH CONFISCATED MY ARMOR AND OTHER GEAR WHEN I WAS REPLACED, AND IT'S BEEN REASSIGNED BY NOW...

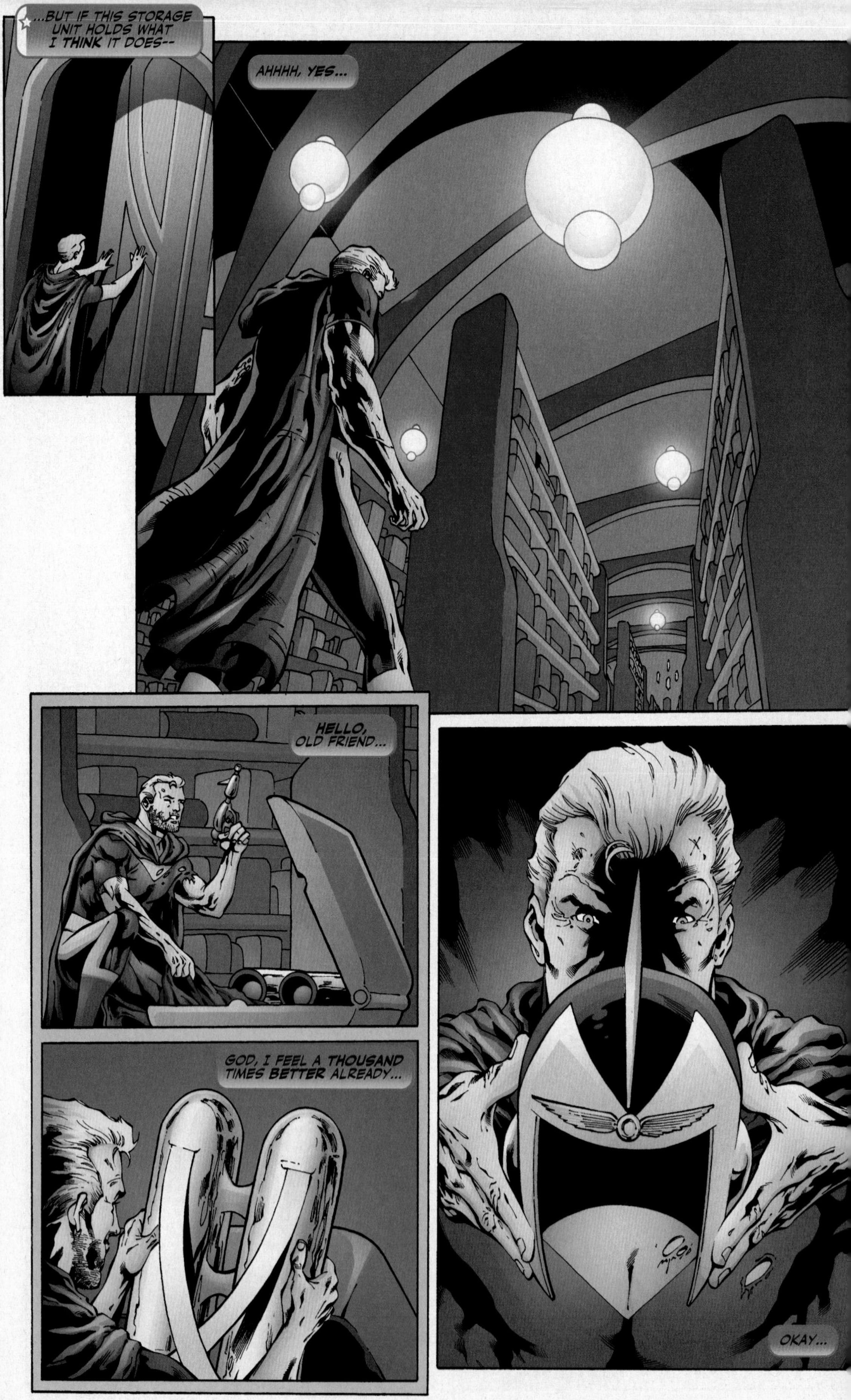
...BUT IF THIS STORAGE UNIT HOLDS WHAT I THINK IT DOES--
AHHHH, YES...
HELLO, OLD FRIEND...
GOD, I FEEL A THOUSAND TIMES BETTER ALREADY...
OKAY...

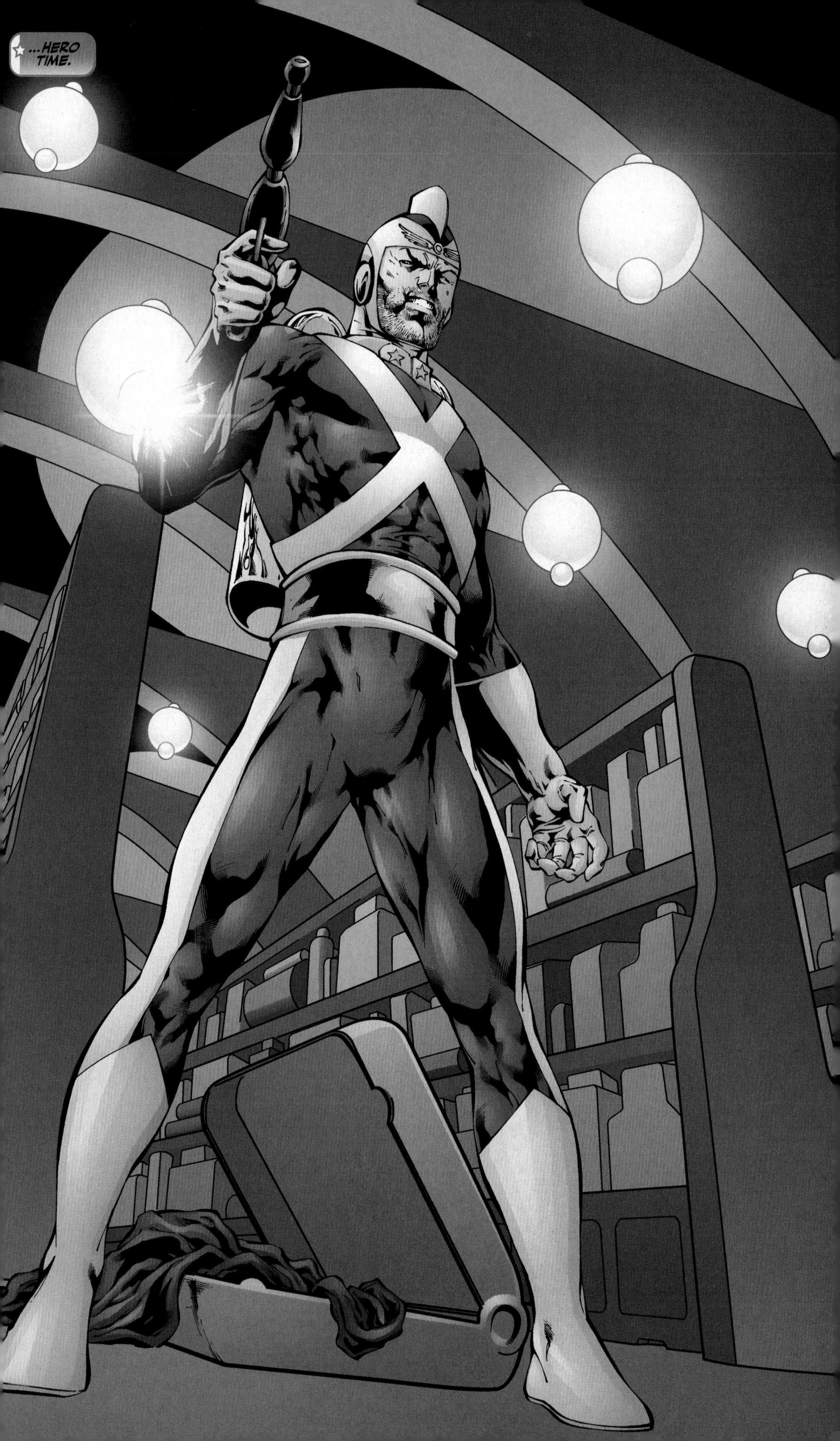
...HERO TIME.

CHAPTER FIVE

PATIENT ZERO

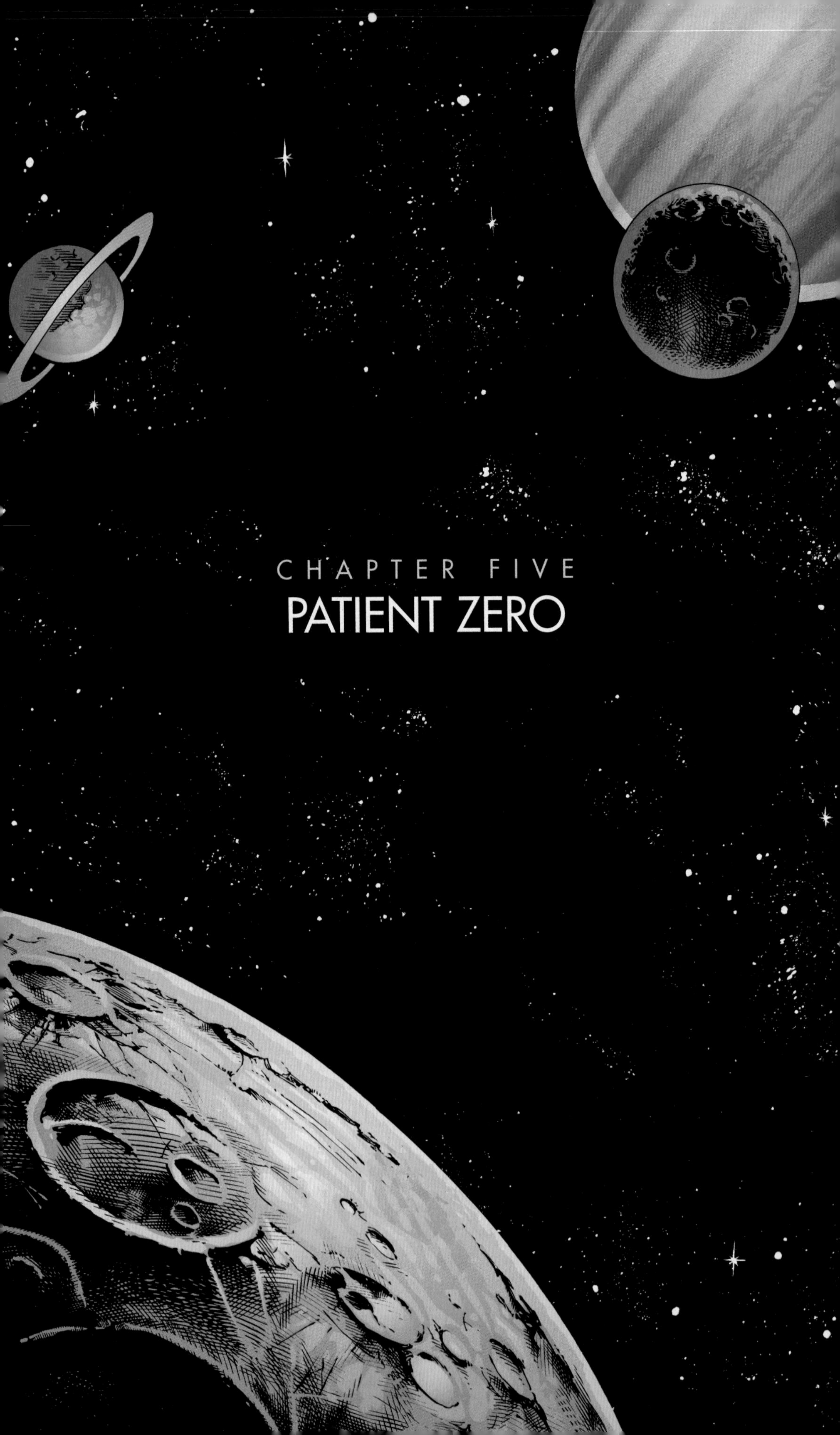

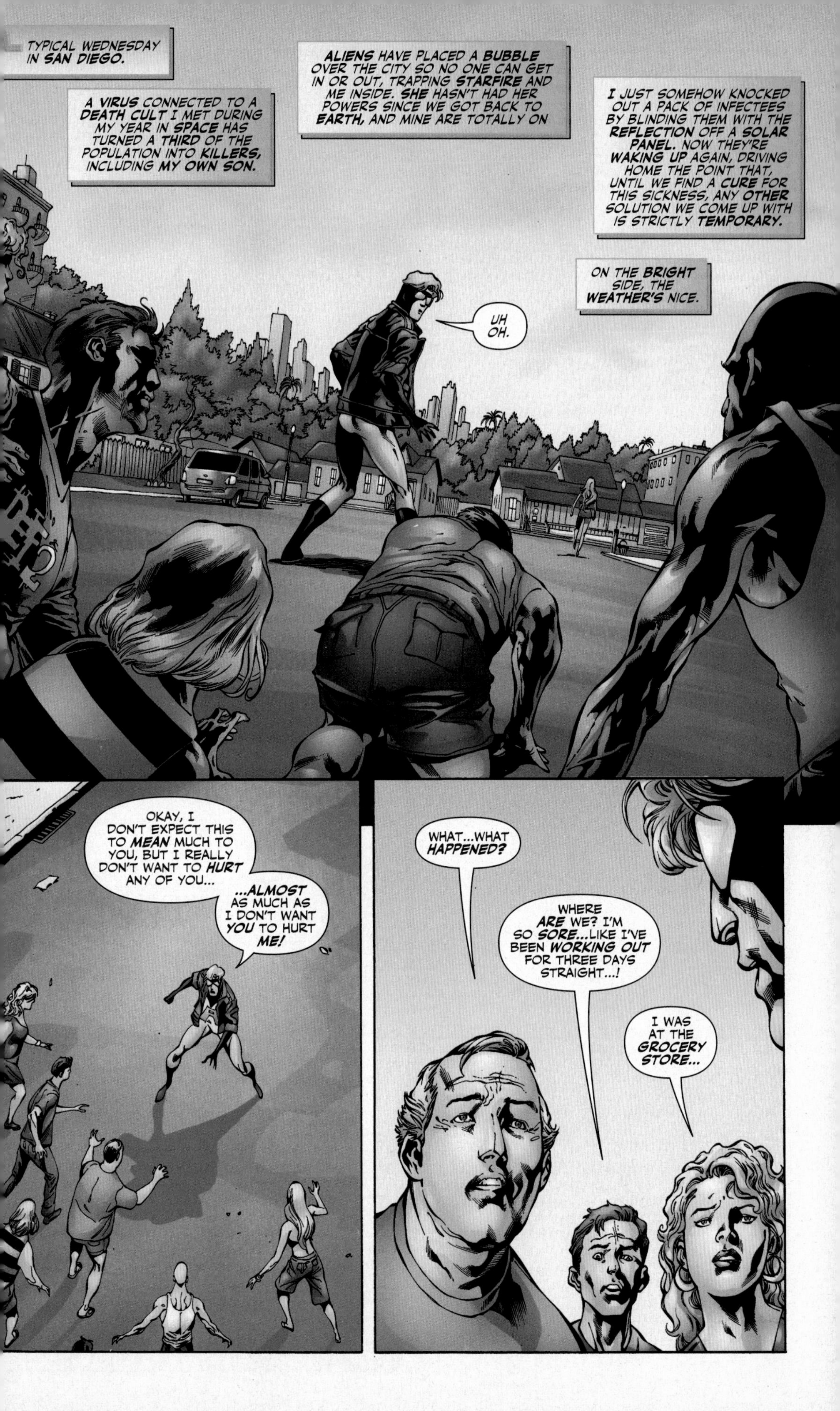

TYPICAL WEDNESDAY IN SAN DIEGO.
A VIRUS CONNECTED TO A DEATH CULT I MET DURING MY YEAR IN SPACE HAS TURNED A THIRD OF THE POPULATION INTO KILLERS, INCLUDING MY OWN SON.
ALIENS HAVE PLACED A BUBBLE OVER THE CITY SO NO ONE CAN GET IN OR OUT, TRAPPING STARFIRE AND ME INSIDE. SHE HASN'T HAD HER POWERS SINCE WE GOT BACK TO EARTH, AND MINE ARE TOTALLY ON
I JUST SOMEHOW KNOCKED OUT A PACK OF INFECTEES BY BLINDING THEM WITH THE REFLECTION OFF A SOLAR PANEL. NOW THEY'RE WAKING UP AGAIN, DRIVING HOME THE POINT THAT, UNTIL WE FIND A CURE FOR THIS SICKNESS, ANY OTHER SOLUTION WE COME UP WITH IS STRICTLY TEMPORARY.
ON THE BRIGHT SIDE, THE WEATHER'S NICE.
UH OH.
OKAY, I DON'T EXPECT THIS TO MEAN MUCH TO YOU, BUT I REALLY DON'T WANT TO HURT ANY OF YOU...
...ALMOST AS MUCH AS I DON'T WANT YOU TO HURT ME!
WHAT...WHAT HAPPENED?
WHERE ARE WE? I'M SO SORE...LIKE I'VE BEEN WORKING OUT FOR THREE DAYS STRAIGHT...!
I WAS AT THE GROCERY STORE...

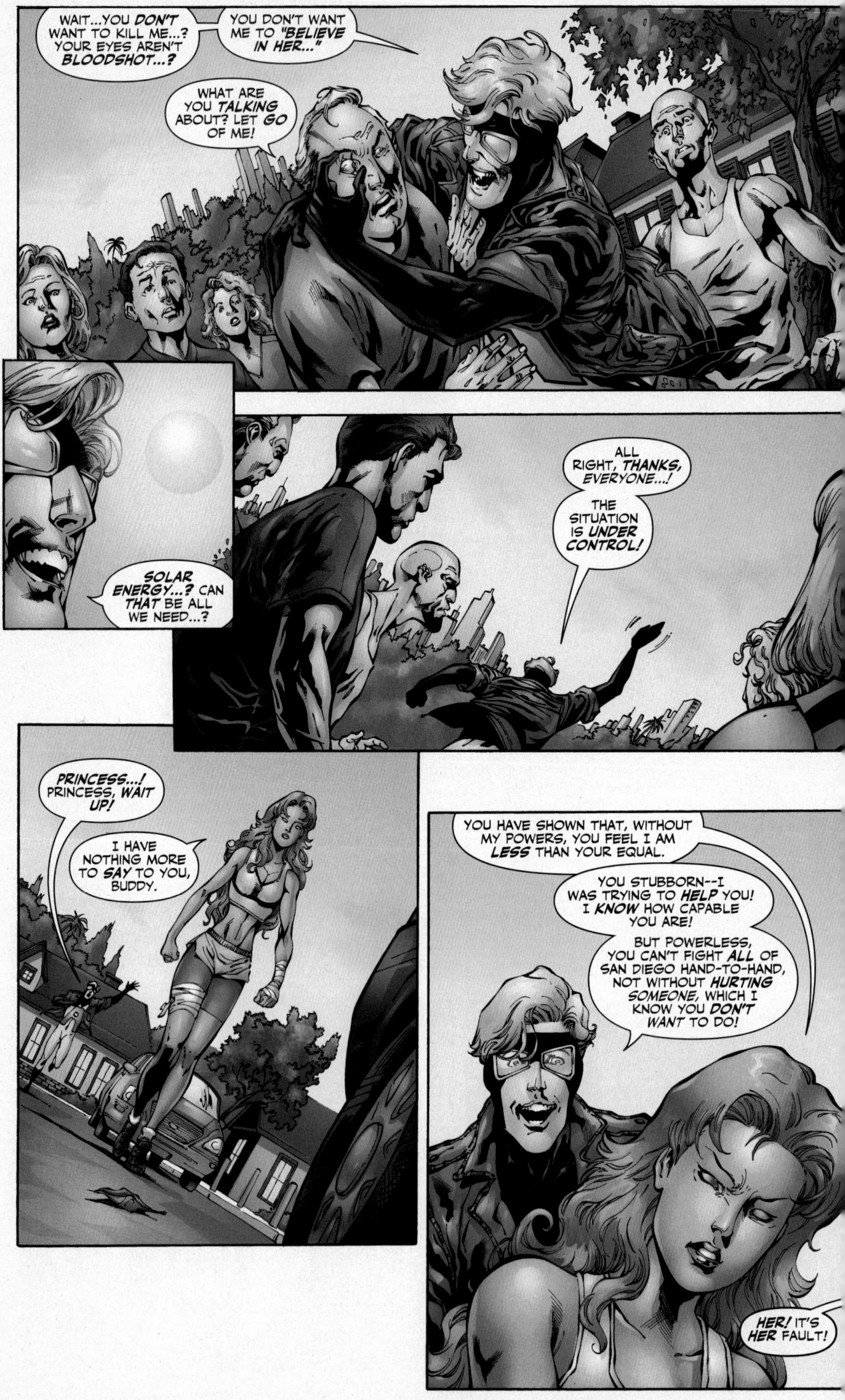
WAIT...YOU DON'T WANT TO KILL ME...? YOUR EYES AREN'T BLOODSHOT...?
YOU DON'T WANT ME TO "BELIEVE IN HER..."
WHAT ARE YOU TALKING ABOUT? LET GO OF ME!
SOLAR ENERGY...? CAN THAT BE ALL WE NEED...?
ALL RIGHT, THANKS, EVERYONE...!
THE SITUATION IS UNDER CONTROL!
PRINCESS...! PRINCESS, WAIT UP!
I HAVE NOTHING MORE TO SAY TO YOU, BUDDY.
YOU HAVE SHOWN THAT, WITHOUT MY POWERS, YOU FEEL I AM LESS THAN YOUR EQUAL.
YOU STUBBORN--I WAS TRYING TO HELP YOU! I KNOW HOW CAPABLE YOU ARE!
BUT POWERLESS, YOU CAN'T FIGHT ALL OF SAN DIEGO HAND-TO-HAND, NOT WITHOUT HURTING SOMEONE, WHICH I KNOW YOU DON'T WANT TO DO!
HER! IT'S HER FAULT!

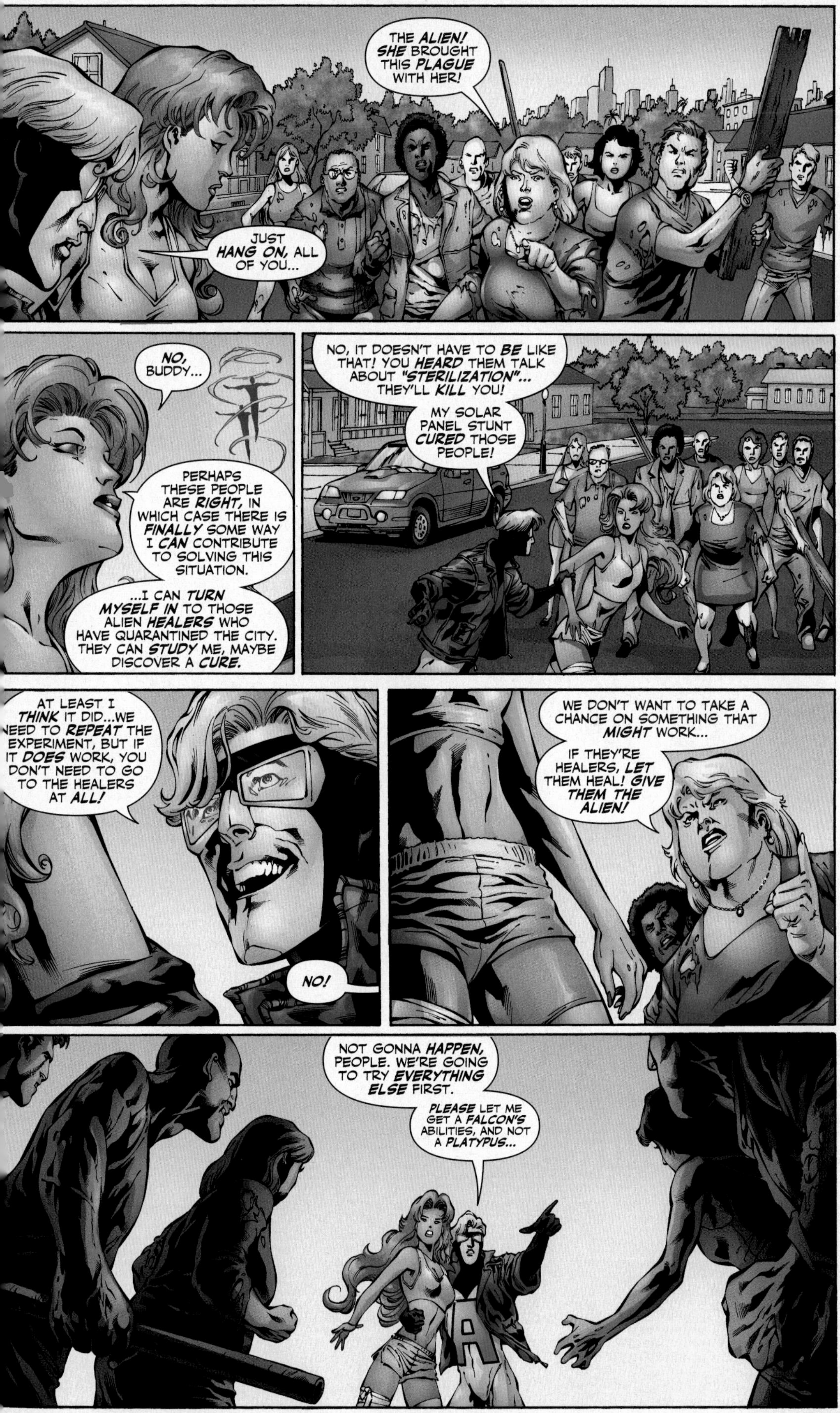
THE ALIEN! SHE BROUGHT THIS PLAGUE WITH HER!
JUST HANG ON, ALL OF YOU...
NO, BUDDY...
PERHAPS THESE PEOPLE ARE RIGHT, IN WHICH CASE THERE IS FINALLY SOME WAY I CAN CONTRIBUTE TO SOLVING THIS SITUATION.
...I CAN TURN MYSELF IN TO THOSE ALIEN HEALERS WHO HAVE QUARANTINED THE CITY. THEY CAN STUDY ME, MAYBE DISCOVER A CURE.
NO, IT DOESN'T HAVE TO BE LIKE THAT! YOU HEARD THEM TALK ABOUT "STERILIZATION"... THEY'LL KILL YOU!
MY SOLAR PANEL STUNT CURED THOSE PEOPLE!
AT LEAST I THINK IT DID...WE NEED TO REPEAT THE EXPERIMENT, BUT IF IT DOES WORK, YOU DON'T NEED TO GO TO THE HEALERS AT ALL!
NO!
WE DON'T WANT TO TAKE A CHANCE ON SOMETHING THAT MIGHT WORK...
IF THEY'RE HEALERS, LET THEM HEAL! GIVE THEM THE ALIEN!
NOT GONNA HAPPEN, PEOPLE. WE'RE GOING TO TRY EVERYTHING ELSE FIRST.
PLEASE LET ME GET A FALCON'S ABILITIES, AND NOT A PLATYPUS...

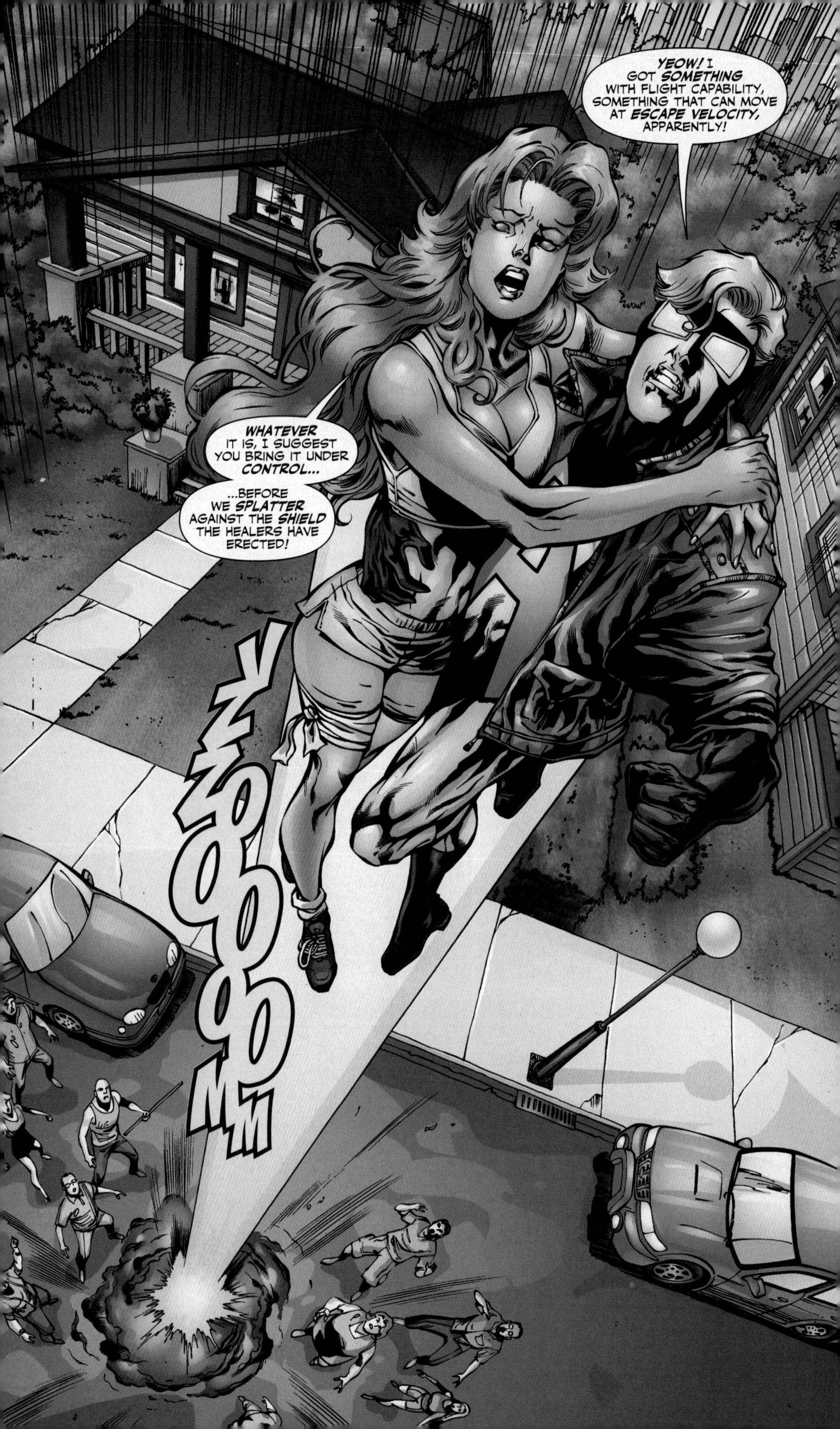

YEOW! I GOT SOMETHING WITH FLIGHT CAPABILITY, SOMETHING THAT CAN MOVE AT ESCAPE VELOCITY, APPARENTLY!
WHATEVER IT IS, I SUGGEST YOU BRING IT UNDER CONTROL...
...BEFORE WE SPLATTER AGAINST THE SHIELD THE HEALERS HAVE ERECTED!
VROOOOOM

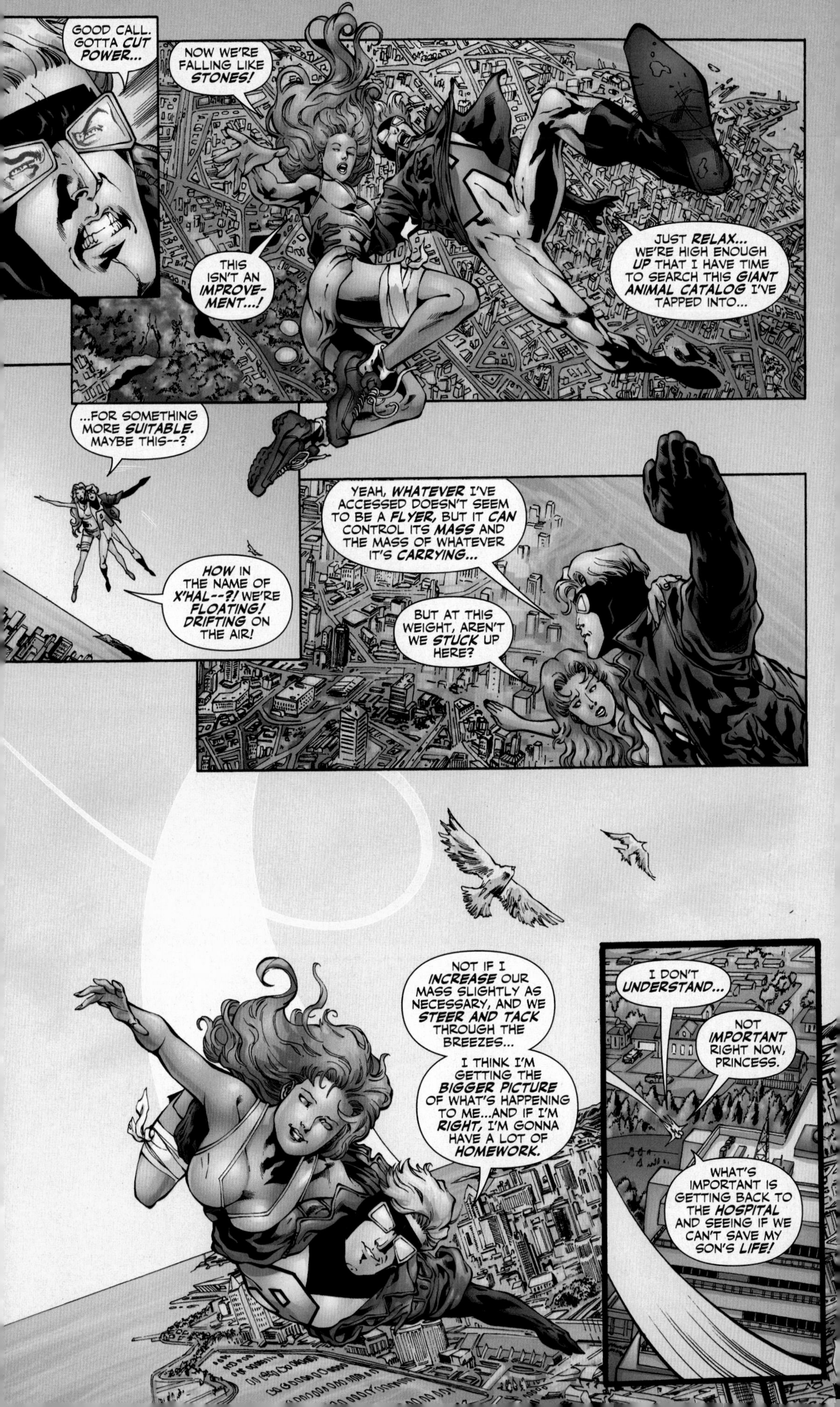

GOOD CALL. GOTTA CUT POWER...
NOW WE'RE FALLING LIKE STONES!
THIS ISN'T AN IMPROVEMENT...!
JUST RELAX... WE'RE HIGH ENOUGH UP THAT I HAVE TIME TO SEARCH THIS GIANT ANIMAL CATALOG I'VE TAPPED INTO...
...FOR SOMETHING MORE SUITABLE. MAYBE THIS--?
HOW IN THE NAME OF X'HAL--?! WE'RE FLOATING! DRIFTING ON THE AIR!
YEAH, WHATEVER I'VE ACCESSED DOESN'T SEEM TO BE A FLYER, BUT IT CAN CONTROL ITS MASS AND THE MASS OF WHATEVER IT'S CARRYING...
BUT AT THIS WEIGHT, AREN'T WE STUCK UP HERE?
NOT IF I INCREASE OUR MASS SLIGHTLY AS NECESSARY, AND WE STEER AND TACK THROUGH THE BREEZES...
I THINK I'M GETTING THE BIGGER PICTURE OF WHAT'S HAPPENING TO ME...AND IF I'M RIGHT, I'M GONNA HAVE A LOT OF HOMEWORK.
I DON'T UNDERSTAND...
NOT IMPORTANT RIGHT NOW, PRINCESS.
WHAT'S IMPORTANT IS GETTING BACK TO THE HOSPITAL AND SEEING IF WE CAN'T SAVE MY SON'S LIFE!

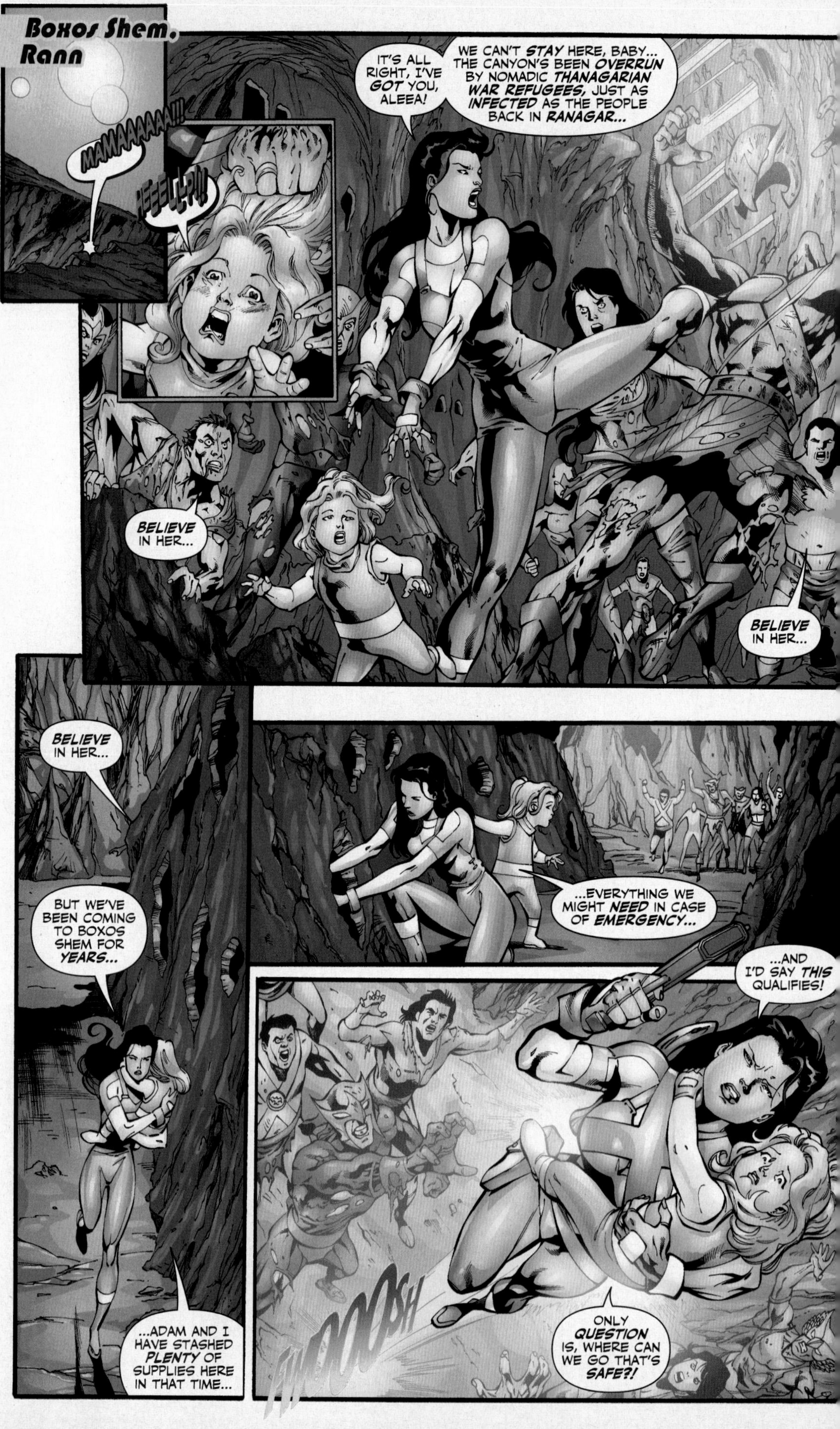
Boxos Shem, Rann
MAMAAAAAA!!!
HEEELLP!!!
IT'S ALL RIGHT, I'VE GOT YOU, ALEEA!
WE CAN'T STAY HERE, BABY... THE CANYON'S BEEN OVERRUN BY NOMADIC THANAGARIAN WAR REFUGEES, JUST AS INFECTED AS THE PEOPLE BACK IN RANAGAR...
BELIEVE IN HER...
BELIEVE IN HER...
BELIEVE IN HER...
BUT WE'VE BEEN COMING TO BOXOS SHEM FOR YEARS...
...ADAM AND I HAVE STASHED PLENTY OF SUPPLIES HERE IN THAT TIME...
...EVERYTHING WE MIGHT NEED IN CASE OF EMERGENCY...
...AND I'D SAY THIS QUALIFIES!
ONLY QUESTION IS, WHERE CAN WE GO THAT'S SAFE?!
FWOOOOSH

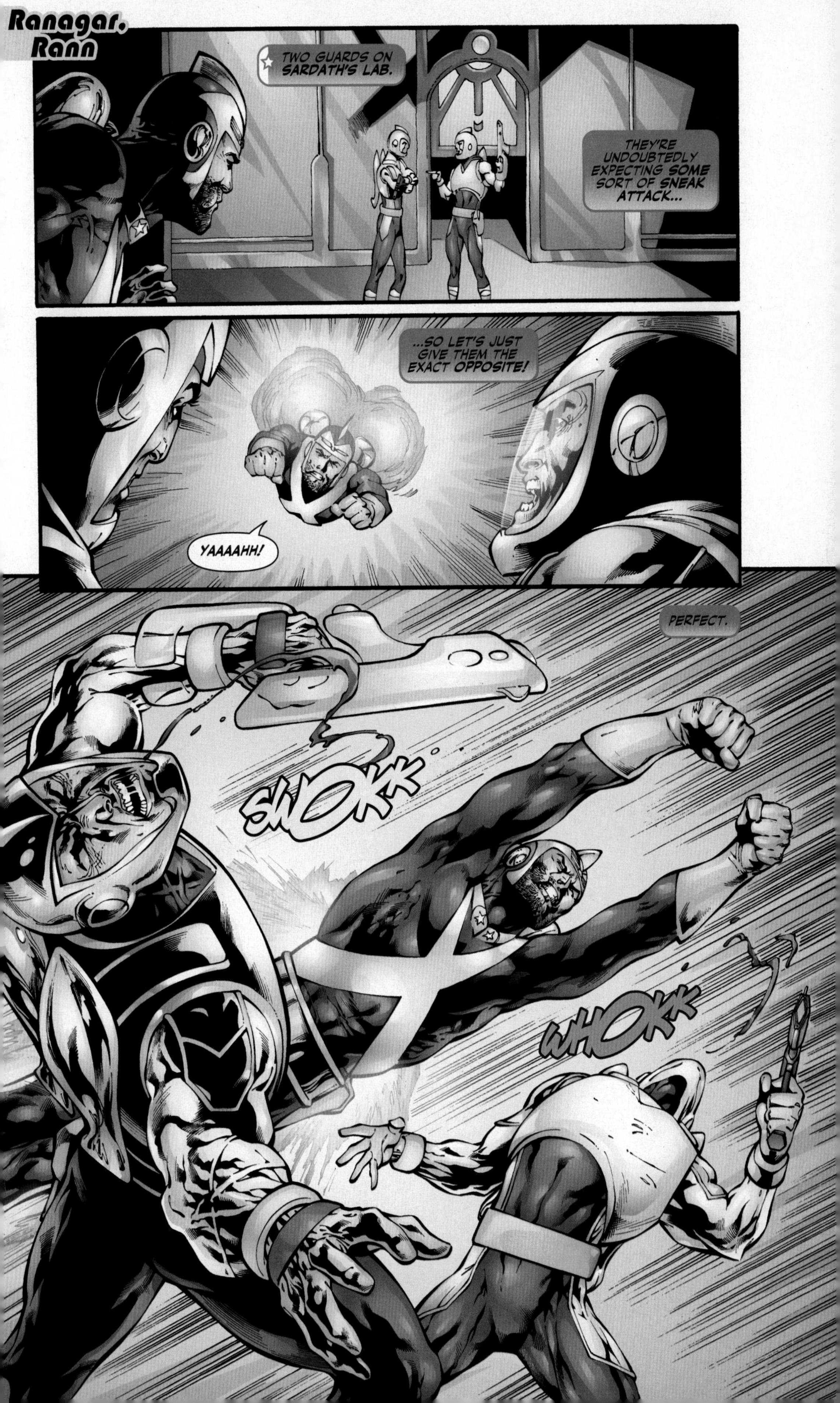
Ranagar, Rann
TWO GUARDS ON SARDATH'S LAB.
THEY'RE UNDOUBTEDLY EXPECTING SOME SORT OF SNEAK ATTACK...
...SO LET'S JUST GIVE THEM THE EXACT OPPOSITE!
YAAAAHH!
PERFECT.
SWOKK
WHOKK

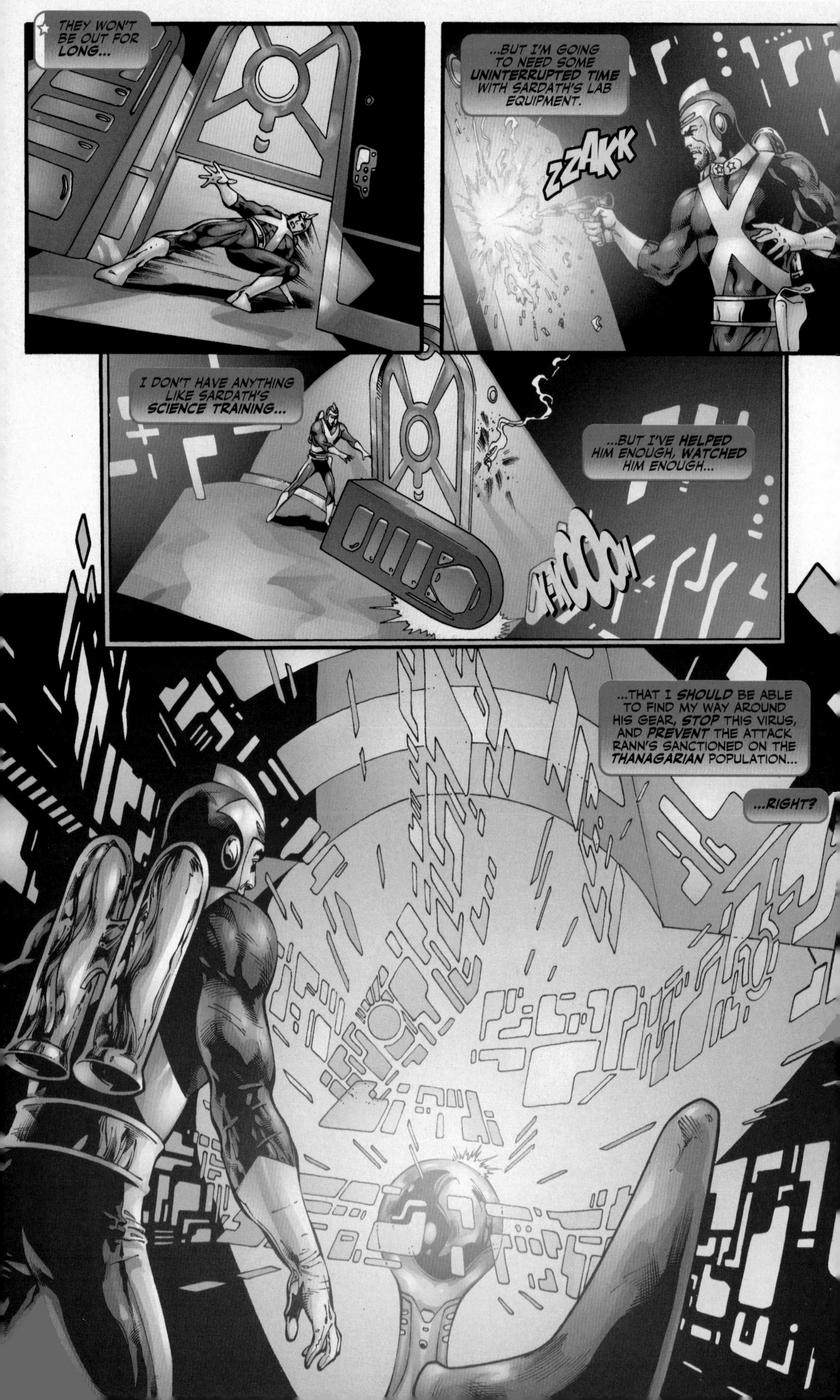
THEY WON'T BE OUT FOR LONG...
...BUT I'M GOING TO NEED SOME UNINTERRUPTED TIME WITH SARDATH'S LAB EQUIPMENT.
ZZAKK
I DON'T HAVE ANYTHING LIKE SARDATH'S SCIENCE TRAINING...
...BUT I'VE HELPED HIM ENOUGH, WATCHED HIM ENOUGH...
...THAT I SHOULD BE ABLE TO FIND MY WAY AROUND HIS GEAR, STOP THIS VIRUS, AND PREVENT THE ATTACK RANN'S SANCTIONED ON THE THANAGARIAN POPULATION...
...RIGHT?

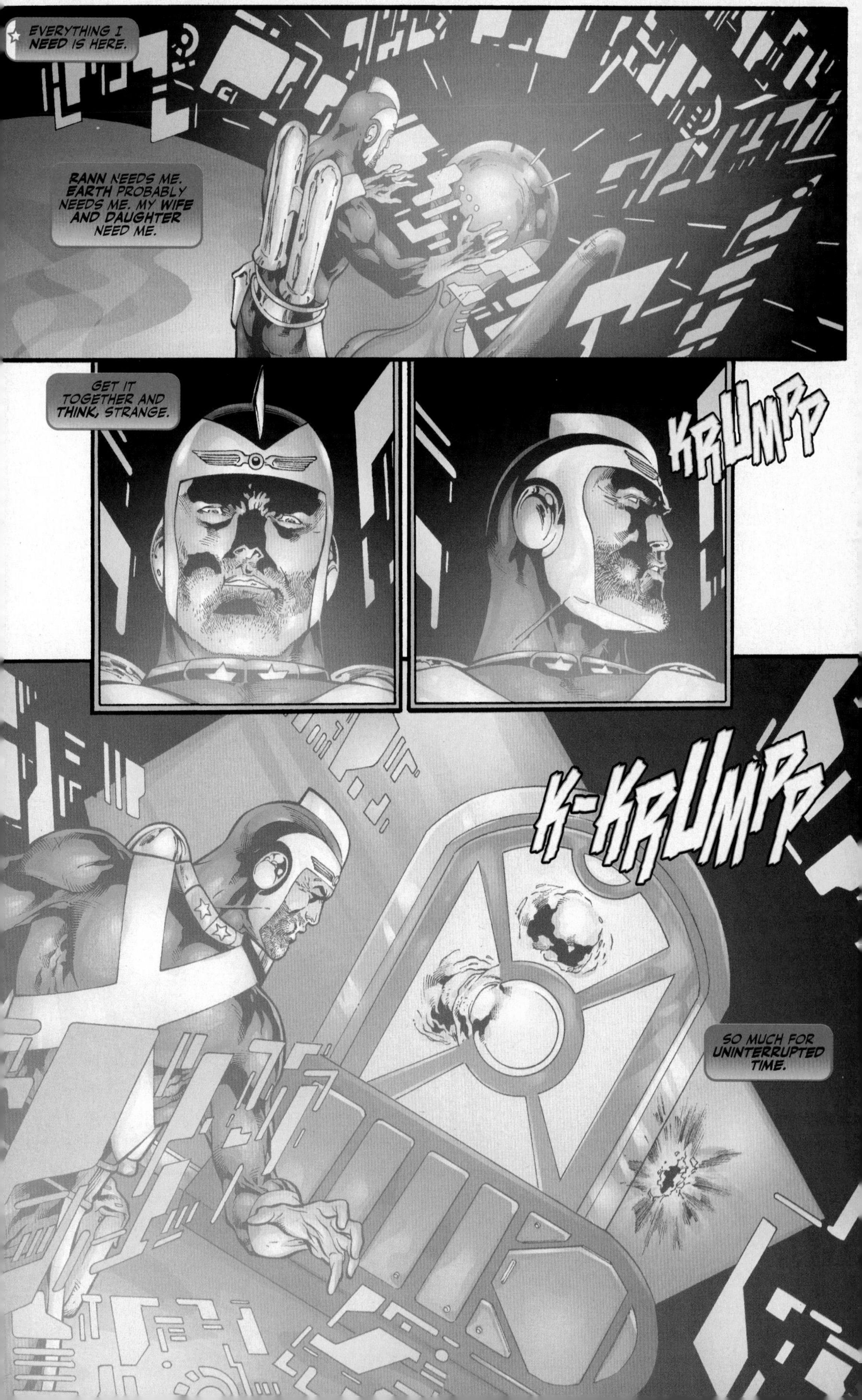
EVERYTHING I NEED IS HERE.
RANN NEEDS ME. EARTH PROBABLY NEEDS ME. MY WIFE AND DAUGHTER NEED ME.
GET IT TOGETHER AND THINK, STRANGE.
KRUMPP
K-KRUMPP
SO MUCH FOR UNINTERRUPTED TIME.

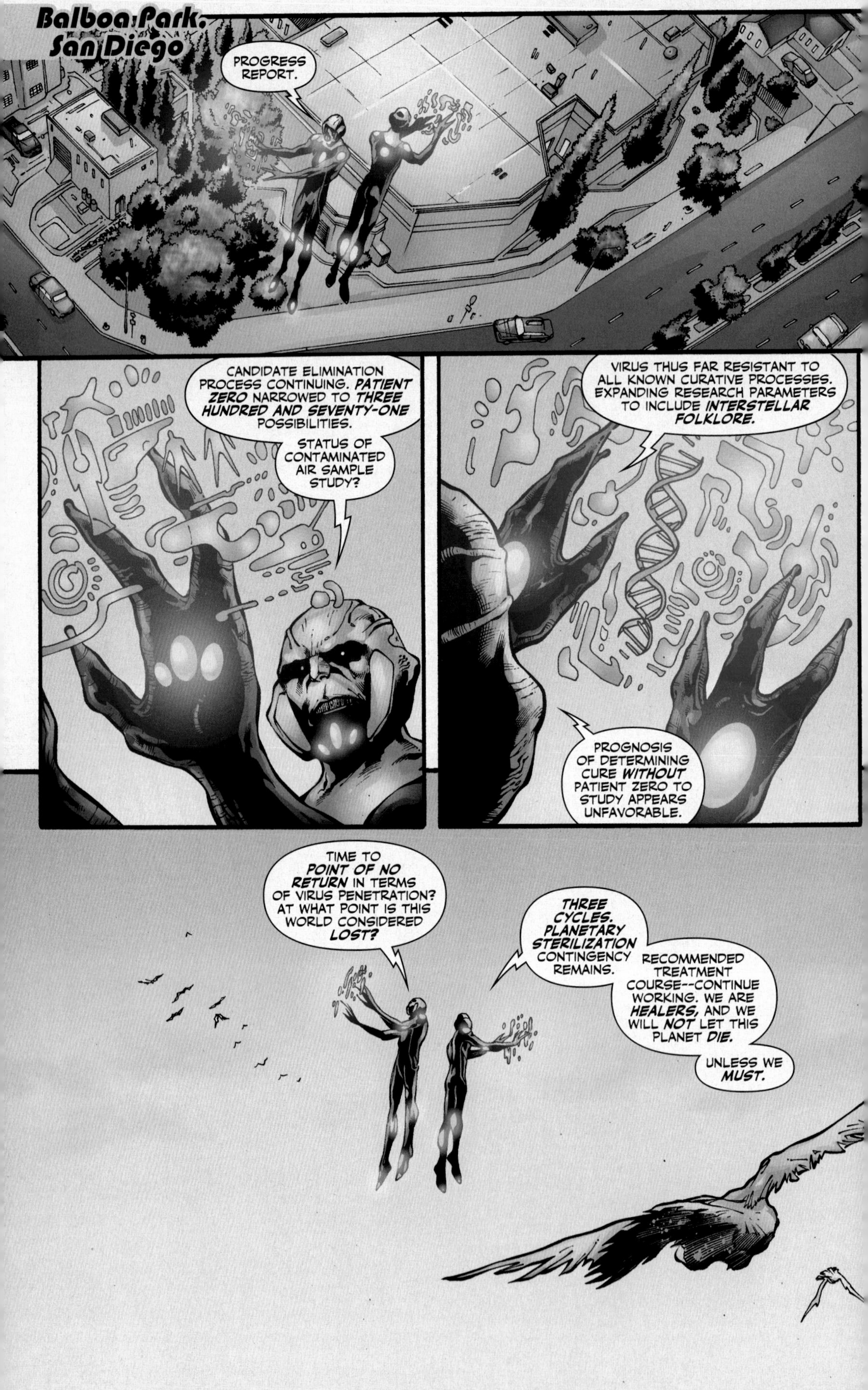

Balboa Park, San Diego
PROGRESS REPORT.
CANDIDATE ELIMINATION PROCESS CONTINUING. PATIENT ZERO NARROWED TO THREE HUNDRED AND SEVENTY-ONE POSSIBILITIES.
STATUS OF CONTAMINATED AIR SAMPLE STUDY?
VIRUS THUS FAR RESISTANT TO ALL KNOWN CURATIVE PROCESSES. EXPANDING RESEARCH PARAMETERS TO INCLUDE INTERSTELLAR FOLKLORE.
PROGNOSIS OF DETERMINING CURE WITHOUT PATIENT ZERO TO STUDY APPEARS UNFAVORABLE.
TIME TO POINT OF NO RETURN IN TERMS OF VIRUS PENETRATION? AT WHAT POINT IS THIS WORLD CONSIDERED LOST?
THREE CYCLES. PLANETARY STERILIZATION CONTINGENCY REMAINS.
RECOMMENDED TREATMENT COURSE--CONTINUE WORKING. WE ARE HEALERS, AND WE WILL NOT LET THIS PLANET DIE.
UNLESS WE MUST.

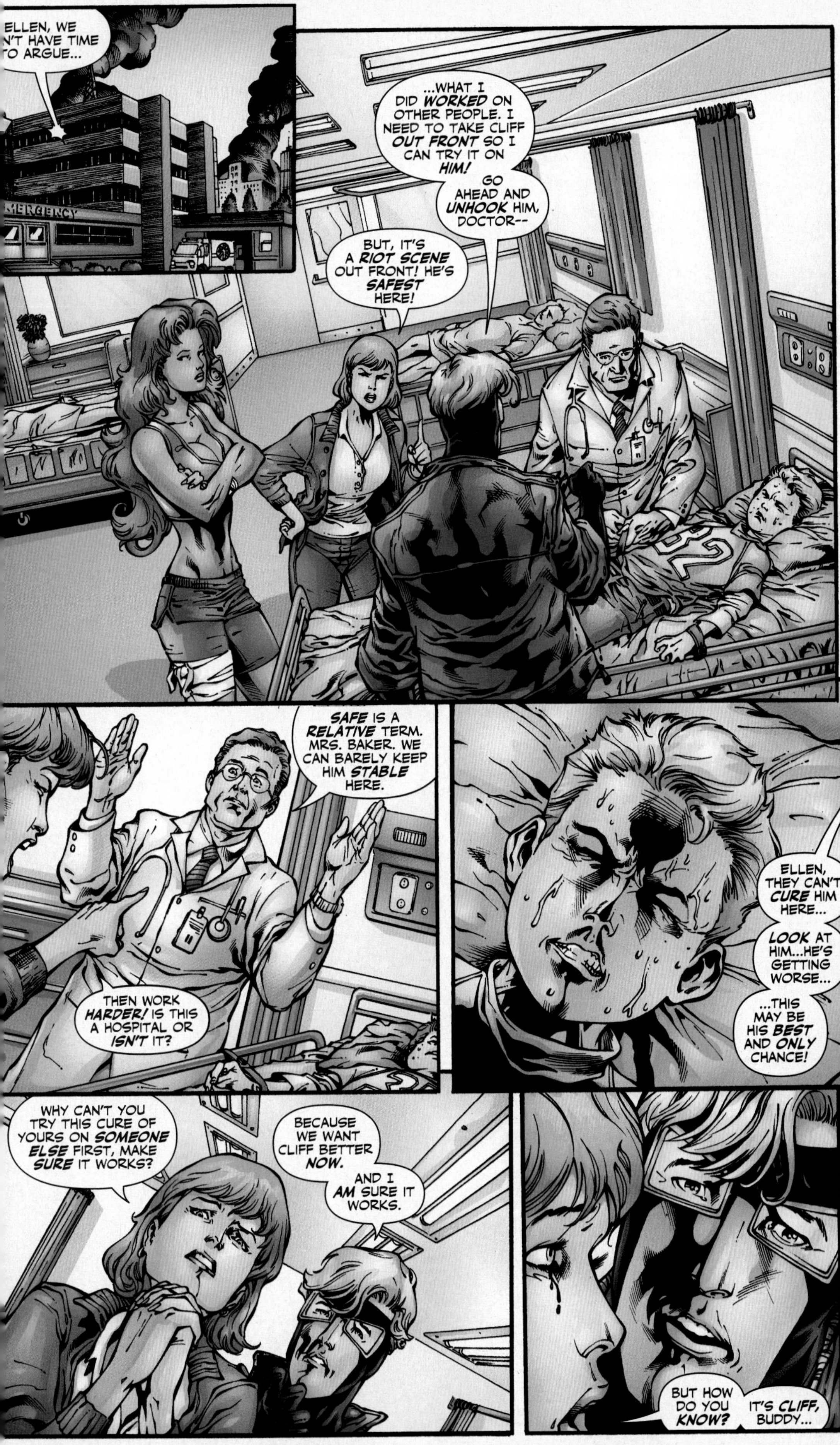

ELLEN, WE N'T HAVE TIME TO ARGUE...
...WHAT I DID WORKED ON OTHER PEOPLE. I NEED TO TAKE CLIFF OUT FRONT SO I CAN TRY IT ON HIM!
GO AHEAD AND UNHOOK HIM, DOCTOR--
BUT, IT'S A RIOT SCENE OUT FRONT! HE'S SAFEST HERE!
MERGENCY
SAFE IS A RELATIVE TERM. MRS. BAKER. WE CAN BARELY KEEP HIM STABLE HERE.
THEN WORK HARDER! IS THIS A HOSPITAL OR ISN'T IT?
ELLEN, THEY CAN'T CURE HIM HERE...
LOOK AT HIM...HE'S GETTING WORSE...
...THIS MAY BE HIS BEST AND ONLY CHANCE!
WHY CAN'T YOU TRY THIS CURE OF YOURS ON SOMEONE ELSE FIRST, MAKE SURE IT WORKS?
BECAUSE WE WANT CLIFF BETTER NOW.
AND I AM SURE IT WORKS.
BUT HOW DO YOU KNOW?
IT'S CLIFF, BUDDY...

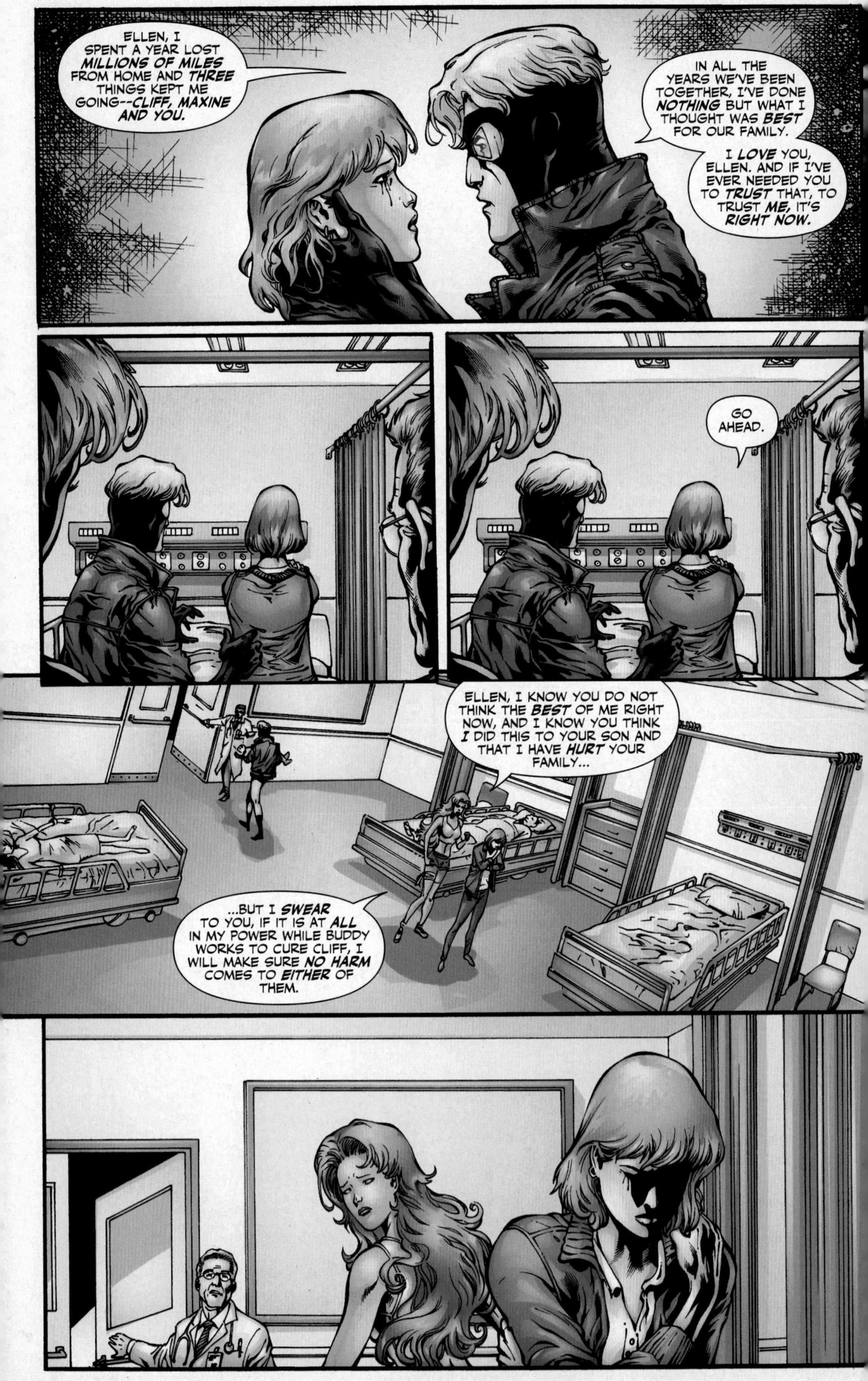
ELLEN, I SPENT A YEAR LOST MILLIONS OF MILES FROM HOME AND THREE THINGS KEPT ME GOING--CLIFF, MAXINE AND YOU.
IN ALL THE YEARS WE'VE BEEN TOGETHER, I'VE DONE NOTHING BUT WHAT I THOUGHT WAS BEST FOR OUR FAMILY.
I LOVE YOU, ELLEN. AND IF I'VE EVER NEEDED YOU TO TRUST THAT, TO TRUST ME, IT'S RIGHT NOW.
GO AHEAD.
ELLEN, I KNOW YOU DO NOT THINK THE BEST OF ME RIGHT NOW, AND I KNOW YOU THINK I DID THIS TO YOUR SON AND THAT I HAVE HURT YOUR FAMILY...
...BUT I SWEAR TO YOU, IF IT IS AT ALL IN MY POWER WHILE BUDDY WORKS TO CURE CLIFF, I WILL MAKE SURE NO HARM COMES TO EITHER OF THEM.

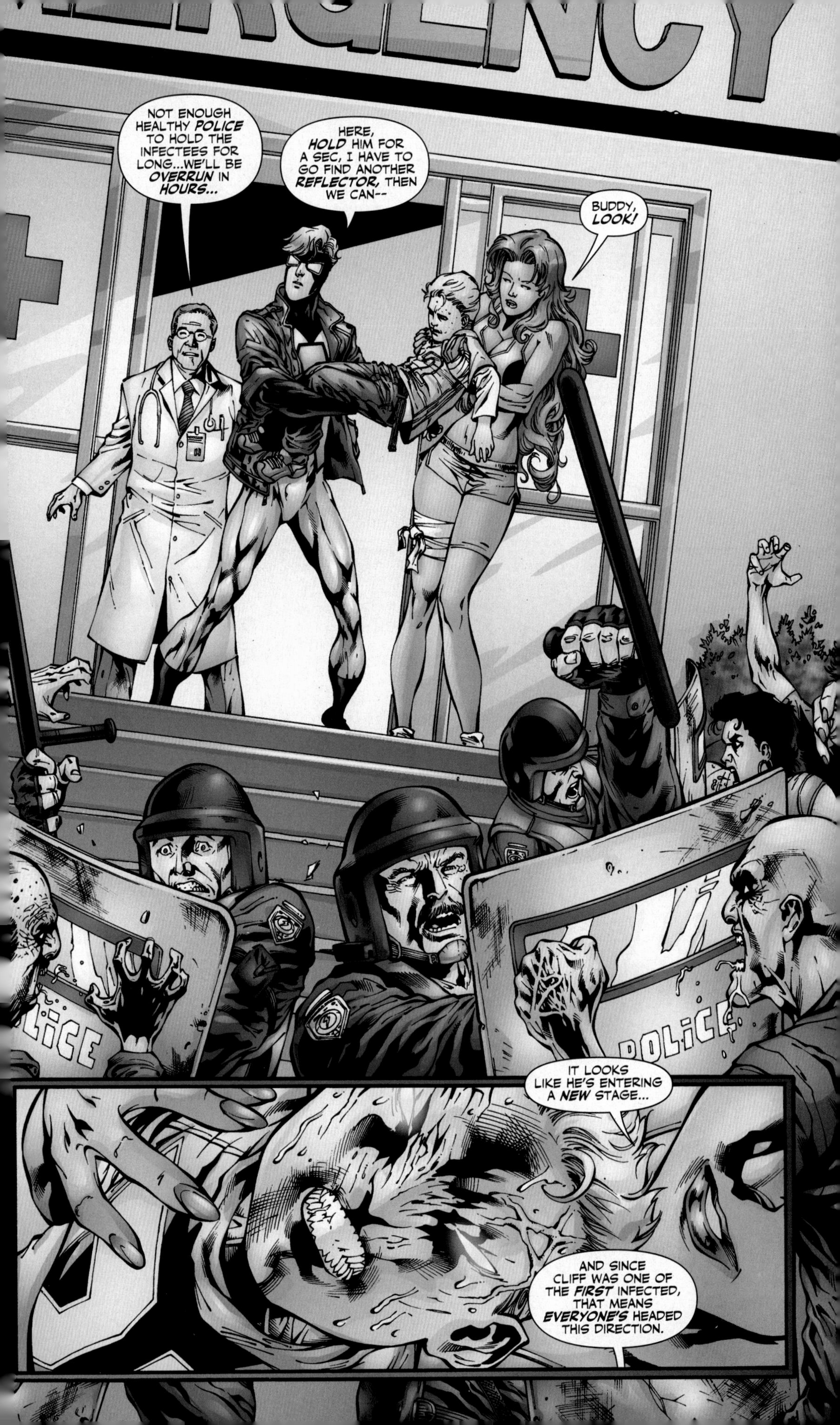

NOT ENOUGH HEALTHY POLICE TO HOLD THE INFECTEES FOR LONG...WE'LL BE OVERRUN IN HOURS...
HERE, HOLD HIM FOR A SEC, I HAVE TO GO FIND ANOTHER REFLECTOR, THEN WE CAN--
BUDDY, LOOK!
POLICE
POLICE
IT LOOKS LIKE HE'S ENTERING A NEW STAGE...
AND SINCE CLIFF WAS ONE OF THE FIRST INFECTED, THAT MEANS EVERYONE'S HEADED THIS DIRECTION.

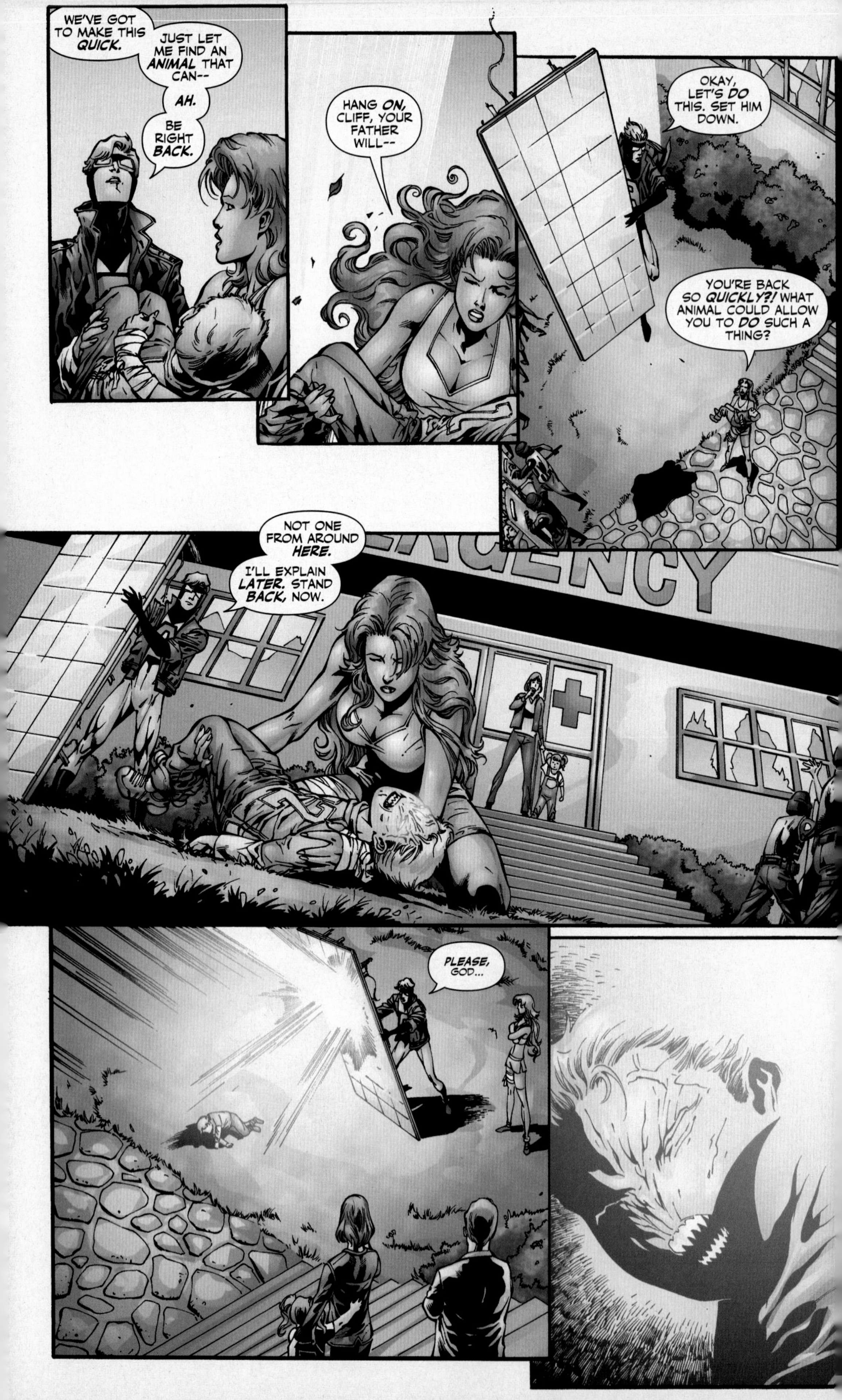
WE'VE GOT TO MAKE THIS *QUICK.*
JUST LET ME FIND AN *ANIMAL* THAT CAN--
AH.
BE RIGHT *BACK.*
HANG *ON,* CLIFF, YOUR FATHER WILL--
OKAY, LET'S *DO* THIS. SET HIM DOWN.
YOU'RE BACK SO *QUICKLY?!* WHAT ANIMAL COULD ALLOW YOU TO *DO* SUCH A THING?
NOT ONE FROM AROUND *HERE.*
I'LL EXPLAIN *LATER.* STAND *BACK,* NOW.
PLEASE, GOD...

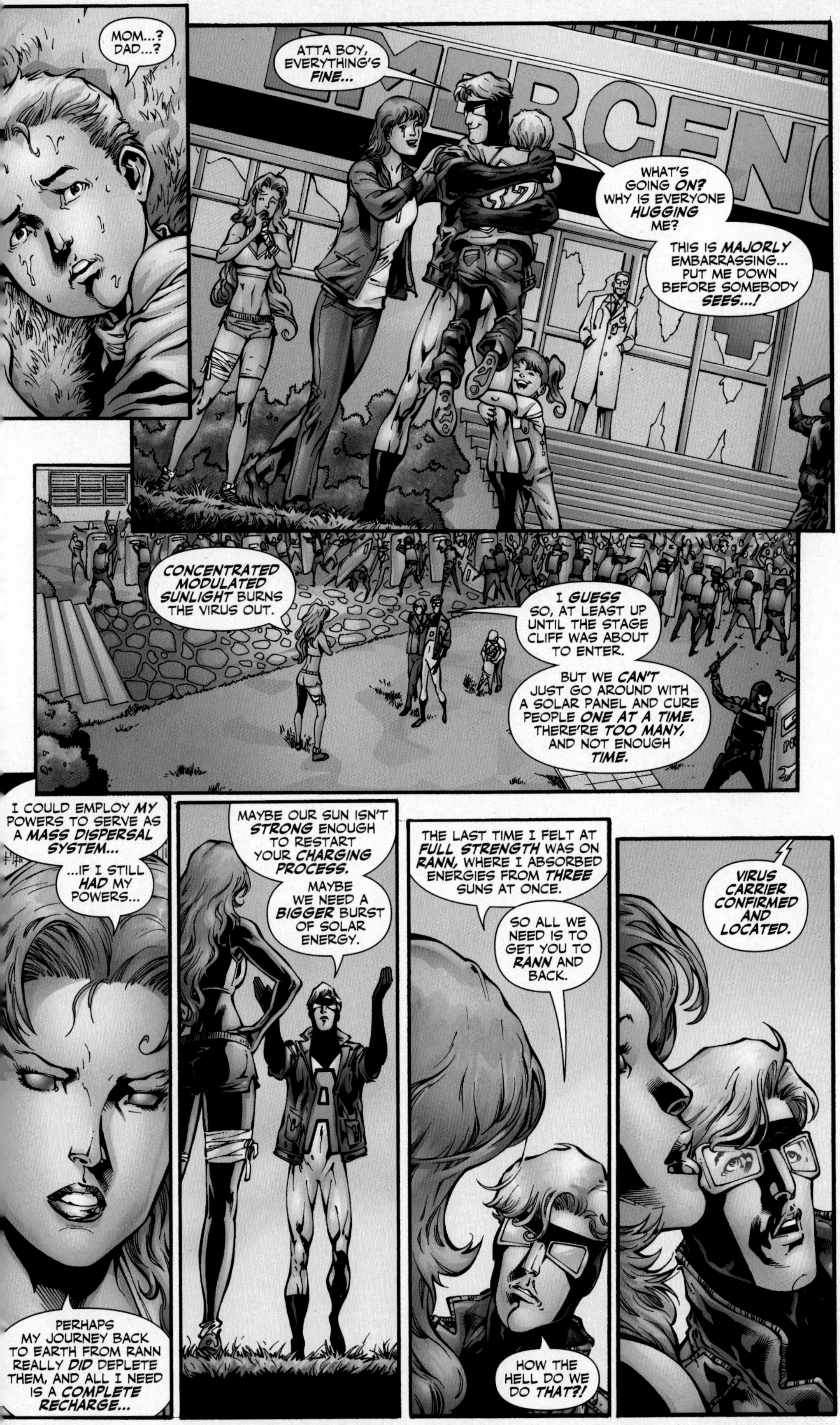
MOM...? DAD...?
ATTA BOY, EVERYTHING'S FINE...
WHAT'S GOING ON? WHY IS EVERYONE HUGGING ME?
THIS IS MAJORLY EMBARRASSING... PUT ME DOWN BEFORE SOMEBODY SEES...!
CONCENTRATED MODULATED SUNLIGHT BURNS THE VIRUS OUT.
I GUESS SO, AT LEAST UP UNTIL THE STAGE CLIFF WAS ABOUT TO ENTER.
BUT WE CAN'T JUST GO AROUND WITH A SOLAR PANEL AND CURE PEOPLE ONE AT A TIME. THERE'RE TOO MANY, AND NOT ENOUGH TIME.
I COULD EMPLOY MY POWERS TO SERVE AS A MASS DISPERSAL SYSTEM...
...IF I STILL HAD MY POWERS...
PERHAPS MY JOURNEY BACK TO EARTH FROM RANN REALLY DID DEPLETE THEM, AND ALL I NEED IS A COMPLETE RECHARGE...
MAYBE OUR SUN ISN'T STRONG ENOUGH TO RESTART YOUR CHARGING PROCESS.
MAYBE WE NEED A BIGGER BURST OF SOLAR ENERGY.
THE LAST TIME I FELT AT FULL STRENGTH WAS ON RANN, WHERE I ABSORBED ENERGIES FROM THREE SUNS AT ONCE.
SO ALL WE NEED IS TO GET YOU TO RANN AND BACK.
HOW THE HELL DO WE DO THAT?!
VIRUS CARRIER CONFIRMED AND LOCATED.

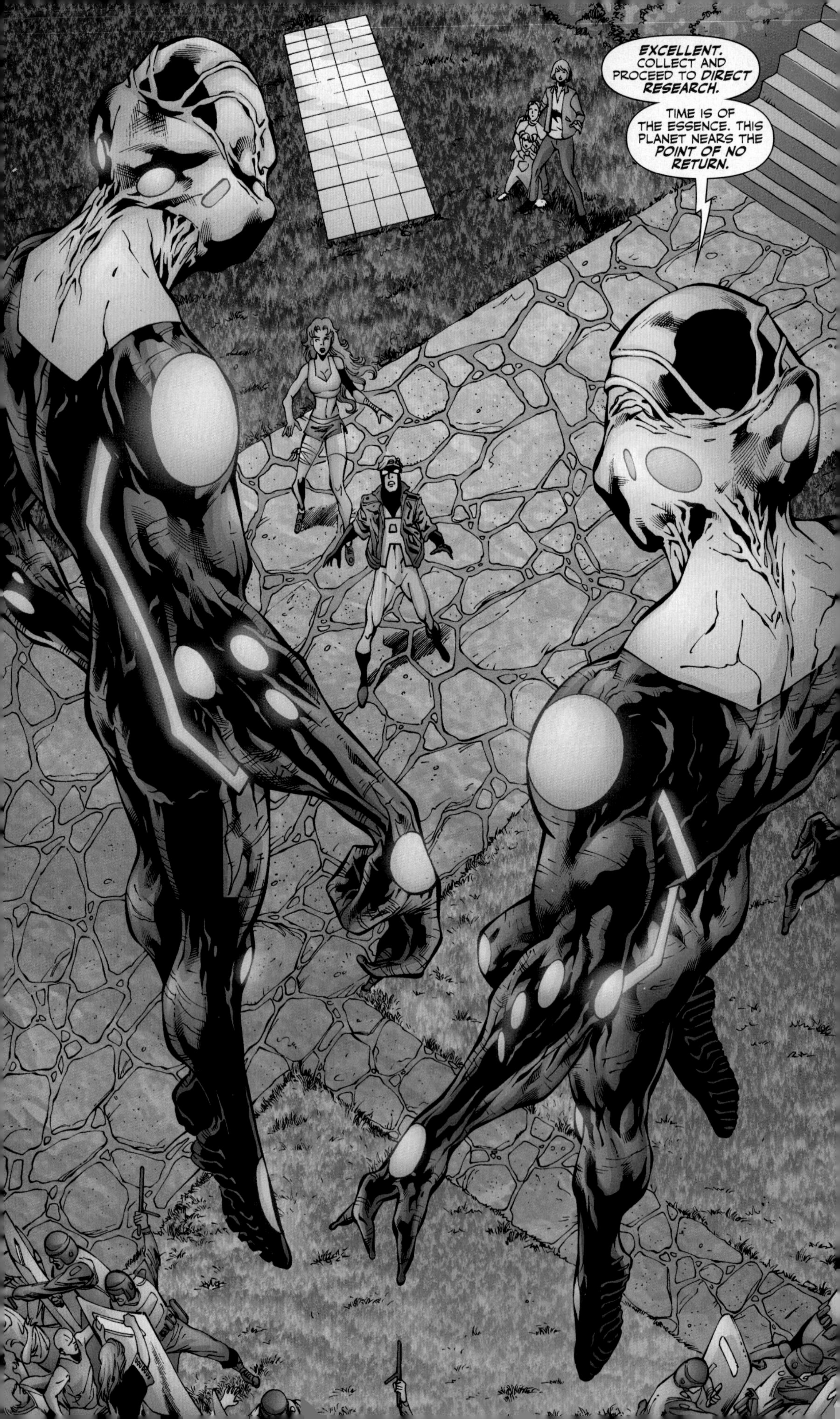
EXCELLENT. COLLECT AND PROCEED TO DIRECT RESEARCH.
TIME IS OF THE ESSENCE. THIS PLANET NEARS THE POINT OF NO RETURN.

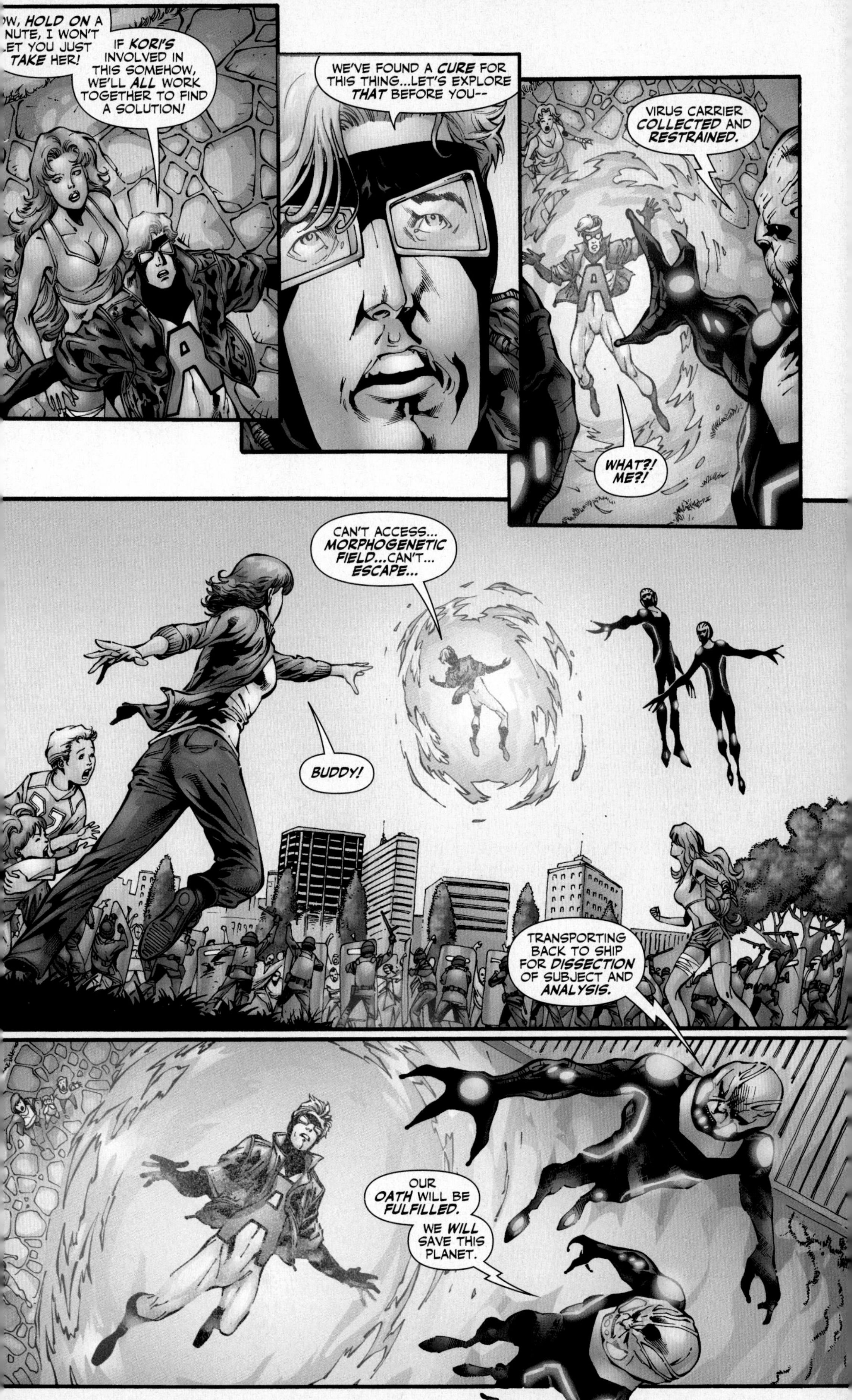

W, HOLD ON A NUTE, I WON'T LET YOU JUST TAKE HER!
IF KORI'S INVOLVED IN THIS SOMEHOW, WE'LL ALL WORK TOGETHER TO FIND A SOLUTION!
WE'VE FOUND A CURE FOR THIS THING...LET'S EXPLORE THAT BEFORE YOU--
VIRUS CARRIER COLLECTED AND RESTRAINED.
WHAT?! ME?!
CAN'T ACCESS... MORPHOGENETIC FIELD...CAN'T... ESCAPE...
BUDDY!
TRANSPORTING BACK TO SHIP FOR DISSECTION OF SUBJECT AND ANALYSIS.
OUR OATH WILL BE FULFILLED.
WE WILL SAVE THIS PLANET.

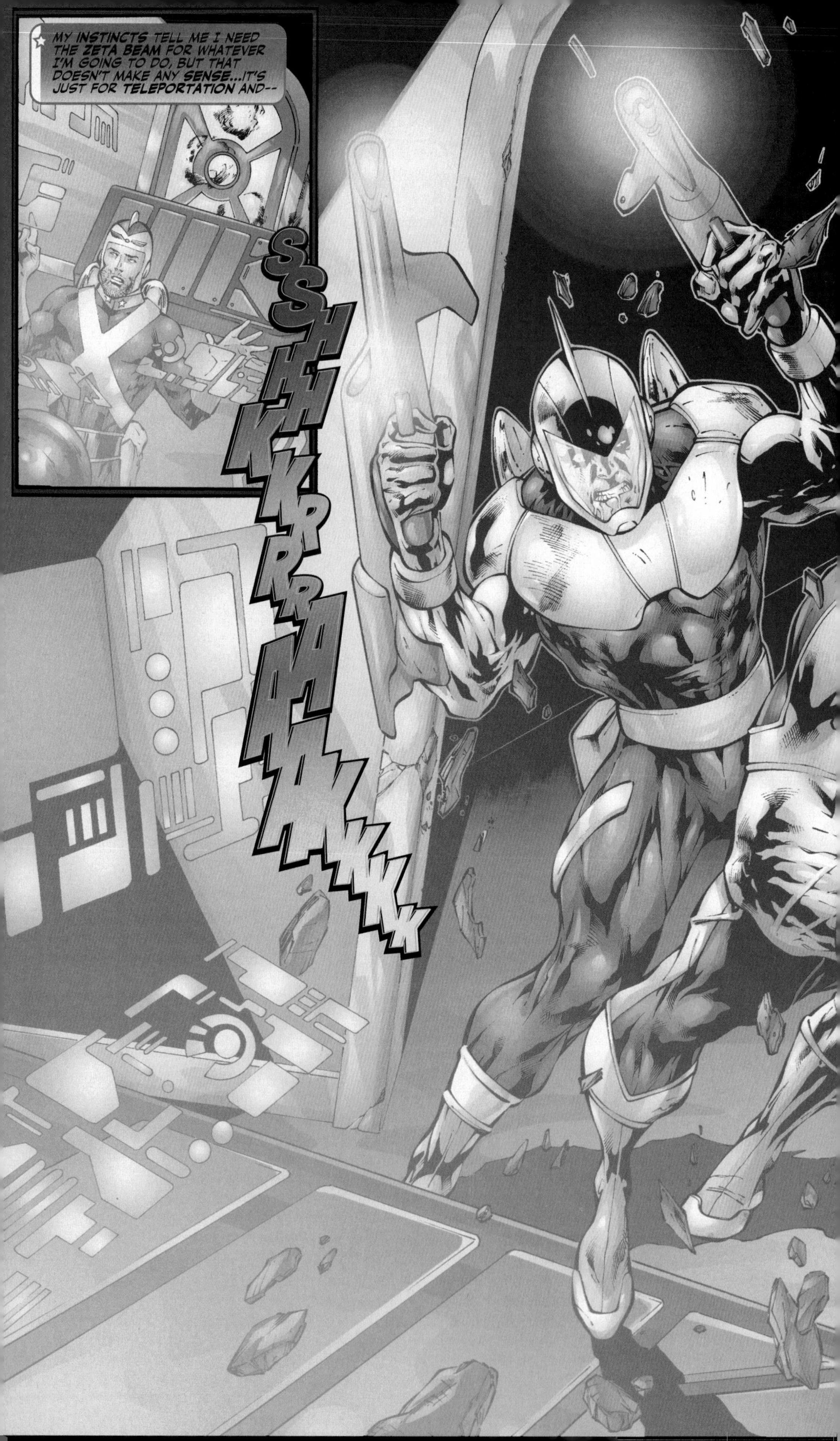
MY INSTINCTS TELL ME I NEED THE ZETA BEAM FOR WHATEVER I'M GOING TO DO, BUT THAT DOESN'T MAKE ANY SENSE...IT'S JUST FOR TELEPORTATION AND--
SSHHHKKRRRAAAKKKK

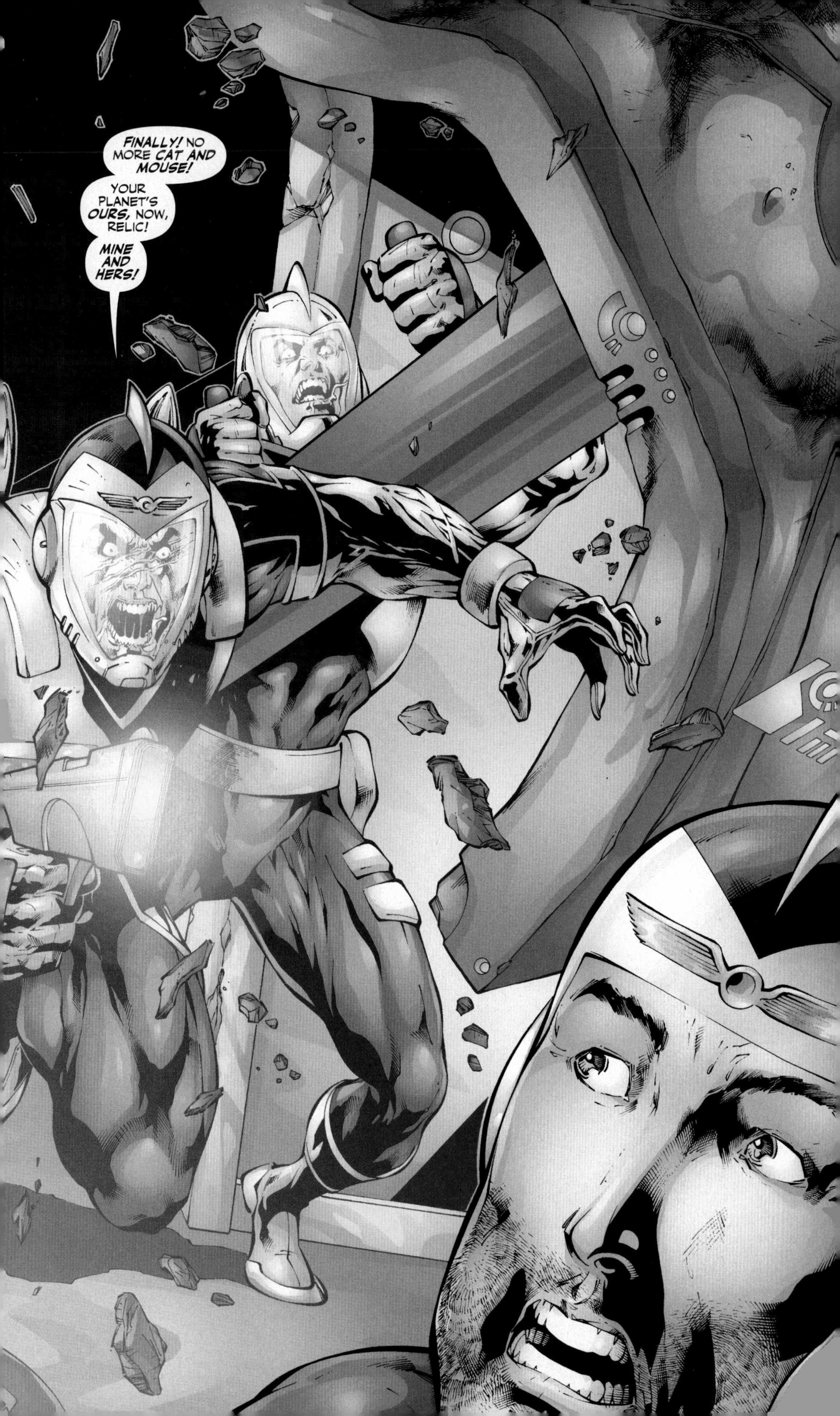
FINALLY! NO MORE CAT AND MOUSE!
YOUR PLANET'S OURS, NOW, RELIC!
MINE AND HERS!

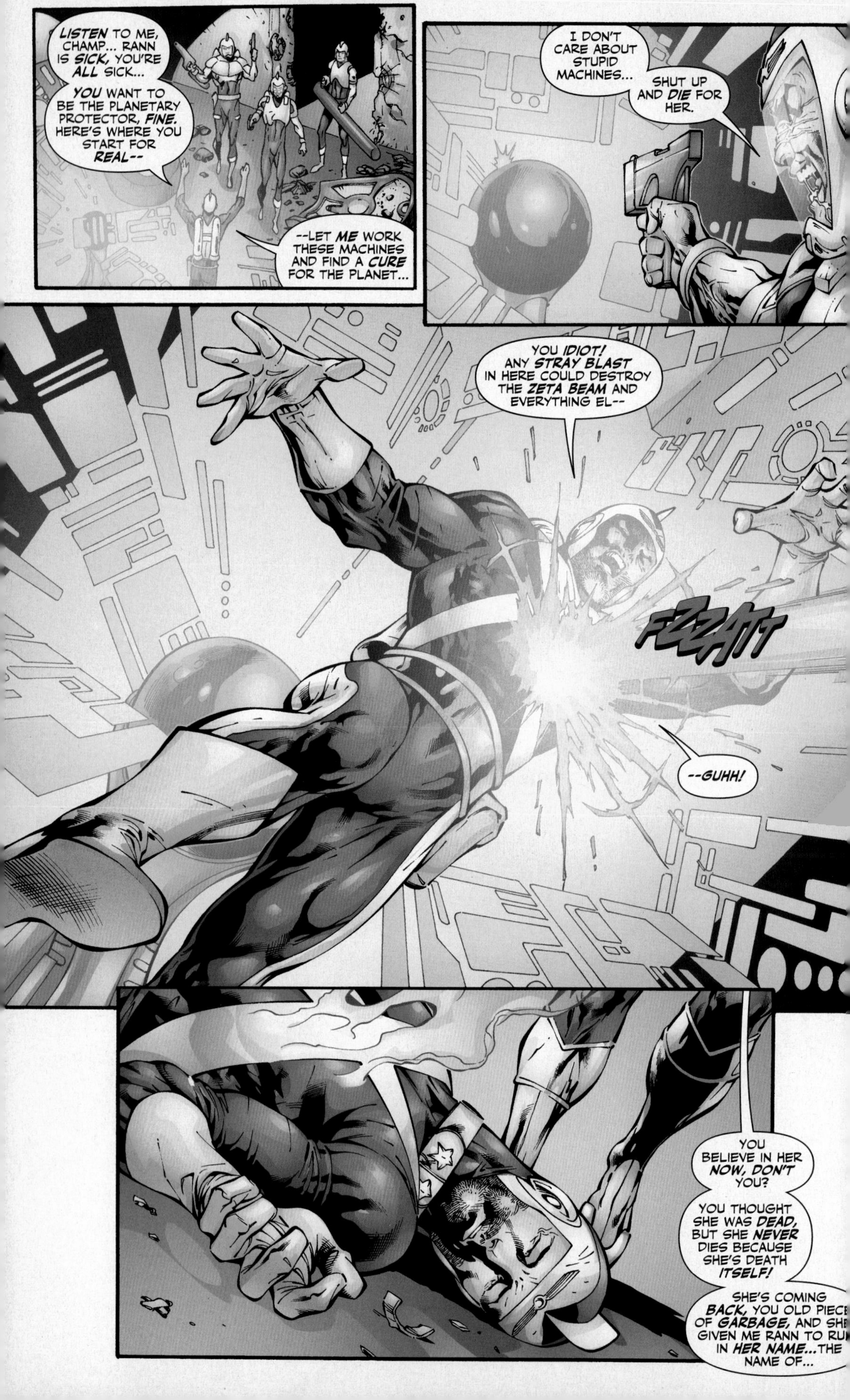
LISTEN TO ME, CHAMP... RANN IS SICK, YOU'RE ALL SICK...
YOU WANT TO BE THE PLANETARY PROTECTOR, FINE. HERE'S WHERE YOU START FOR REAL--
--LET ME WORK THESE MACHINES AND FIND A CURE FOR THE PLANET...
I DON'T CARE ABOUT STUPID MACHINES...
SHUT UP AND DIE FOR HER.
YOU IDIOT! ANY STRAY BLAST IN HERE COULD DESTROY THE ZETA BEAM AND EVERYTHING EL--
FZZZATT
--GUHH!
YOU BELIEVE IN HER NOW, DON'T YOU?
YOU THOUGHT SHE WAS DEAD, BUT SHE NEVER DIES BECAUSE SHE'S DEATH ITSELF!
SHE'S COMING BACK, YOU OLD PIECE OF GARBAGE, AND SHE'S GIVEN ME RANN TO RULE IN HER NAME...THE NAME OF...

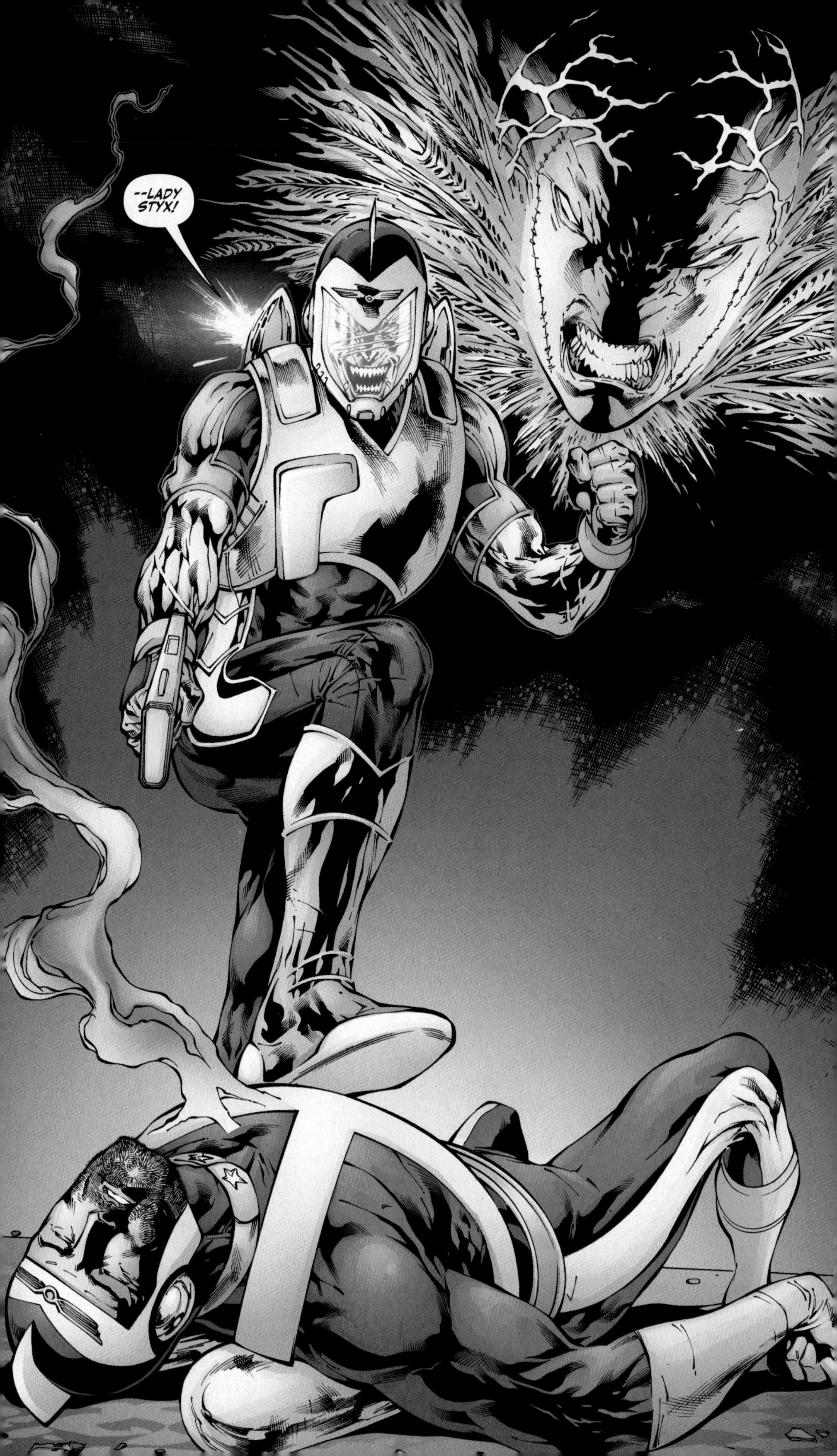
--LADY STYX!

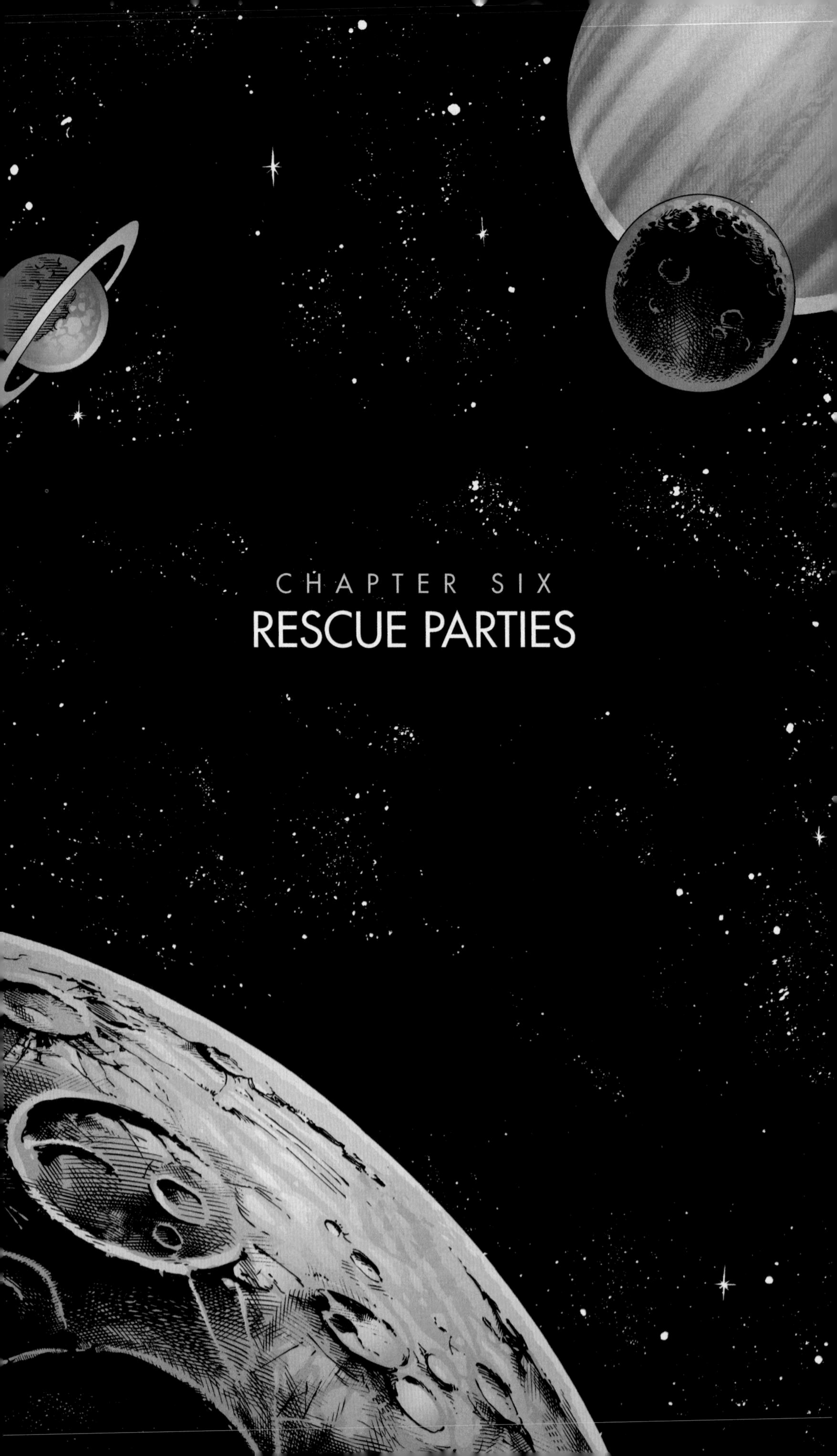

CHAPTER SIX

RESCUE PARTIES

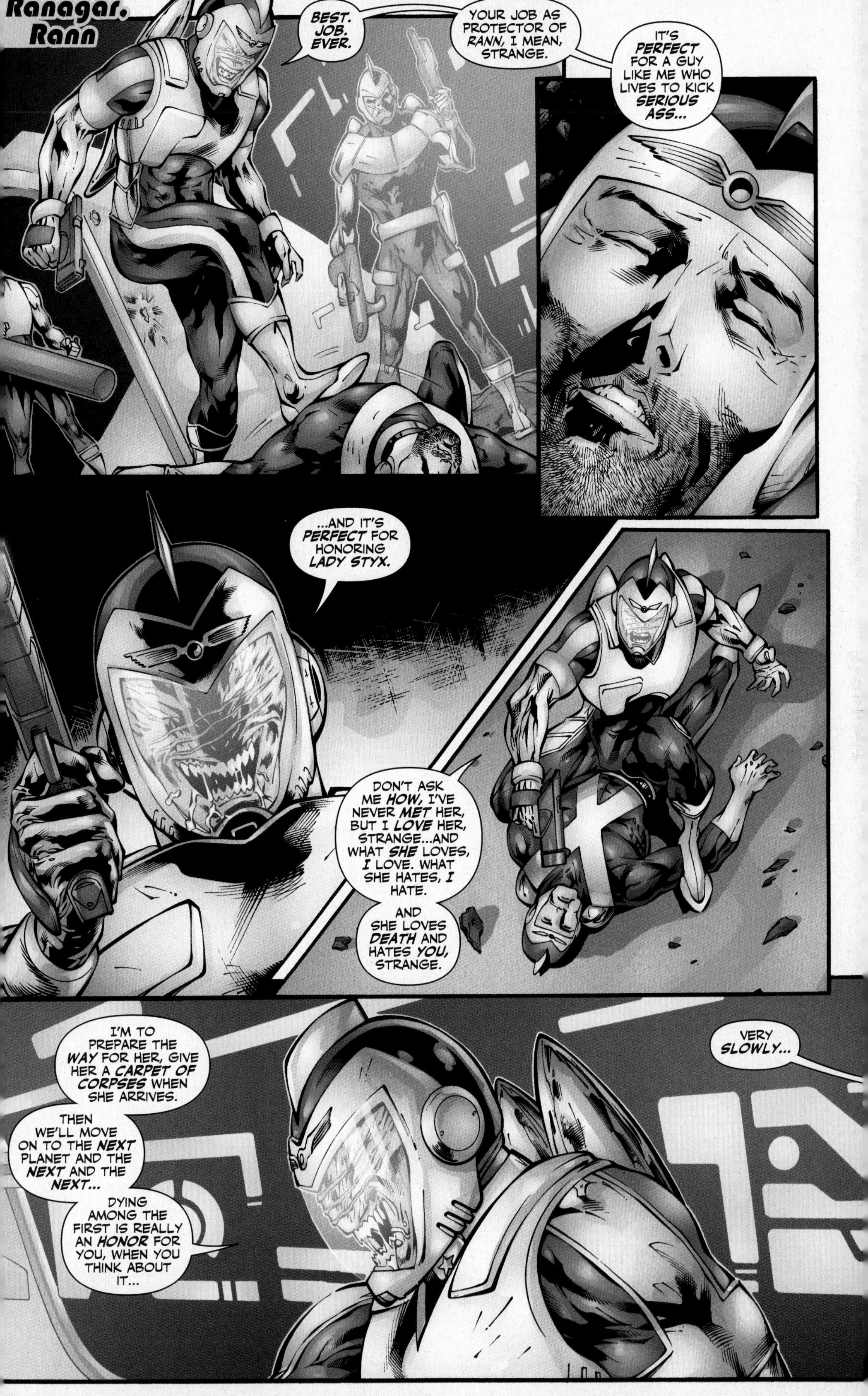
Ranagar, Rann
BEST. JOB. EVER.
YOUR JOB AS PROTECTOR OF RANN, I MEAN, STRANGE.
IT'S PERFECT FOR A GUY LIKE ME WHO LIVES TO KICK SERIOUS ASS...
...AND IT'S PERFECT FOR HONORING LADY STYX.
DON'T ASK ME HOW, I'VE NEVER MET HER, BUT I LOVE HER, STRANGE...AND WHAT SHE LOVES, I LOVE. WHAT SHE HATES, I HATE.
AND SHE LOVES DEATH AND HATES YOU, STRANGE.
I'M TO PREPARE THE WAY FOR HER, GIVE HER A CARPET OF CORPSES WHEN SHE ARRIVES.
THEN WE'LL MOVE ON TO THE NEXT PLANET AND THE NEXT AND THE NEXT...
DYING AMONG THE FIRST IS REALLY AN HONOR FOR YOU, WHEN YOU THINK ABOUT IT...
VERY SLOWLY...

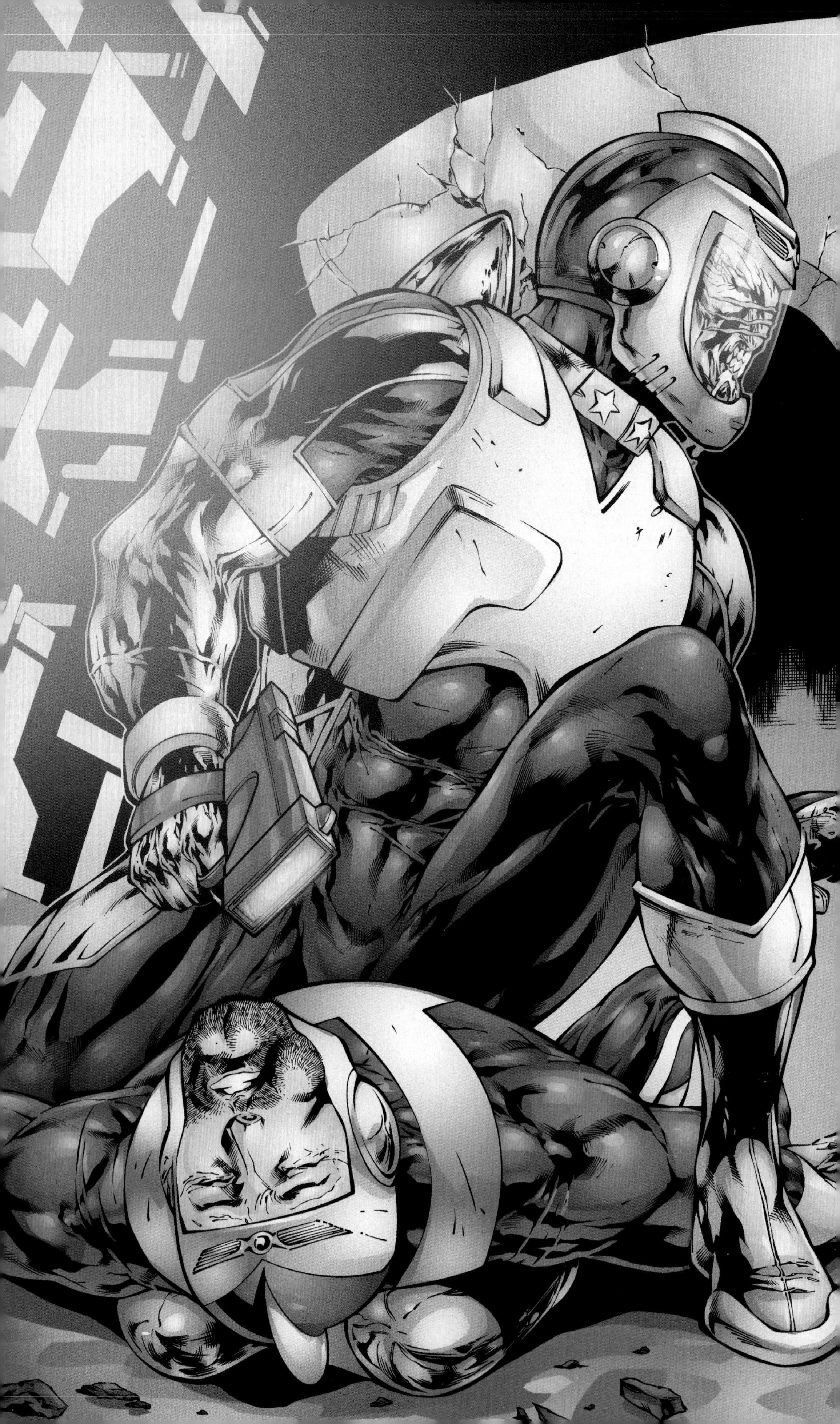

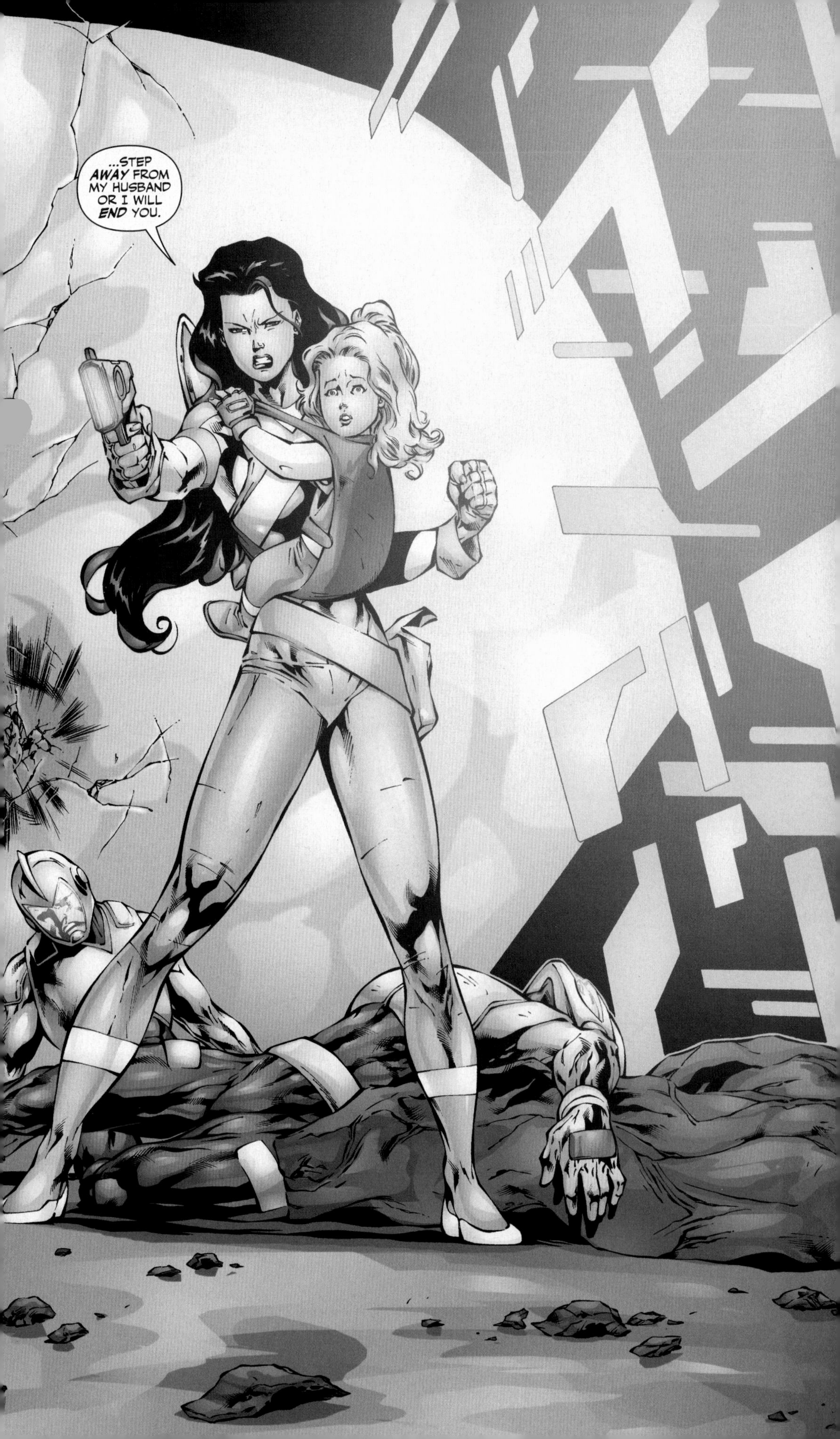
...STEP AWAY FROM MY HUSBAND OR I WILL END YOU.

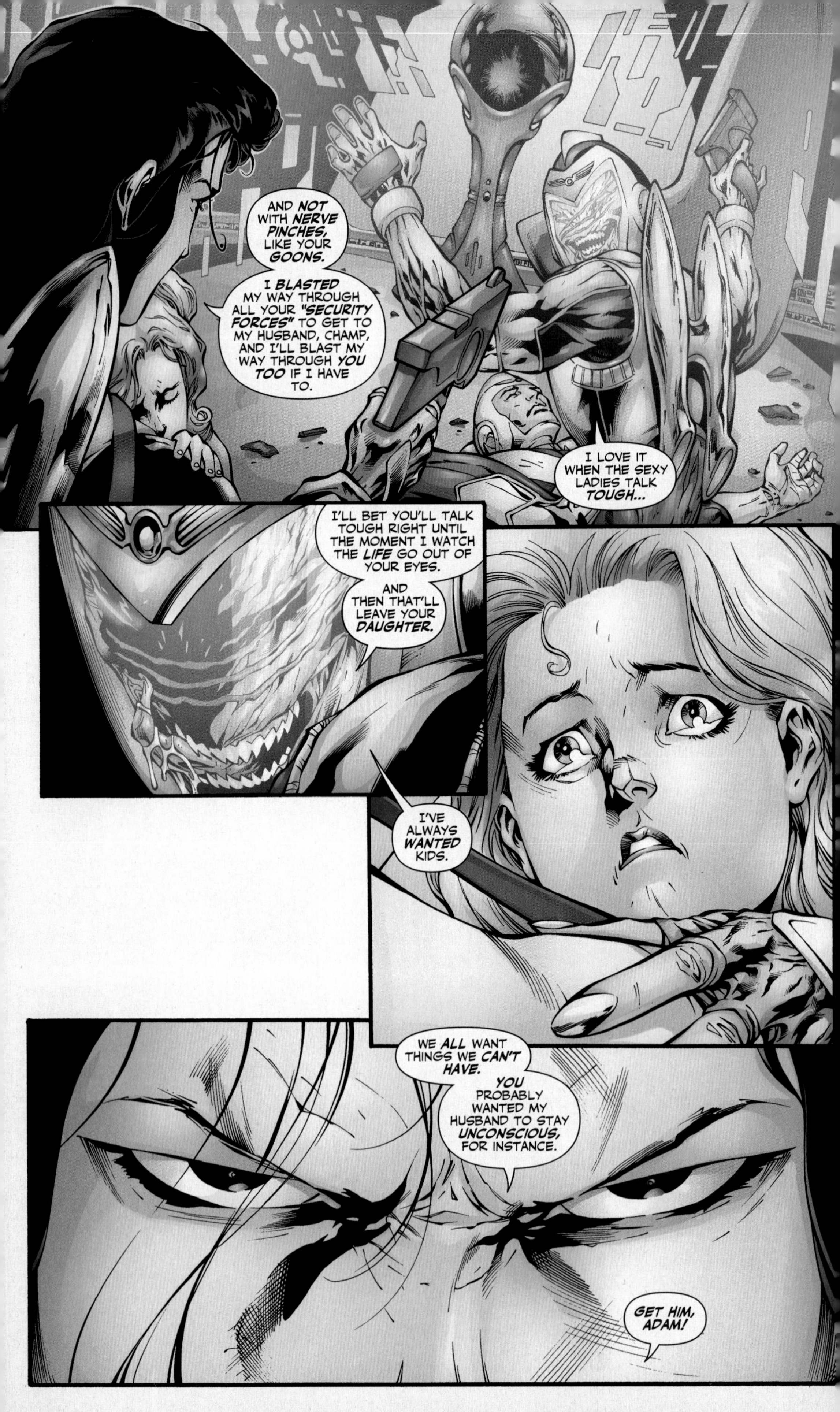
AND NOT WITH NERVE PINCHES, LIKE YOUR GOONS.
I BLASTED MY WAY THROUGH ALL YOUR "SECURITY FORCES" TO GET TO MY HUSBAND, CHAMP, AND I'LL BLAST MY WAY THROUGH YOU TOO IF I HAVE TO.
I LOVE IT WHEN THE SEXY LADIES TALK TOUGH...
I'LL BET YOU'LL TALK TOUGH RIGHT UNTIL THE MOMENT I WATCH THE LIFE GO OUT OF YOUR EYES.
AND THEN THAT'LL LEAVE YOUR DAUGHTER.
I'VE ALWAYS WANTED KIDS.
WE ALL WANT THINGS WE CAN'T HAVE.
YOU PROBABLY WANTED MY HUSBAND TO STAY UNCONSCIOUS, FOR INSTANCE.
GET HIM, ADAM!

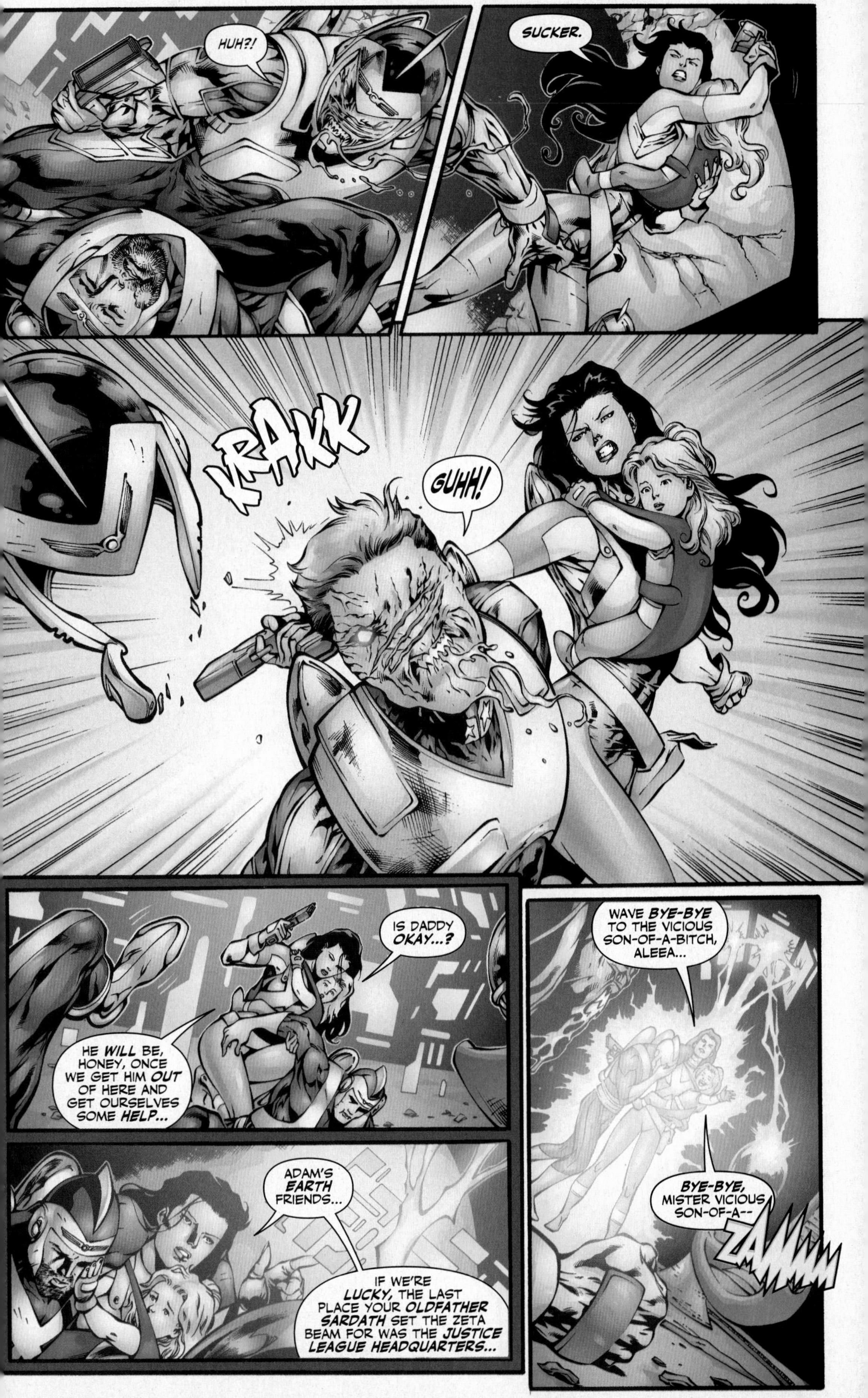
HUH?!
SUCKER.
KRAKK
GUHH!
IS DADDY OKAY...?
HE WILL BE, HONEY, ONCE WE GET HIM OUT OF HERE AND GET OURSELVES SOME HELP...
ADAM'S EARTH FRIENDS...
IF WE'RE LUCKY, THE LAST PLACE YOUR OLDFATHER SARDATH SET THE ZETA BEAM FOR WAS THE JUSTICE LEAGUE HEADQUARTERS...
WAVE BYE-BYE TO THE VICIOUS SON-OF-A-BITCH, ALEEA...
BYE-BYE, MISTER VICIOUS SON-OF-A--
ZAMMM

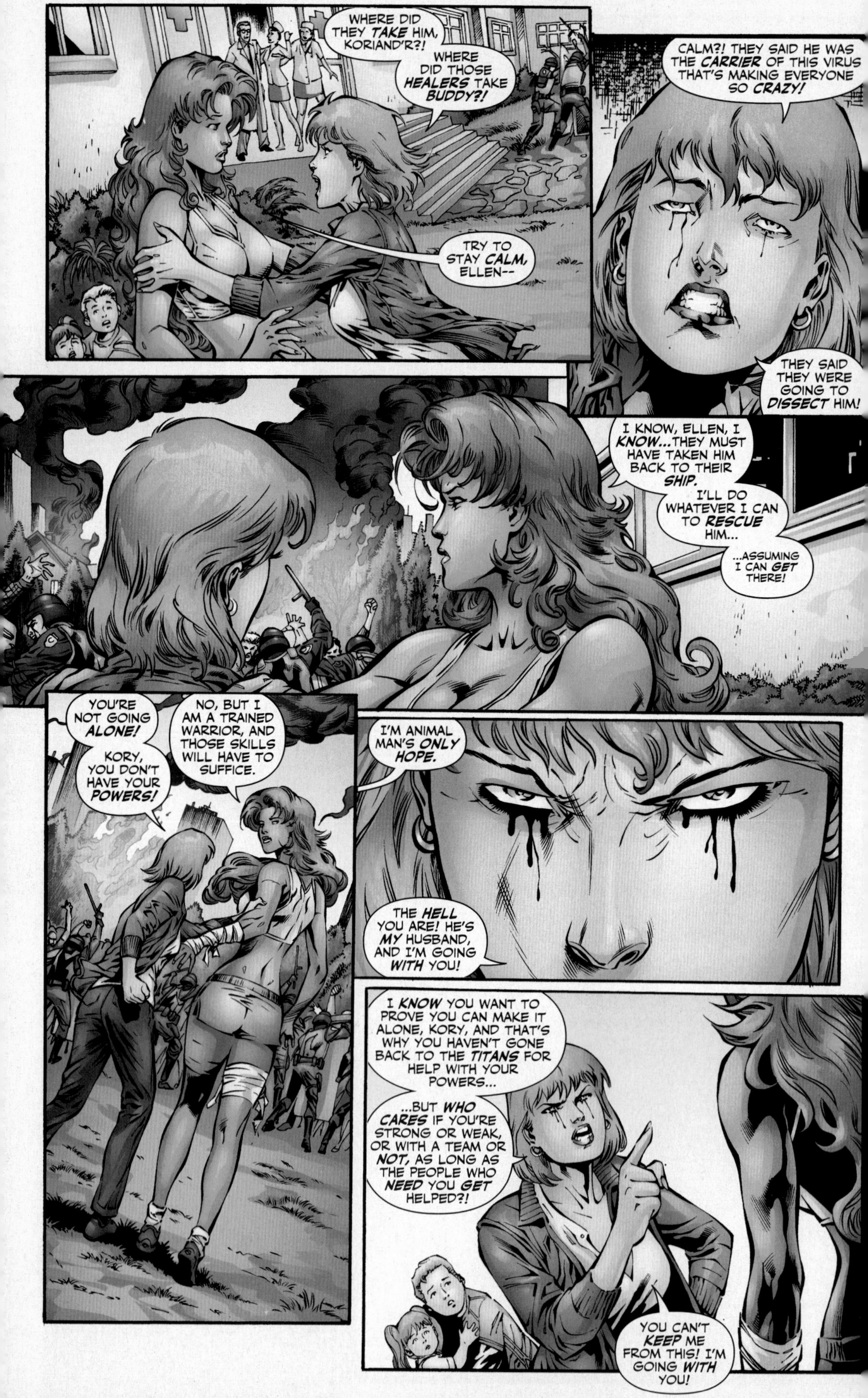
WHERE DID THEY TAKE HIM, KORIAND'R?!
WHERE DID THOSE HEALERS TAKE BUDDY?!
TRY TO STAY CALM, ELLEN--
CALM?! THEY SAID HE WAS THE CARRIER OF THIS VIRUS THAT'S MAKING EVERYONE SO CRAZY!
THEY SAID THEY WERE GOING TO DISSECT HIM!
I KNOW, ELLEN, I KNOW... THEY MUST HAVE TAKEN HIM BACK TO THEIR SHIP.
I'LL DO WHATEVER I CAN TO RESCUE HIM...
...ASSUMING I CAN GET THERE!
YOU'RE NOT GOING ALONE!
KORY, YOU DON'T HAVE YOUR POWERS!
NO, BUT I AM A TRAINED WARRIOR, AND THOSE SKILLS WILL HAVE TO SUFFICE.
I'M ANIMAL MAN'S ONLY HOPE.
THE HELL YOU ARE! HE'S MY HUSBAND, AND I'M GOING WITH YOU!
I KNOW YOU WANT TO PROVE YOU CAN MAKE IT ALONE, KORY, AND THAT'S WHY YOU HAVEN'T GONE BACK TO THE TITANS FOR HELP WITH YOUR POWERS...
...BUT WHO CARES IF YOU'RE STRONG OR WEAK, OR WITH A TEAM OR NOT, AS LONG AS THE PEOPLE WHO NEED YOU GET HELPED?!
YOU CAN'T KEEP ME FROM THIS! I'M GOING WITH YOU!

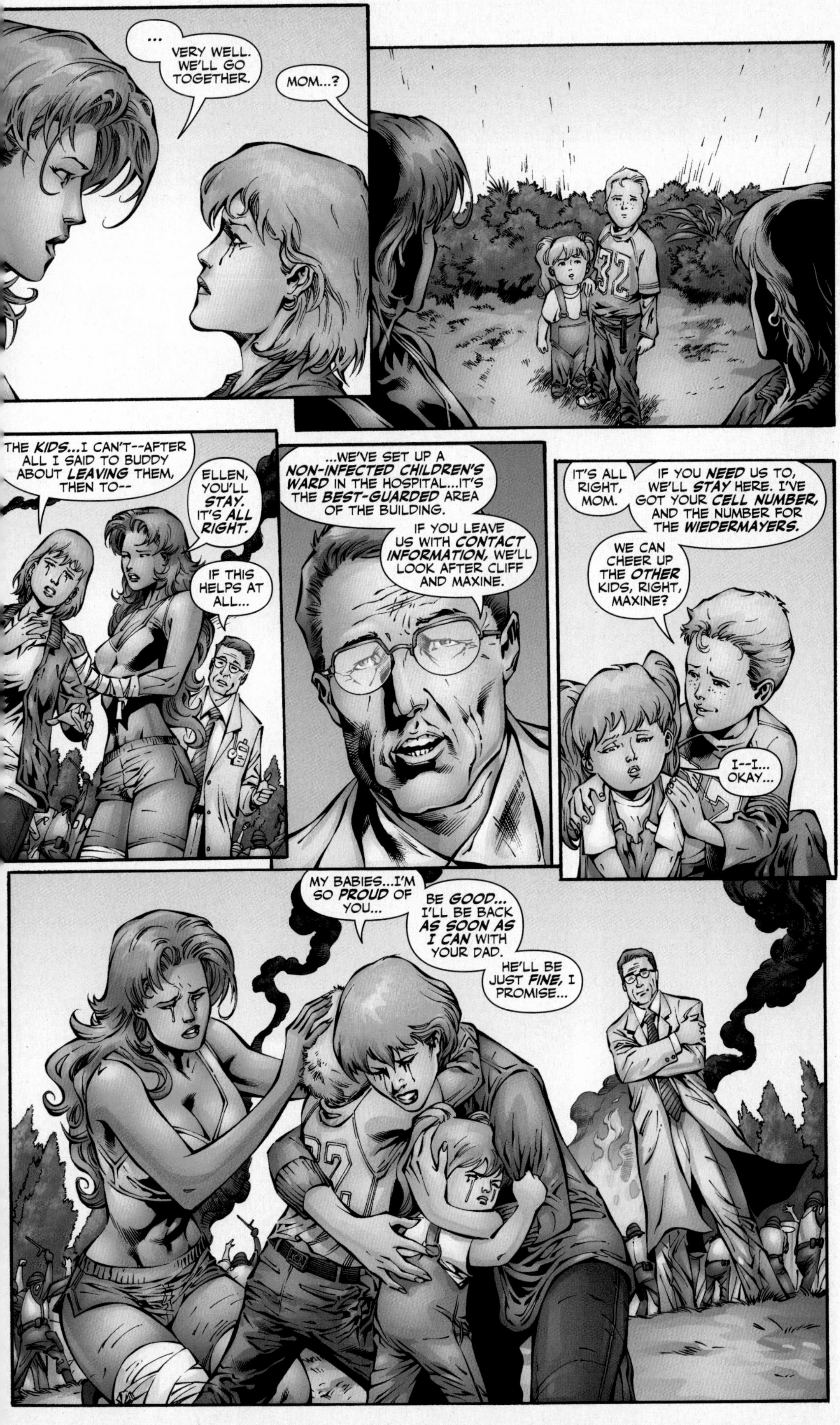
...
VERY WELL. WE'LL GO TOGETHER.
MOM...?
THE KIDS...I CAN'T--AFTER ALL I SAID TO BUDDY ABOUT LEAVING THEM, THEN TO--
ELLEN, YOU'LL STAY. IT'S ALL RIGHT.
IF THIS HELPS AT ALL...
...WE'VE SET UP A NON-INFECTED CHILDREN'S WARD IN THE HOSPITAL...IT'S THE BEST-GUARDED AREA OF THE BUILDING.
IF YOU LEAVE US WITH CONTACT INFORMATION, WE'LL LOOK AFTER CLIFF AND MAXINE.
IT'S ALL RIGHT, MOM.
IF YOU NEED US TO, WE'LL STAY HERE. I'VE GOT YOUR CELL NUMBER, AND THE NUMBER FOR THE WIEDERMAYERS.
WE CAN CHEER UP THE OTHER KIDS, RIGHT, MAXINE?
I--I... OKAY...
MY BABIES...I'M SO PROUD OF YOU...
BE GOOD... I'LL BE BACK AS SOON AS I CAN WITH YOUR DAD.
HE'LL BE JUST FINE, I PROMISE...

THOUGH A *CARRIER* OF THE VIRUS, HE DOES NOT SHOW *SYMPTOMS.*

PATIENT ZERO APPEARS TO BE *REVIVING.* SHALL WE *RE-ANESTHETIZE?*

NOT *REQUIRED.* WE CANNOT AFFORD THE *TIME* IT WOULD TAKE. THE EQUIPMENT IS *PREPARED* AND *STANDING BY.*

THE *OPERATING THEATER* IS PREPARED AND READY.

WHA-- WHERE AM I...?

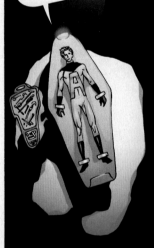

UNNNHH...

PREPARE FOR *DISSECTION.*

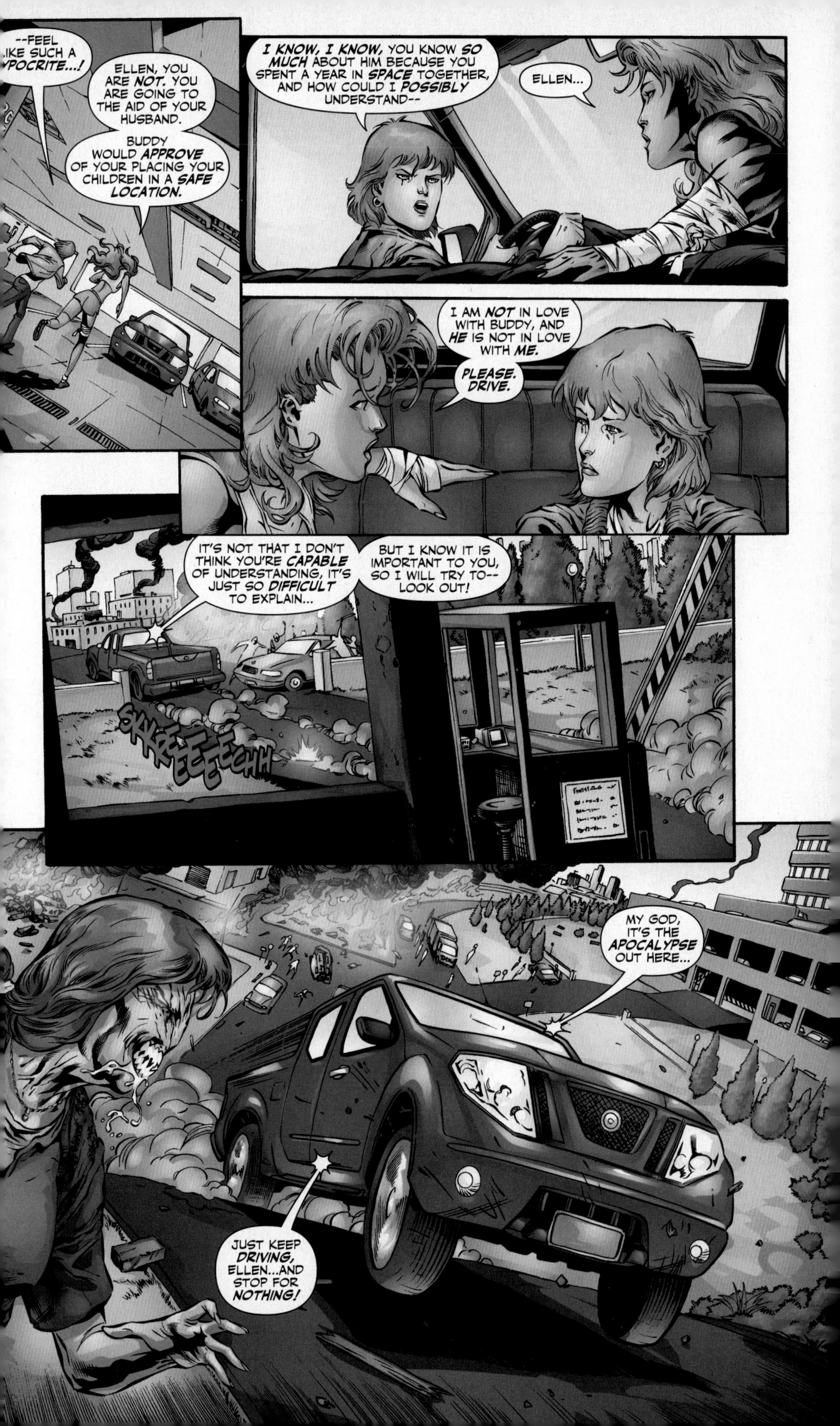
--FEEL
LIKE SUCH A
HYPOCRITE...!
ELLEN, YOU ARE NOT. YOU ARE GOING TO THE AID OF YOUR HUSBAND.
BUDDY WOULD APPROVE OF YOUR PLACING YOUR CHILDREN IN A SAFE LOCATION.
I KNOW, I KNOW, YOU KNOW SO MUCH ABOUT HIM BECAUSE YOU SPENT A YEAR IN SPACE TOGETHER, AND HOW COULD I POSSIBLY UNDERSTAND--
ELLEN...
I AM NOT IN LOVE WITH BUDDY, AND HE IS NOT IN LOVE WITH ME.
PLEASE. DRIVE.
IT'S NOT THAT I DON'T THINK YOU'RE CAPABLE OF UNDERSTANDING, IT'S JUST SO DIFFICULT TO EXPLAIN...
BUT I KNOW IT IS IMPORTANT TO YOU, SO I WILL TRY TO-- LOOK OUT!
SKKREEEEEECHH
MY GOD, IT'S THE APOCALYPSE OUT HERE...
JUST KEEP DRIVING, ELLEN...AND STOP FOR NOTHING!

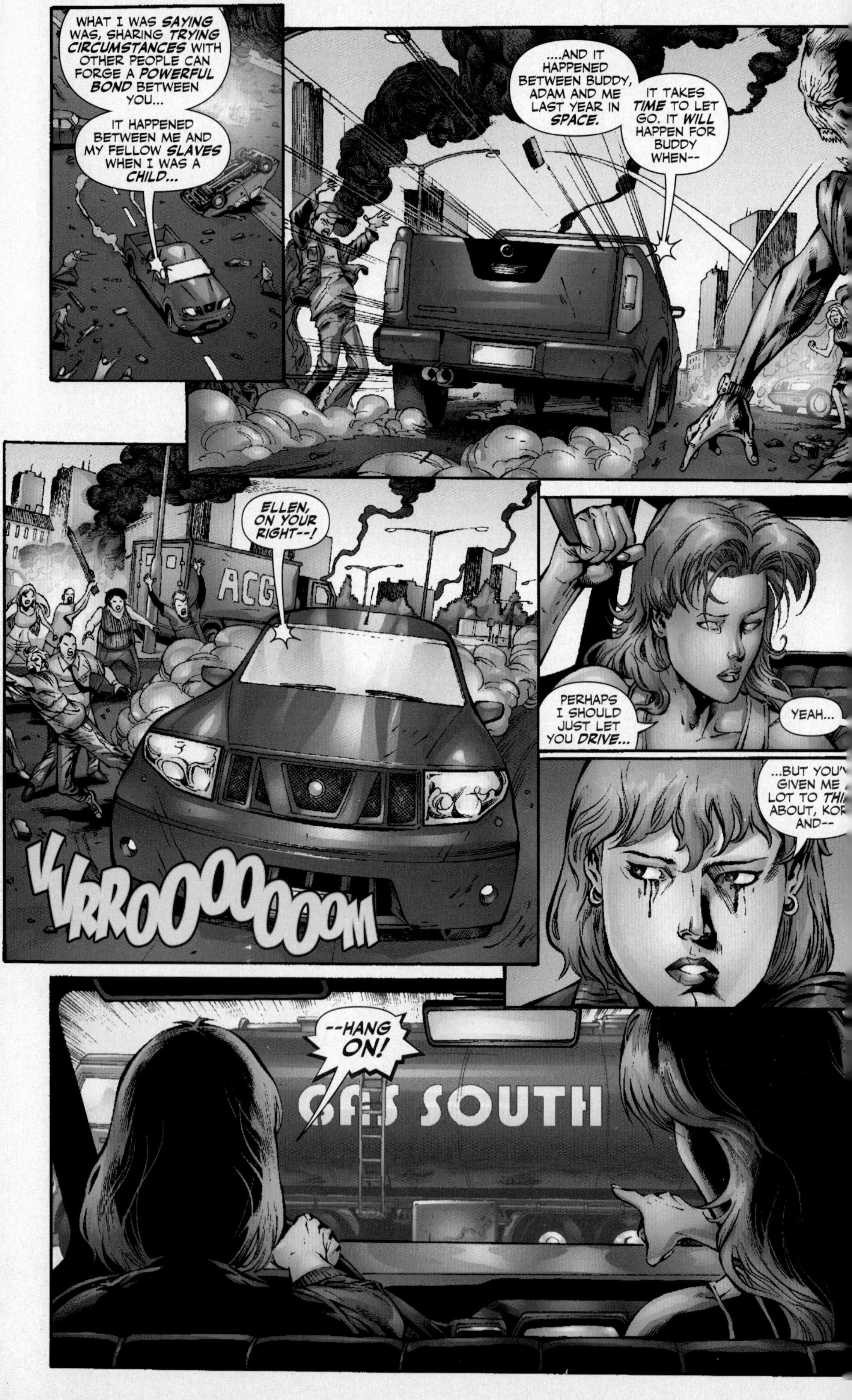
WHAT I WAS SAYING WAS, SHARING TRYING CIRCUMSTANCES WITH OTHER PEOPLE CAN FORGE A POWERFUL BOND BETWEEN YOU...
IT HAPPENED BETWEEN ME AND MY FELLOW SLAVES WHEN I WAS A CHILD...
....AND IT HAPPENED BETWEEN BUDDY, ADAM AND ME LAST YEAR IN SPACE.
IT TAKES TIME TO LET GO. IT WILL HAPPEN FOR BUDDY WHEN--
ELLEN, ON YOUR RIGHT--!
ACG
VVRROOOOOOOM
PERHAPS I SHOULD JUST LET YOU DRIVE...
YEAH...
...BUT YOU'
GIVEN ME
LOT TO THI
ABOUT, KOR
AND--
--HANG ON!
GAS SOUTH

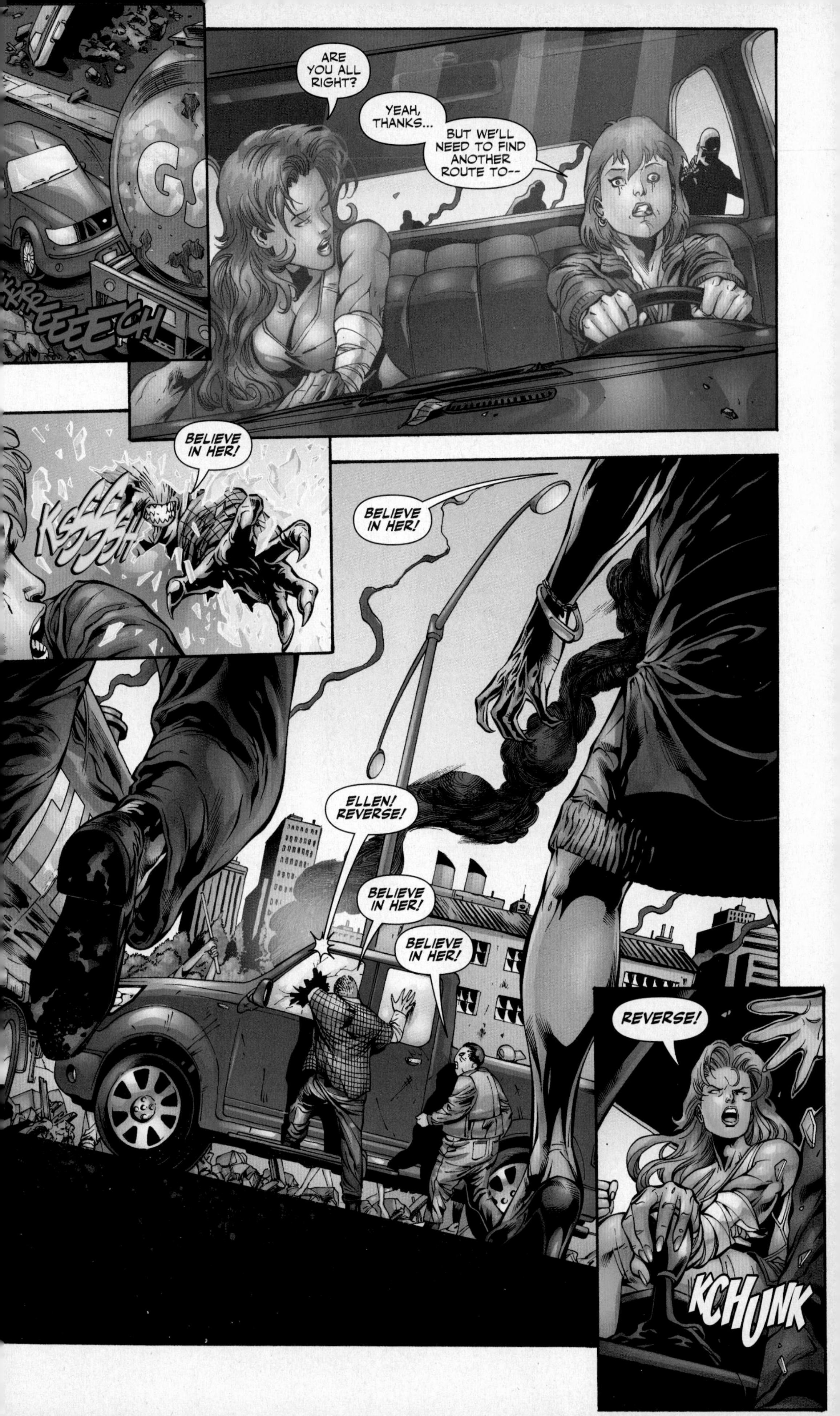
SKREEEEECH
GO
ARE YOU ALL RIGHT?
YEAH, THANKS...
BUT WE'LL NEED TO FIND ANOTHER ROUTE TO--
BELIEVE IN HER!
KSSSSH
BELIEVE IN HER!
ELLEN! REVERSE!
BELIEVE IN HER!
BELIEVE IN HER!
REVERSE!
KCHUNK

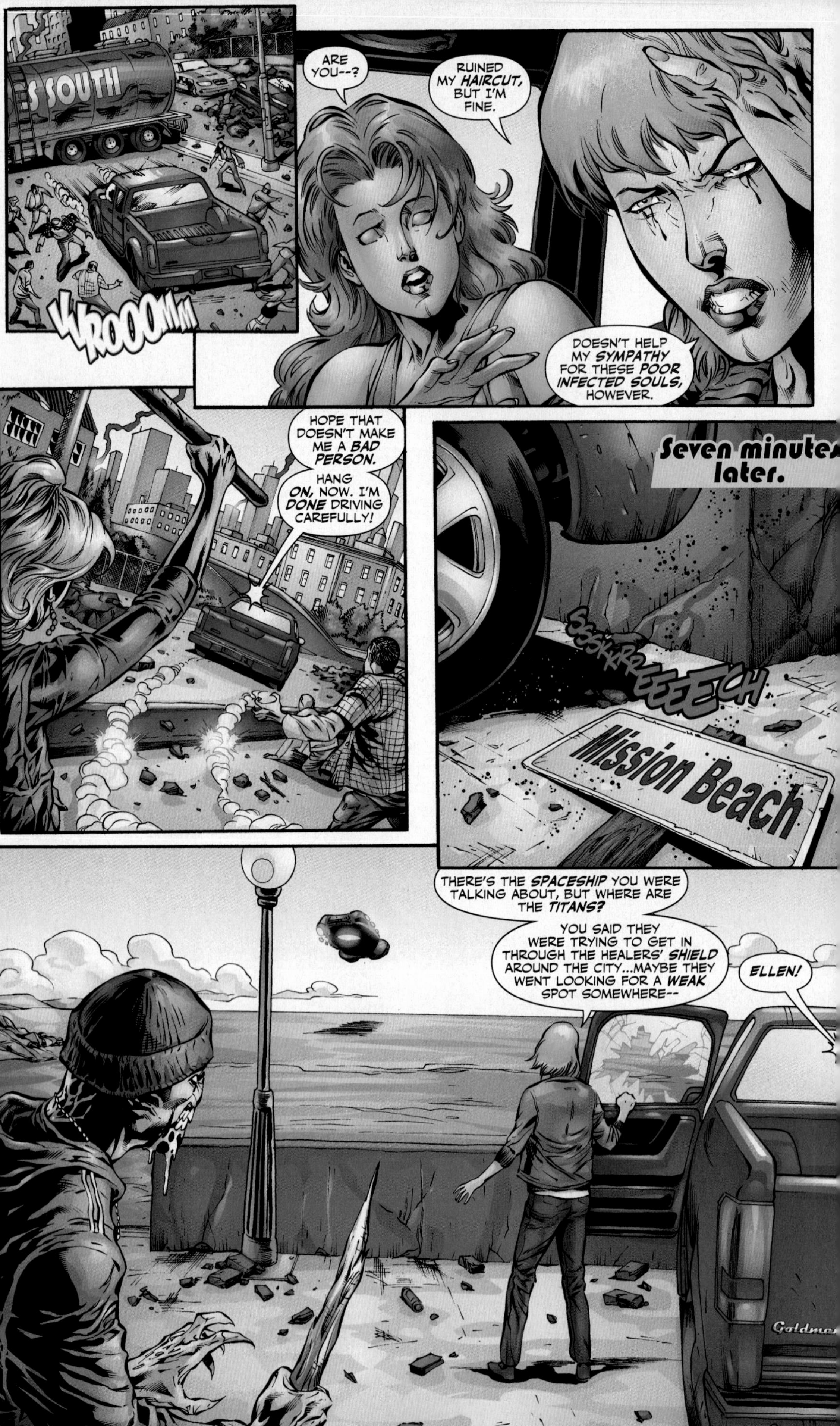
S SOUTH
VROOOMM
ARE YOU--?
RUINED MY HAIRCUT, BUT I'M FINE.
DOESN'T HELP MY SYMPATHY FOR THESE POOR INFECTED SOULS, HOWEVER.
HOPE THAT DOESN'T MAKE ME A BAD PERSON.
HANG ON, NOW. I'M DONE DRIVING CAREFULLY!
Seven minutes later.
SSSKKRREEEEECH
Mission Beach
THERE'S THE SPACESHIP YOU WERE TALKING ABOUT, BUT WHERE ARE THE TITANS?
YOU SAID THEY WERE TRYING TO GET IN THROUGH THE HEALERS' SHIELD AROUND THE CITY...MAYBE THEY WENT LOOKING FOR A WEAK SPOT SOMEWHERE--
ELLEN!

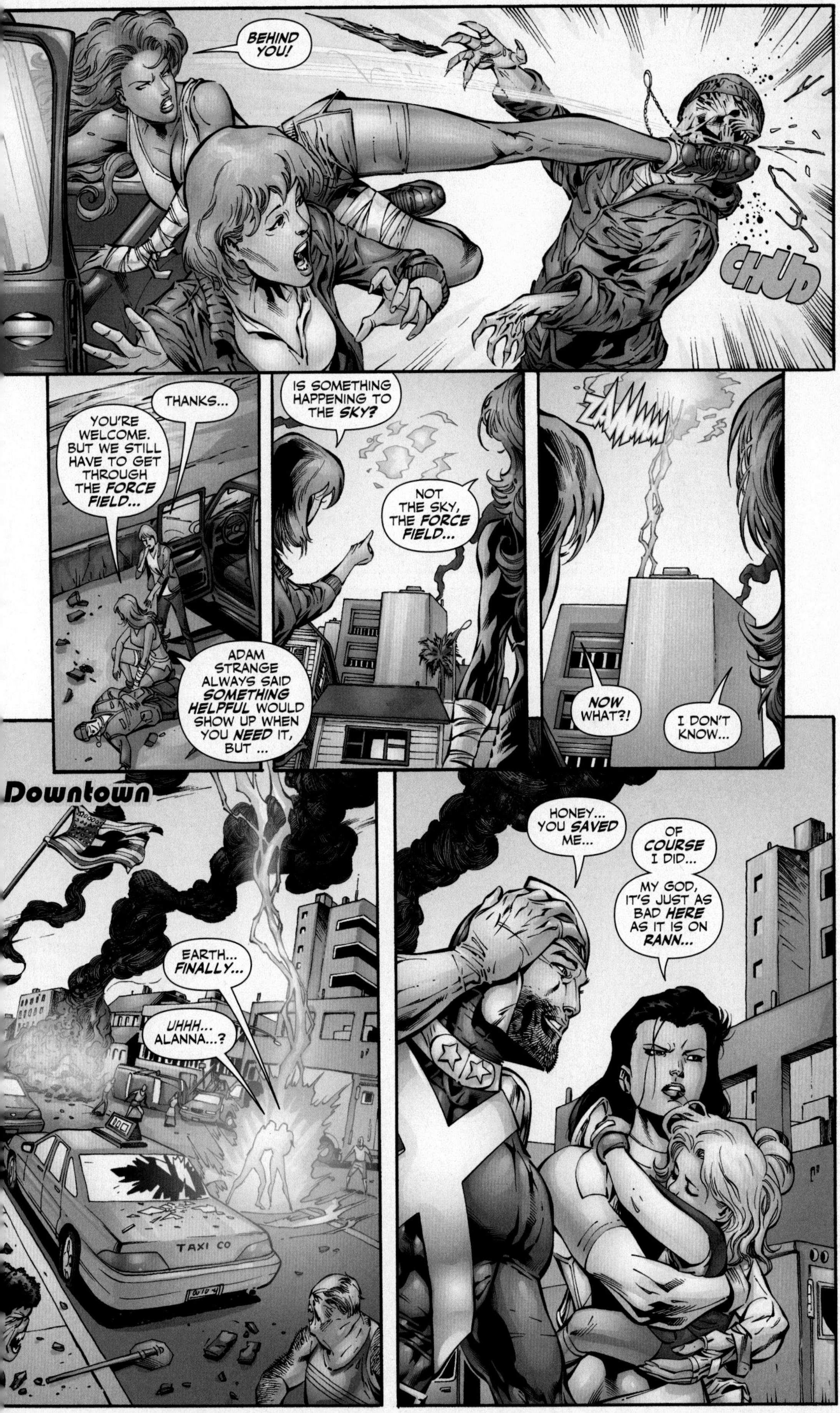
BEHIND YOU!
CHUD
THANKS...
YOU'RE WELCOME. BUT WE STILL HAVE TO GET THROUGH THE FORCE FIELD...
ADAM STRANGE ALWAYS SAID SOMETHING HELPFUL WOULD SHOW UP WHEN YOU NEED IT, BUT ...
IS SOMETHING HAPPENING TO THE SKY?
NOT THE SKY, THE FORCE FIELD...
ZAMMM
NOW WHAT?!
I DON'T KNOW...
Downtown
EARTH... FINALLY...
UHHH... ALANNA...?
TAXI CO
HONEY... YOU SAVED ME...
OF COURSE I DID...
MY GOD, IT'S JUST AS BAD HERE AS IT IS ON RANN...

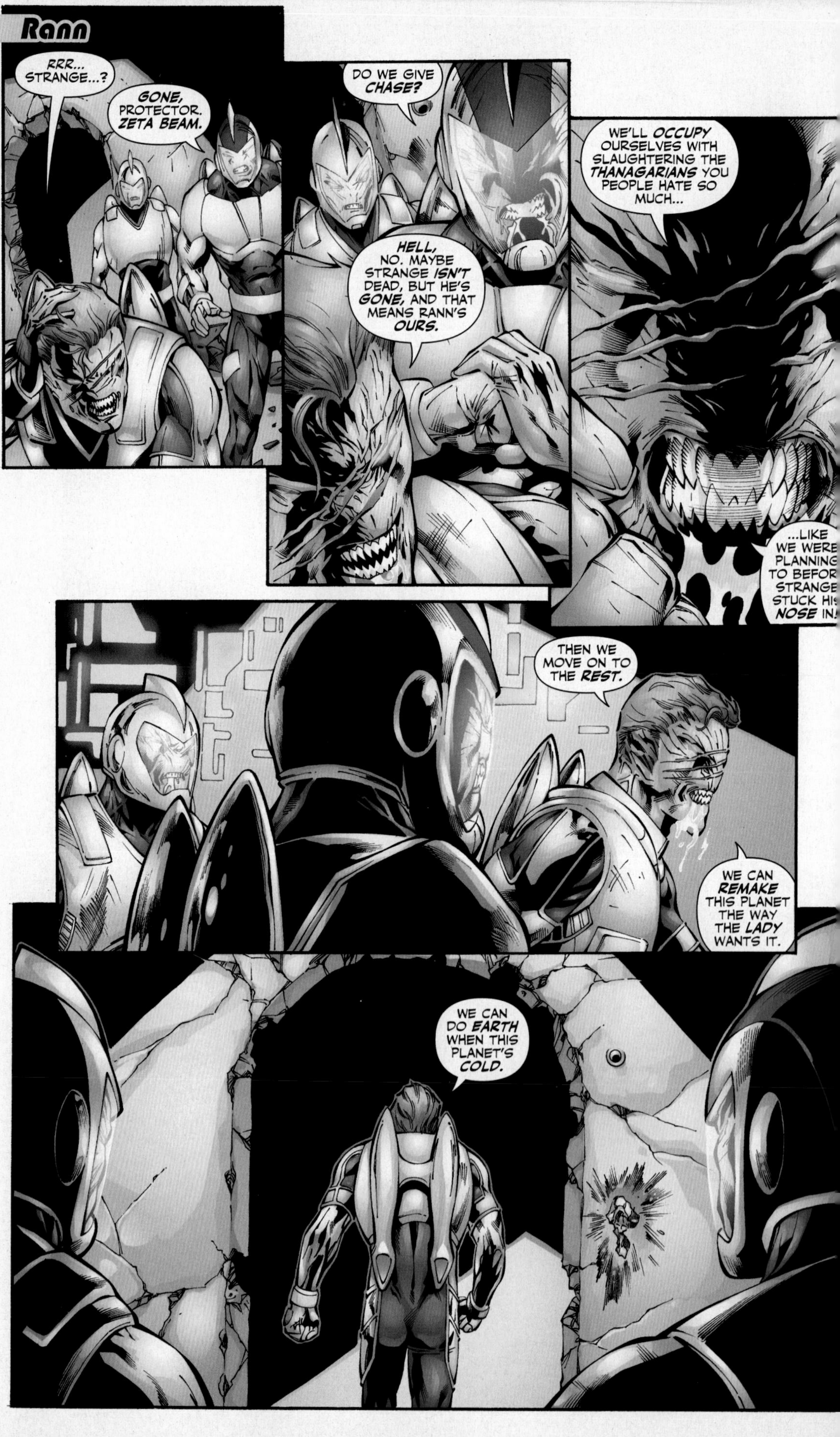
Rann
RRR... STRANGE...?
GONE, PROTECTOR. ZETA BEAM.
DO WE GIVE CHASE?
HELL, NO. MAYBE STRANGE ISN'T DEAD, BUT HE'S GONE, AND THAT MEANS RANN'S OURS.
WE'LL OCCUPY OURSELVES WITH SLAUGHTERING THE THANAGARIANS YOU PEOPLE HATE SO MUCH...
...LIKE WE WERE PLANNING TO BEFOR STRANGE STUCK HIS NOSE IN.
THEN WE MOVE ON TO THE REST.
WE CAN REMAKE THIS PLANET THE WAY THE LADY WANTS IT.
WE CAN DO EARTH WHEN THIS PLANET'S COLD.

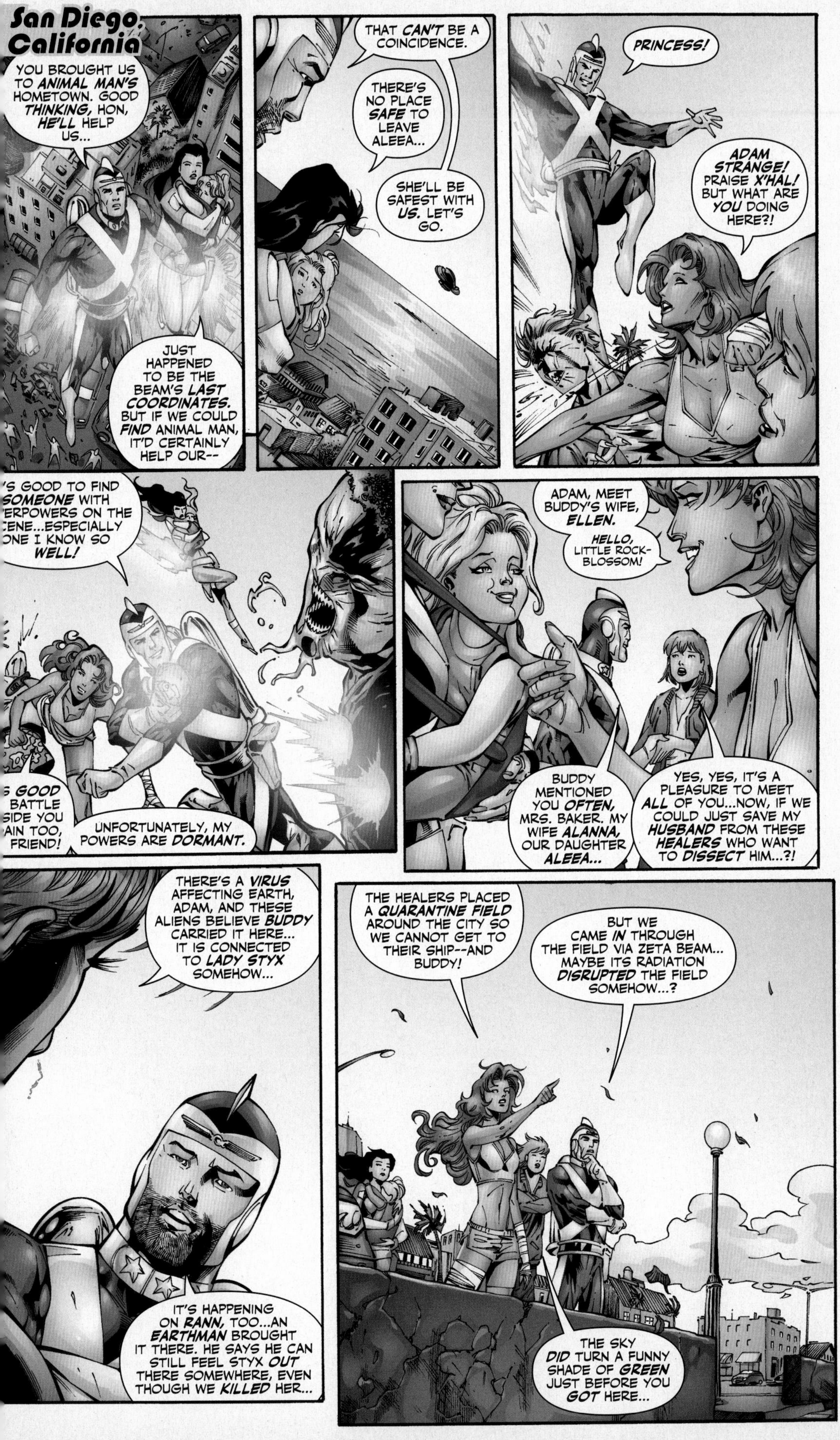
San Diego, California
YOU BROUGHT US TO ANIMAL MAN'S HOMETOWN. GOOD THINKING, HON, HE'LL HELP US...
JUST HAPPENED TO BE THE BEAM'S LAST COORDINATES. BUT IF WE COULD FIND ANIMAL MAN, IT'D CERTAINLY HELP OUR--
THAT CAN'T BE A COINCIDENCE.
THERE'S NO PLACE SAFE TO LEAVE ALEEA...
SHE'LL BE SAFEST WITH US. LET'S GO.
PRINCESS!
ADAM STRANGE! PRAISE X'HAL! BUT WHAT ARE YOU DOING HERE?!
'S GOOD TO FIND SOMEONE WITH ERPOWERS ON THE CENE...ESPECIALLY ONE I KNOW SO WELL!
S GOOD BATTLE SIDE YOU AIN TOO, FRIEND!
UNFORTUNATELY, MY POWERS ARE DORMANT.
ADAM, MEET BUDDY'S WIFE, ELLEN.
HELLO, LITTLE ROCK-BLOSSOM!
BUDDY MENTIONED YOU OFTEN, MRS. BAKER. MY WIFE ALANNA, OUR DAUGHTER ALEEA...
YES, YES, IT'S A PLEASURE TO MEET ALL OF YOU...NOW, IF WE COULD JUST SAVE MY HUSBAND FROM THESE HEALERS WHO WANT TO DISSECT HIM...?!
THERE'S A VIRUS AFFECTING EARTH, ADAM, AND THESE ALIENS BELIEVE BUDDY CARRIED IT HERE... IT IS CONNECTED TO LADY STYX SOMEHOW...
IT'S HAPPENING ON RANN, TOO...AN EARTHMAN BROUGHT IT THERE. HE SAYS HE CAN STILL FEEL STYX OUT THERE SOMEWHERE, EVEN THOUGH WE KILLED HER...
THE HEALERS PLACED A QUARANTINE FIELD AROUND THE CITY SO WE CANNOT GET TO THEIR SHIP--AND BUDDY!
BUT WE CAME IN THROUGH THE FIELD VIA ZETA BEAM... MAYBE ITS RADIATION DISRUPTED THE FIELD SOMEHOW...?
THE SKY DID TURN A FUNNY SHADE OF GREEN JUST BEFORE YOU GOT HERE...

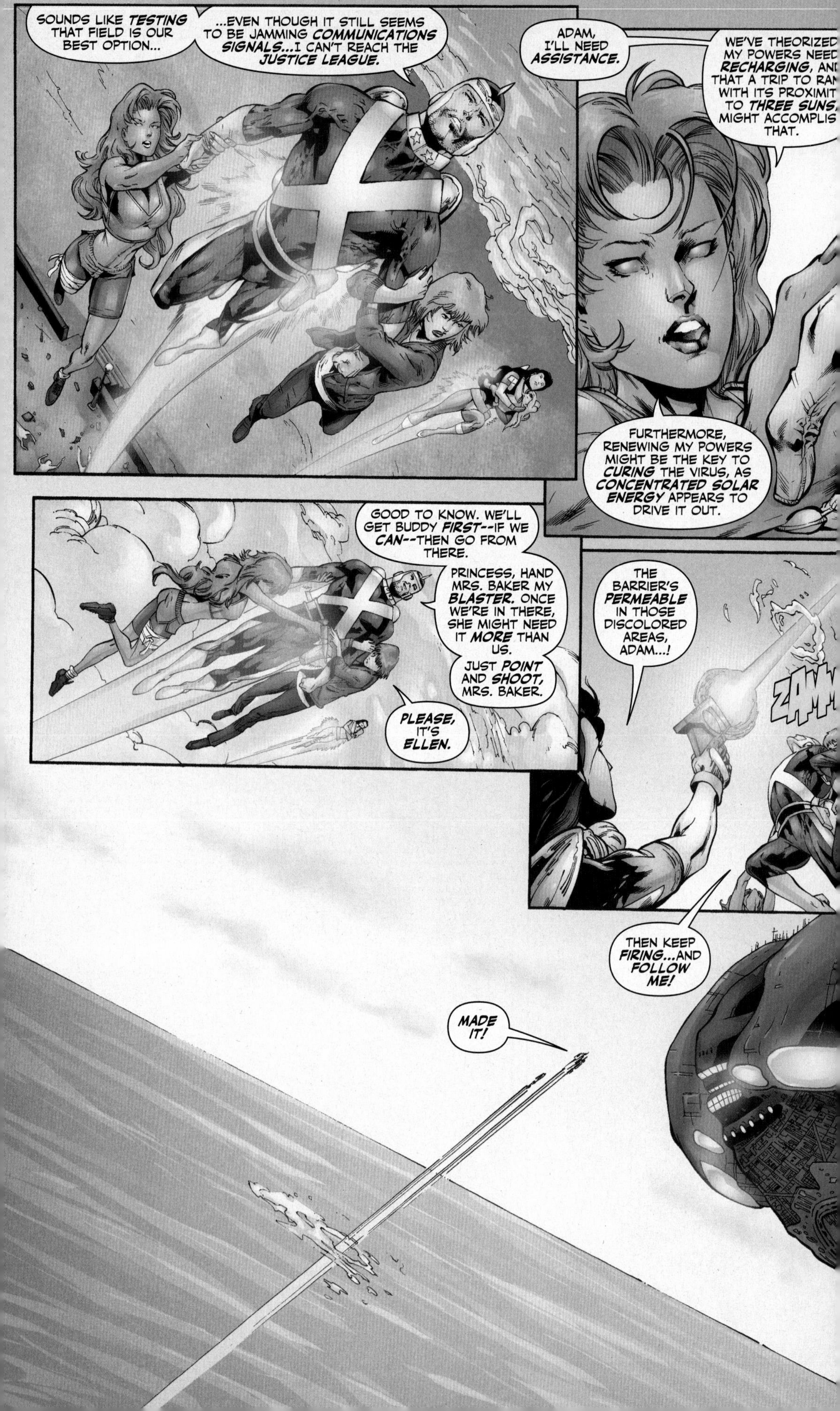
SOUNDS LIKE TESTING THAT FIELD IS OUR BEST OPTION...
...EVEN THOUGH IT STILL SEEMS TO BE JAMMING COMMUNICATIONS SIGNALS...I CAN'T REACH THE JUSTICE LEAGUE.
ADAM, I'LL NEED ASSISTANCE.
WE'VE THEORIZED MY POWERS NEED RECHARGING, AND THAT A TRIP TO RAN WITH ITS PROXIMIT TO THREE SUNS, MIGHT ACCOMPLIS THAT.
FURTHERMORE, RENEWING MY POWERS MIGHT BE THE KEY TO CURING THE VIRUS, AS CONCENTRATED SOLAR ENERGY APPEARS TO DRIVE IT OUT.
GOOD TO KNOW. WE'LL GET BUDDY FIRST--IF WE CAN--THEN GO FROM THERE.
PRINCESS, HAND MRS. BAKER MY BLASTER. ONCE WE'RE IN THERE, SHE MIGHT NEED IT MORE THAN US.
JUST POINT AND SHOOT, MRS. BAKER.
PLEASE, IT'S ELLEN.
THE BARRIER'S PERMEABLE IN THOSE DISCOLORED AREAS, ADAM...!
THEN KEEP FIRING...AND FOLLOW ME!
MADE IT!

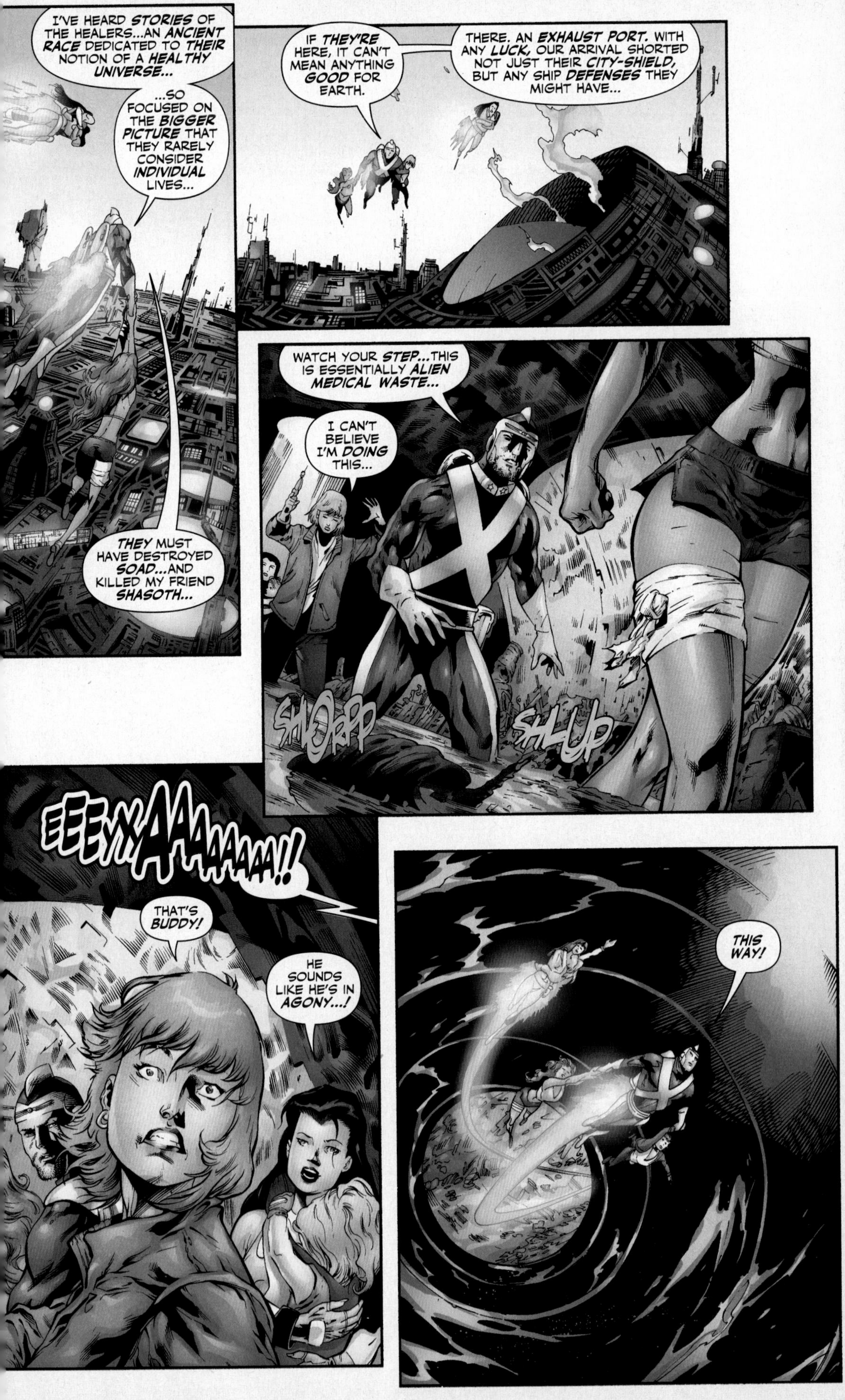

I'VE HEARD STORIES OF THE HEALERS...AN ANCIENT RACE DEDICATED TO THEIR NOTION OF A HEALTHY UNIVERSE...
...SO FOCUSED ON THE BIGGER PICTURE THAT THEY RARELY CONSIDER INDIVIDUAL LIVES...
THEY MUST HAVE DESTROYED SOAD...AND KILLED MY FRIEND SHASOTH...
IF THEY'RE HERE, IT CAN'T MEAN ANYTHING GOOD FOR EARTH.
THERE. AN EXHAUST PORT. WITH ANY LUCK, OUR ARRIVAL SHORTED NOT JUST THEIR CITY-SHIELD, BUT ANY SHIP DEFENSES THEY MIGHT HAVE...
WATCH YOUR STEP...THIS IS ESSENTIALLY ALIEN MEDICAL WASTE...
I CAN'T BELIEVE I'M DOING THIS...
SHLORPP
SHLUP
EEEYYAAAAAAAA!!
THAT'S BUDDY!
HE SOUNDS LIKE HE'S IN AGONY...!
THIS WAY!

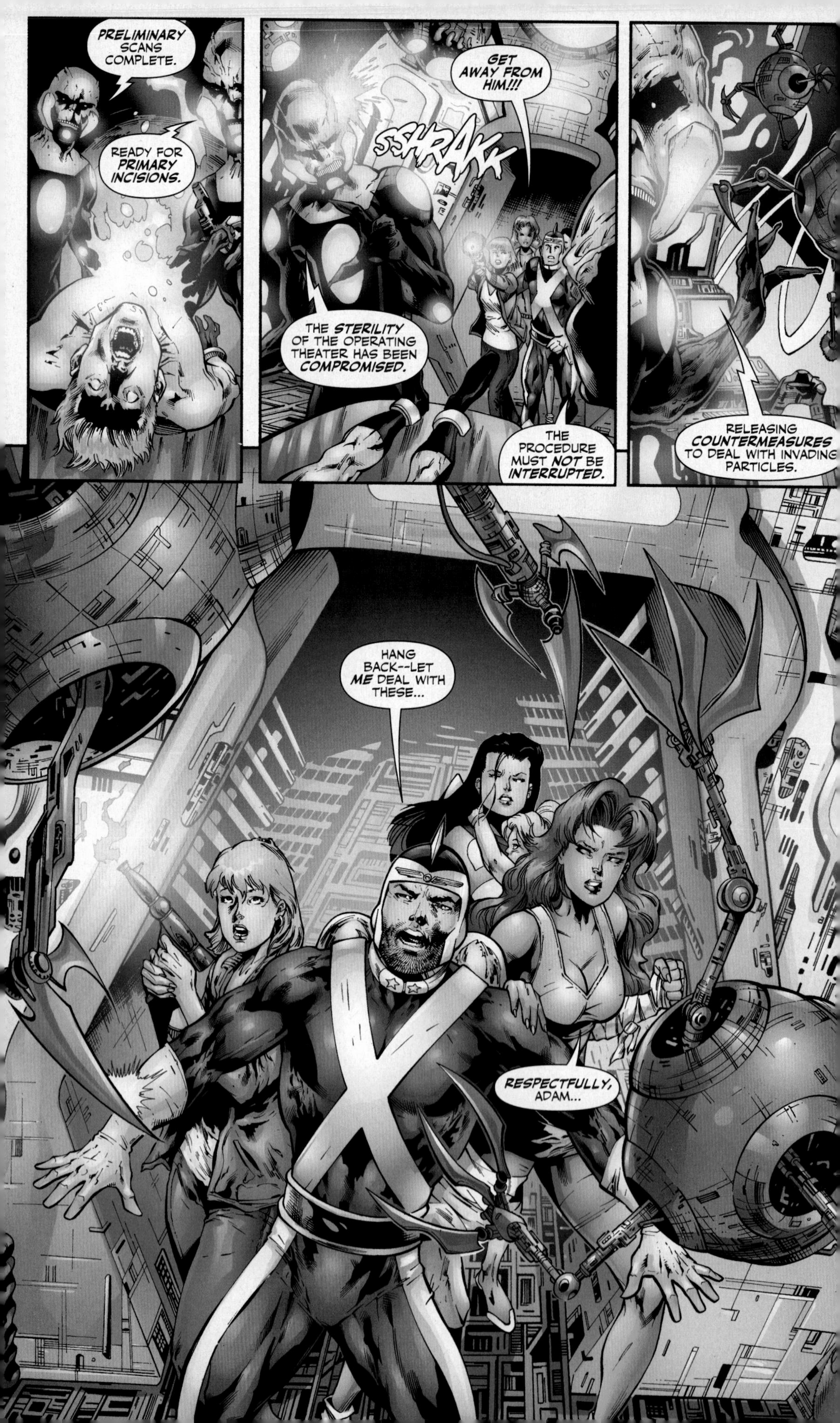
PRELIMINARY SCANS COMPLETE.
READY FOR PRIMARY INCISIONS.
GET AWAY FROM HIM!!!
SSHRAKK
THE STERILITY OF THE OPERATING THEATER HAS BEEN COMPROMISED.
THE PROCEDURE MUST NOT BE INTERRUPTED.
RELEASING COUNTERMEASURES TO DEAL WITH INVADING PARTICLES.
HANG BACK--LET ME DEAL WITH THESE...
RESPECTFULLY, ADAM...

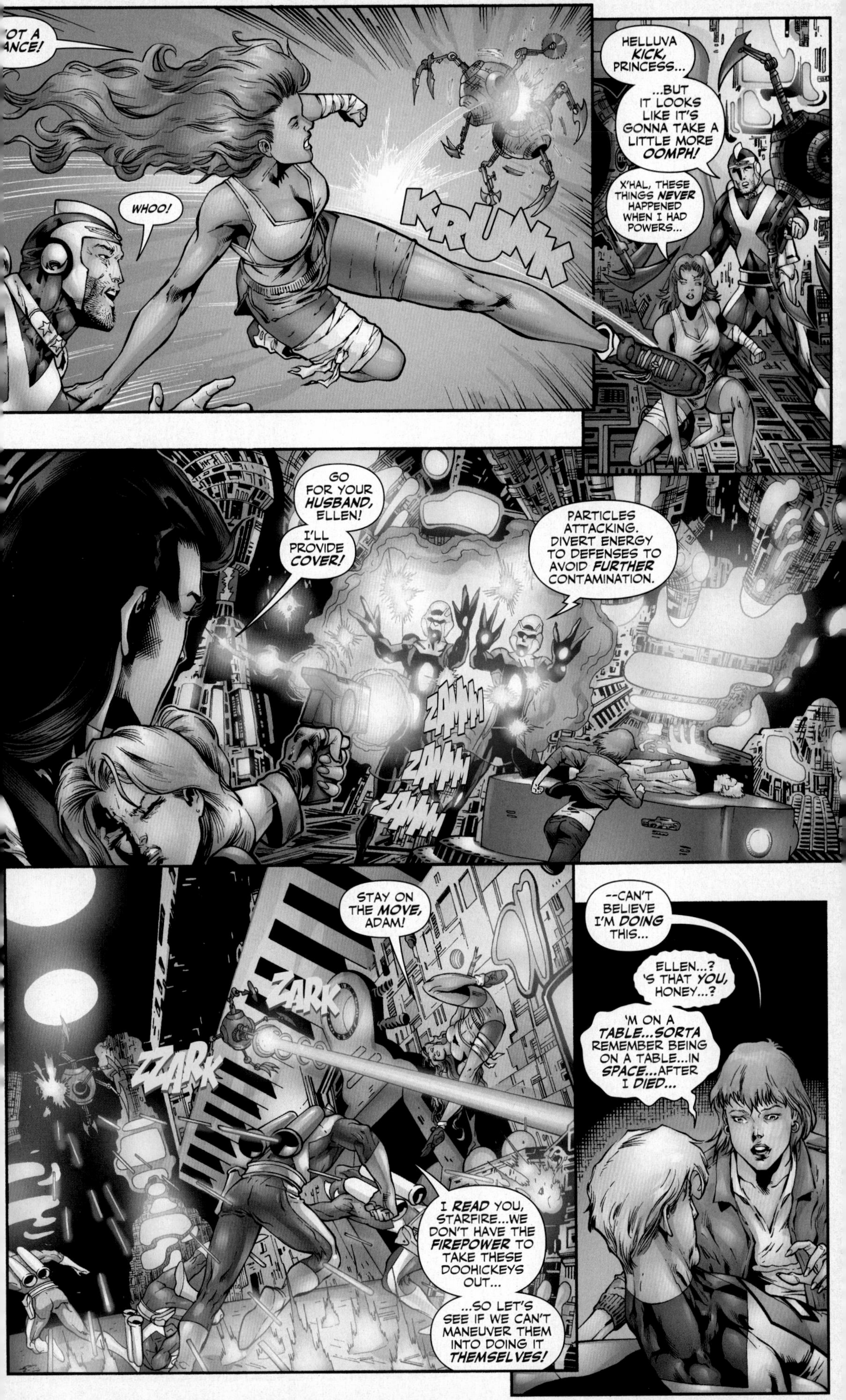

...OT A
...ANCE!
WHOO!
KRUNK
HELLUVA KICK, PRINCESS...
...BUT IT LOOKS LIKE IT'S GONNA TAKE A LITTLE MORE OOMPH!
X'HAL, THESE THINGS NEVER HAPPENED WHEN I HAD POWERS...
GO FOR YOUR HUSBAND, ELLEN!
I'LL PROVIDE COVER!
PARTICLES ATTACKING. DIVERT ENERGY TO DEFENSES TO AVOID FURTHER CONTAMINATION.
ZAMMM
ZAMMM
ZAMMM
STAY ON THE MOVE, ADAM!
ZARK
ZZARK
I READ YOU, STARFIRE...WE DON'T HAVE THE FIREPOWER TO TAKE THESE DOOHICKEYS OUT...
...SO LET'S SEE IF WE CAN'T MANEUVER THEM INTO DOING IT THEMSELVES!
--CAN'T BELIEVE I'M DOING THIS...
ELLEN...? 'S THAT YOU, HONEY...?
'M ON A TABLE...SORTA REMEMBER BEING ON A TABLE...IN SPACE...AFTER I DIED...

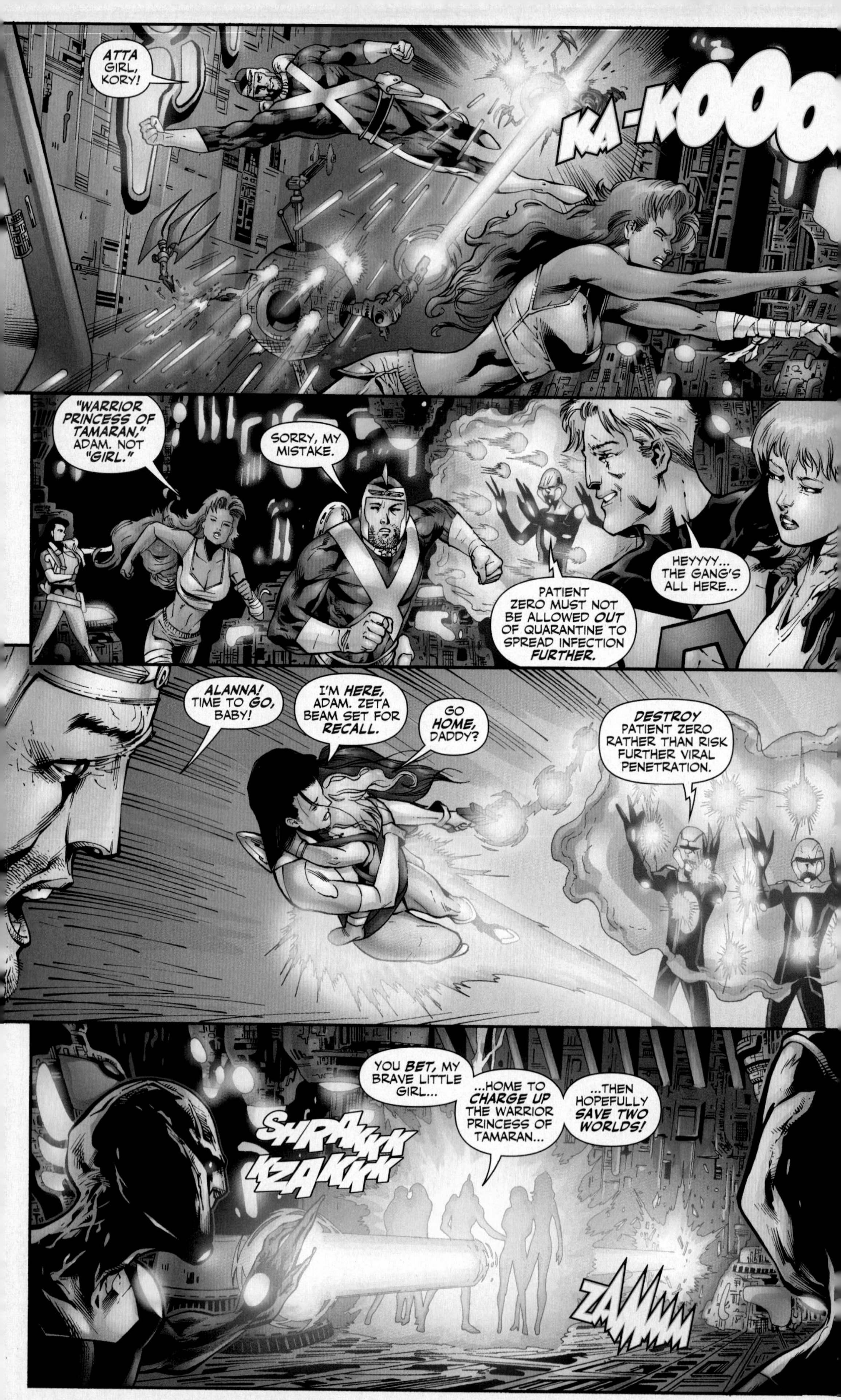
ATTA GIRL, KORY!
KA-KOOOO
"WARRIOR PRINCESS OF TAMARAN," ADAM. NOT "GIRL."
SORRY, MY MISTAKE.
PATIENT ZERO MUST NOT BE ALLOWED OUT OF QUARANTINE TO SPREAD INFECTION FURTHER.
HEYYYY... THE GANG'S ALL HERE...
ALANNA! TIME TO GO, BABY!
I'M HERE, ADAM. ZETA BEAM SET FOR RECALL.
GO HOME, DADDY?
DESTROY PATIENT ZERO RATHER THAN RISK FURTHER VIRAL PENETRATION.
YOU BET, MY BRAVE LITTLE GIRL...
...HOME TO CHARGE UP THE WARRIOR PRINCESS OF TAMARAN...
...THEN HOPEFULLY SAVE TWO WORLDS!
SHRAKKK
KZAKKK
ZAMMM

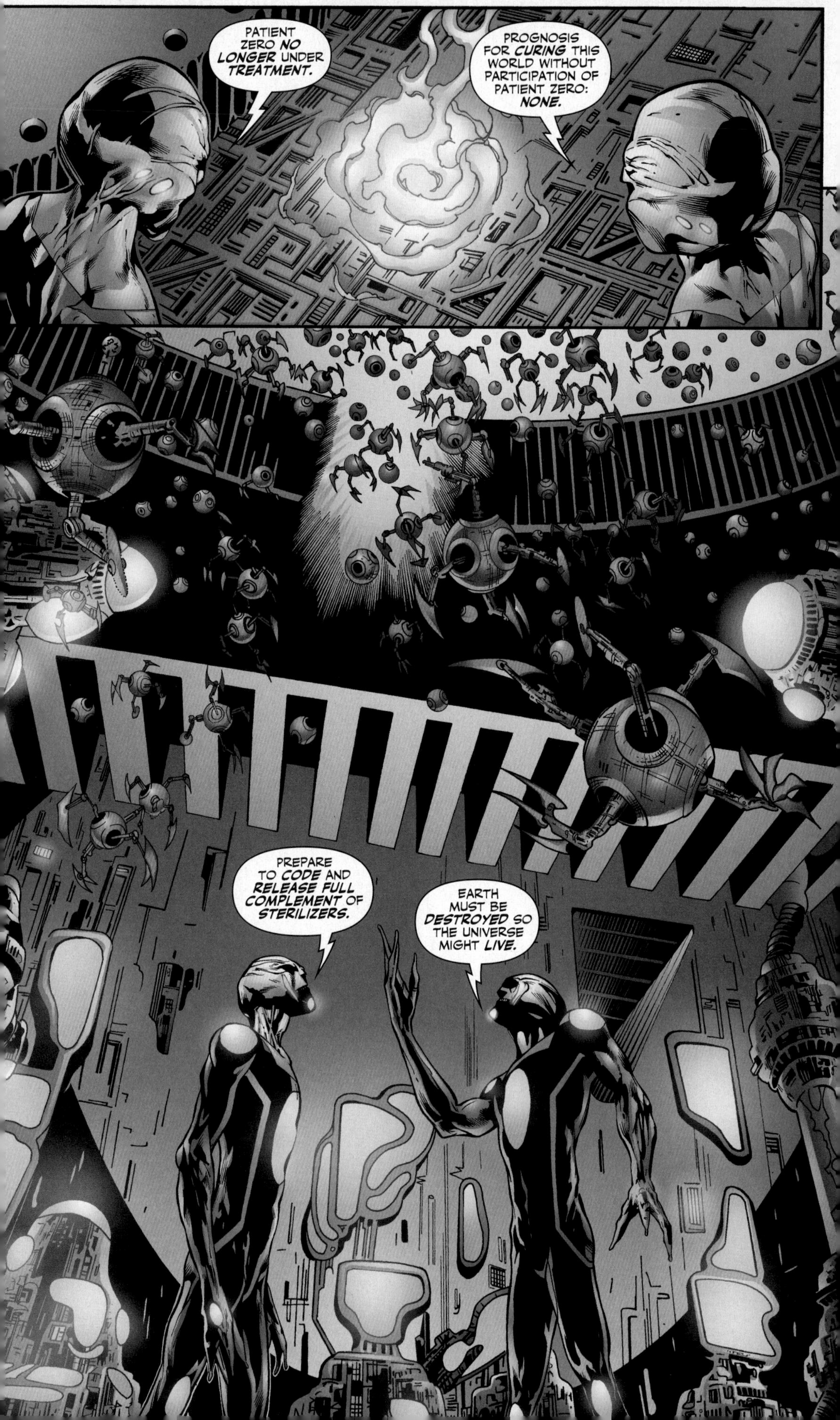
PATIENT ZERO NO LONGER UNDER TREATMENT.
PROGNOSIS FOR CURING THIS WORLD WITHOUT PARTICIPATION OF PATIENT ZERO: NONE.
PREPARE TO CODE AND RELEASE FULL COMPLEMENT OF STERILIZERS.
EARTH MUST BE DESTROYED SO THE UNIVERSE MIGHT LIVE.

CHAPTER SEVEN

TO SERVE RANN

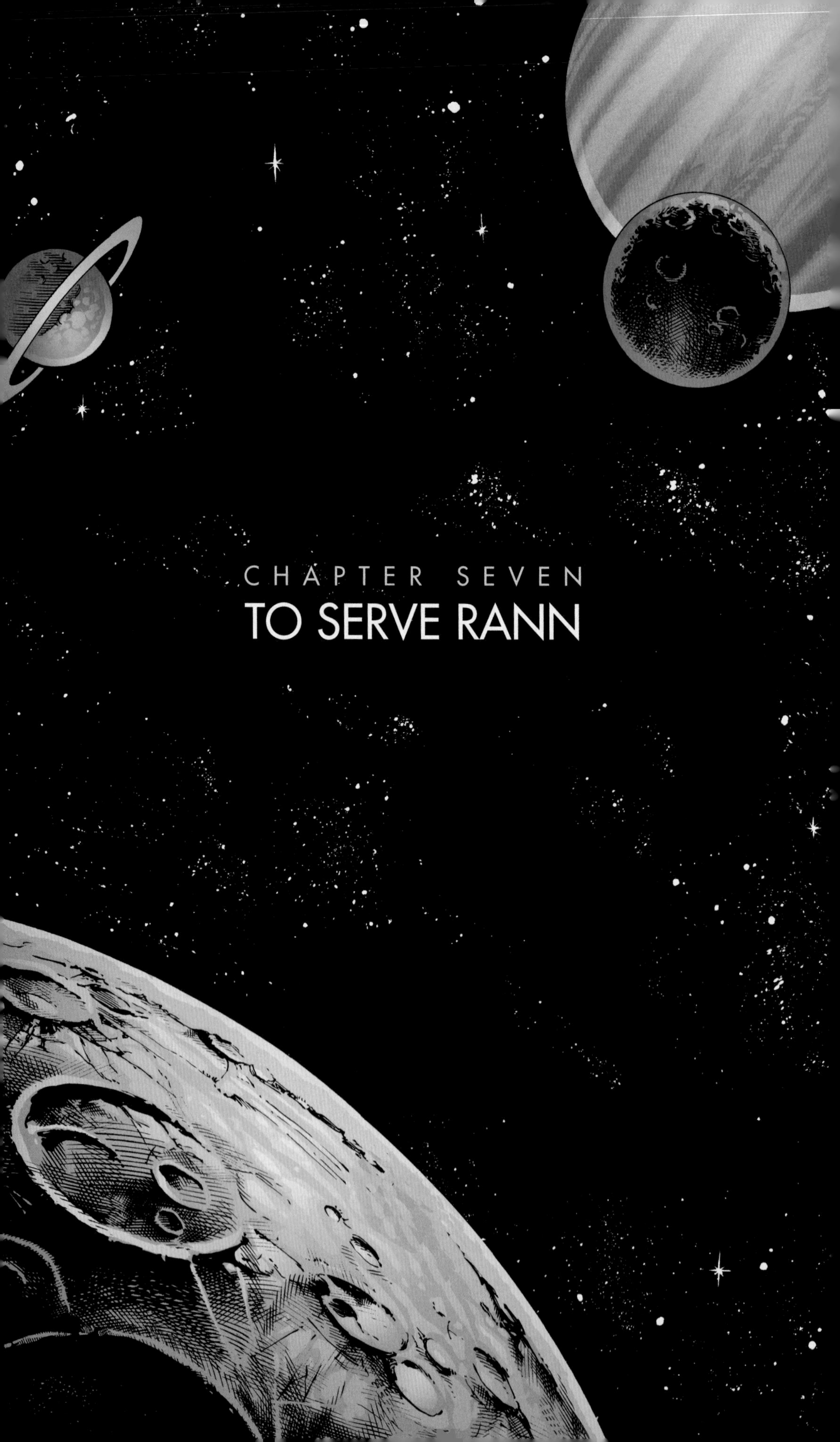

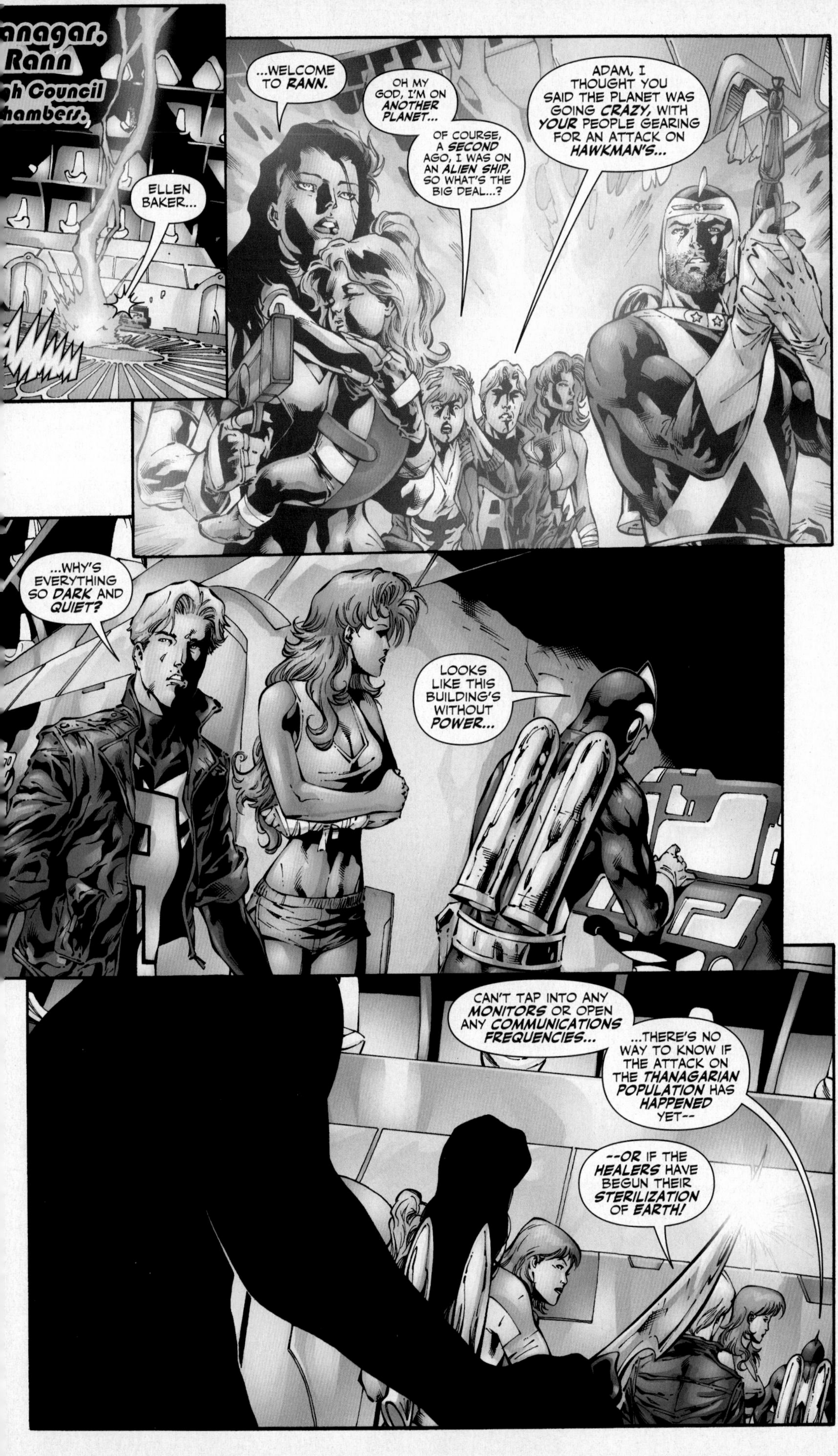
anagar.
Rann
gh Council
hambers.
ELLEN BAKER...
...WELCOME TO RANN.
OH MY GOD, I'M ON ANOTHER PLANET...
OF COURSE, A SECOND AGO, I WAS ON AN ALIEN SHIP, SO WHAT'S THE BIG DEAL...?
ADAM, I THOUGHT YOU SAID THE PLANET WAS GOING CRAZY, WITH YOUR PEOPLE GEARING FOR AN ATTACK ON HAWKMAN'S...
...WHY'S EVERYTHING SO DARK AND QUIET?
LOOKS LIKE THIS BUILDING'S WITHOUT POWER...
CAN'T TAP INTO ANY MONITORS OR OPEN ANY COMMUNICATIONS FREQUENCIES...
...THERE'S NO WAY TO KNOW IF THE ATTACK ON THE THANAGARIAN POPULATION HAS HAPPENED YET--
--OR IF THE HEALERS HAVE BEGUN THEIR STERILIZATION OF EARTH!

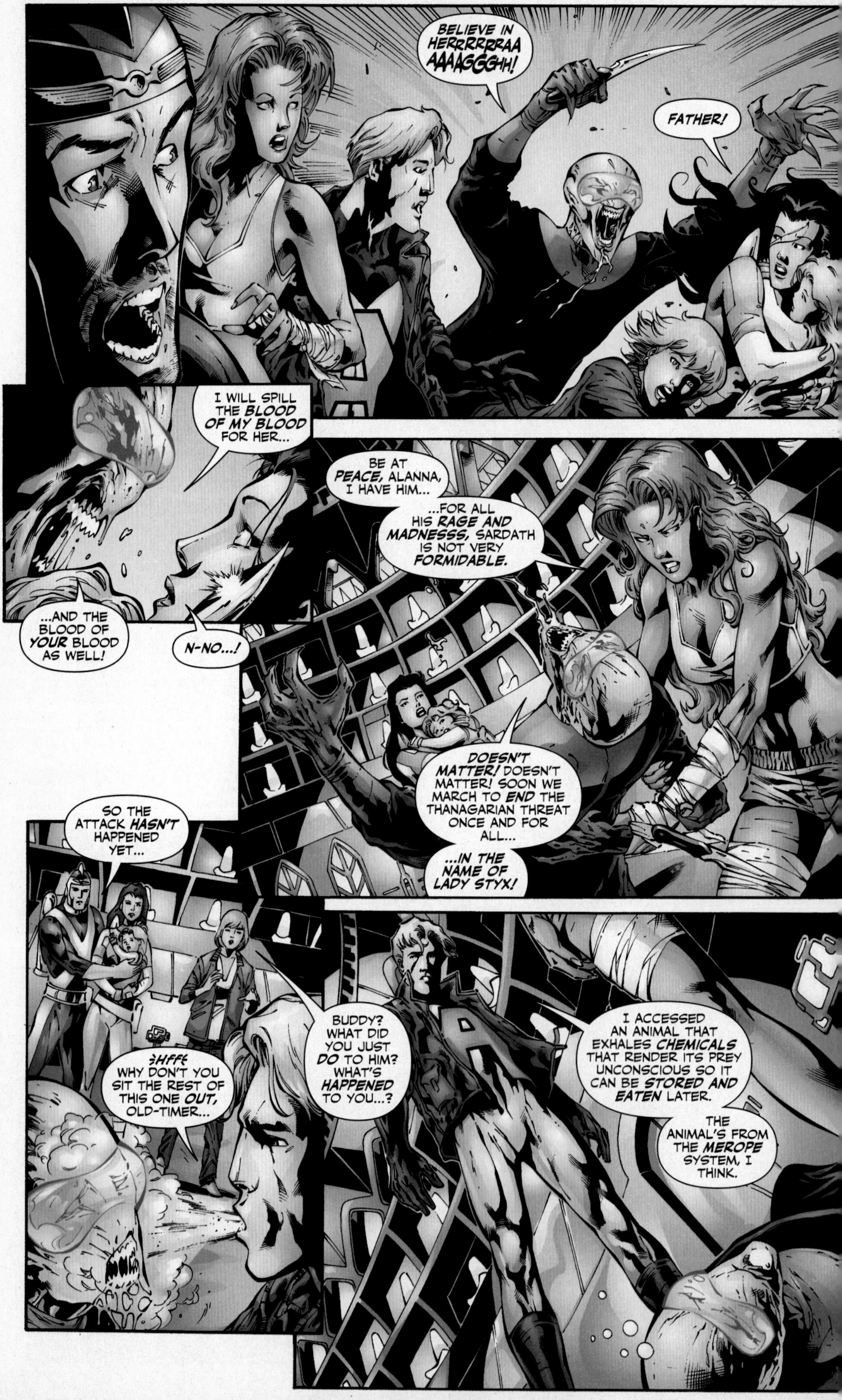
BELIEVE IN HERRRRRRAA AAAAGGGHH!
FATHER!
I WILL SPILL THE BLOOD OF MY BLOOD FOR HER...
...AND THE BLOOD OF YOUR BLOOD AS WELL!
N-NO...!
BE AT PEACE, ALANNA, I HAVE HIM...
...FOR ALL HIS RAGE AND MADNESSS, SARDATH IS NOT VERY FORMIDABLE.
DOESN'T MATTER! DOESN'T MATTER! SOON WE MARCH TO END THE THANAGARIAN THREAT ONCE AND FOR ALL...
...IN THE NAME OF LADY STYX!
SO THE ATTACK HASN'T HAPPENED YET...
ƺHFFƸ WHY DON'T YOU SIT THE REST OF THIS ONE OUT, OLD-TIMER...
BUDDY? WHAT DID YOU JUST DO TO HIM? WHAT'S HAPPENED TO YOU...?
I ACCESSED AN ANIMAL THAT EXHALES CHEMICALS THAT RENDER ITS PREY UNCONSCIOUS SO IT CAN BE STORED AND EATEN LATER.
THE ANIMAL'S FROM THE MEROPE SYSTEM, I THINK.

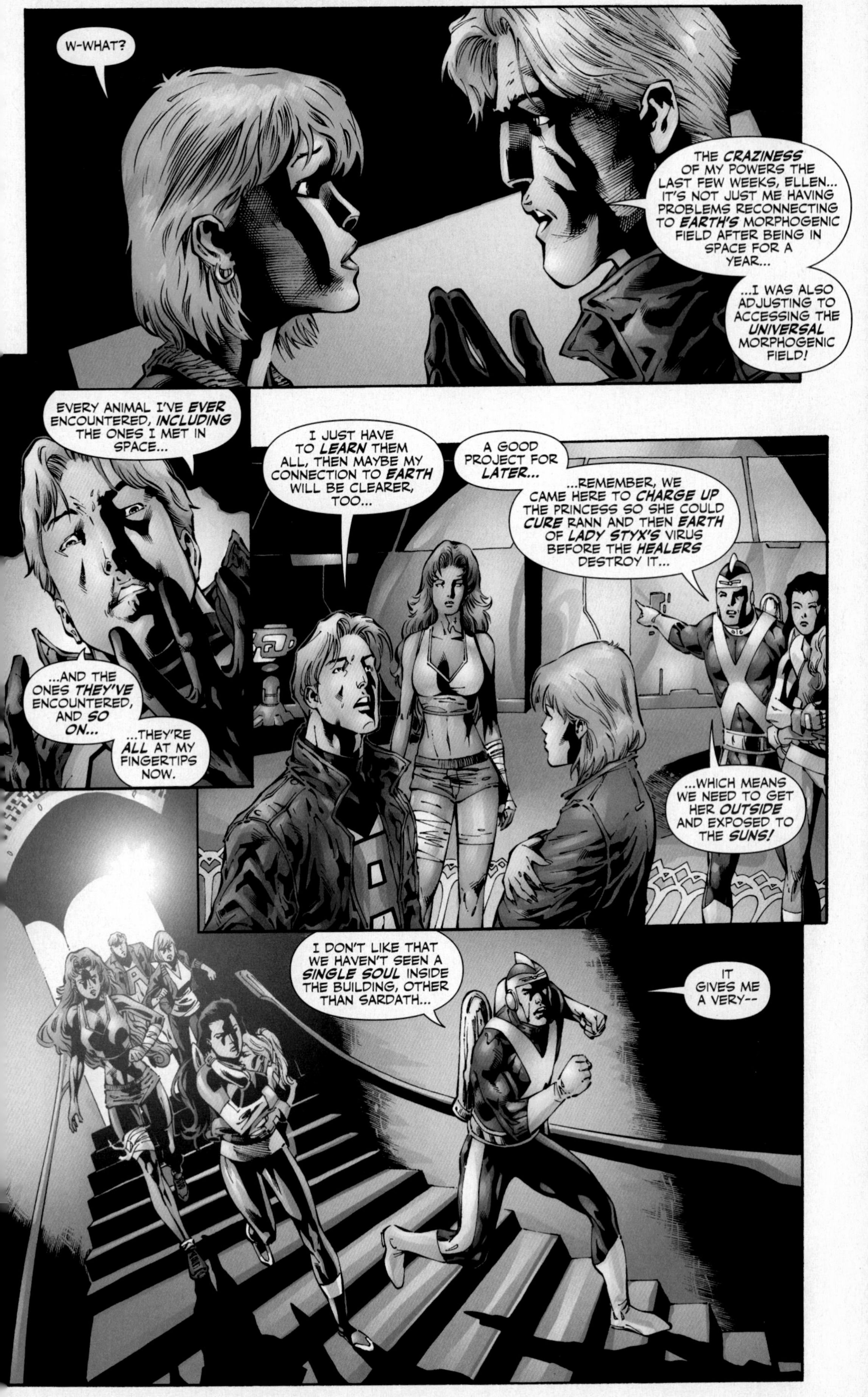
W-WHAT?
THE CRAZINESS OF MY POWERS THE LAST FEW WEEKS, ELLEN... IT'S NOT JUST ME HAVING PROBLEMS RECONNECTING TO EARTH'S MORPHOGENIC FIELD AFTER BEING IN SPACE FOR A YEAR...
...I WAS ALSO ADJUSTING TO ACCESSING THE UNIVERSAL MORPHOGENIC FIELD!
EVERY ANIMAL I'VE EVER ENCOUNTERED, INCLUDING THE ONES I MET IN SPACE...
...AND THE ONES THEY'VE ENCOUNTERED, AND SO ON...
...THEY'RE ALL AT MY FINGERTIPS NOW.
I JUST HAVE TO LEARN THEM ALL, THEN MAYBE MY CONNECTION TO EARTH WILL BE CLEARER, TOO...
A GOOD PROJECT FOR LATER...
...REMEMBER, WE CAME HERE TO CHARGE UP THE PRINCESS SO SHE COULD CURE RANN AND THEN EARTH OF LADY STYX'S VIRUS BEFORE THE HEALERS DESTROY IT...
...WHICH MEANS WE NEED TO GET HER OUTSIDE AND EXPOSED TO THE SUNS!
I DON'T LIKE THAT WE HAVEN'T SEEN A SINGLE SOUL INSIDE THE BUILDING, OTHER THAN SARDATH...
IT GIVES ME A VERY--

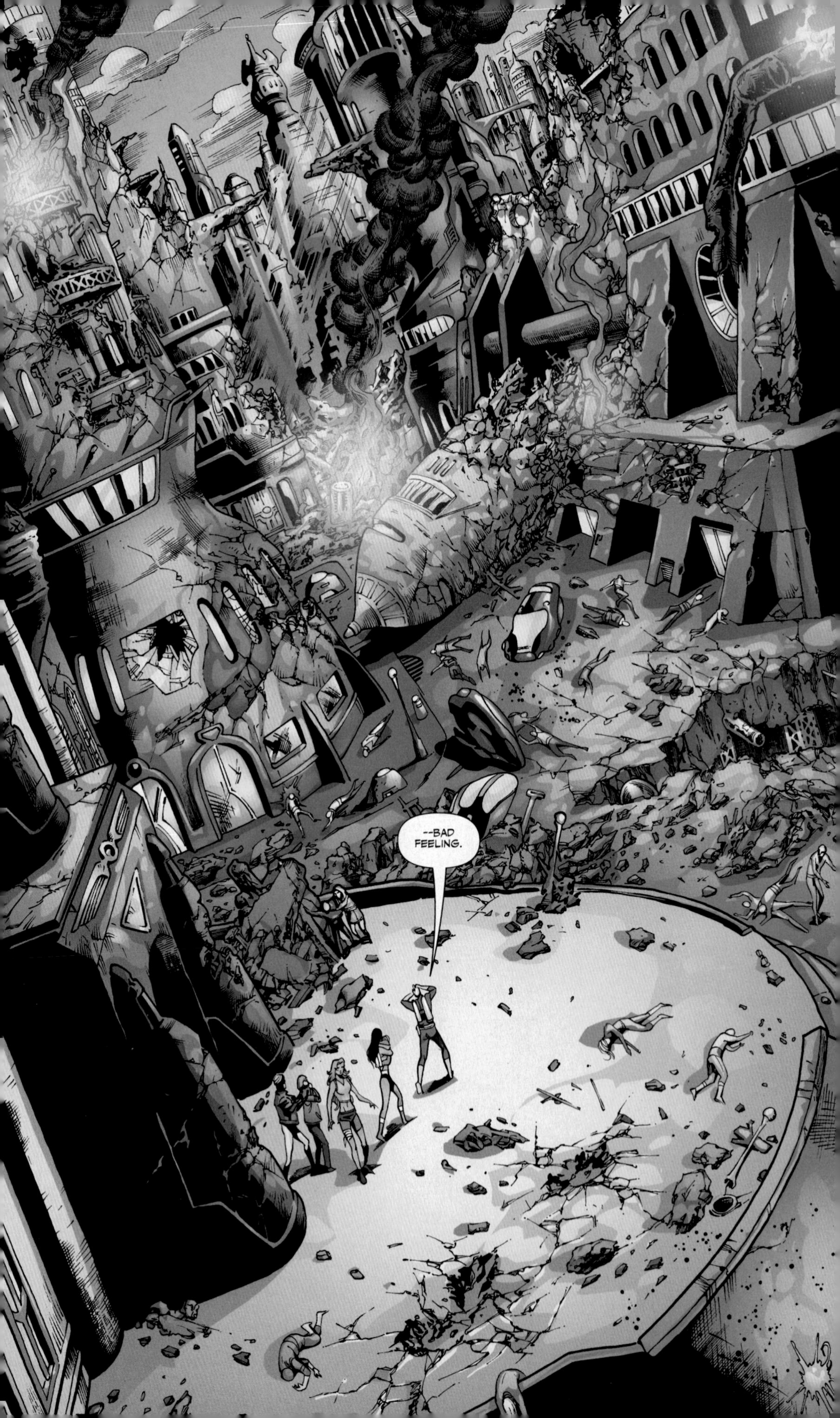
--BAD FEELING.

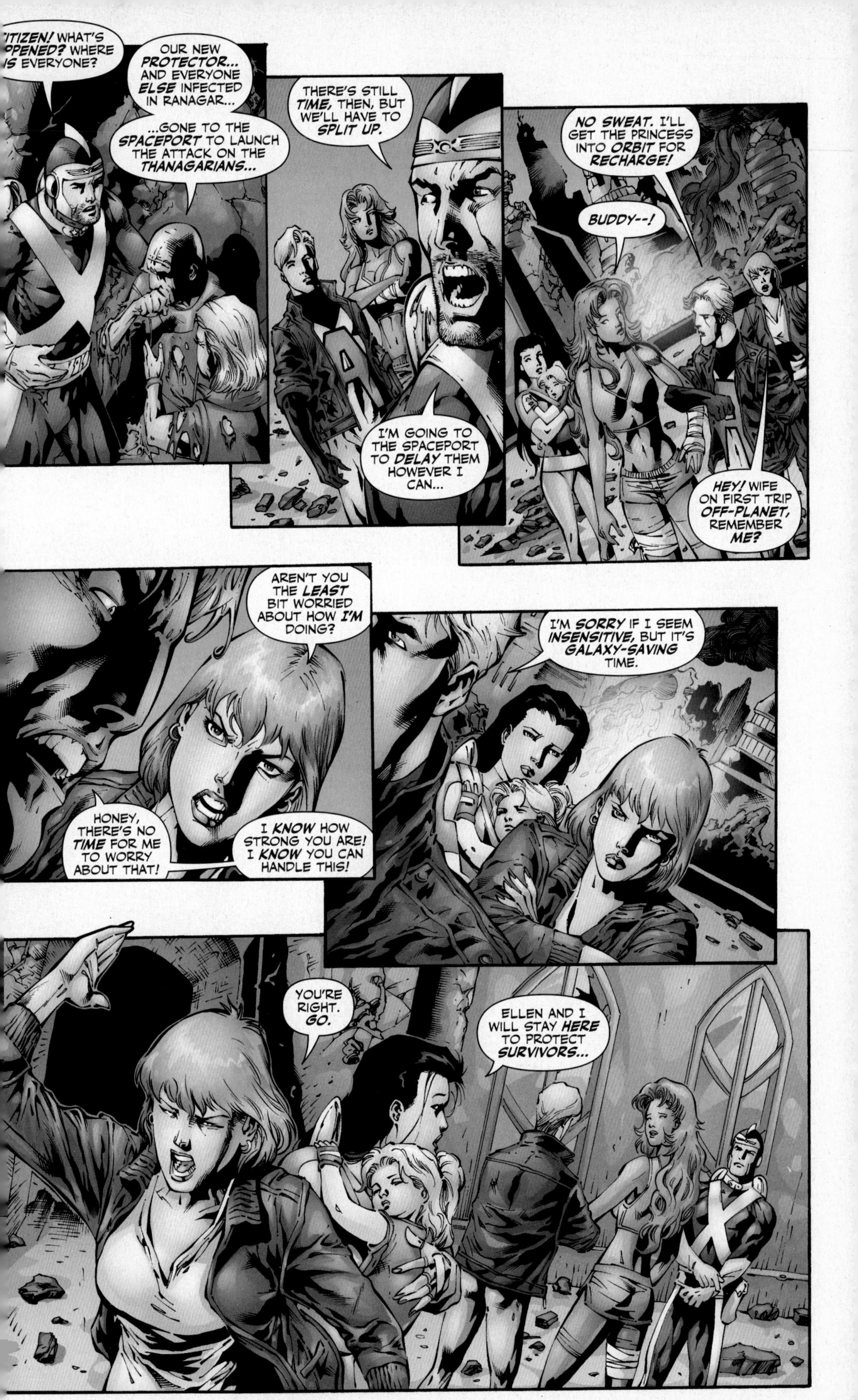

...TIZEN! WHAT'S ...PPENED? WHERE ...S EVERYONE?
OUR NEW PROTECTOR... AND EVERYONE ELSE INFECTED IN RANAGAR...
...GONE TO THE SPACEPORT TO LAUNCH THE ATTACK ON THE THANAGARIANS...
THERE'S STILL TIME, THEN, BUT WE'LL HAVE TO SPLIT UP.
I'M GOING TO THE SPACEPORT TO DELAY THEM HOWEVER I CAN...
NO SWEAT. I'LL GET THE PRINCESS INTO ORBIT FOR RECHARGE!
BUDDY--!
HEY! WIFE ON FIRST TRIP OFF-PLANET, REMEMBER ME?
AREN'T YOU THE LEAST BIT WORRIED ABOUT HOW I'M DOING?
HONEY, THERE'S NO TIME FOR ME TO WORRY ABOUT THAT!
I KNOW HOW STRONG YOU ARE! I KNOW YOU CAN HANDLE THIS!
I'M SORRY IF I SEEM INSENSITIVE, BUT IT'S GALAXY-SAVING TIME.
YOU'RE RIGHT. GO.
ELLEN AND I WILL STAY HERE TO PROTECT SURVIVORS...

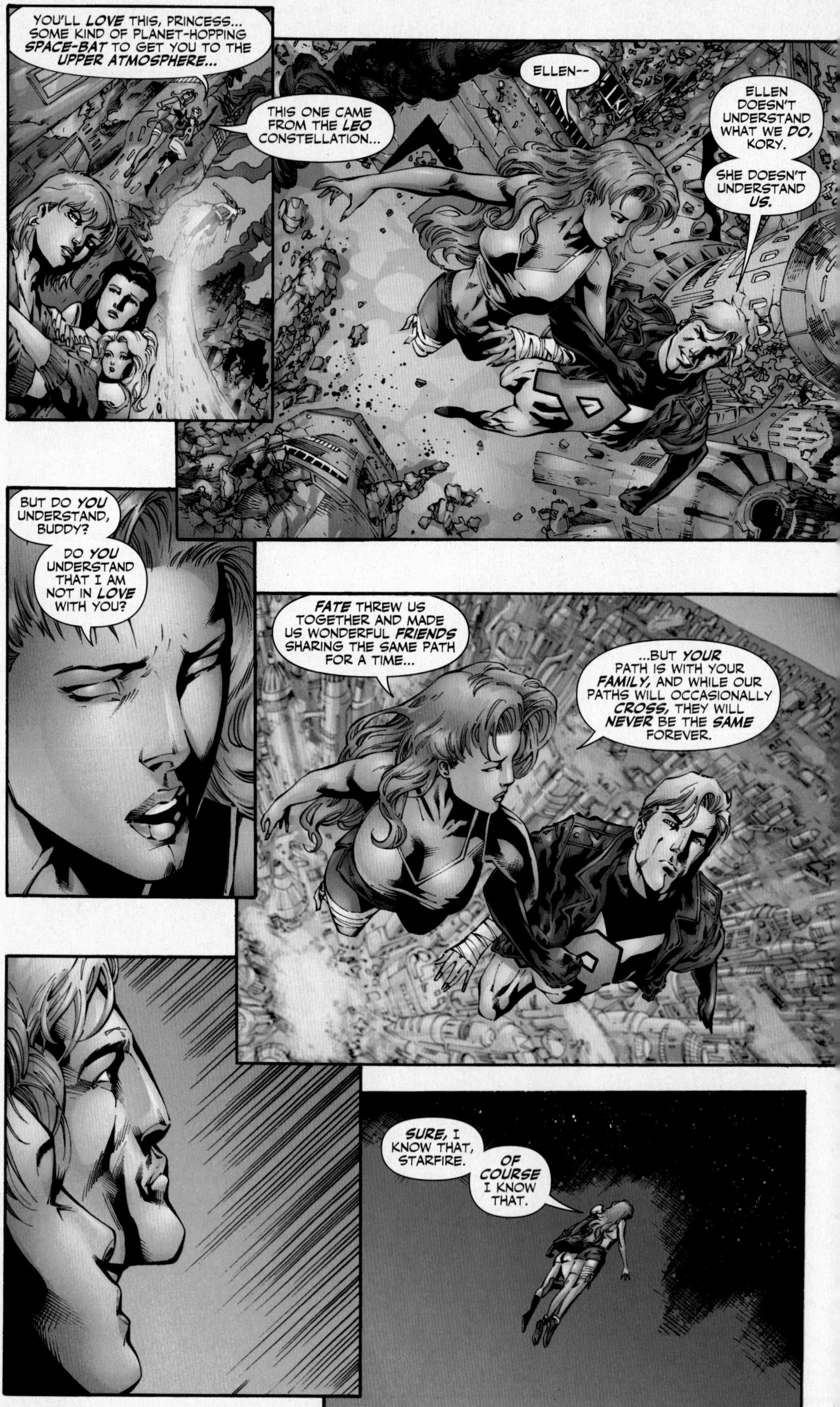
YOU'LL LOVE THIS, PRINCESS... SOME KIND OF PLANET-HOPPING SPACE-BAT TO GET YOU TO THE UPPER ATMOSPHERE...
THIS ONE CAME FROM THE LEO CONSTELLATION...
ELLEN--
ELLEN DOESN'T UNDERSTAND WHAT WE DO, KORY.
SHE DOESN'T UNDERSTAND US.
BUT DO YOU UNDERSTAND, BUDDY?
DO YOU UNDERSTAND THAT I AM NOT IN LOVE WITH YOU?
FATE THREW US TOGETHER AND MADE US WONDERFUL FRIENDS SHARING THE SAME PATH FOR A TIME...
...BUT YOUR PATH IS WITH YOUR FAMILY, AND WHILE OUR PATHS WILL OCCASIONALLY CROSS, THEY WILL NEVER BE THE SAME FOREVER.
SURE, I KNOW THAT, STARFIRE.
OF COURSE I KNOW THAT.

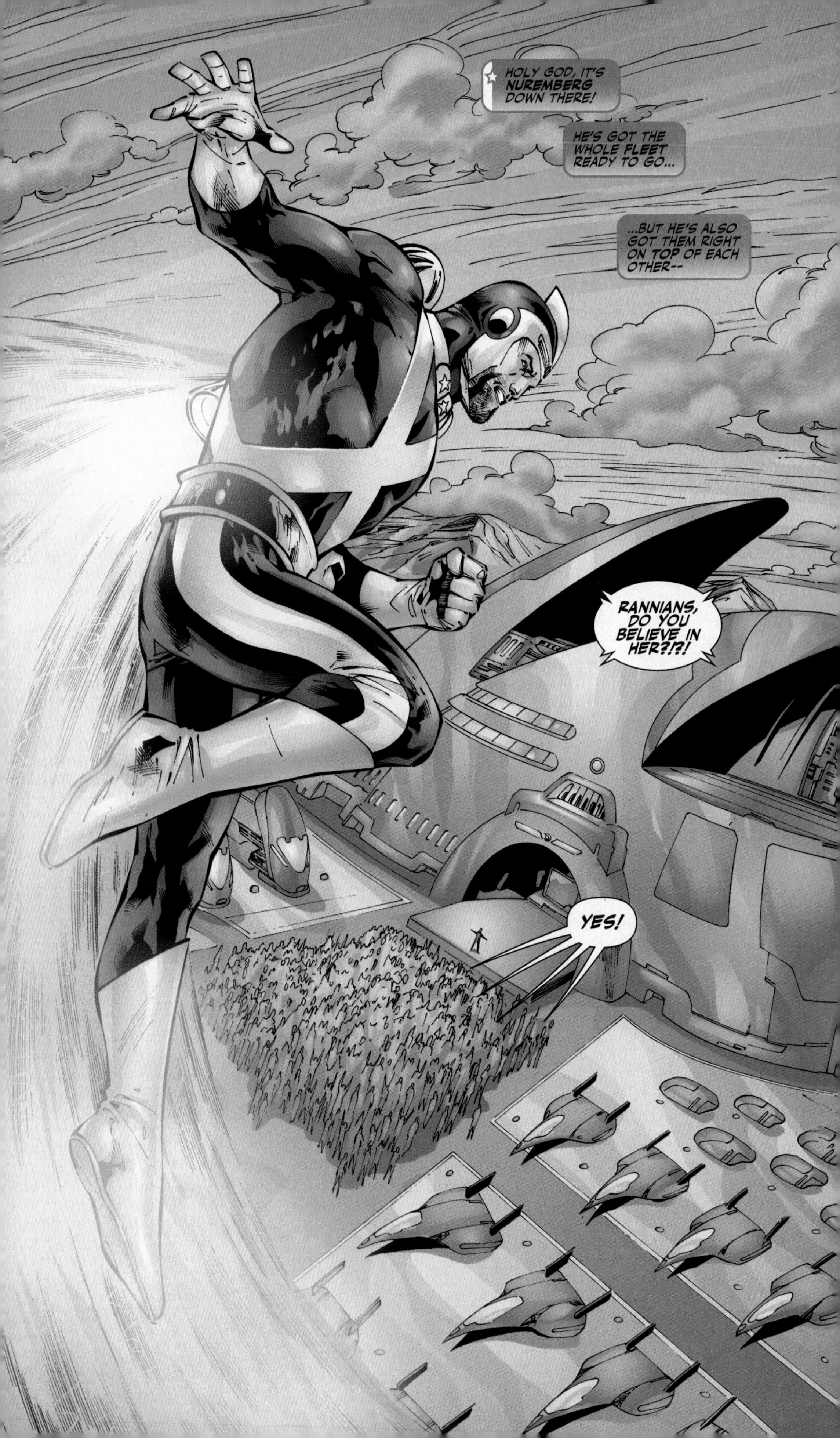
HOLY GOD, IT'S NUREMBERG DOWN THERE!
HE'S GOT THE WHOLE FLEET READY TO GO...
...BUT HE'S ALSO GOT THEM RIGHT ON TOP OF EACH OTHER--
RANNIANS, DO YOU BELIEVE IN HER?!?!
YES!

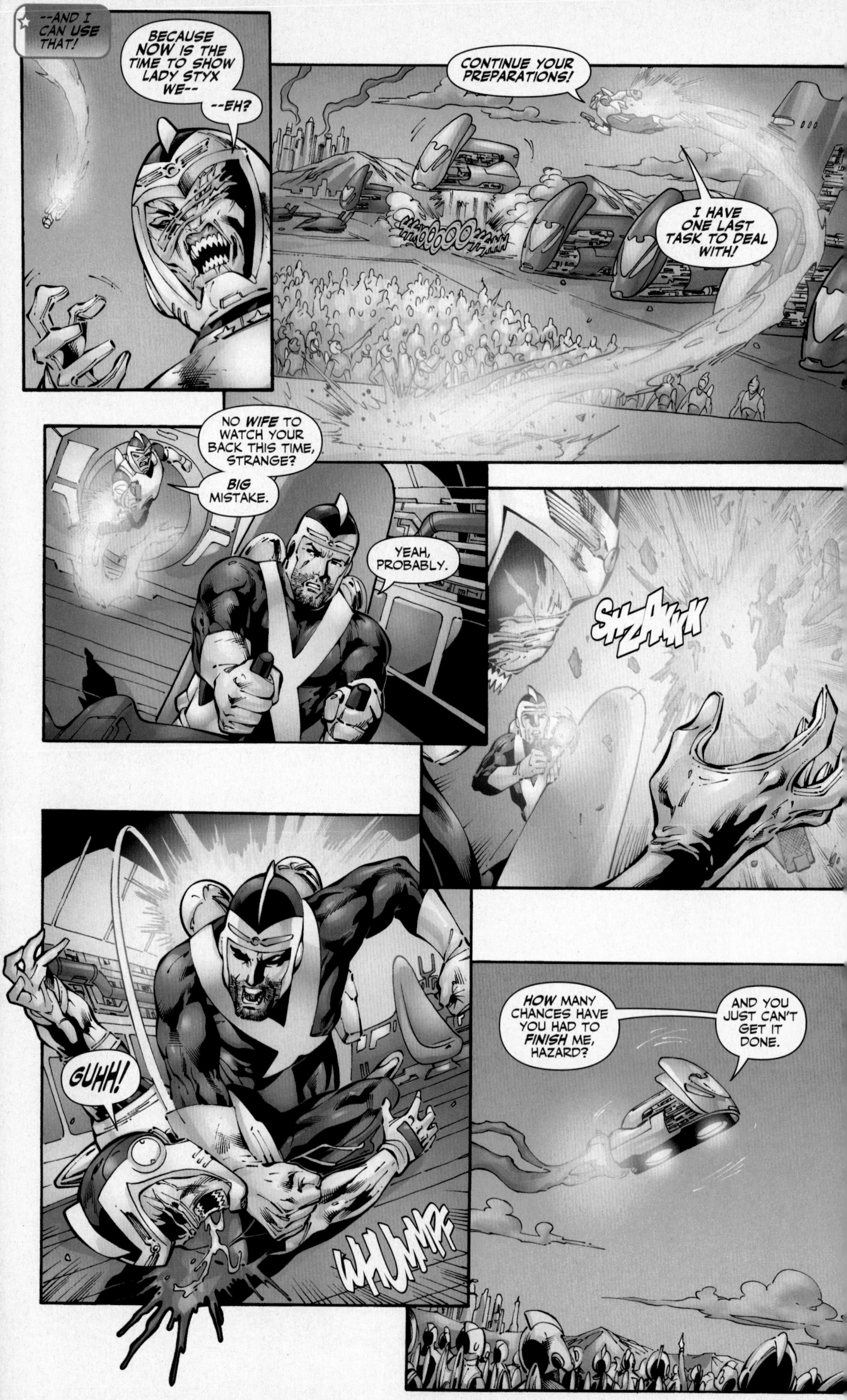
--AND I CAN USE THAT!
BECAUSE NOW IS THE TIME TO SHOW LADY STYX WE--
--EH?
CONTINUE YOUR PREPARATIONS!
I HAVE ONE LAST TASK TO DEAL WITH!
SHHHOOOOOOSHHHH
NO WIFE TO WATCH YOUR BACK THIS TIME, STRANGE?
BIG MISTAKE.
YEAH, PROBABLY.
SHZAKKK
GUHH!
WHUMPF
HOW MANY CHANCES HAVE YOU HAD TO FINISH ME, HAZARD?
AND YOU JUST CAN'T GET IT DONE.

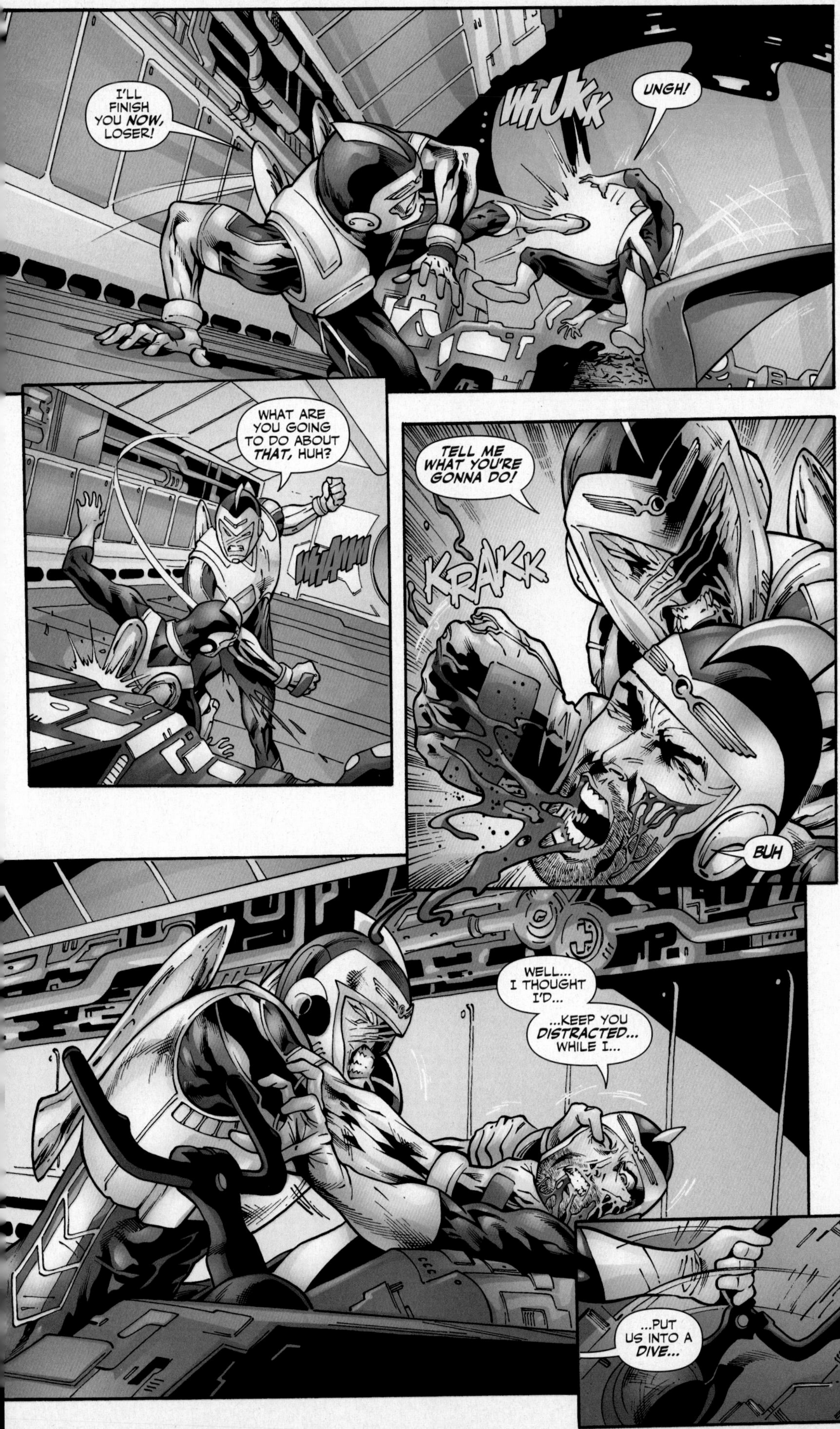
I'LL FINISH YOU NOW, LOSER!
WHUKK
UNGH!
WHAT ARE YOU GOING TO DO ABOUT THAT, HUH?
WHAMM
TELL ME WHAT YOU'RE GONNA DO!
KRAKK
BUH
WELL... I THOUGHT I'D...
...KEEP YOU DISTRACTED... WHILE I...
...PUT US INTO A DIVE...

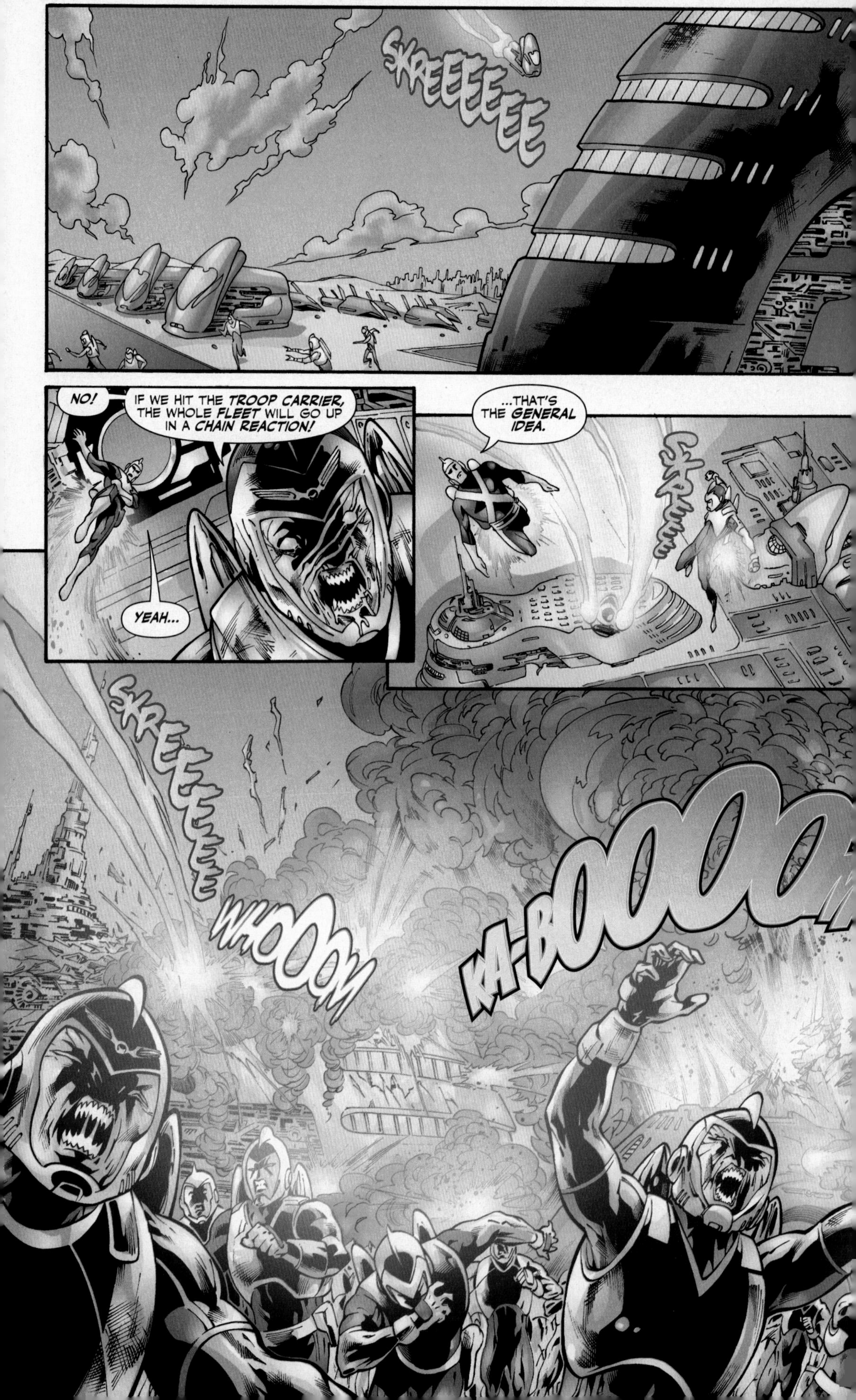
SKREEEEEEEE
NO!
IF WE HIT THE TROOP CARRIER, THE WHOLE FLEET WILL GO UP IN A CHAIN REACTION!
YEAH...
...THAT'S THE GENERAL IDEA.
SKREEEEEEE
WHOOOOM
KA-BOOOOM

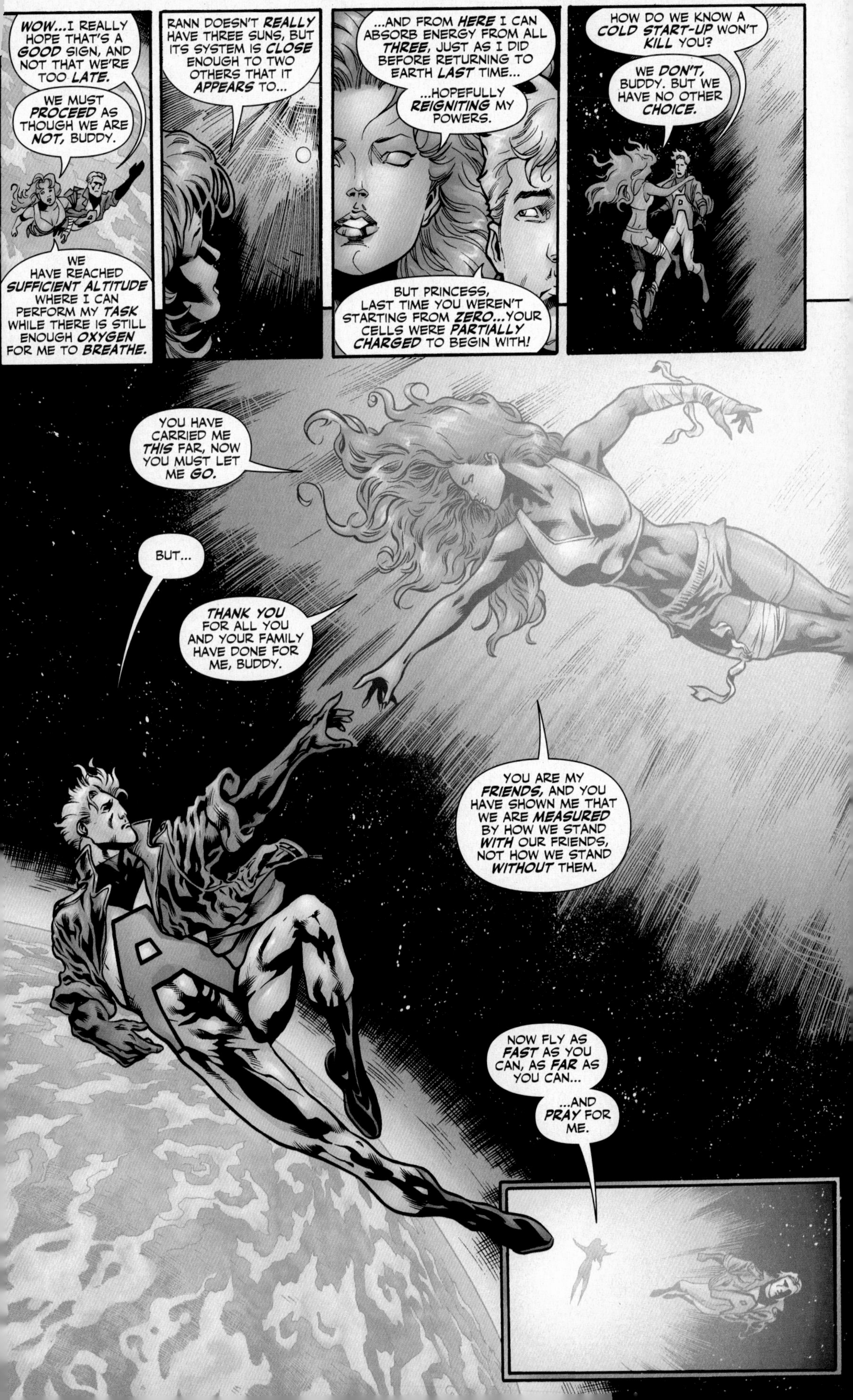
WOW...I REALLY HOPE THAT'S A GOOD SIGN, AND NOT THAT WE'RE TOO LATE.
WE MUST PROCEED AS THOUGH WE ARE NOT, BUDDY.
WE HAVE REACHED SUFFICIENT ALTITUDE WHERE I CAN PERFORM MY TASK WHILE THERE IS STILL ENOUGH OXYGEN FOR ME TO BREATHE.
RANN DOESN'T REALLY HAVE THREE SUNS, BUT ITS SYSTEM IS CLOSE ENOUGH TO TWO OTHERS THAT IT APPEARS TO...
...AND FROM HERE I CAN ABSORB ENERGY FROM ALL THREE, JUST AS I DID BEFORE RETURNING TO EARTH LAST TIME...
...HOPEFULLY REIGNITING MY POWERS.
BUT PRINCESS, LAST TIME YOU WEREN'T STARTING FROM ZERO...YOUR CELLS WERE PARTIALLY CHARGED TO BEGIN WITH!
HOW DO WE KNOW A COLD START-UP WON'T KILL YOU?
WE DON'T, BUDDY. BUT WE HAVE NO OTHER CHOICE.
YOU HAVE CARRIED ME THIS FAR, NOW YOU MUST LET ME GO.
BUT...
THANK YOU FOR ALL YOU AND YOUR FAMILY HAVE DONE FOR ME, BUDDY.
YOU ARE MY FRIENDS, AND YOU HAVE SHOWN ME THAT WE ARE MEASURED BY HOW WE STAND WITH OUR FRIENDS, NOT HOW WE STAND WITHOUT THEM.
NOW FLY AS FAST AS YOU CAN, AS FAR AS YOU CAN...
...AND PRAY FOR ME.

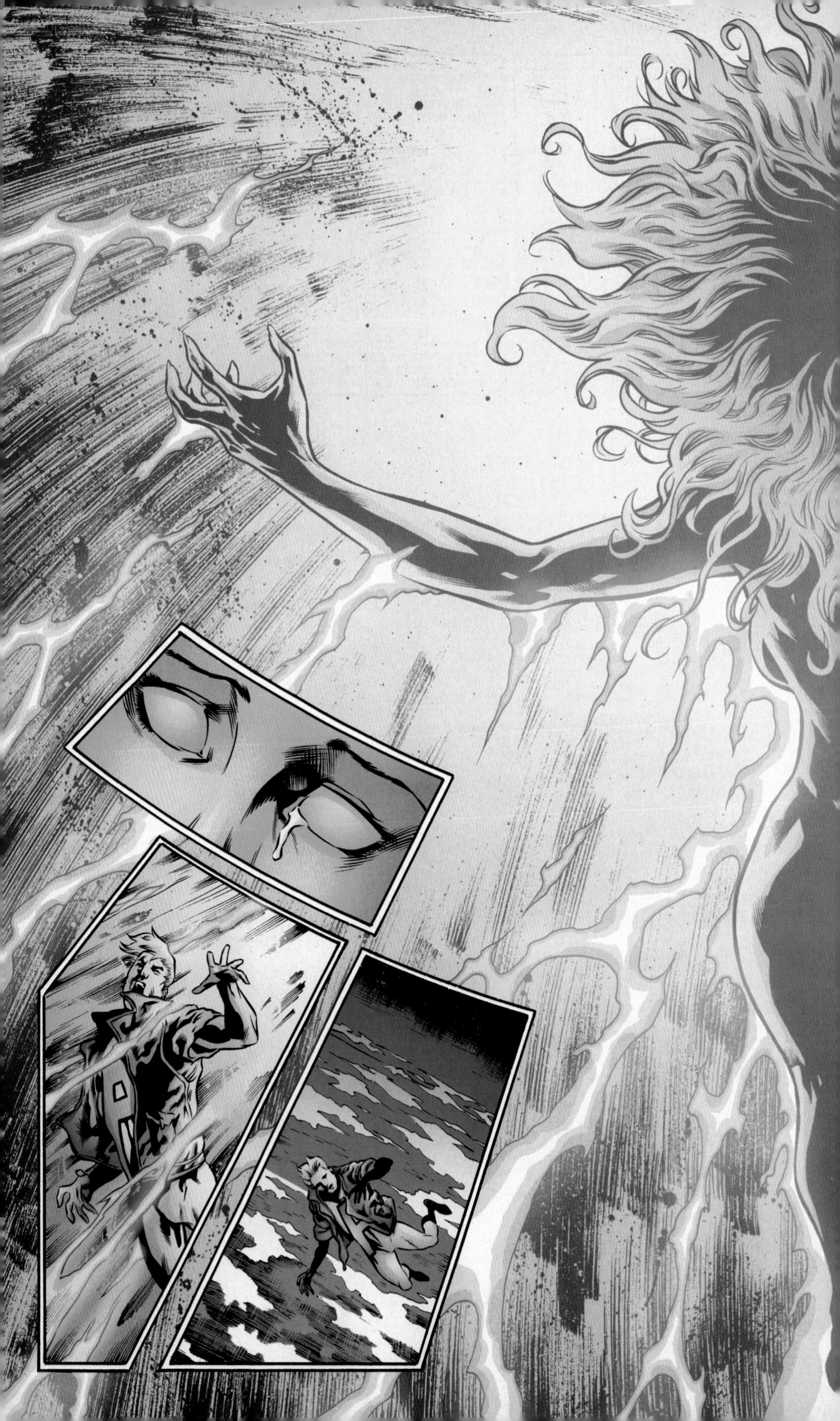

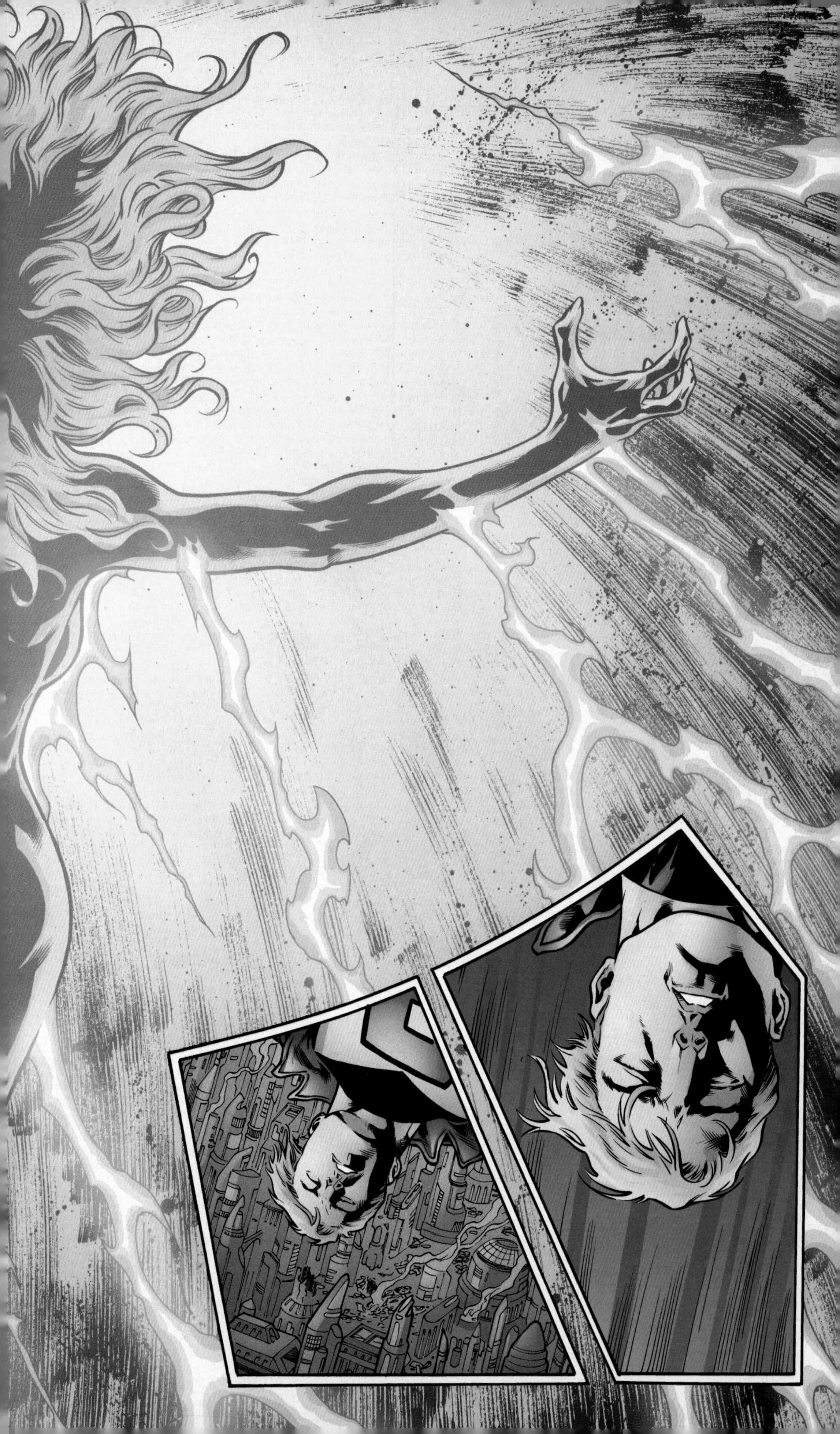

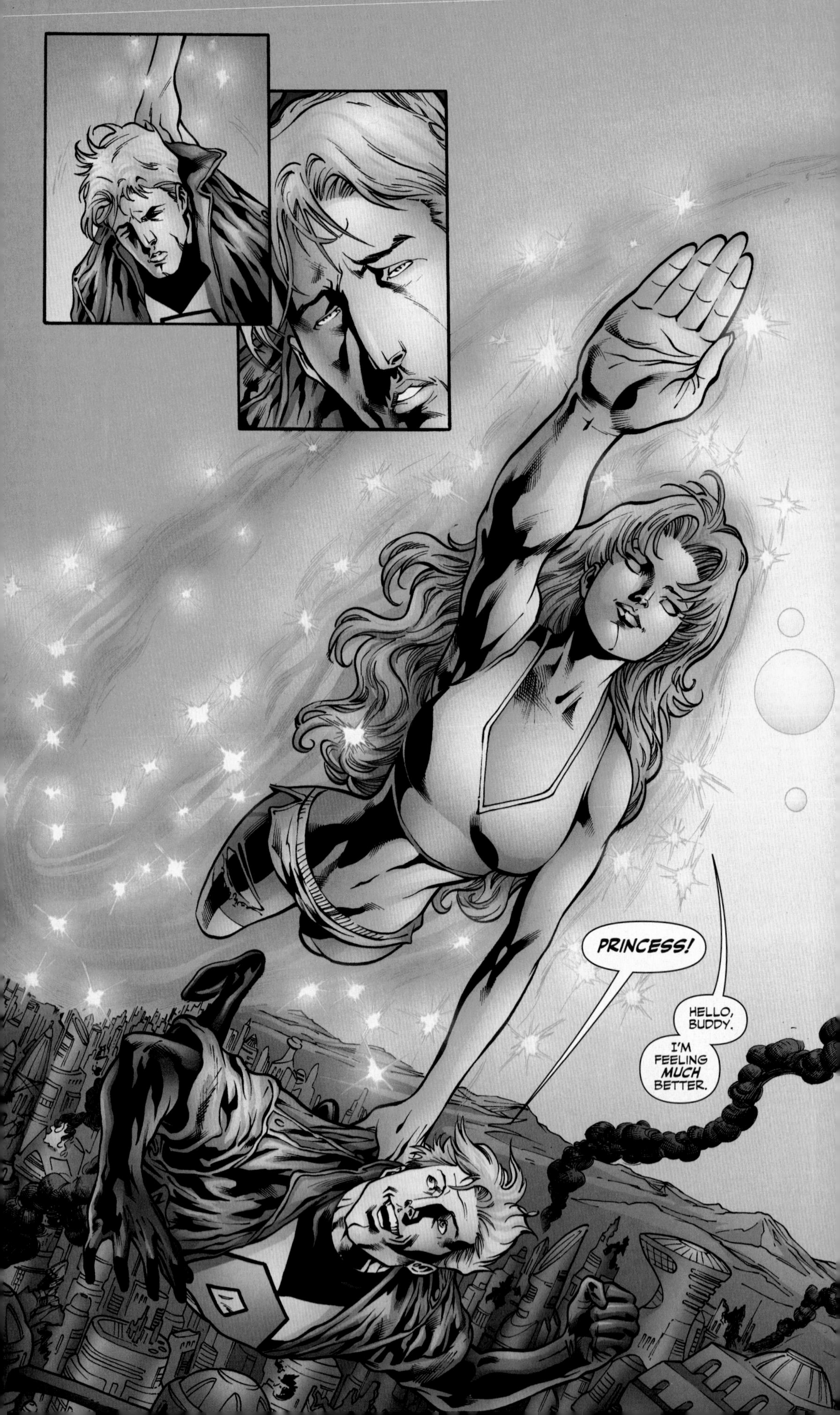
PRINCESS!
HELLO, BUDDY.
I'M FEELING MUCH BETTER.

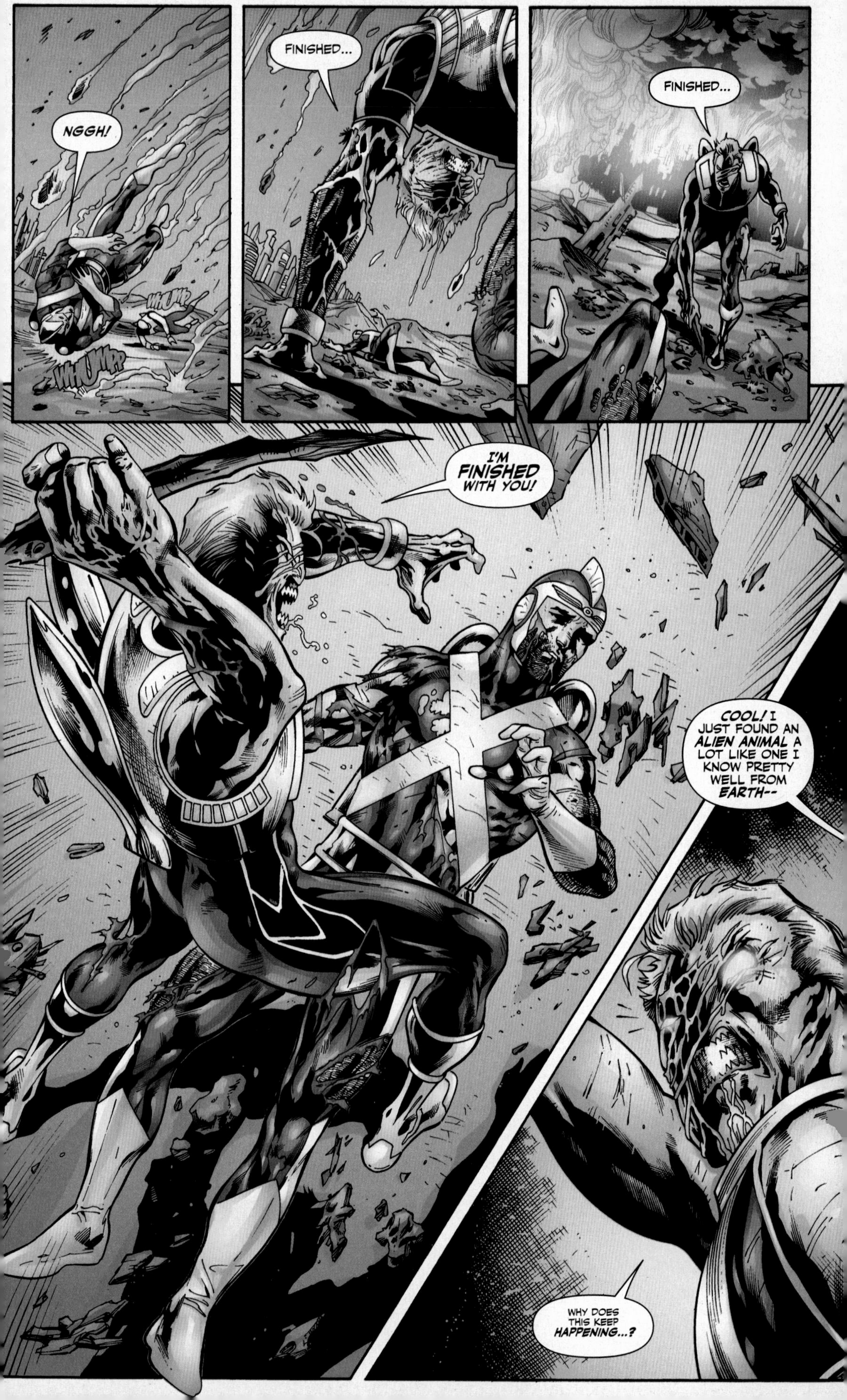
NGGH!
WHUMP
WHUMPP
FINISHED...
FINISHED...
I'M FINISHED WITH YOU!
COOL! I JUST FOUND AN ALIEN ANIMAL A LOT LIKE ONE I KNOW PRETTY WELL FROM EARTH--
WHY DOES THIS KEEP HAPPENING...?

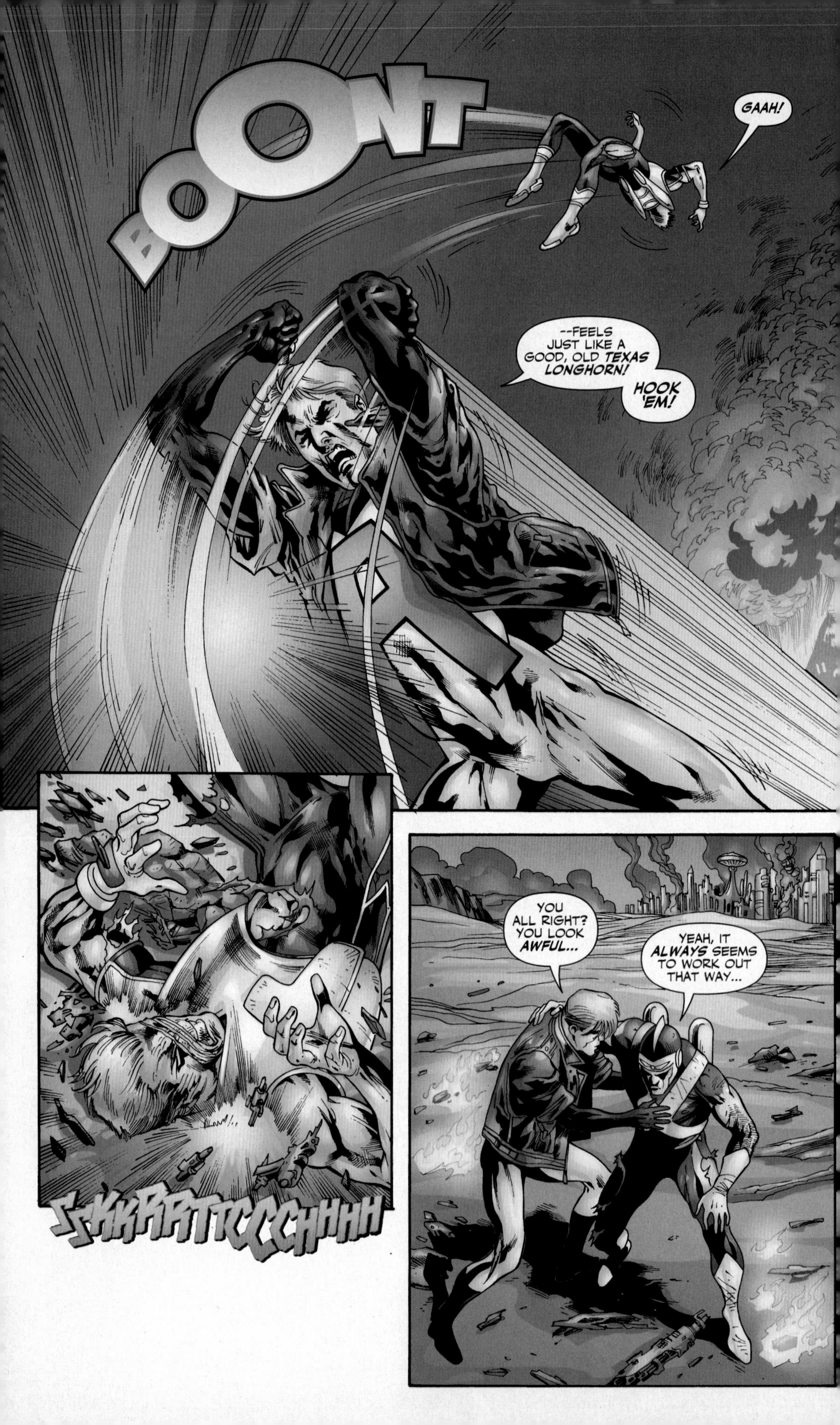
BOOOMT
GAAH!
--FEELS JUST LIKE A GOOD, OLD TEXAS LONGHORN!
HOOK 'EM!
SSKKRRTTCCCHHHH
YOU ALL RIGHT? YOU LOOK AWFUL...
YEAH, IT ALWAYS SEEMS TO WORK OUT THAT WAY...

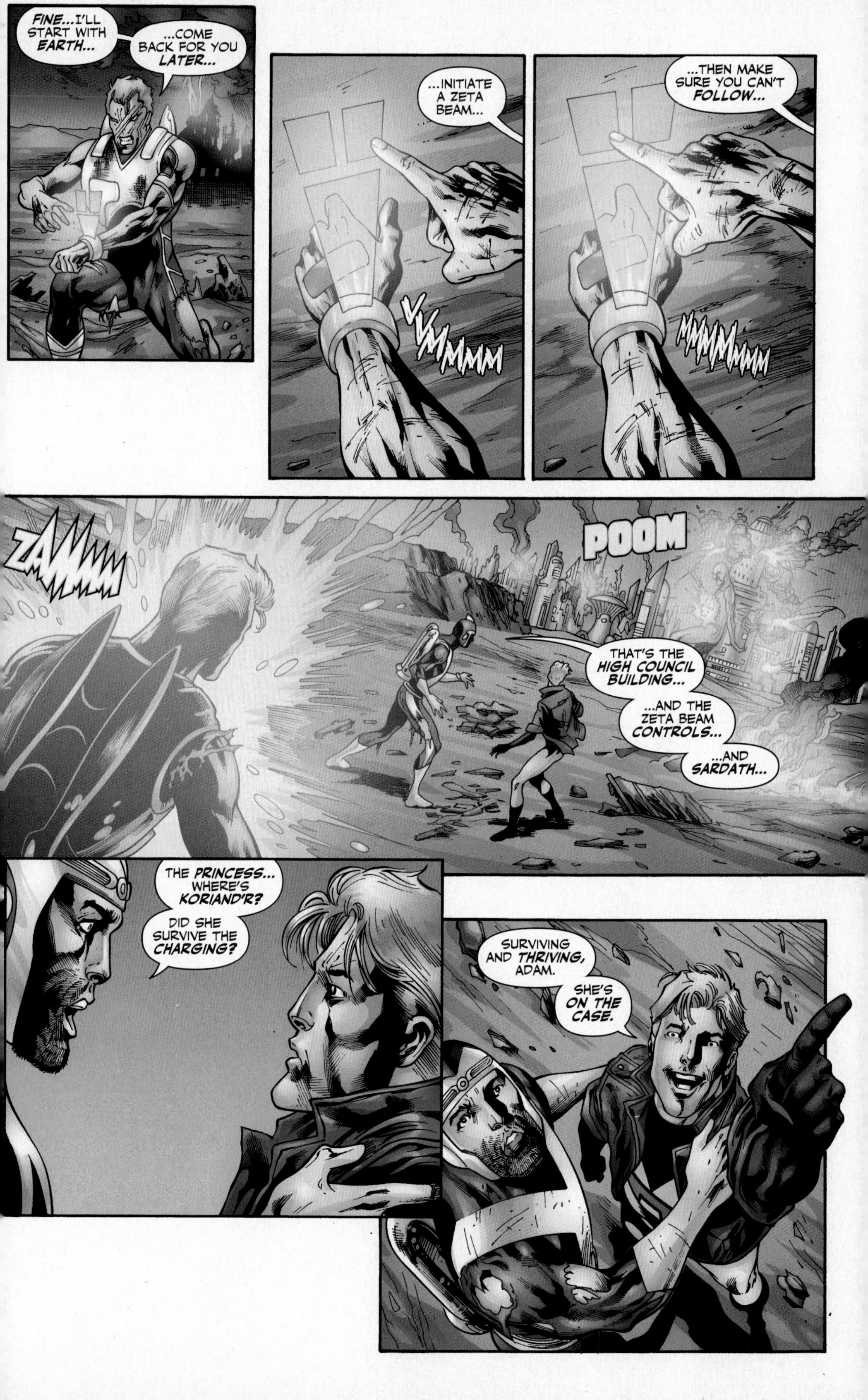
FINE...I'LL START WITH EARTH...
...COME BACK FOR YOU LATER...
...INITIATE A ZETA BEAM...
VVMMMM
...THEN MAKE SURE YOU CAN'T FOLLOW...
MMMMMMM
ZAMMM
POOM
THAT'S THE HIGH COUNCIL BUILDING...
...AND THE ZETA BEAM CONTROLS...
...AND SARDATH...
THE PRINCESS... WHERE'S KORIAND'R?
DID SHE SURVIVE THE CHARGING?
SURVIVING AND THRIVING, ADAM.
SHE'S ON THE CASE.

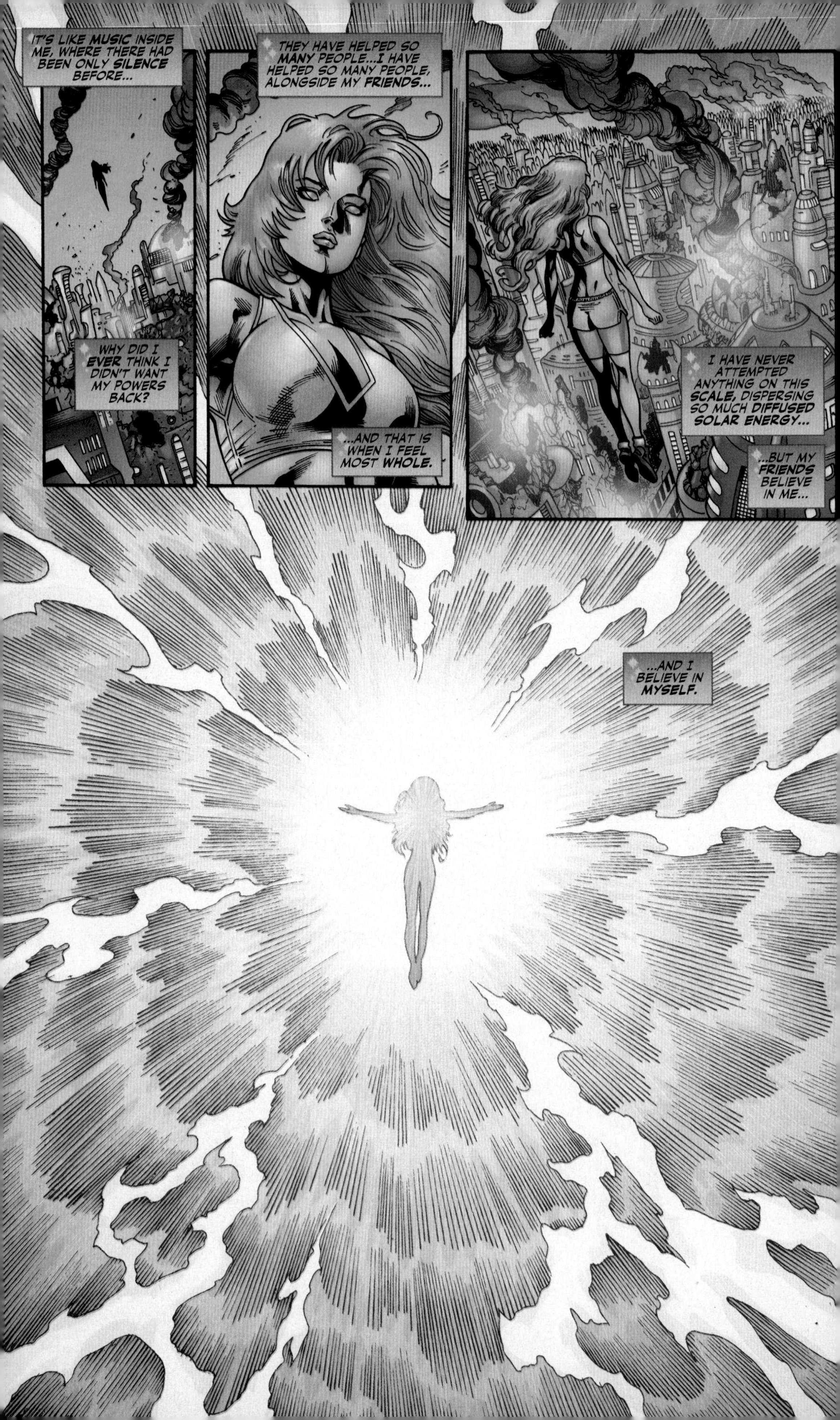
IT'S LIKE MUSIC INSIDE ME, WHERE THERE HAD BEEN ONLY SILENCE BEFORE...
WHY DID I EVER THINK I DIDN'T WANT MY POWERS BACK?
THEY HAVE HELPED SO MANY PEOPLE...I HAVE HELPED SO MANY PEOPLE, ALONGSIDE MY FRIENDS...
...AND THAT IS WHEN I FEEL MOST WHOLE.
I HAVE NEVER ATTEMPTED ANYTHING ON THIS SCALE, DISPERSING SO MUCH DIFFUSED SOLAR ENERGY...
...BUT MY FRIENDS BELIEVE IN ME...
...AND I BELIEVE IN MYSELF.

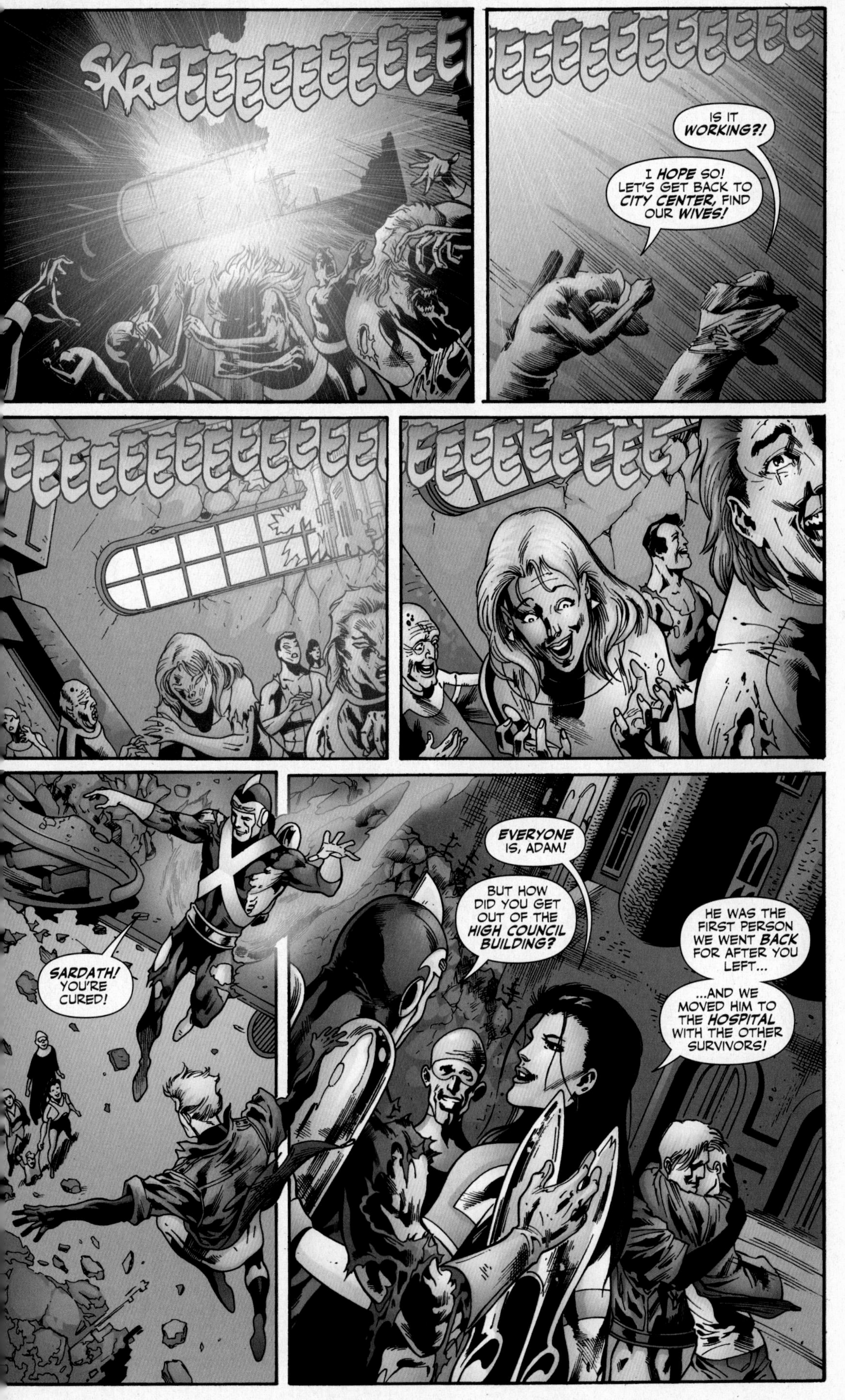
SKREEEEEEEEEEEE
EEEEEEEEEEEEEE
IS IT WORKING?!
I HOPE SO! LET'S GET BACK TO CITY CENTER, FIND OUR WIVES!
EEEEEEEEEEEEEEE
EEEEEEEEEEE
SARDATH! YOU'RE CURED!
EVERYONE IS, ADAM!
BUT HOW DID YOU GET OUT OF THE HIGH COUNCIL BUILDING?
HE WAS THE FIRST PERSON WE WENT BACK FOR AFTER YOU LEFT...
...AND WE MOVED HIM TO THE HOSPITAL WITH THE OTHER SURVIVORS!

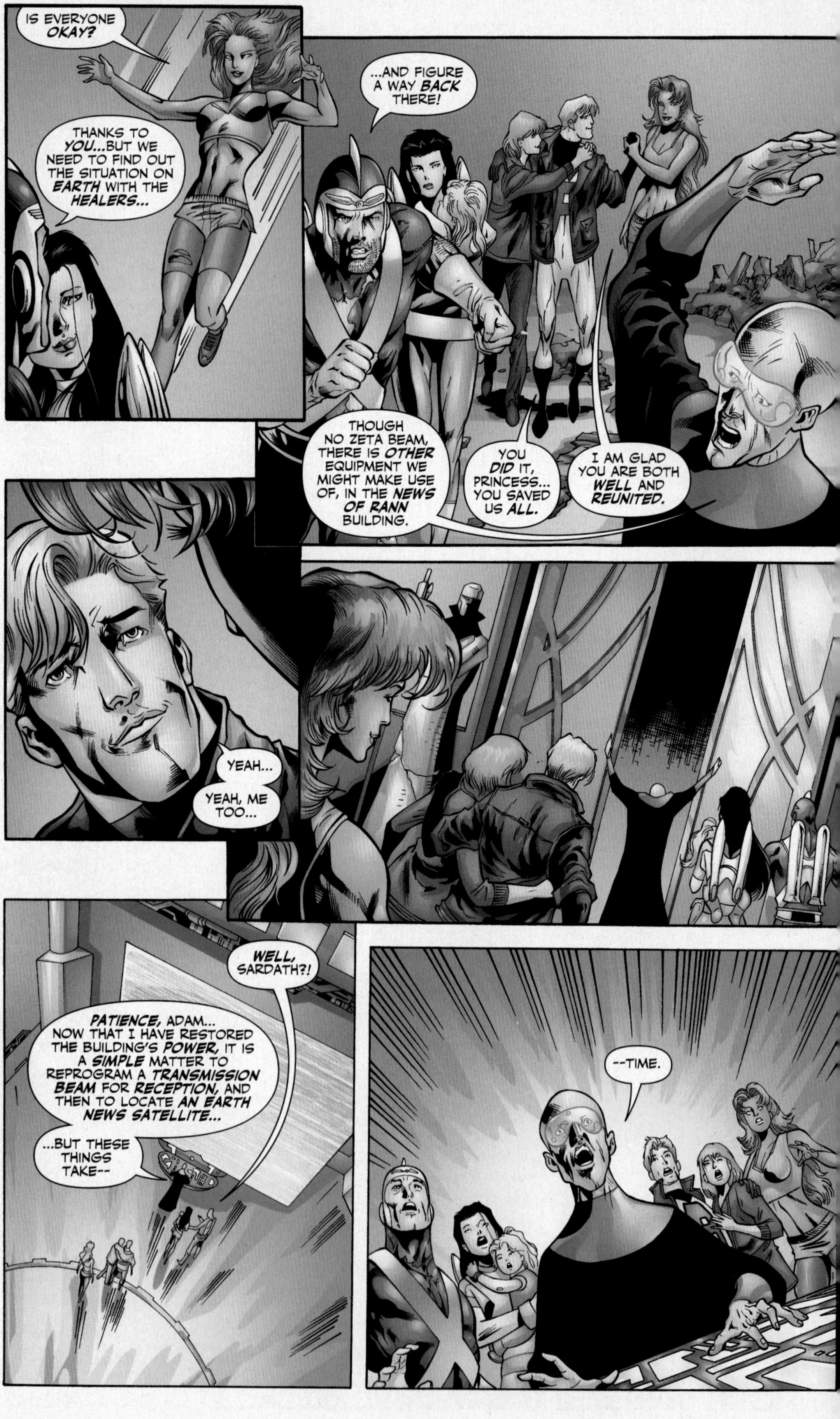
IS EVERYONE OKAY?
THANKS TO YOU...BUT WE NEED TO FIND OUT THE SITUATION ON EARTH WITH THE HEALERS...
...AND FIGURE A WAY BACK THERE!
THOUGH NO ZETA BEAM, THERE IS OTHER EQUIPMENT WE MIGHT MAKE USE OF, IN THE NEWS OF RANN BUILDING.
YOU DID IT, PRINCESS... YOU SAVED US ALL.
I AM GLAD YOU ARE BOTH WELL AND REUNITED.
YEAH...
YEAH, ME TOO...
WELL, SARDATH?!
PATIENCE, ADAM... NOW THAT I HAVE RESTORED THE BUILDING'S POWER, IT IS A SIMPLE MATTER TO REPROGRAM A TRANSMISSION BEAM FOR RECEPTION, AND THEN TO LOCATE AN EARTH NEWS SATELLITE...
...BUT THESE THINGS TAKE--
--TIME.

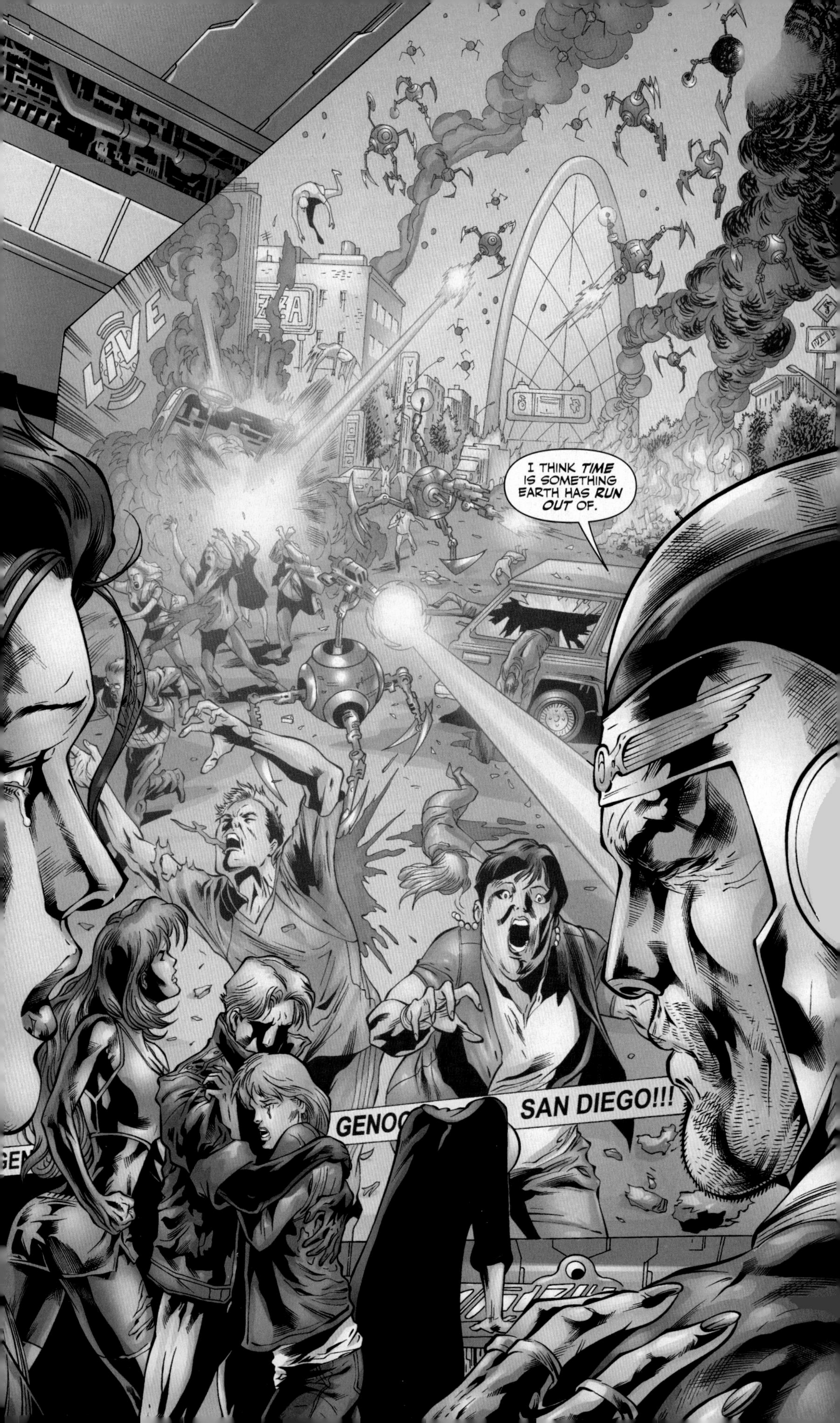

LIVE
I THINK *TIME* IS SOMETHING EARTH HAS *RUN OUT* OF.
GENOC
SAN DIEGO!!!

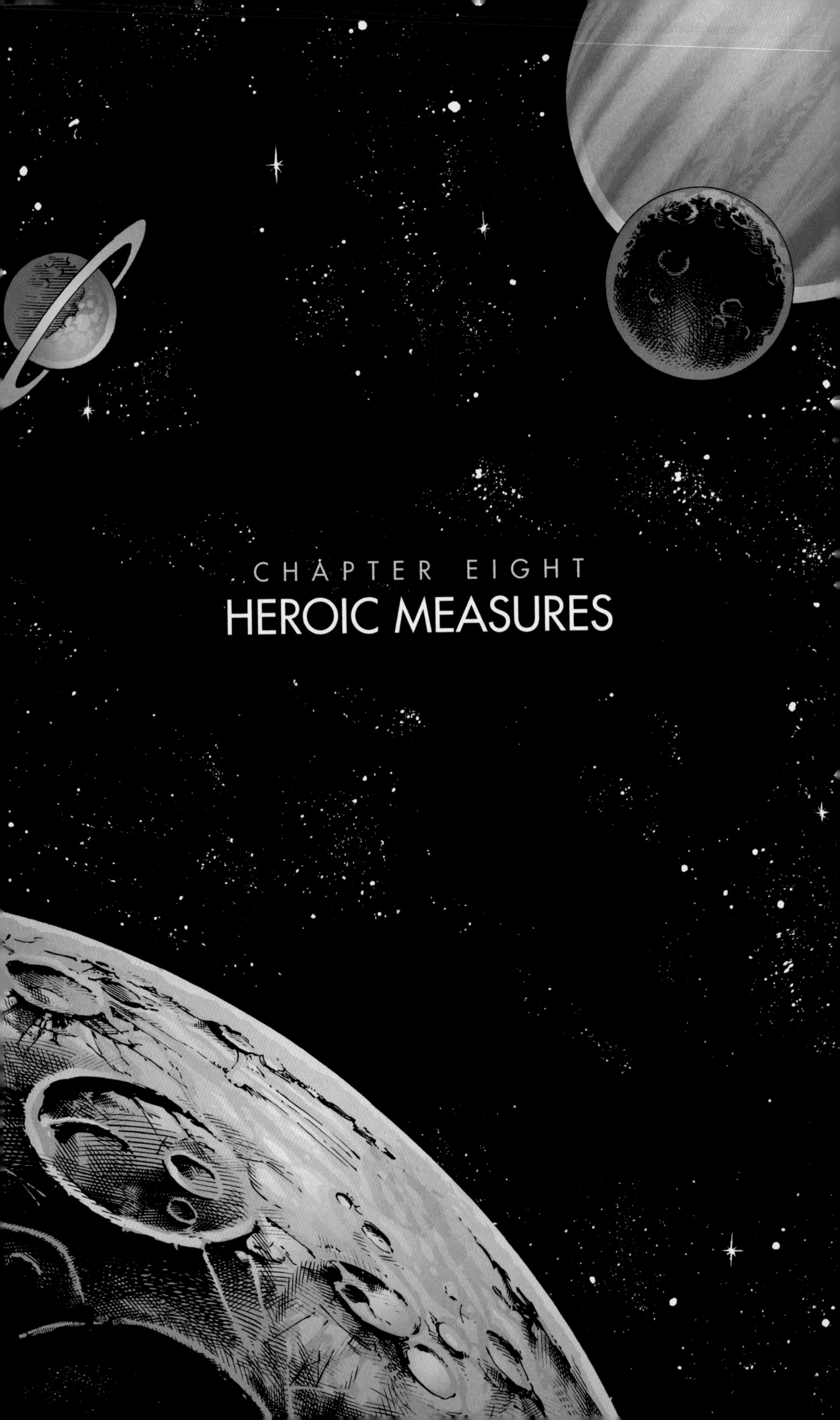

CHAPTER EIGHT

HEROIC MEASURES

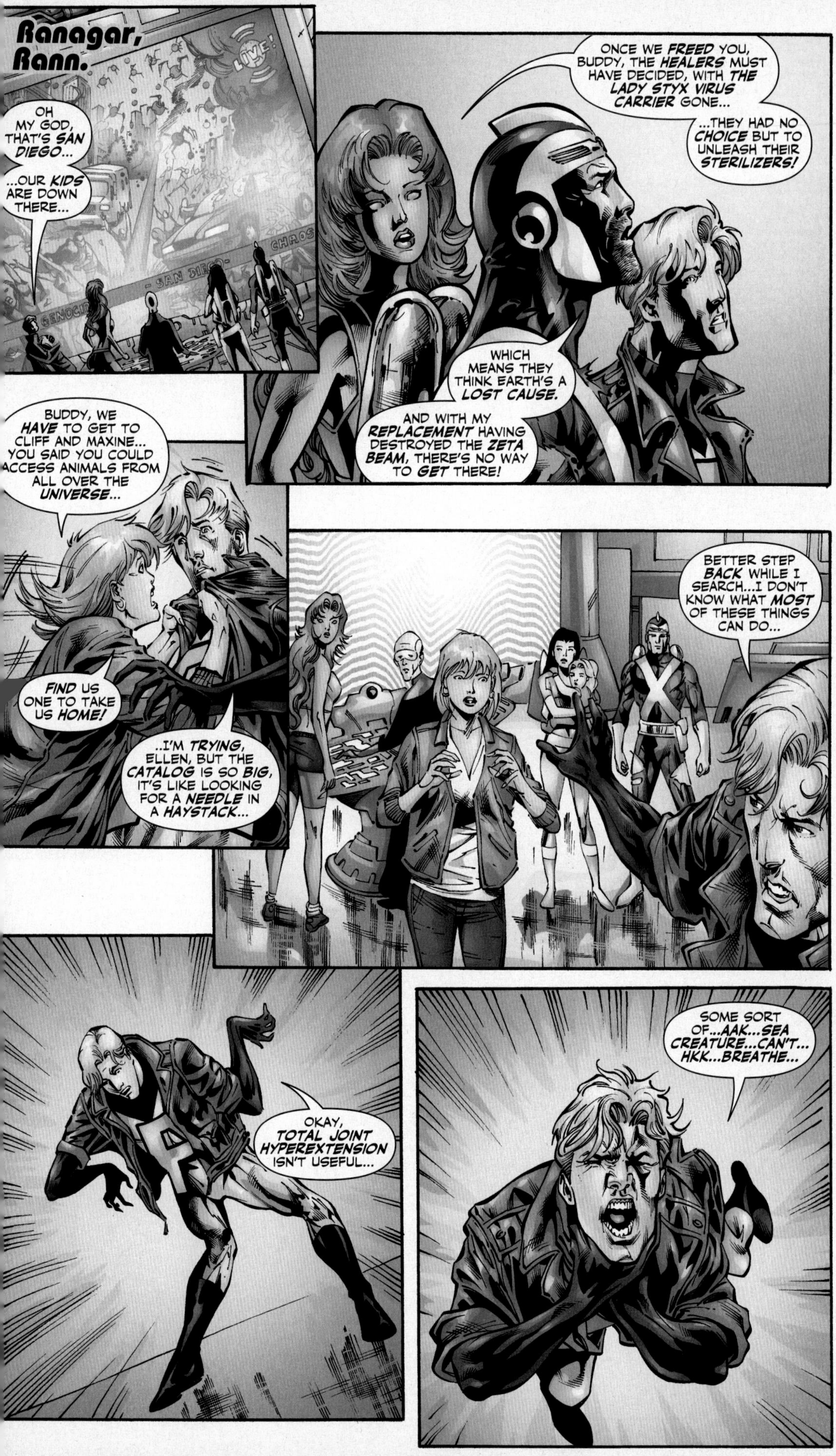
Ranagar, Rann.
LIVE!
CHAOS
SAN DIEGO
GENOCIDE
OH MY GOD, THAT'S SAN DIEGO...
...OUR KIDS ARE DOWN THERE...
ONCE WE FREED YOU, BUDDY, THE HEALERS MUST HAVE DECIDED, WITH THE LADY STYX VIRUS CARRIER GONE...
...THEY HAD NO CHOICE BUT TO UNLEASH THEIR STERILIZERS!
WHICH MEANS THEY THINK EARTH'S A LOST CAUSE.
AND WITH MY REPLACEMENT HAVING DESTROYED THE ZETA BEAM, THERE'S NO WAY TO GET THERE!
BUDDY, WE HAVE TO GET TO CLIFF AND MAXINE... YOU SAID YOU COULD ACCESS ANIMALS FROM ALL OVER THE UNIVERSE...
FIND US ONE TO TAKE US HOME!
..I'M TRYING, ELLEN, BUT THE CATALOG IS SO BIG, IT'S LIKE LOOKING FOR A NEEDLE IN A HAYSTACK...
BETTER STEP BACK WHILE I SEARCH...I DON'T KNOW WHAT MOST OF THESE THINGS CAN DO...
OKAY, TOTAL JOINT HYPEREXTENSION ISN'T USEFUL...
SOME SORT OF...AAK...SEA CREATURE...CAN'T... HKK...BREATHE...

BETTER...BUT NOW I CAN *SMELL* HALFWAY ACROSS THE *PLANET*... *OVER-WHELMING...OVER-LOADED...*

BUDDY, *STOP...!*

SNIF SNIF

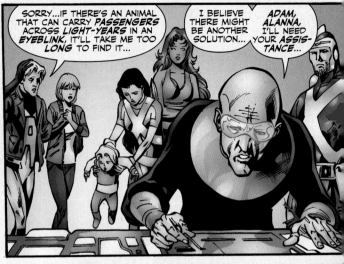

SORRY...IF THERE'S AN ANIMAL THAT CAN CARRY *PASSENGERS* ACROSS *LIGHT-YEARS* IN AN *EYEBLINK*, IT'LL TAKE ME TOO *LONG* TO FIND IT...

I BELIEVE THERE MIGHT BE ANOTHER SOLUTION...

ADAM, ALANNA, I'LL NEED YOUR *ASSISTANCE...*

ATTACH THOSE *CABLES* TO THAT *DIGITIZER*, AND SET THE INPUTS TO THE *THIRD LEVEL,* PLEASE.

WHAT ARE YOU *DOING?*

THIS IS THE *NEWS OF RANN* BUILDING, WITH CONTROLS FOR *DATA TRANSMISSION.*

I BELIEVE I CAN *RECALIBRATE* THE TRANSMITTERS TO *DIGITIZE SOLID MASS*, AND RELAY IT THROUGH THE *EARTH SATELLITE* WE'VE TAPPED TO BE *RECONSTRUCTED* ON YOUR PLANET.

ELLEN, YOU'RE STAYING *HERE.*

THE *HELL* I AM!

HONEY, YOU HEARD HIM...HE *BELIEVES* HE CAN DO THIS. IF HE'S *WRONG,* AND SOMETHING *HAPPENS* TO US, THE KIDS WILL BE *ALONE!*

IF SOMETHING GOES WRONG FOR YOU IN THE BEAM AND I'M *STUCK* HERE, THE KIDS ARE ALONE *ANYWAY!* IF YOU GO AND GET *KILLED,* SAME THING!

WE GO *TOGETHER,* BUDDY! IT'S THE KIDS' *BEST CHANCE!*

ALL RIGHT... OKAY...

I BELIEVE WE ARE *READY...*

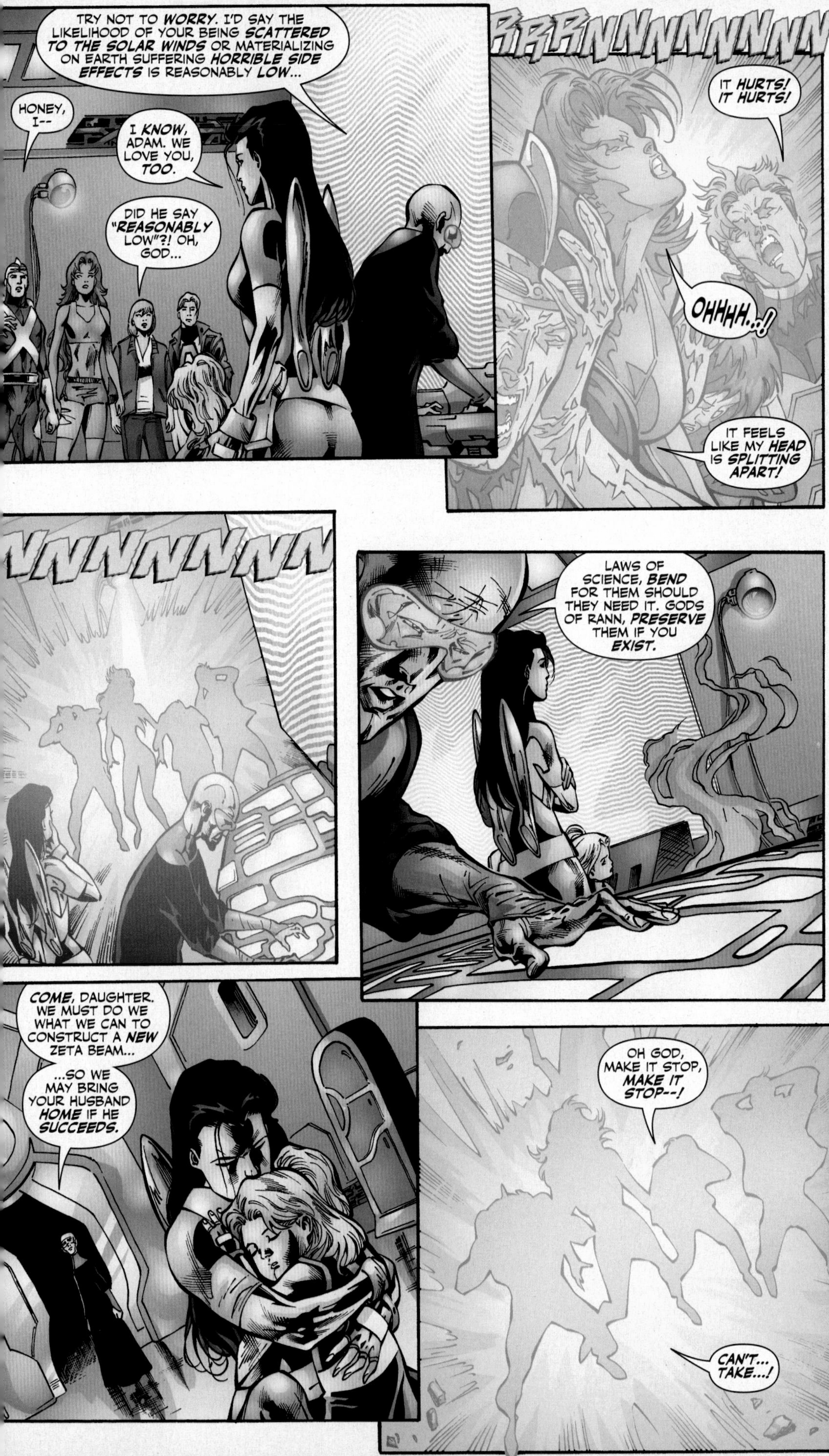
TRY NOT TO WORRY. I'D SAY THE LIKELIHOOD OF YOUR BEING SCATTERED TO THE SOLAR WINDS OR MATERIALIZING ON EARTH SUFFERING HORRIBLE SIDE EFFECTS IS REASONABLY LOW...
HONEY, I--
I KNOW, ADAM. WE LOVE YOU, TOO.
DID HE SAY "REASONABLY LOW"?! OH, GOD...
RRRNNNNNNNNN
IT HURTS! IT HURTS!
OHHHH...!
IT FEELS LIKE MY HEAD IS SPLITTING APART!
NNNNNNNNN
LAWS OF SCIENCE, BEND FOR THEM SHOULD THEY NEED IT. GODS OF RANN, PRESERVE THEM IF YOU EXIST.
COME, DAUGHTER. WE MUST DO WE WHAT WE CAN TO CONSTRUCT A NEW ZETA BEAM...
...SO WE MAY BRING YOUR HUSBAND HOME IF HE SUCCEEDS.
OH GOD, MAKE IT STOP, MAKE IT STOP--!
CAN'T... TAKE...!

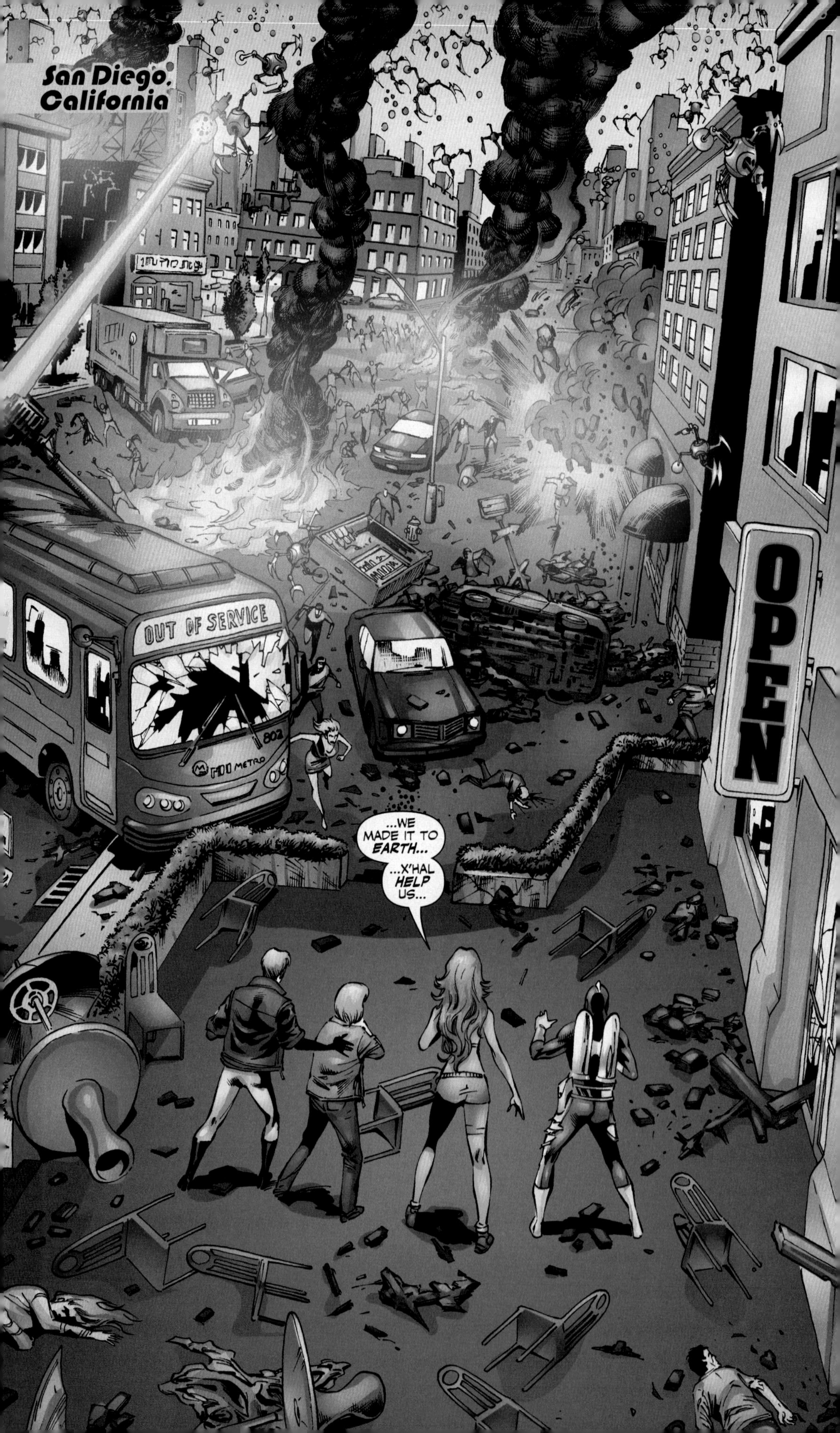
San Diego, California
OUT OF SERVICE
802
METRO
OPEN
...WE MADE IT TO EARTH...
...X'HAL HELP US...

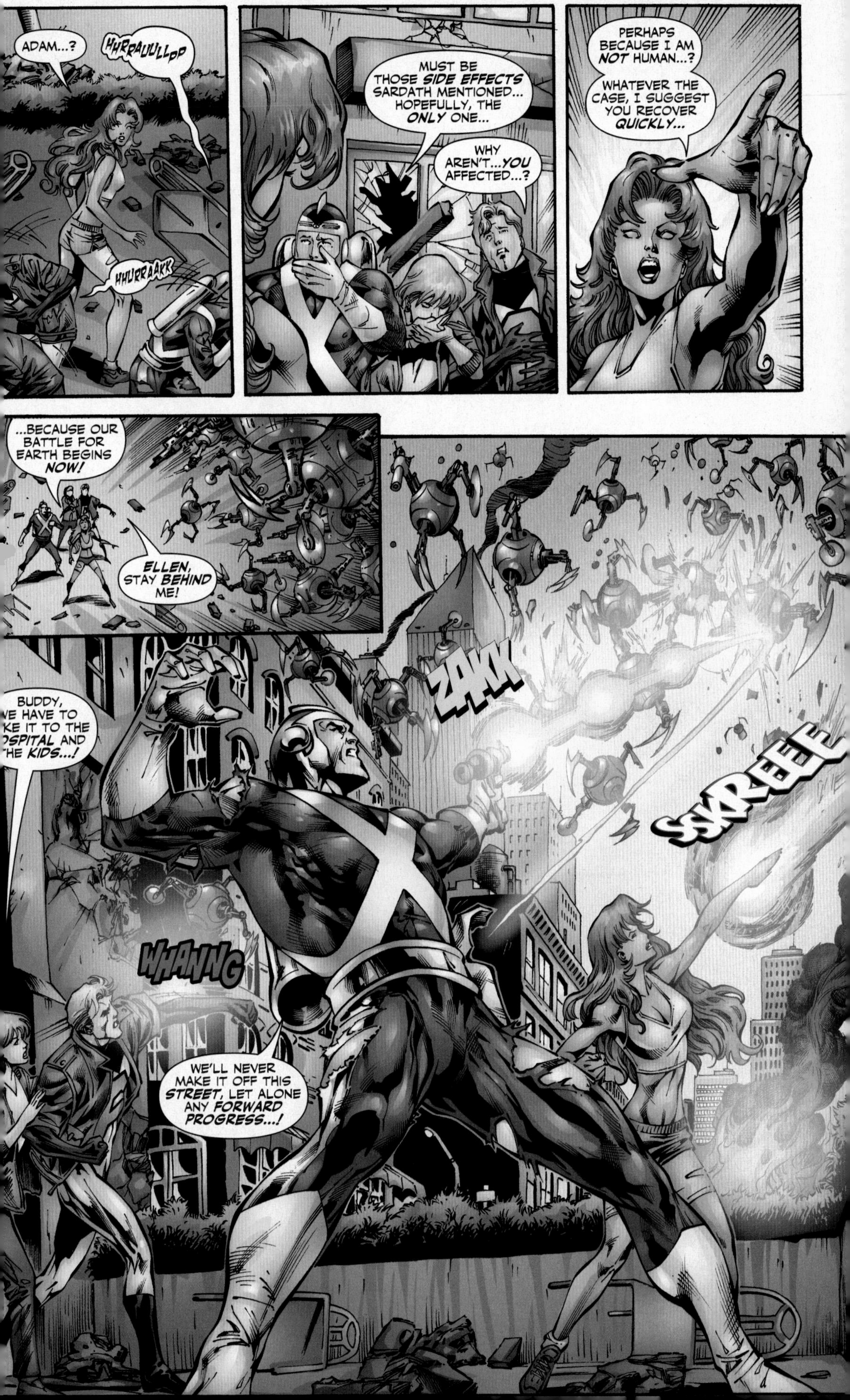
ADAM...?
HHRRAUULLPP
HHURRAAKK
MUST BE THOSE SIDE EFFECTS SARDATH MENTIONED... HOPEFULLY, THE ONLY ONE...
WHY AREN'T...YOU AFFECTED...?
PERHAPS BECAUSE I AM NOT HUMAN...?
WHATEVER THE CASE, I SUGGEST YOU RECOVER QUICKLY...
...BECAUSE OUR BATTLE FOR EARTH BEGINS NOW!
ELLEN, STAY BEHIND ME!
ZAKK
BUDDY, WE HAVE TO KE IT TO THE OSPITAL AND THE KIDS...!
SSKREEE
WHANNG
WE'LL NEVER MAKE IT OFF THIS STREET, LET ALONE ANY FORWARD PROGRESS...!

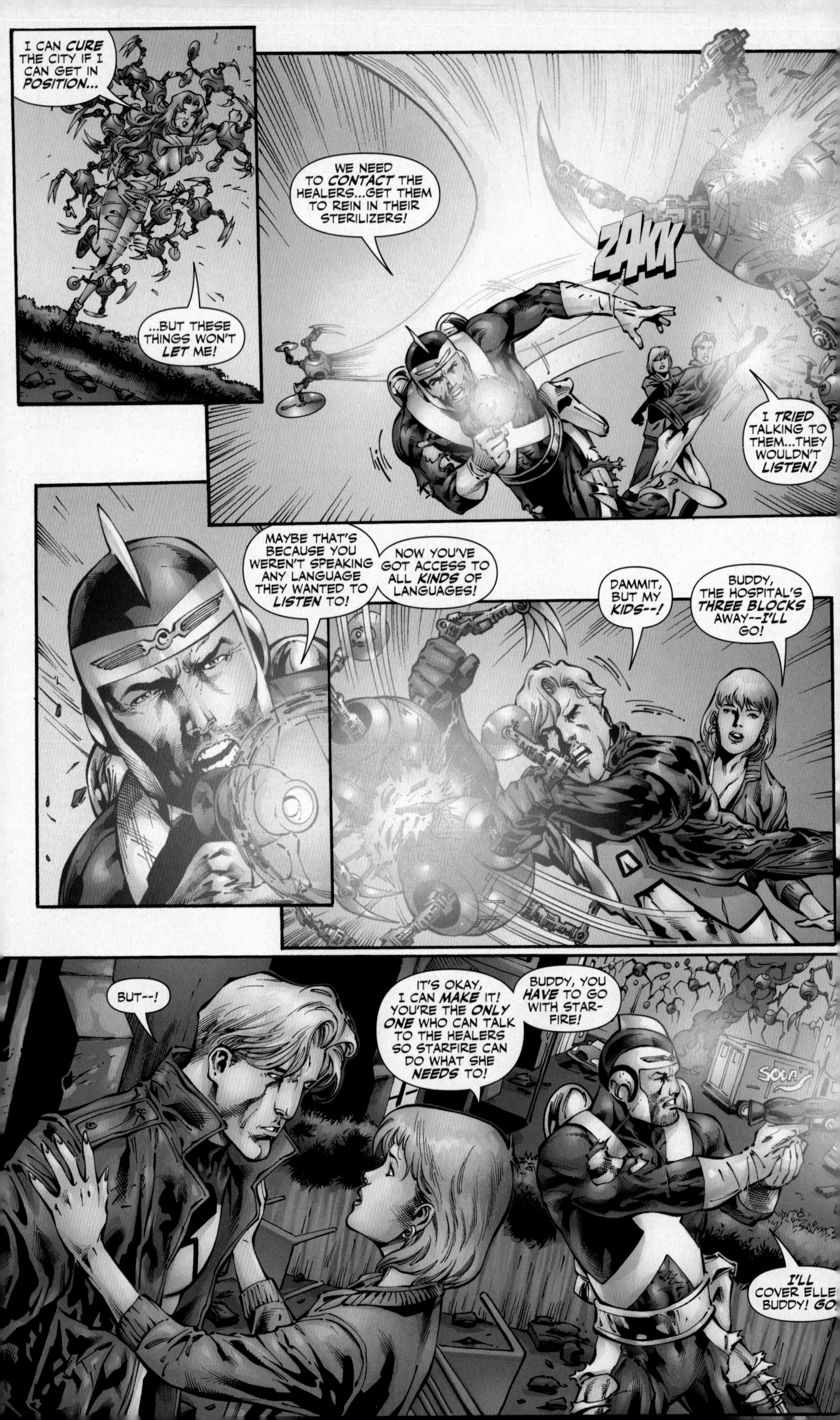
I CAN CURE THE CITY IF I CAN GET IN POSITION...
...BUT THESE THINGS WON'T LET ME!
WE NEED TO CONTACT THE HEALERS...GET THEM TO REIN IN THEIR STERILIZERS!
ZAKK
I TRIED TALKING TO THEM...THEY WOULDN'T LISTEN!
MAYBE THAT'S BECAUSE YOU WEREN'T SPEAKING ANY LANGUAGE THEY WANTED TO LISTEN TO!
NOW YOU'VE GOT ACCESS TO ALL KINDS OF LANGUAGES!
DAMMIT, BUT MY KIDS--!
BUDDY, THE HOSPITAL'S THREE BLOCKS AWAY--I'LL GO!
BUT--!
IT'S OKAY, I CAN MAKE IT! YOU'RE THE ONLY ONE WHO CAN TALK TO THE HEALERS SO STARFIRE CAN DO WHAT SHE NEEDS TO!
BUDDY, YOU HAVE TO GO WITH STAR-FIRE!
SODA
I'LL COVER ELLE BUDDY! GO

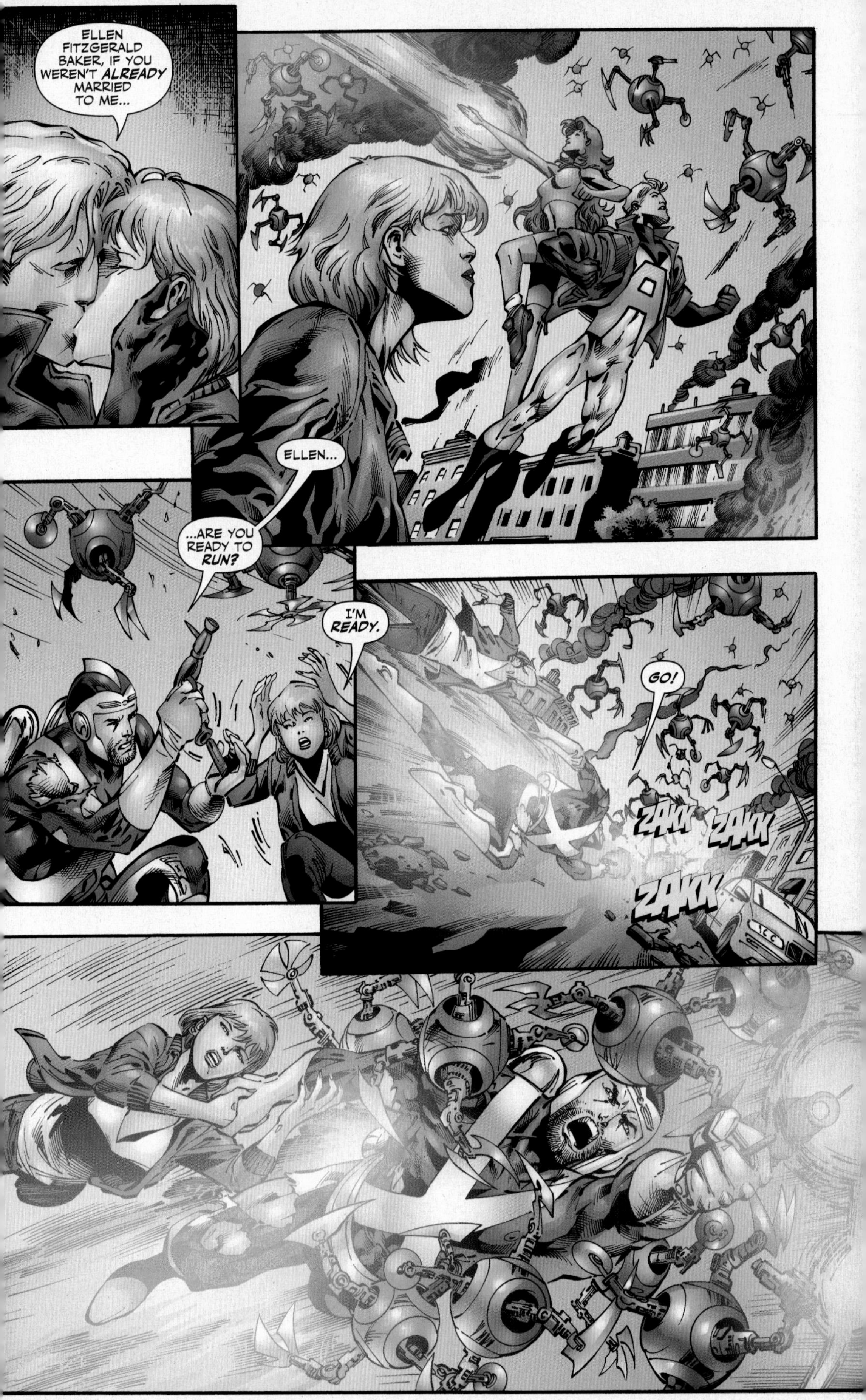
ELLEN FITZGERALD BAKER, IF YOU WEREN'T ALREADY MARRIED TO ME...
ELLEN...
...ARE YOU READY TO RUN?
I'M READY.
GO!
ZAKK ZAKK
ZAKK

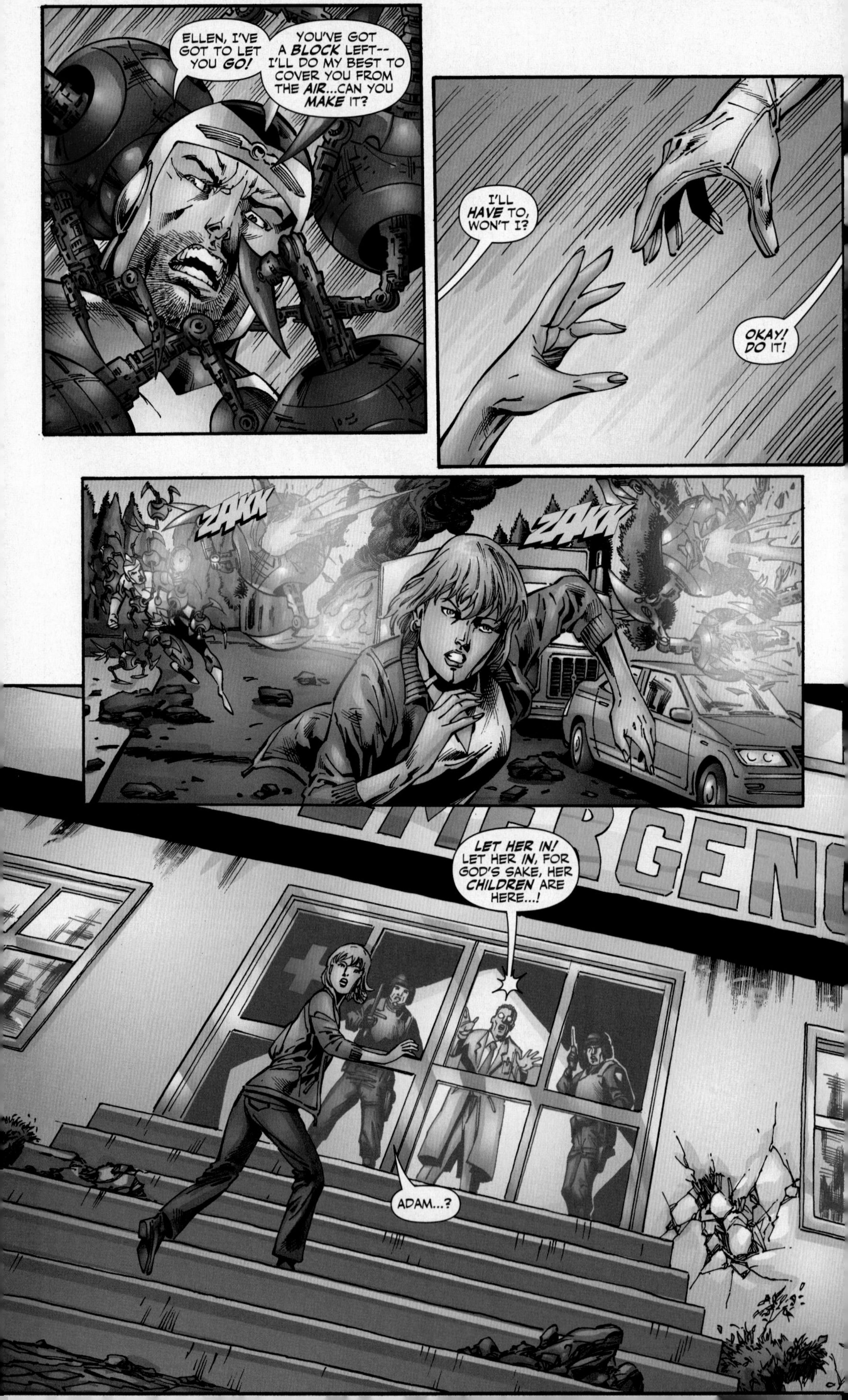
ELLEN, I'VE GOT TO LET YOU GO!
YOU'VE GOT A BLOCK LEFT-- I'LL DO MY BEST TO COVER YOU FROM THE AIR...CAN YOU MAKE IT?
I'LL HAVE TO, WON'T I?
OKAY! DO IT!
ZAKK
ZAKK
LET HER IN! LET HER IN, FOR GOD'S SAKE, HER CHILDREN ARE HERE...!
ADAM...?

ADAM!
I'M FINE! GO TO YOUR KIDS! I'LL BE FINE!
DAMMIT!
IF I CAN GET TO MY JET PACK CONTROLS...RIG THE TANKS TO EXPLODE OUT...
...I MIGHT BLOW THESE THINGS OFF ME SO I CAN GET SOME BREATHING ROOM...IF I SURVIVE THE EXPLOSION...
NO...TOO FAST...
ALANNA...ALEEA... I LOVE YOU...
WHA BOOOM

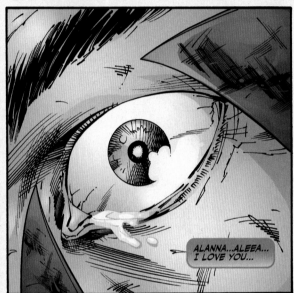

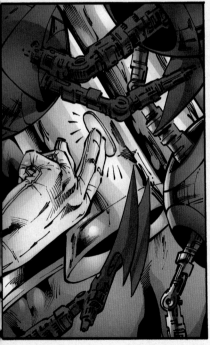

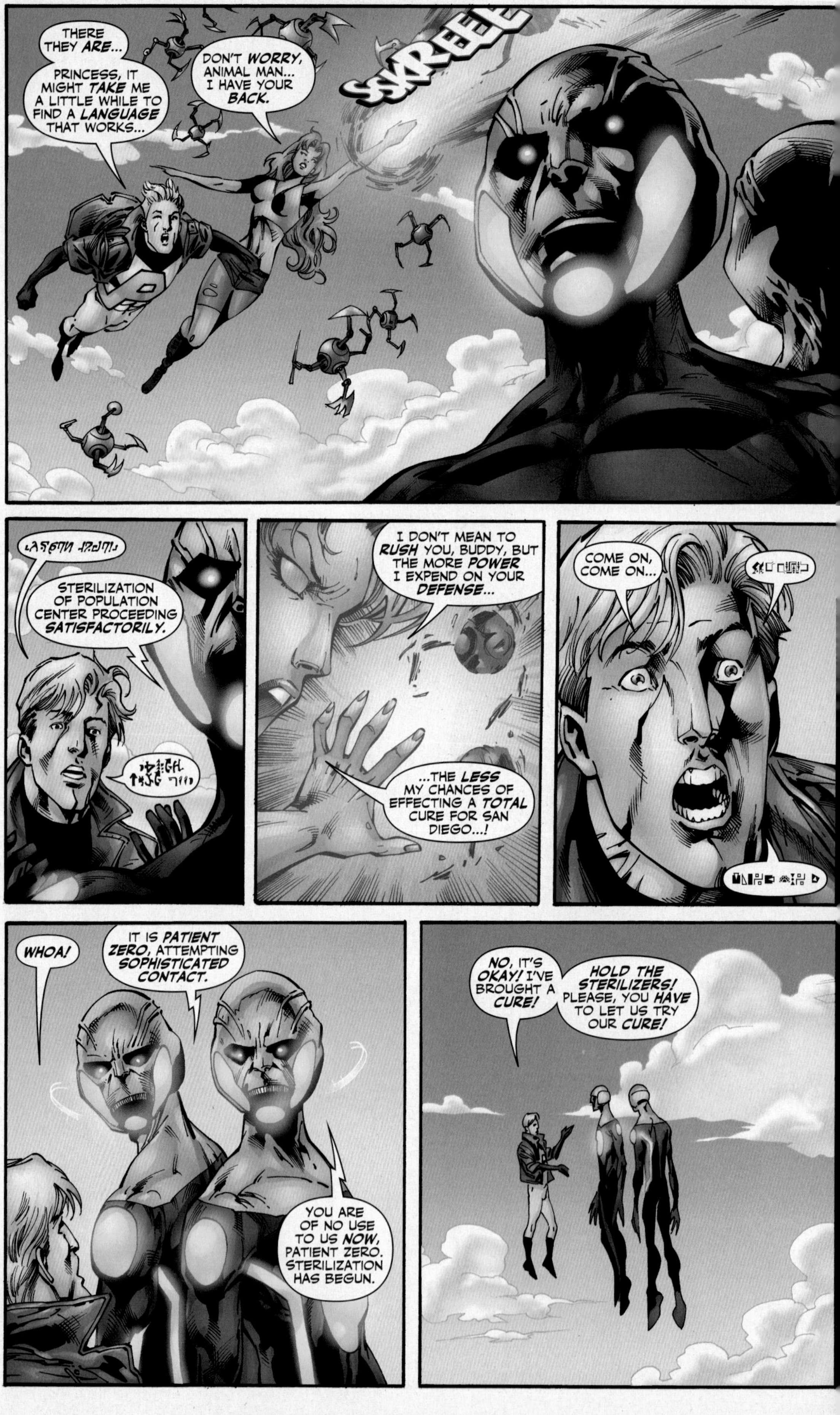
THERE THEY ARE...
PRINCESS, IT MIGHT TAKE ME A LITTLE WHILE TO FIND A LANGUAGE THAT WORKS...
DON'T WORRY, ANIMAL MAN... I HAVE YOUR BACK.
SSKREEE
STERILIZATION OF POPULATION CENTER PROCEEDING SATISFACTORILY.
I DON'T MEAN TO RUSH YOU, BUDDY, BUT THE MORE POWER I EXPEND ON YOUR DEFENSE...
...THE LESS MY CHANCES OF EFFECTING A TOTAL CURE FOR SAN DIEGO...!
COME ON, COME ON...
WHOA!
IT IS PATIENT ZERO, ATTEMPTING SOPHISTICATED CONTACT.
YOU ARE OF NO USE TO US NOW, PATIENT ZERO. STERILIZATION HAS BEGUN.
NO, IT'S OKAY! I'VE BROUGHT A CURE!
HOLD THE STERILIZERS! PLEASE, YOU HAVE TO LET US TRY OUR CURE!

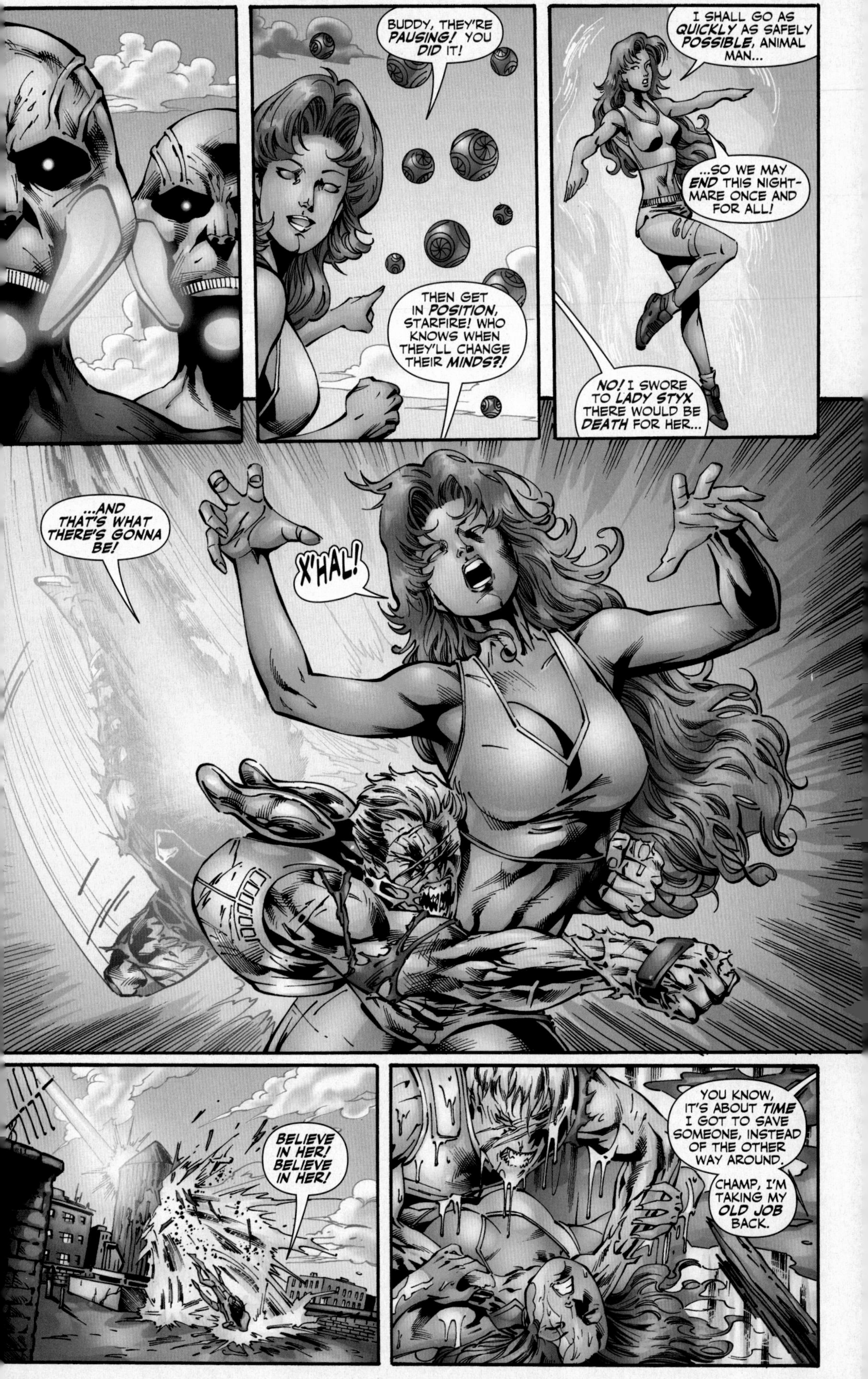
BUDDY, THEY'RE PAUSING! YOU DID IT!
THEN GET IN POSITION, STARFIRE! WHO KNOWS WHEN THEY'LL CHANGE THEIR MINDS?!
I SHALL GO AS QUICKLY AS SAFELY POSSIBLE, ANIMAL MAN...
...SO WE MAY END THIS NIGHTMARE ONCE AND FOR ALL!
NO! I SWORE TO LADY STYX THERE WOULD BE DEATH FOR HER...
...AND THAT'S WHAT THERE'S GONNA BE!
X'HAL!
BELIEVE IN HER! BELIEVE IN HER!
YOU KNOW, IT'S ABOUT TIME I GOT TO SAVE SOMEONE, INSTEAD OF THE OTHER WAY AROUND.
CHAMP, I'M TAKING MY OLD JOB BACK.

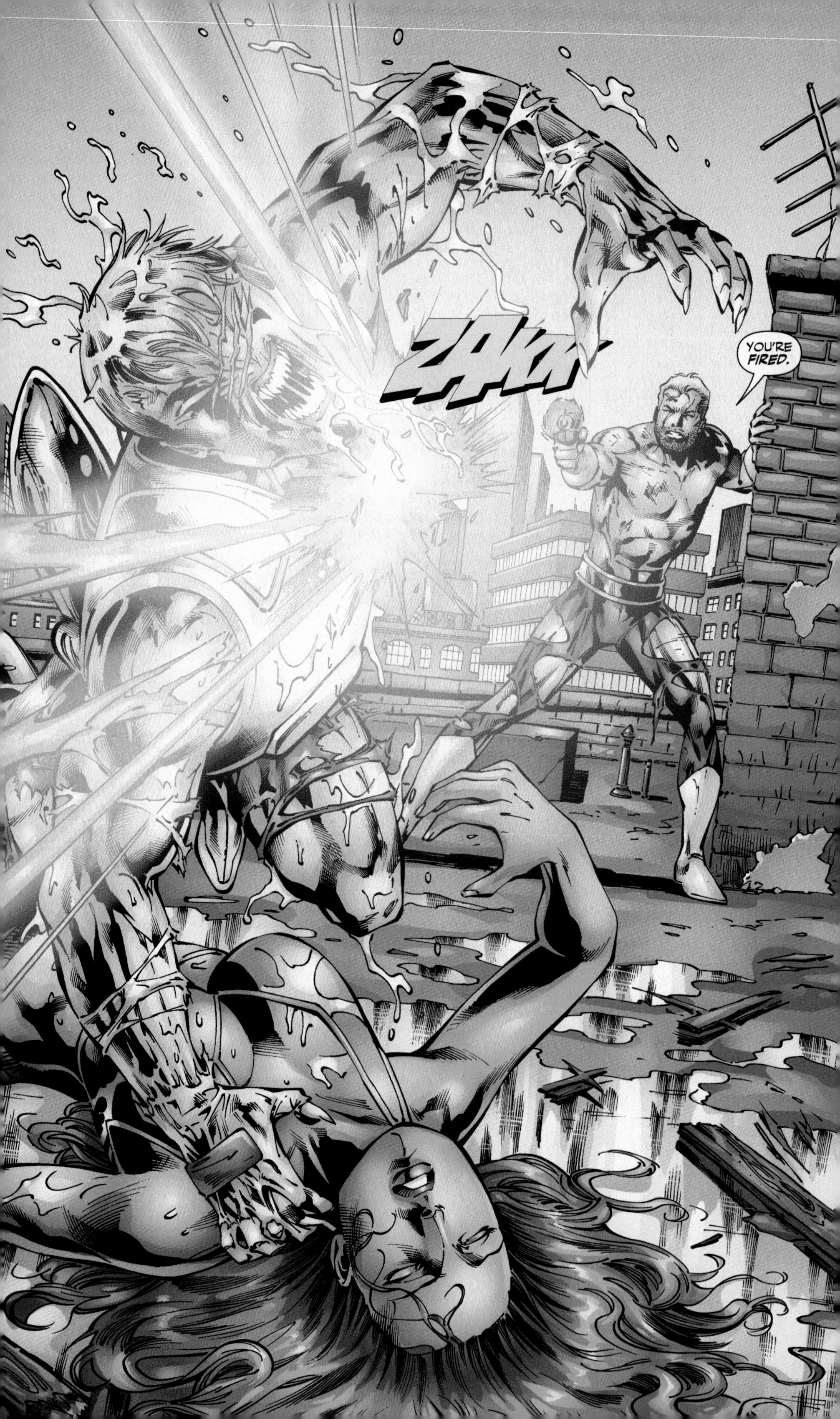
ZAKK
YOU'RE FIRED.

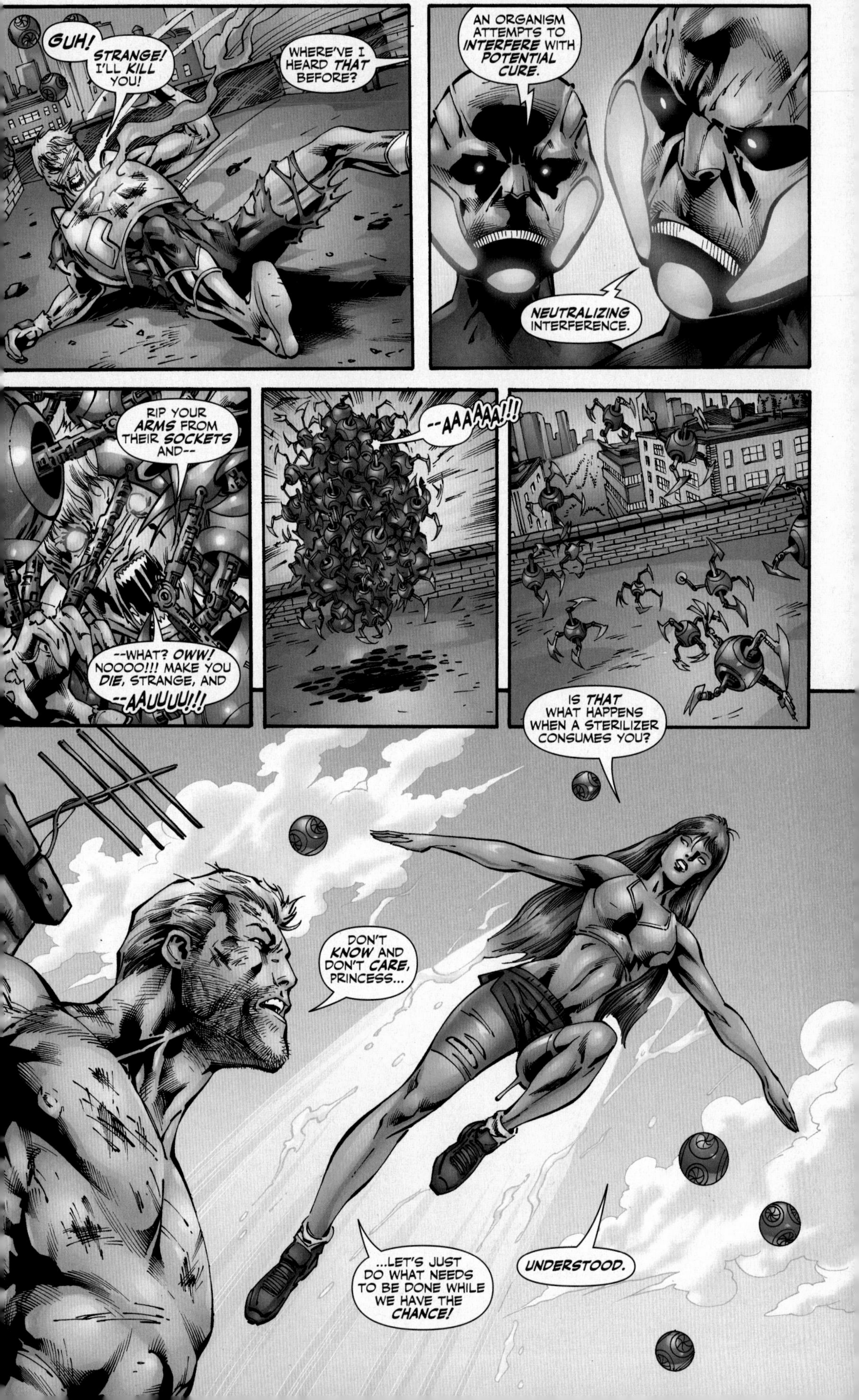
GUH! STRANGE! I'LL KILL YOU!
WHERE'VE I HEARD THAT BEFORE?
AN ORGANISM ATTEMPTS TO INTERFERE WITH POTENTIAL CURE.
NEUTRALIZING INTERFERENCE.
RIP YOUR ARMS FROM THEIR SOCKETS AND--
--WHAT? OWW! NOOOO!!! MAKE YOU DIE, STRANGE, AND --AAUUUU!!!
--AAAAAA!!!
IS THAT WHAT HAPPENS WHEN A STERILIZER CONSUMES YOU?
DON'T KNOW AND DON'T CARE, PRINCESS...
...LET'S JUST DO WHAT NEEDS TO BE DONE WHILE WE HAVE THE CHANCE!
UNDERSTOOD.

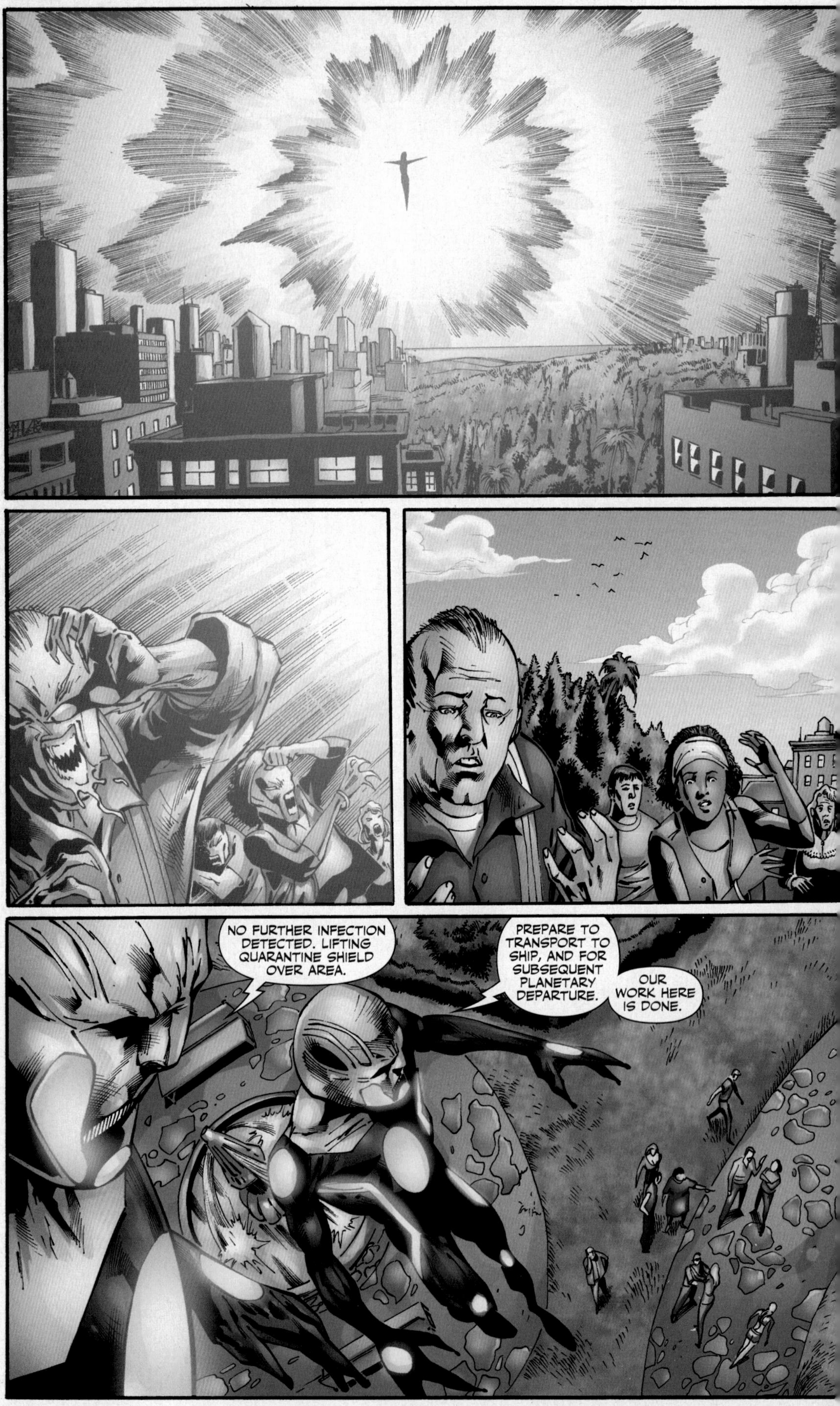
NO FURTHER INFECTION DETECTED. LIFTING QUARANTINE SHIELD OVER AREA.
PREPARE TO TRANSPORT TO SHIP, AND FOR SUBSEQUENT PLANETARY DEPARTURE.
OUR WORK HERE IS DONE.

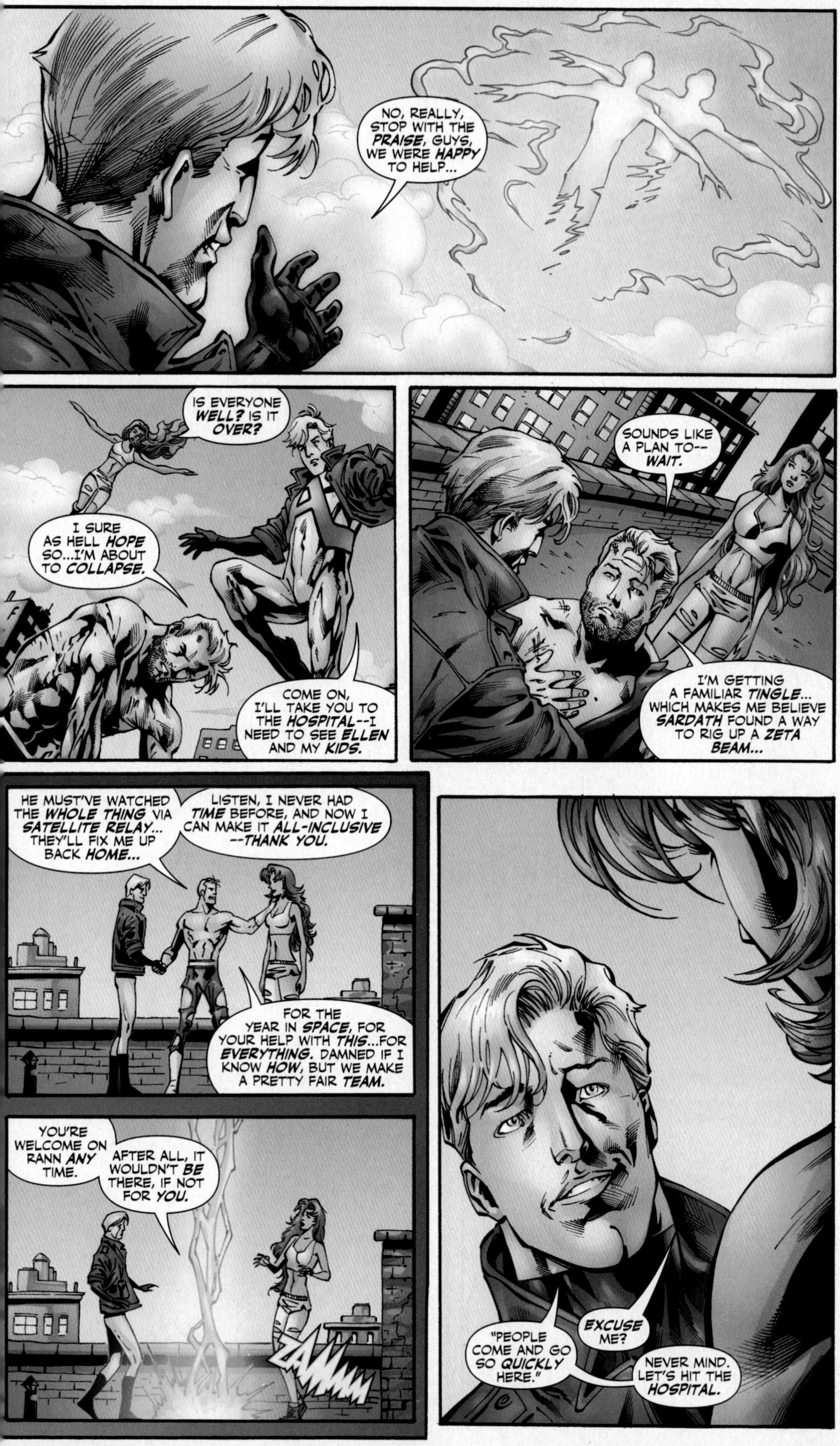
NO, REALLY, STOP WITH THE PRAISE, GUYS, WE WERE HAPPY TO HELP...
IS EVERYONE WELL? IS IT OVER?
I SURE AS HELL HOPE SO...I'M ABOUT TO COLLAPSE.
COME ON, I'LL TAKE YOU TO THE HOSPITAL--I NEED TO SEE ELLEN AND MY KIDS.
SOUNDS LIKE A PLAN TO-- WAIT.
I'M GETTING A FAMILIAR TINGLE... WHICH MAKES ME BELIEVE SARDATH FOUND A WAY TO RIG UP A ZETA BEAM...
HE MUST'VE WATCHED THE WHOLE THING VIA SATELLITE RELAY... THEY'LL FIX ME UP BACK HOME...
LISTEN, I NEVER HAD TIME BEFORE, AND NOW I CAN MAKE IT ALL-INCLUSIVE --THANK YOU.
FOR THE YEAR IN SPACE, FOR YOUR HELP WITH THIS...FOR EVERYTHING. DAMNED IF I KNOW HOW, BUT WE MAKE A PRETTY FAIR TEAM.
YOU'RE WELCOME ON RANN ANY TIME.
AFTER ALL, IT WOULDN'T BE THERE, IF NOT FOR YOU.
ZAMMM
"PEOPLE COME AND GO SO QUICKLY HERE."
EXCUSE ME?
NEVER MIND. LET'S HIT THE HOSPITAL.

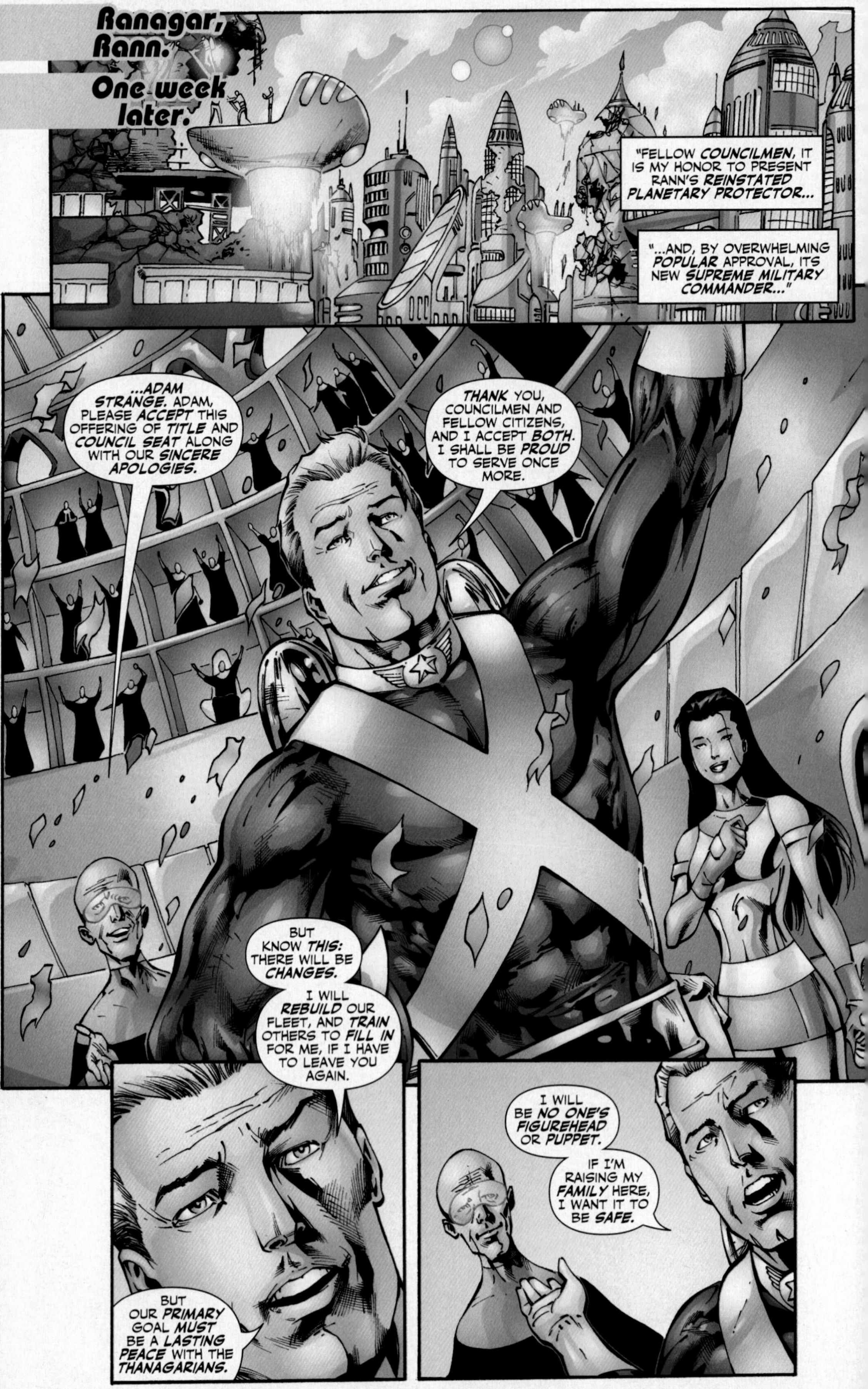
Ranagar, Rann.
One week later.
"FELLOW COUNCILMEN, IT IS MY HONOR TO PRESENT RANN'S REINSTATED PLANETARY PROTECTOR...
"...AND, BY OVERWHELMING POPULAR APPROVAL, ITS NEW SUPREME MILITARY COMMANDER..."
...ADAM STRANGE. ADAM, PLEASE ACCEPT THIS OFFERING OF TITLE AND COUNCIL SEAT ALONG WITH OUR SINCERE APOLOGIES.
THANK YOU, COUNCILMEN AND FELLOW CITIZENS, AND I ACCEPT BOTH. I SHALL BE PROUD TO SERVE ONCE MORE.
BUT KNOW THIS: THERE WILL BE CHANGES.
I WILL REBUILD OUR FLEET, AND TRAIN OTHERS TO FILL IN FOR ME, IF I HAVE TO LEAVE YOU AGAIN.
BUT OUR PRIMARY GOAL MUST BE A LASTING PEACE WITH THE THANAGARIANS.
I WILL BE NO ONE'S FIGUREHEAD OR PUPPET.
IF I'M RAISING MY FAMILY HERE, I WANT IT TO BE SAFE.

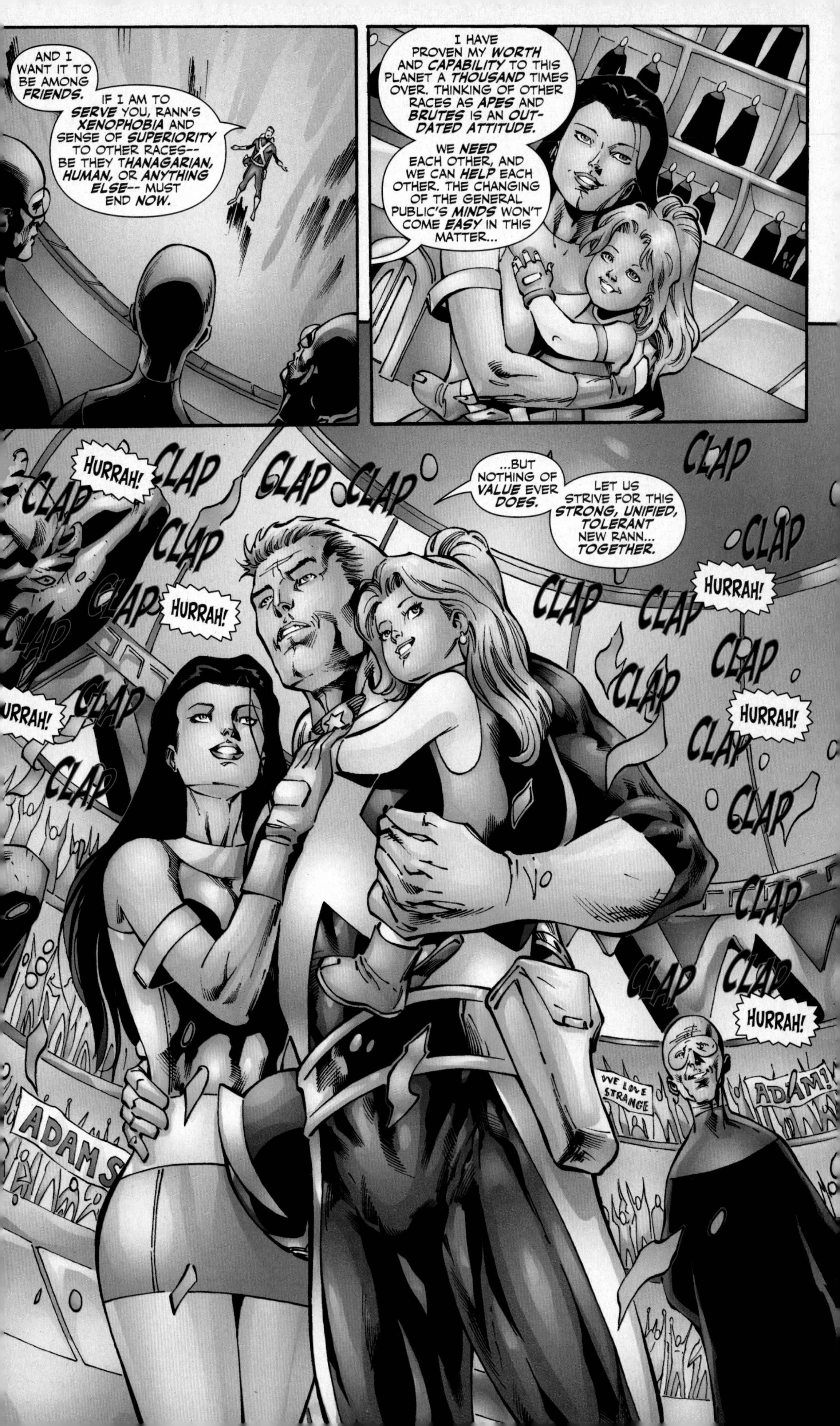
AND I WANT IT TO BE AMONG FRIENDS.
IF I AM TO SERVE YOU, RANN'S XENOPHOBIA AND SENSE OF SUPERIORITY TO OTHER RACES-- BE THEY THANAGARIAN, HUMAN, OR ANYTHING ELSE-- MUST END NOW.
I HAVE PROVEN MY WORTH AND CAPABILITY TO THIS PLANET A THOUSAND TIMES OVER. THINKING OF OTHER RACES AS APES AND BRUTES IS AN OUT-DATED ATTITUDE.
WE NEED EACH OTHER, AND WE CAN HELP EACH OTHER. THE CHANGING OF THE GENERAL PUBLIC'S MINDS WON'T COME EASY IN THIS MATTER...
...BUT NOTHING OF VALUE EVER DOES.
LET US STRIVE FOR THIS STRONG, UNIFIED, TOLERANT NEW RANN... TOGETHER.
HURRAH!
CLAP CLAP CLAP CLAP
HURRAH!
HURRAH!
HURRAH!
HURRAH!
HURRAH!
WE LOVE STRANGE
ADAMS
ADAM!

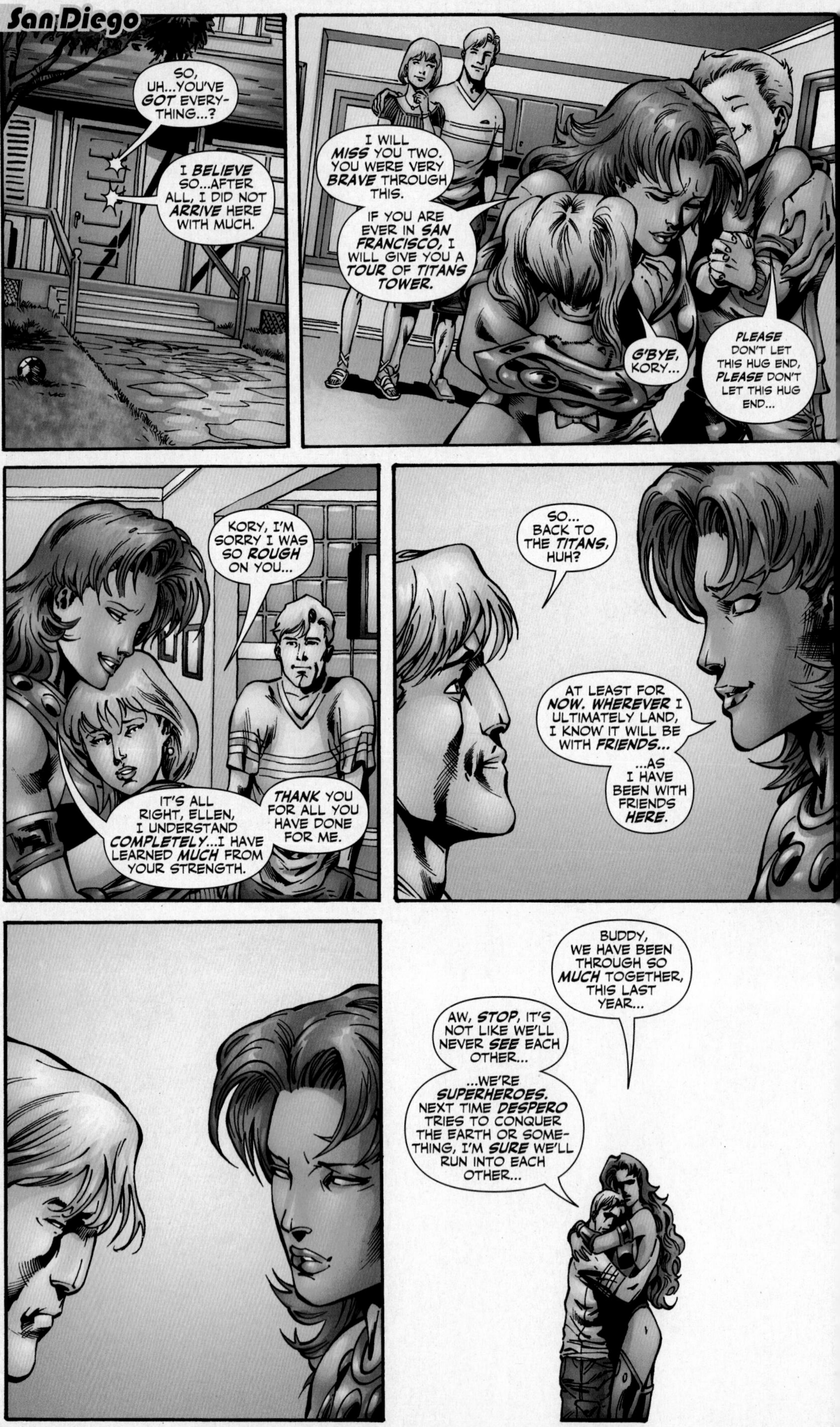
San Diego
SO, UH...YOU'VE GOT EVERYTHING...?
I BELIEVE SO...AFTER ALL, I DID NOT ARRIVE HERE WITH MUCH.
I WILL MISS YOU TWO. YOU WERE VERY BRAVE THROUGH THIS.
IF YOU ARE EVER IN SAN FRANCISCO, I WILL GIVE YOU A TOUR OF TITANS TOWER.
G'BYE, KORY...
PLEASE DON'T LET THIS HUG END, PLEASE DON'T LET THIS HUG END...
KORY, I'M SORRY I WAS SO ROUGH ON YOU...
IT'S ALL RIGHT, ELLEN, I UNDERSTAND COMPLETELY...I HAVE LEARNED MUCH FROM YOUR STRENGTH.
THANK YOU FOR ALL YOU HAVE DONE FOR ME.
SO... BACK TO THE TITANS, HUH?
AT LEAST FOR NOW. WHEREVER I ULTIMATELY LAND, I KNOW IT WILL BE WITH FRIENDS...
...AS I HAVE BEEN WITH FRIENDS HERE.
BUDDY, WE HAVE BEEN THROUGH SO MUCH TOGETHER, THIS LAST YEAR...
AW, STOP, IT'S NOT LIKE WE'LL NEVER SEE EACH OTHER...
...WE'RE SUPERHEROES. NEXT TIME DESPERO TRIES TO CONQUER THE EARTH OR SOMETHING, I'M SURE WE'LL RUN INTO EACH OTHER...

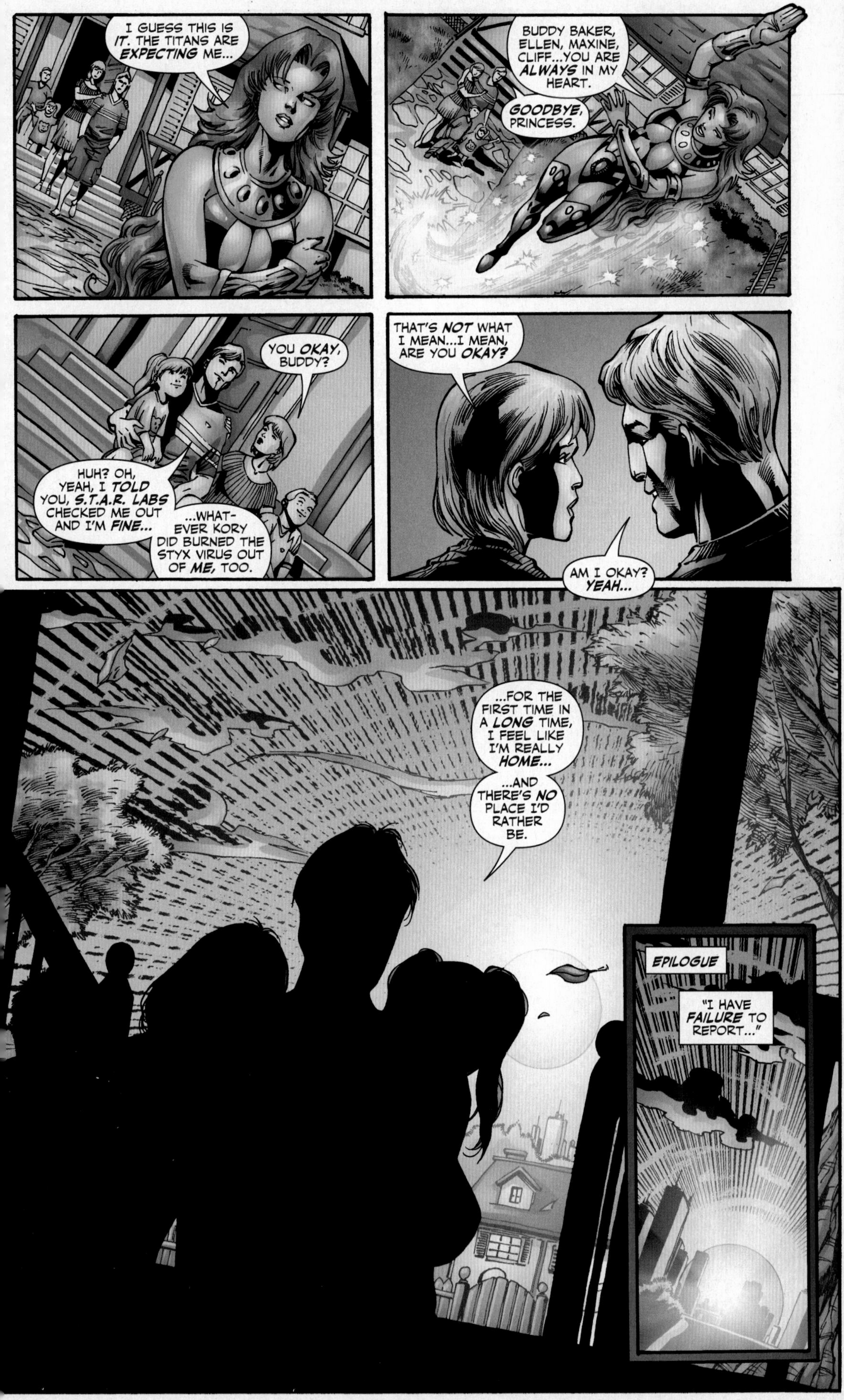
I GUESS THIS IS IT. THE TITANS ARE EXPECTING ME...
BUDDY BAKER, ELLEN, MAXINE, CLIFF...YOU ARE ALWAYS IN MY HEART.
GOODBYE, PRINCESS.
YOU OKAY, BUDDY?
HUH? OH, YEAH, I TOLD YOU, S.T.A.R. LABS CHECKED ME OUT AND I'M FINE...
...WHAT-EVER KORY DID BURNED THE STYX VIRUS OUT OF ME, TOO.
THAT'S NOT WHAT I MEAN...I MEAN, ARE YOU OKAY?
AM I OKAY? YEAH...
...FOR THE FIRST TIME IN A LONG TIME, I FEEL LIKE I'M REALLY HOME...
...AND THERE'S NO PLACE I'D RATHER BE.
EPILOGUE
"I HAVE FAILURE TO REPORT..."

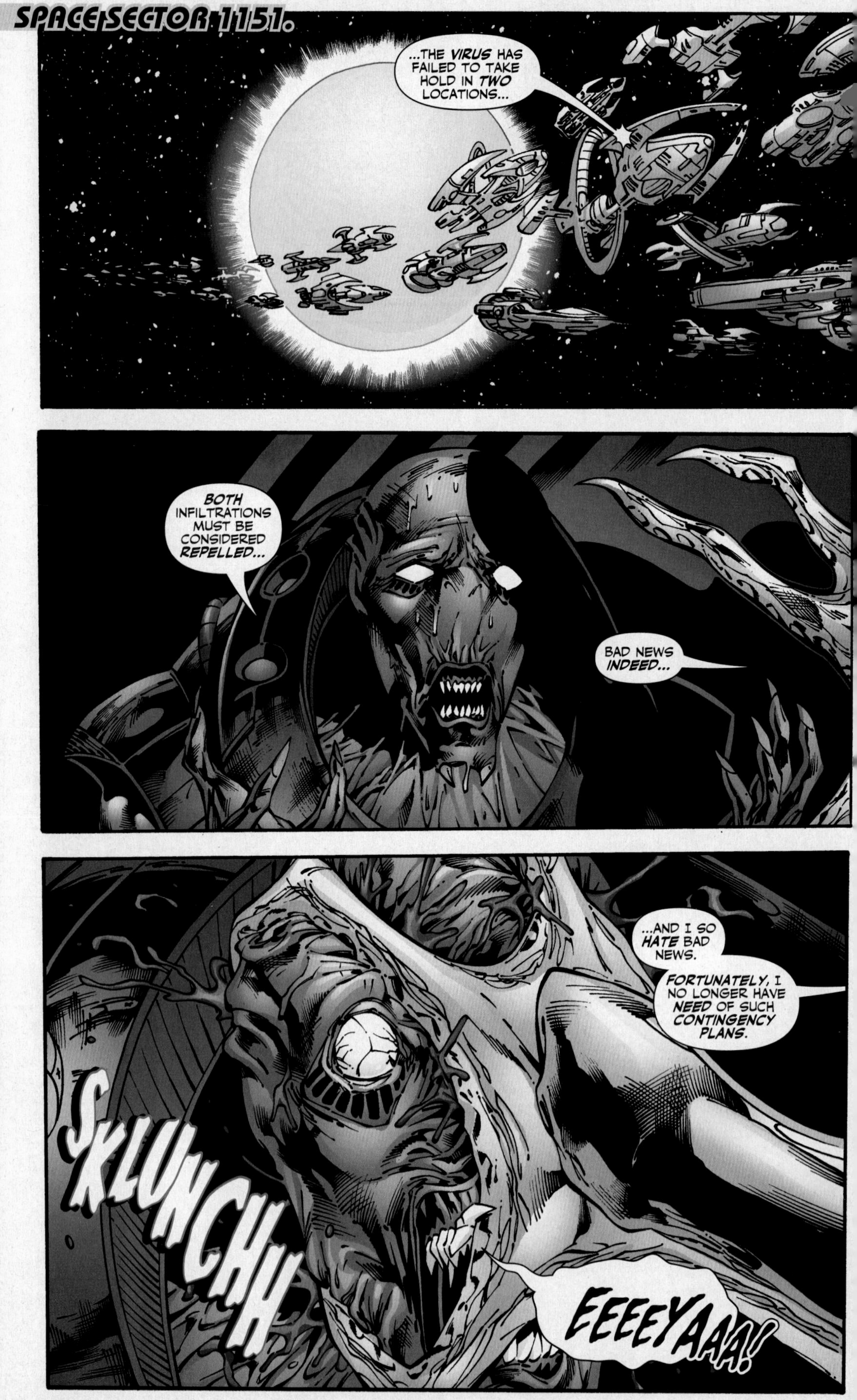
SPACE SECTOR 1151.
...THE VIRUS HAS FAILED TO TAKE HOLD IN TWO LOCATIONS...
BOTH INFILTRATIONS MUST BE CONSIDERED REPELLED...
BAD NEWS INDEED...
...AND I SO HATE BAD NEWS.
FORTUNATELY, I NO LONGER HAVE NEED OF SUCH CONTINGENCY PLANS.
SKLUNCHH
EEEEYAAA!

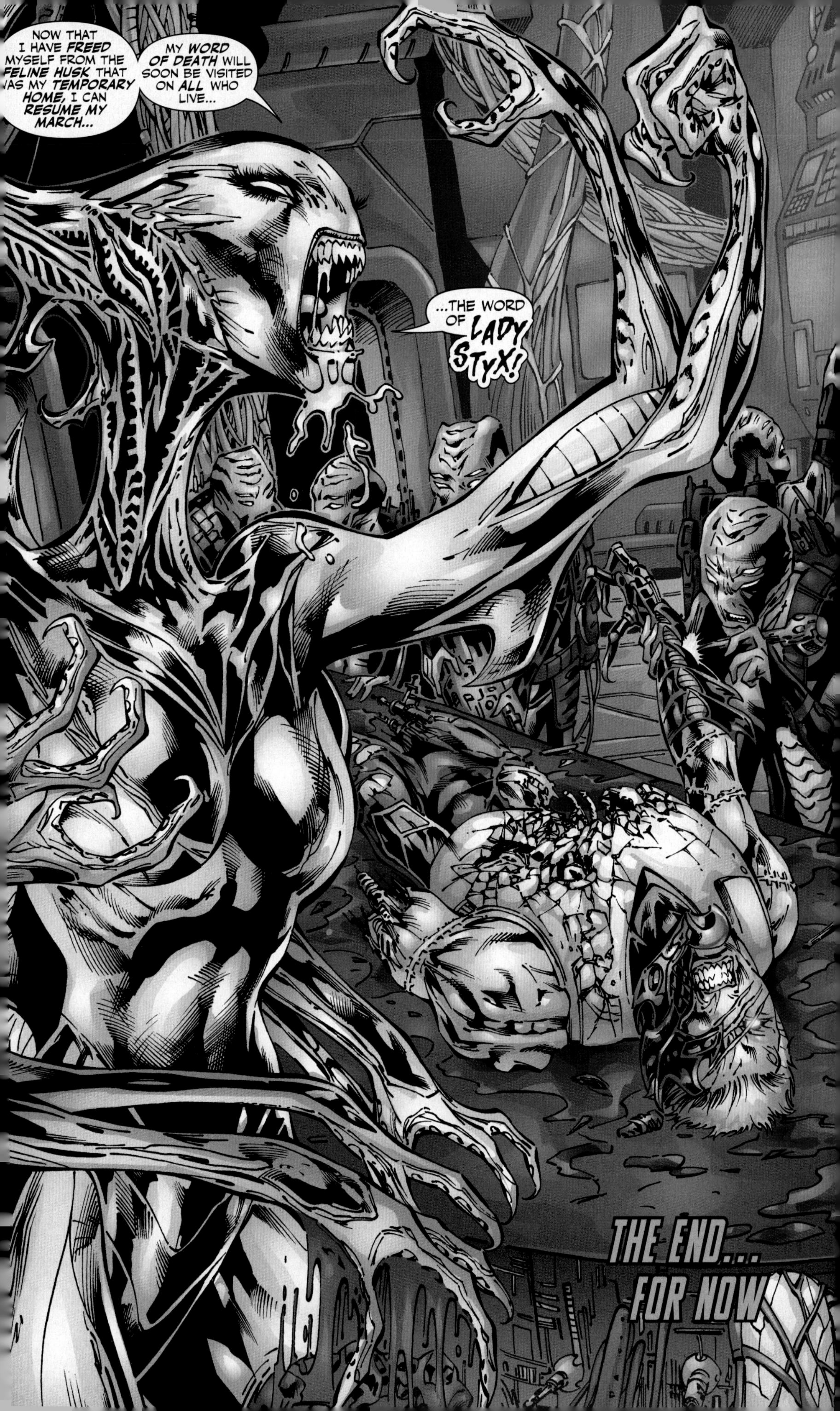
NOW THAT I HAVE FREED MYSELF FROM THE FELINE HUSK THAT WAS MY TEMPORARY HOME, I CAN RESUME MY MARCH...
MY WORD OF DEATH WILL SOON BE VISITED ON ALL WHO LIVE...
...THE WORD OF LADY STYX!
THE END... FOR NOW

COVER GALLERY

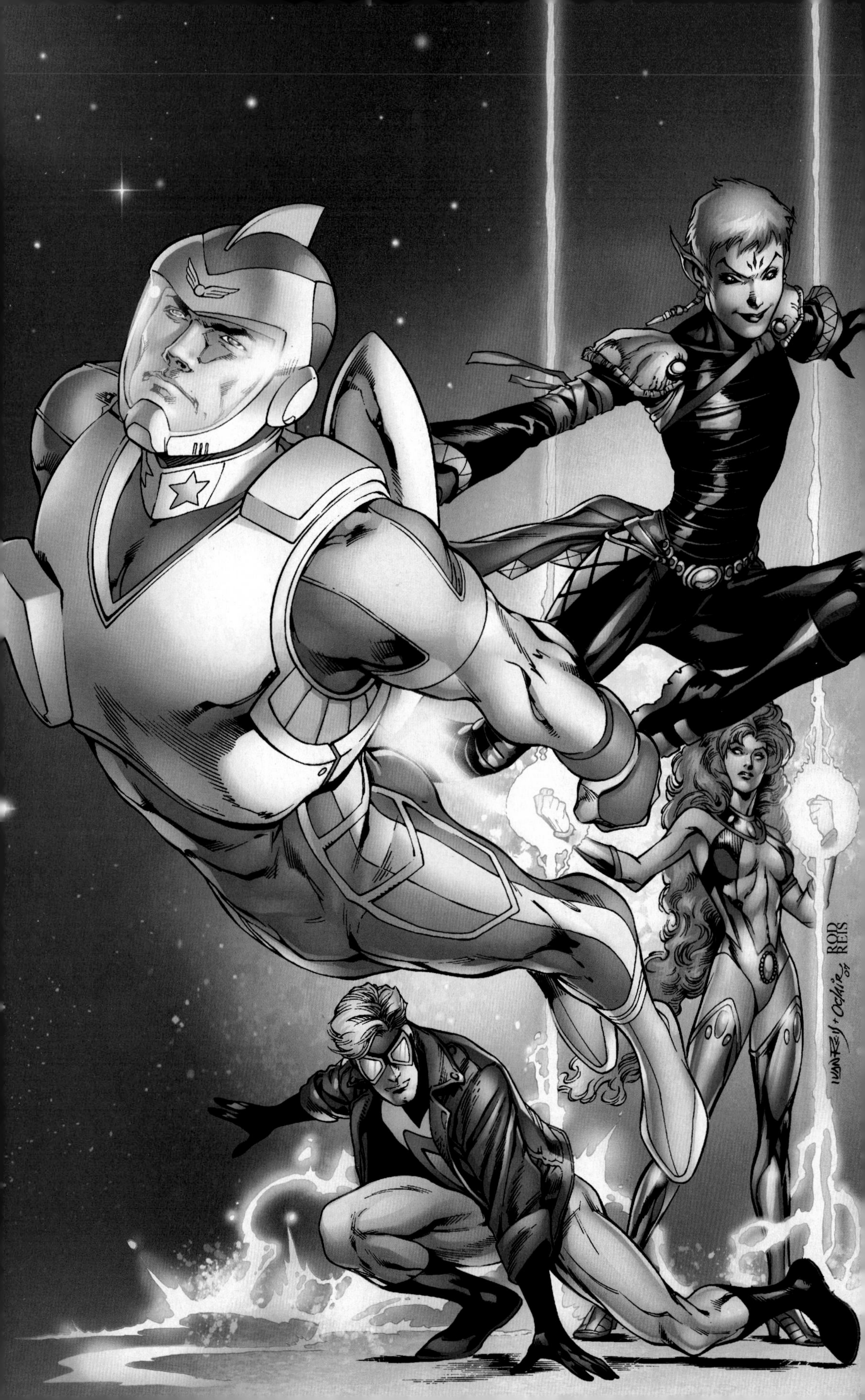
ROD REIS

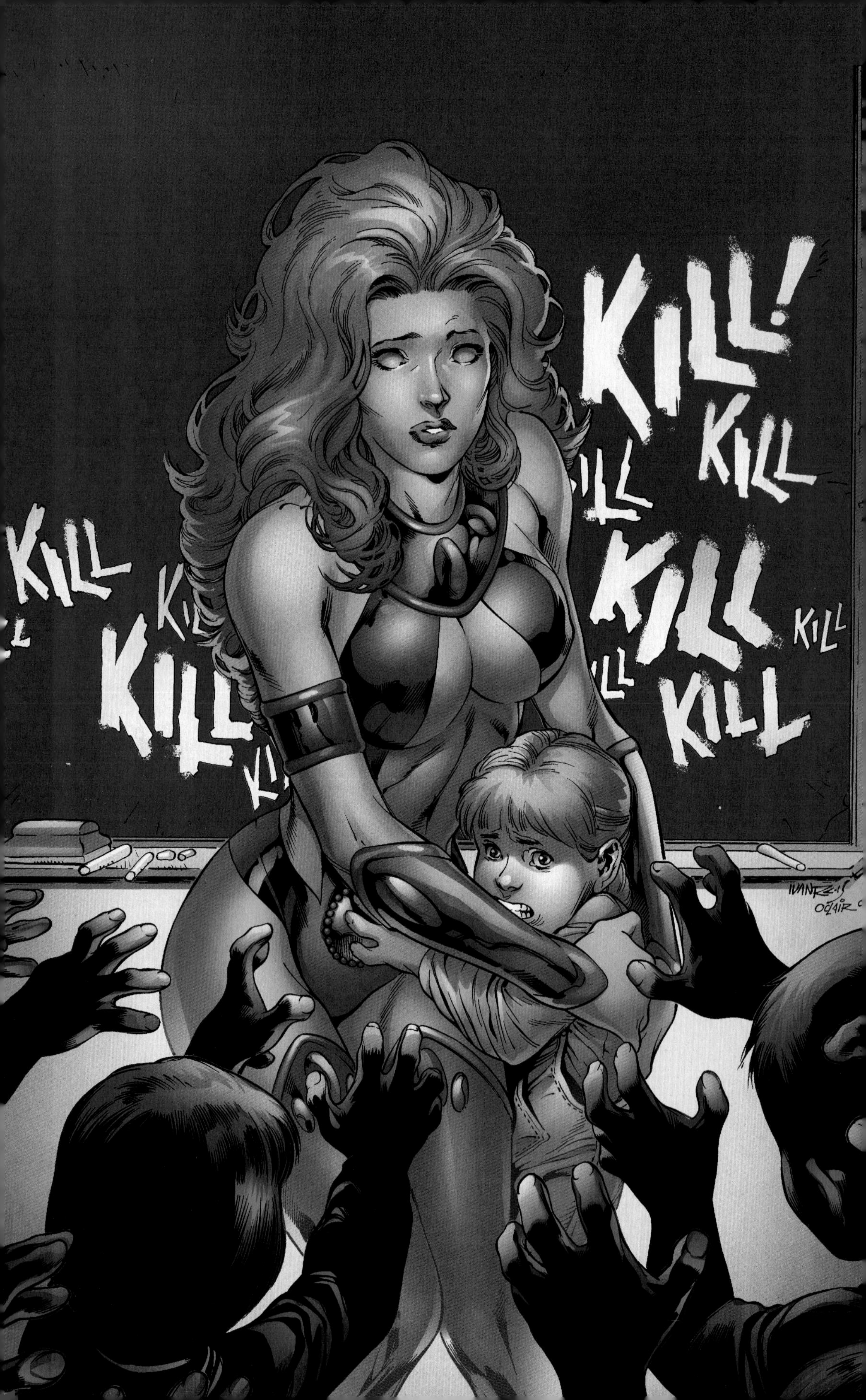

KILL!
KILL
KILL
KILL
KILL
KILL
KILL
KILL

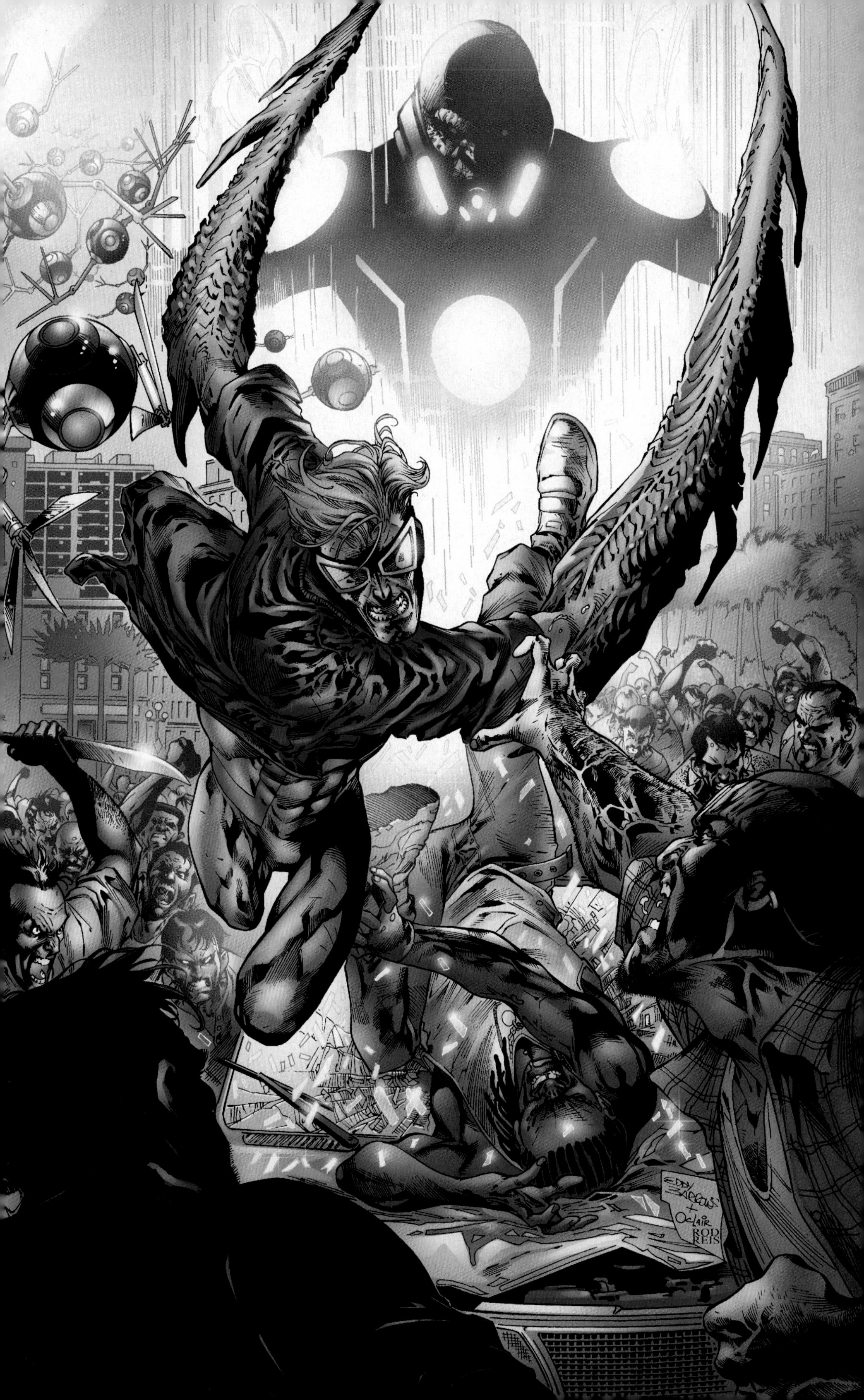
EDDY BARROWS
+
OCLAIR
ROD REIS

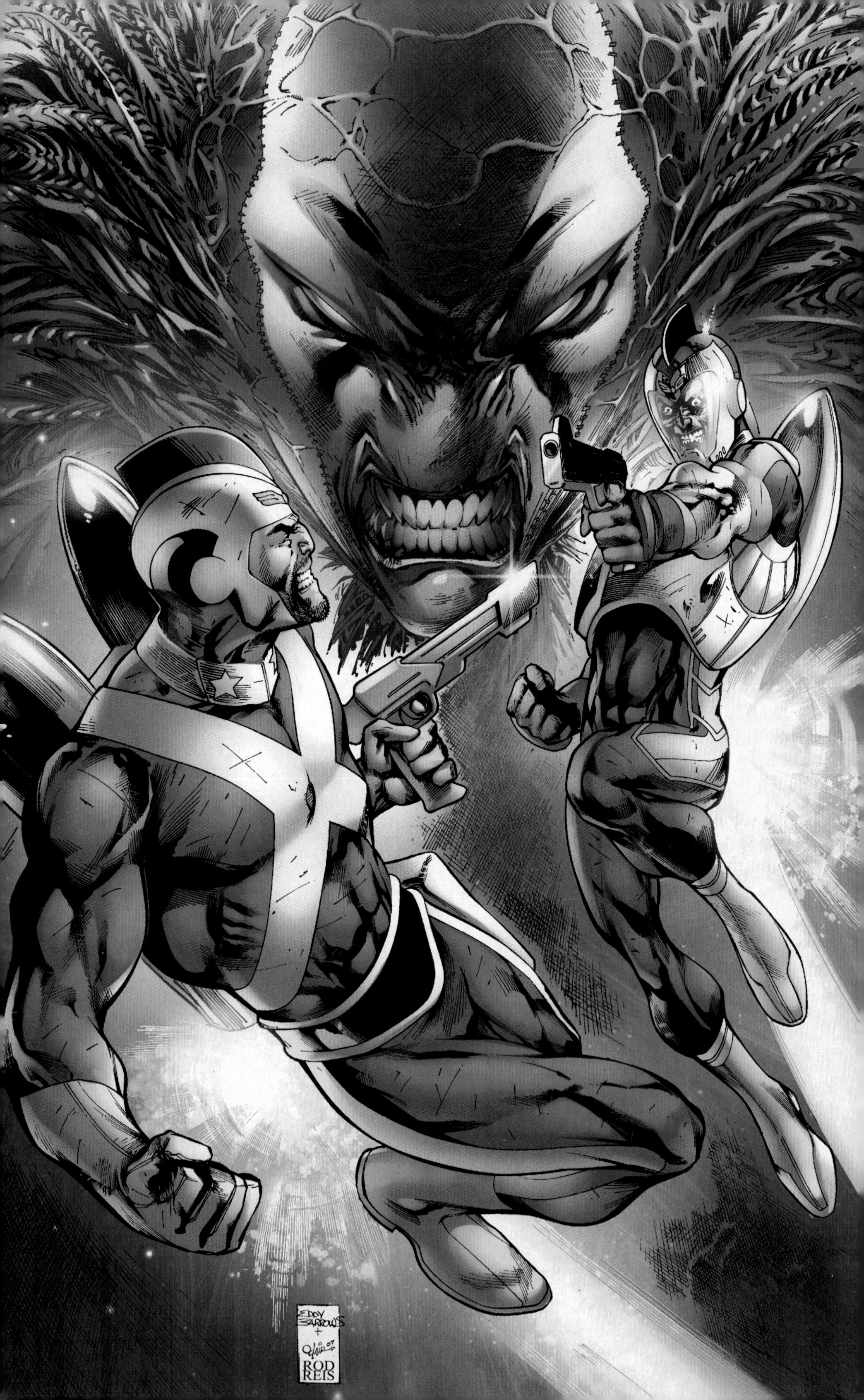
EDDY BARROWS
+
ROD REIS

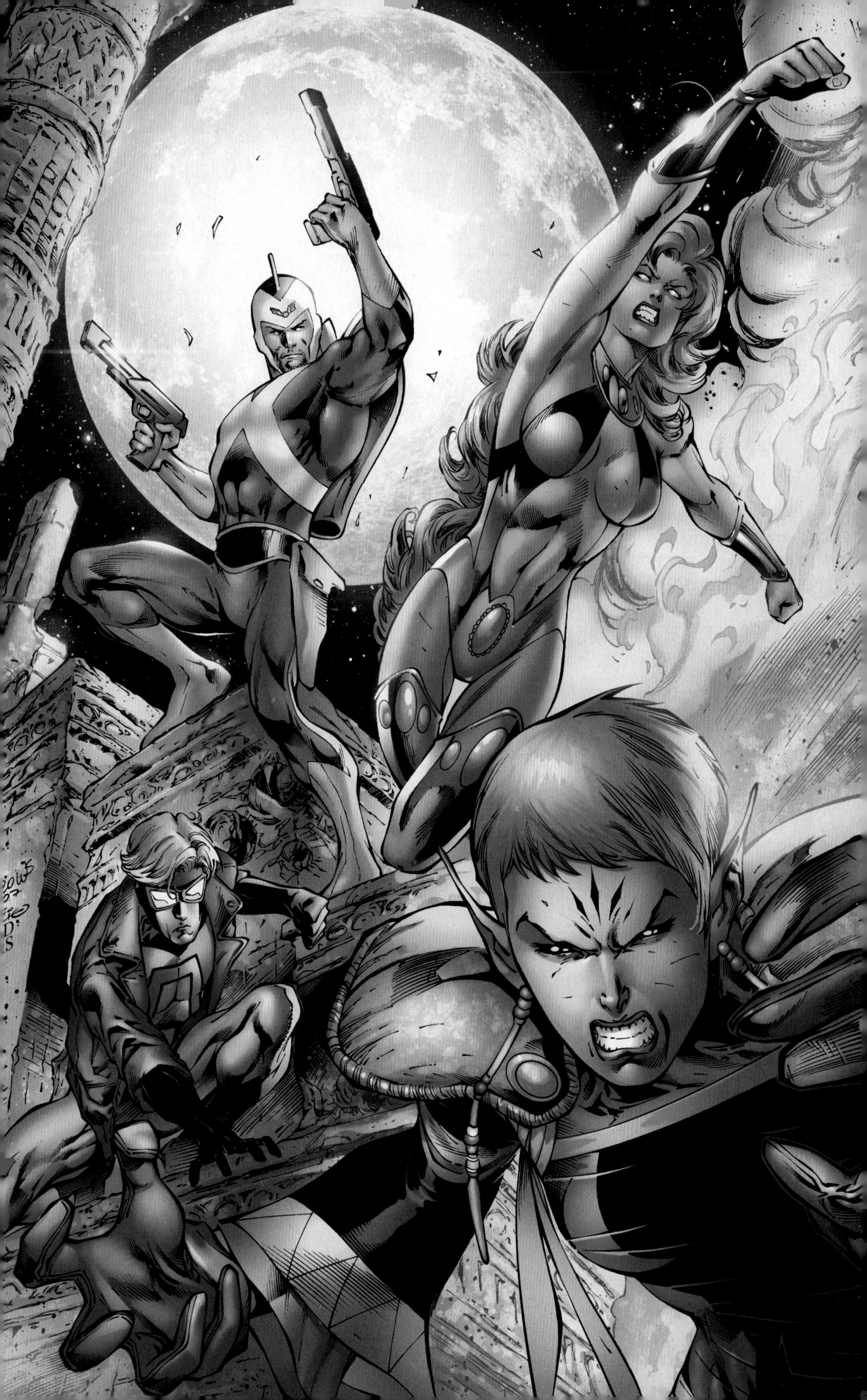

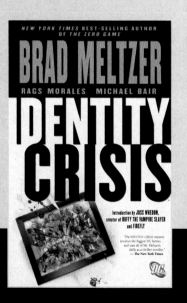

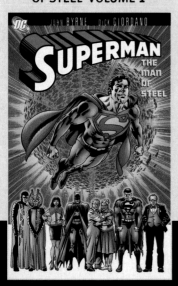
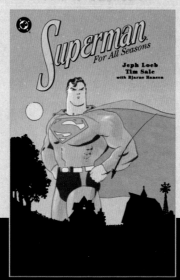